THE CAMBRIDGE COMPANION Ͳ
NELSON MAN

Nelson Mandela was one of the most revereɑ
himself to a compelling political cause, suffer
his violent and divided country to a peaceful ɪ
however, is not uncontested: his decision to em
1960s, his solitary talks with apartheid officials   ...ɪc economic
policies adopted during his presidency still spɪ   ...ɪtense debate. The essays
in this *Companion*, written by experts in history, anthropology, jurisprudence,
cinema, literature, and visual studies, address these and other issues. They
examine how Mandela became the icon he is today and ponder the meanings
and uses of his internationally recognizable image. Their overarching concerns
include Mandela's relation to "tradition" and "modernity," the impact of his
most famous public performances, the oscillation between Africanist and
non-racial positions in South Africa, and the politics of gender and national
sentiment. The volume concludes with a meditation on Mandela's legacy in the
twenty-first century and a detailed guide to further reading.

RITA BARNARD is Professor of English and Comparative Literature at the
University of Pennsylvania and Professor Extraordinaire at Stellenbosch
University, South Africa. She is the author of *The Great Depression and the
Culture of Abundance* and *Apartheid and Beyond: South African Writers and
the Politics of Place*. Her work has appeared in several important collections
about South African literature and culture and in journals such as *Novel,
Contemporary Literature, Cultural Studies, Research in African Literatures,* and
Modern Fiction Studies.

A complete list of books in the series is at the back of this book.

THE CAMBRIDGE
COMPANION TO
NELSON MANDELA

THE CAMBRIDGE COMPANION TO
NELSON MANDELA

EDITED BY

RITA BARNARD
University of Pennsylvania

CAMBRIDGE
UNIVERSITY PRESS

CAMBRIDGE
UNIVERSITY PRESS

32 Avenue of the Americas, New York, NY 10013-2473, USA

Cambridge University Press is part of the University of Cambridge.

It furthers the University's mission by disseminating knowledge in the pursuit of
education, learning, and research at the highest international levels of excellence.

www.cambridge.org
Information on this title: www.cambridge.org/9781107600959

© Cambridge University Press 2014

First published 2014

Printed in the United States of America

A catalog record for this publication is available from the British Library.

Library of Congress Cataloging in Publication data
The Cambridge companion to Nelson Mandela / [edited by] Rita Barnard.
pages cm
Includes bibliographical references and index.
ISBN 978-1-107-01311-7 (hardback) – ISBN 978-1-107-60095-9 (paperback)
1. Mandela, Nelson, 1918– 2. Mandela, Nelson, 1918– – Political and social
views. 3. Mandela, Nelson, 1918– – Influence. 4. Statesmen – South Africa –
Biography. 5. Anti-apartheid activists – South Africa – Biography. 6. Anti-apartheid
movements – South Africa – History. 7. South Africa – Politics and government.
8. South Africa – Race relations. I. Barnard, Rita.
DT1974.C36 2014
968.065092–dc23 2013044145

ISBN 978-1-107-01311-7 Hardback
ISBN 978-1-107-60095-9 Paperback

CONTENTS

ILLUSTRATIONS

NOTES ON CONTRIBUTORS

RITA BARNARD is Professor of English and Comparative Literature at the University of Pennsylvania and Professor Extraordinaire at the University of Stellenbosch. She is the author of *The Great Depression and the Culture of Abundance* and *Apartheid and Beyond: South African Writers and the Politics of Place*, as well as many essays on South African culture and American and global modernisms. She is co-editor of *After the Thrill Is Gone: Ten Years of Democracy in South Africa*, a special issue of *South Atlantic Quarterly*, and *Safundi: The Journal of South African and American Studies*.

PHILIP BONNER is Emeritus Professor of History at the University of the Witwatersrand and until recently held the National Research Foundation Chair in Local Histories and Present Realities. He has published widely on urban and labor history. As Chair of the Wits History Workshop, he was principal organizer of several important conferences, including the 1999 History Workshop on the Truth and Reconciliation Report, entitled "Commissioning the Past." He has served as co-curator of the Apartheid Museum in Johannesburg and as historical consultant to and executive producer of a six-part documentary television series entitled *Soweto: A History*, which was screened on Channel 4 in Britain, SBS in Australia, and SABC TV 1 to critical acclaim.

JONATHAN HYSLOP received his MA degrees from the University of Oxford and the University of Birmingham and his PhD from the University of the Witwatersrand. He is Professor of Sociology and Anthropology at Colgate University and holds the honorary position of Extraordinary Professor in the Sociology Department at the University of Pretoria. He worked for many years at the University of the Witwatersrand, where he was a committee member of the History Workshop and Deputy Director of the Wits Institute of Social and Economic Research. He is the author of *The Notorious Syndicalist* and has published numerous articles on South African social history in journals, such as the *Journal of Global History*, the *Journal of Historical Sociology*, the *History Workshop Journal*, and the *Journal of African History*.

ACHILLE MBEMBE is a philosopher, political scientist, and public intellectual. He obtained his PhD in history at the Sorbonne in Paris and a DEA in political science at the Institut d'Études Politiques. He is currently Research Professor in History and Politics at the University of the Witwatersrand and is affiliated with the Wits Institute of Social and Economic Research, as well as Duke University, where he teaches each fall. He is a contributing editor to *Public Culture* and co-convener of the Johannesburg Workshop in Theory and Criticism. Mbembe has written extensively on African history and politics, most notably for English readers, in his book *On the Postcolony*. His recent work includes *Sortir de la grande nuit: Essai sur l'Afrique décolonisée*, soon to be released in English by Columbia University Press.

LITHEKO MODISANE earned his PhD from the University of the Witwatersrand, where he teaches in the Department of African Literature. He was formerly a Postdoctoral Associate in the Archive and Public Culture Research Initiative at the University of Cape Town, as well as a Visiting Scholar at the University of Michigan. His interests range widely in the fields of literature, film, television, and theater. His book, *South Africa's Renegade Reels: The Making and Public Lives of Black-Centered Films*, explores the role of films as catalysts for public reflection on social and political issues germane to anti-apartheid politics and fledgling democracies.

BRENNA MUNRO holds a PhD from the University of Virginia and is Associate Professor of English at the University of Miami. She is a specialist in gender studies and queer theory, as well as African, Anglophone, and Caribbean literature. Munro is the author of *South Africa and the Dream of Love to Come: Queer Sexuality and the Struggle for Freedom* and many articles on gender and sexuality in post-apartheid writing. These include "Queer Futures: The Coming-out Novel in South Africa," in Tejumola Olaniyan and Ato Quayson's collection, *African Criticism and Theory*.

SIFISO MXOLISI NDLOVU received his PhD in history from the University of the Witwatersrand. He is Executive Director of the South African Democracy Education Trust (SADET), set up in 2000 to record the history of the liberation struggle in South Africa. He has published book chapters in SADET's *Road to Democracy in South Africa* series and is the author of *The Soweto Uprisings: Counter-memories of 16 June 1976*. His other research interests include the precolonial history of South Africa and the history of football, and he has published articles in these fields in the *South African Historical Journal*, *History and Theory*, and *Soccer and Society*. He is a member of UNESCO's Scientific Committee responsible for revising the *History of Africa* series.

ZOLANI NGWANE holds an MA in theology and a PhD in anthropology from the University of Chicago and is an Associate Professor at Haverford College. His research interests, which frequently take him back to the Eastern Cape, include social reproduction and intergenerational politics, including social institutions like chiefly courts and male initiation rites. He is working on a study of South African nation building in the 1990s and teaches courses on the new faces of tradition and modernity, black South African writing and ethnography, education, and religion. His publications include essays in the *Journal of South African Studies*, *Journal of Religion in Africa*, *Interventions*, and *Safundi*.

SARAH NUTTALL, who holds a DPhil from Oxford University, is Professor of Literary and Cultural Studies and Director of the Wits Institute for Social and Economic Research in Johannesburg. She teaches at Duke University each fall semester. She is the editor of several groundbreaking volumes on contemporary South African literature and culture, including *Negotiating the Past: The Making of Memory in South Africa*, *Senses of Culture: South African Culture Studies*, *Beautiful/Ugly: African and Diaspora Aesthetics*, and, with Achille Mbembe, *Johannesburg: The Elusive Metropolis*. Her monograph, *Entanglement: Literary and Cultural Reflections on Postapartheid*, appeared in 2009.

DEBORAH POSEL received her DPhil from Oxford University. She taught for many years at the University of the Witwatersrand, where she was founding director of the Wits Institute for Social and Economic Research. She is currently Professor of Sociology at the University of Cape Town and Director of the Institute for Humanities in Africa. She has written and published widely on many aspects of South African politics and society during and beyond the apartheid years, including *The Making of Apartheid*; *Apartheid's Genesis*, with Philip Bonner and Peter Delius; and *Commissioning the Past: Understanding South Africa's Truth and Reconciliation Commission*, with Graeme Simpson.

DANIEL ROUX received his PhD from the University of Cape Town and is a Senior Lecturer at the University of Stellenbosch. His research interests are South African life writing and journalism, prison writing, and postcolonial theory. He has published articles on various prison narratives, including Jonny Steinberg's *The Number* and Nelson Mandela's *Long Walk to Freedom*, as well as the chapter on prison writing for *The Cambridge History of South African Literature*.

DAVID SCHALKWYK received his DPhil from the University of York. He is Director of the Global Shakespeares Project at Queen Mary, University of London, and the University of Warwick. Formerly, he served as Director of Research at the Folger Shakespeare Library and editor of the *Shakespeare Quarterly*. His books include *Shakespeare, Love and Service*, *Literature and the Touch of the Real*, *Speech and Performance in Shakespeare's Sonnets and Plays*, and *Hamlet's Dreams: The Robben Island Shakespeare*.

ADAM SITZE holds a PhD from the University of Minnesota, where he was a MacArthur Scholar. He is currently Assistant Professor of Law, Jurisprudence, and Social Thought at Amherst College. He is the author of *The Impossible Machine: A Genealogy of South Africa's Truth and Reconciliation Commission* and co-editor of *Biopolitics: A Reader*. His essay on Mbeki's AIDS policy and human rights, "Denialism," appeared in *After the Thrill Is Gone: Ten Years of Democracy in South Africa*.

LIZE VAN ROBBROECK earned her MA from the University of the Witwatersrand and her PhD from the University of Stellenbosch, where she is Associate Professor in the Department of Visual Arts. She is one of the editors and writers of *The Visual Century*, a four-volume revisionist history of South African art in the twentieth century. She has published articles on postcoloniality and nationalism in South African visual arts in journals such as *Cultural Studies* and *African Arts*. Her research interests center on postcolonial subjectivities and explore the interface between psychoanalytical and postcolonial theories. She currently serves as the editor-in-chief of *Third Text Africa*.

ACKNOWLEDGMENTS

Mandela's speeches frequently deploy the rhetorical device of listing predecessors, inspirational figures, and comrades-in-arms to be honored. These
acknowledgments may be also seen in that light, as a grateful recognition
that nothing worth accomplishing is ever done alone – certainly not a collection of essays.

The splendid people of the Nelson Mandela Centre of Memory could not
have been more helpful. A warm tribute is due to Verne Harris, for wise
counsel and thoughtful comments, as well as to Lucia Raadschelders and
Razia Saleh.

Many South African colleagues offered insight and support, including the
historians Christopher Saunders, Albert Grundling, Saul Dubow, and Thula
Simpson. Jon Hyslop, Phil Bonner, and David Attwell were especially generous, not only with expert knowledge, but with conversation and comradeship. My two trusty assistants, Ian Duncan and Trevor Margraf, were
indispensable; no one could wish for more intelligent readers and can-do
collaborators. Sally Gaule and Paul Landau graciously fielded urgent questions about references. Several friends commented on the manuscript at difficult moments. For this, I am eternally indebted to Jennifer Wenzel, Jennifer
Glaser, Rob Nixon, Stephen Clingman, Monica Popescu, Lucy Graham, and
Sam Hughes. Daniel Roux was my right-hand man at just the right time:
what a privilege to think and write with him on a back porch with a view
of a manicured garden!

Ray Ryan at Cambridge University Press was the sole instigator of this
project. More than the usual tribute to an editor is therefore his due: his
patience and professionalism made the book much better than it would otherwise have been.

I gratefully acknowledge the following persons and institutions for permission to use photographs and poetry: the Nelson Mandela Centre of
Memory for the photograph of Mandela in his garden and images from
the *Authorised Comic Book*, Jeremy Cronin for his "Poem for Mandela,"

Time-Life Inc. for the 1999 cover image of Mandela as icon, the European Press Photo Agency for the moving photograph of Mandela in mourning, and Arthur Tyrone for the photograph of the aging Mandela. The artists whose work is reproduced in this volume were particularly generous. I am indebted to Yiull Damaso for not only allowing us to use his thought-provoking painting of Mandela on the autopsy table, but also taking the time to read parts of the manuscript and providing us with a high-resolution image of the work. Finally, I extend a very special thank you to Paul Emsley for the use of his magnificent portrait of Mandela both inside the text and as our cover image.

ABBREVIATIONS

ANC	African National Congress
ANCYL	African National Congress Youth League
BC	Black Consciousness
BPA	Black Parents Association
CODESA	Congress for a Democratic South Africa
COSATU	Congress of South African Trades' Unions
CPSA	Communist Party of South Africa
DCR	Democratic Republic of Congo
FNL	National Liberation Front of Algeria (Front de la Libération Nationale)
GNU	Government of National Unity
IFP	Inkatha Freedom Party
MK	Umkhonto we Sizwe
MPLA	Popular Movement for the Liberation of Angola (Movimento Popular de Liberação de Angola)
MUFC	Mandela United Football Club
NEC	National Executive Committee
NP	National Party (Nasionale Party)
OAU	Organization of African Unity
PAC	Pan-Africanist Congress
RDP	Reconstruction and Development Program
RMC	Release Mandela Campaign
SACP	South African Communist Party
SADC	Southern African Development Community
TAC	Treatment Action Campaign
TRC	Truth and Reconciliation Commission
UDF	United Democratic Front

UNESCO	United Nations Educational, Scientific, and Cultural Organization
UNISA	University of South Africa
UNITA	National Union for the Total Independence of Angola (União Nacional para a Independência Total de Angola)
Wits	University of the Witwatersrand

CHRONOLOGY

1910   Union of South Africa is founded on principles negotiated by a racially exclusive National Convention.

1912   Native National Congress, later named African National Congress (ANC), is founded.

1913   Native Land Act is passed, depriving black South Africans of right to own land.

1914   General J. B. M. Hertzog forms National Party (NP).

1915   South Africa occupies the German colony of South-West Africa; later governs it as League of Nations mandate territory.

1918   World War I ends.
        July 18. Rolihlahla Mandela is born at Mvezo, Transkei, son of Noqaphi Nosekeni and Mphakanyiswa Gadla Mandela.

1920   Moves with his mother to Qunu after his father is deposed as headman.
        ANC supports strike by black miners.

1921   Communist Party of South·Africa (CPSA) is founded.

1923   South African Indian Congress (SAIC) is founded.

1925   Mandela attends primary school in Qunu; is named Nelson by a teacher.

1926   Balfour Declaration recognizes South Africa's autonomy within British Empire.

1927   Native Administration Act is passed, setting up a separate legal system for black South Africans and giving sweeping powers to governor-general.

Mandela's father dies from tuberculosis. Mandela moves to Mqekezweni as ward of the regent of the Thembu royal house, Jongintaba Dalindyebo.

1930   Pass-burning campaign is undertaken by Industrial and Commercial Workers Union and Communist Party.

1933   Coalition of Hertzog's NP and General Jan Smuts's South African Party is formed; Smuts agrees to separate voters' rolls for blacks and whites in Cape Province.

1934   Mandela undergoes circumcision ritual and is named Dalibhunga; addressed with other initiates by Chief Meligqili, who questions whether Africans can enjoy full manhood under colonial conditions.

1935   Enrolls at Clarkebury Institute, a Methodist school in Engcobo.

1936   Native Land and Trust Act extends territory set aside for reserves to 13.6 percent.
Representation of Natives Act removes African voters from common roll in Cape Province.

1937   Mandela enrolls at Healdtown Methodist preparatory school in Fort Beaufort.

1938   Is impressed by visit of oral poet S. E. K. Mqhayi; wins prize for best essay in Xhosa.

1939   Begins studying for BA at Fort Hare University. Becomes close friends with Kaizer Matanzima, later leader of Transkei Bantustan.
South Africa enters World War II.
Hertzog resigns; Smuts becomes prime minister.

1940   Hertzog and Dr. D. F. Malan form Herenigde Nasionale Party (Reunited National Party).
Mandela is involved in student protest; expelled from Fort Hare for refusing to serve on Student Representative Council.

1941   Absconds to Johannesburg to avoid arranged marriage.
Serves a brief stint at Crown Mines as compound policeman. Meets Walter Sisulu, who finds him a clerical position at Witkin, Sidelsky, and Edelman. Begins attending ANC meetings.

1942   Joins the ANC. Passes final exams for BA through University of South Africa.

1943   Graduates with BA from Fort Hare. Enrolls as part-time LLB student at University of the Witwatersrand (Wits). Meets longtime friends and political associates Bram Fischer, Ismail Meer, Joe Slovo, Ruth First, and George Bizos.
August. Marches with Alexandra Bus Boycotters.
December. ANC conference delegates vote to approve formation of Youth League (ANCYL).

1944   April. Mandela is elected to Executive Committee of ANCYL.
Marries Evelyn Ntoko Mase. Completes articles and becomes full-time law student at Wits.

1945   Thembekile Madiba, Mandela's first son, is born.

1946   Discriminatory treatment of Indians in South Africa is included on agenda of first session of United Nations General Assembly.
Mandela moves to Orlando West, Soweto. Provides legal advice to James Mpanza's Sofazonke squatters' movement.
African mine workers go on strike.

1947   Mandela is elected to Executive Committee of Transvaal ANC; opposes "Votes for All" campaign because of Communist and Indian participation.
Anton Lembede, influential Africanist thinker in ANCYL, dies.

1948   Makaziwe Mandela is born; dies nine months later.
May 26. Malan's NP wins general election; apartheid era begins.
UN General Assembly adopts Universal Declaration of Human Rights.

1949   Prohibition of Mixed Marriages Act is passed. ANC adopts Programme of Action in response to tightening restrictions.
Indians and Africans clash in Durban; ANC and Indian Congress leaders work together to defuse violence.
Mandela fails LLB exam at Wits.

1950   Key apartheid laws are enacted, including Population Registration Act, Groups Areas Act, and Suppression of

Communism Act, which equates any opposition to apartheid with Communism.

May Day strike is undertaken against Suppression of Communism Act.

Mandela joins ANC's National Executive Committee.

June 26. National Day of Protest and Mourning is called by ANC and SAIC.

Makgatho Lewanika, Mandela's second son, is born.

1951   Mandela is elected president of ANCYL.

1952   June 26. ANC launches Defiance Campaign with Mandela as "volunteer-in-chief."

Mandela is arrested and placed under banning orders for six months.

Passes exams to qualify as attorney and opens law office with Oliver Tambo.

Is elected president of Transvaal ANC, then ANC deputy president. Albert Luthuli becomes ANC president.

1953   Bantu Education Act is passed.

Communist Party reorganizes in secret and renames itself South African Communist Party (SACP). Walter Sisulu tours Communist countries.

Mandela is involved in organizing protests against demolition of Sophiatown and forced removal of residents; declares that time for passive resistance has ended.

Is served with second banning order, restricting him to Johannesburg and prohibiting him from attending gatherings. Devises M-Plan for future underground activities.

1954   Sophiatown demolitions begin, initiating three decades of forced removals.

Pumla Makaziwe, Mandela's first surviving daughter, is born.

1955   June 26. Congress of the People adopts Freedom Chapter; Mandela, still banned, watches proceedings.

ANC's boycott against Bantu education called off.

1956   August 9. 20,000 women march to Union Buildings to protest pass laws.

December. Mandela is arrested with 156 other activists and charged with high treason. The trial, lasting until 1961, cripples his law practice.

Tomlinson Commission Report explores viability of separate "Bantu Homelands."

1957 Evelyn leaves Mandela, taking furniture and children with her.

1958 Mandela is divorced from Evelyn.
June 14. Marries Winifred Nomzano Madikizela.
Dr. H. F. Verwoerd is elected prime minister of South Africa.

1959 Pan-Africanist Congress (PAC), led by Potlake Leballo and Robert Sobukwe, is formed.
Extension of University Education Act is passed, leading to racially segregated universities. Verwoerd begins to implement "Bantu Homeland" policies of territorial segregation on a tribal basis.
Anti-Apartheid Movement (AAM) is founded in London.
Mandela's daughter Zenani is born.

1960 March 21. Sixty-nine demonstrators are massacred by police at Sharpeville. State of emergency is declared; ANC and PAC are banned.
Mandela burns his pass in Orlando; is arrested and detained under emergency regulations.
South West African People's Organization (SWAPO) is founded by Andimba Toivo ya Toivo, who is later imprisoned on Robben Island.
August 3. Mandela testifies at treason trial in Pretoria.
Mandela's daughter Zindziswa "Zindzi" is born.

1961 March 29. Mandela is acquitted along with other treason trial defendants; goes underground.
April 31. Republic of South Africa is declared; leaves British Commonwealth.
Three-day strike is organized in response; Mandela calls it off after first day.
Mandela is interviewed by BBC television.
December 16. Umkhonto we Sizwe (MK) launches sabotage campaign.

1962 January–July. Mandela travels widely in Africa and England to organize support for ANC and acquire military training.
August 5. Is arrested outside Pietermaritzburg; charged with incitement and leaving South Africa illegally.

Receives five-year sentence. Spends time in solitary confinement at Pretoria Central Prison for refusing to wear shorts but soon asks to rejoin other prisoners.

1963   Is transferred to Robben Island; brought back to Pretoria after police raid on Liliesleaf Farm, Rivonia, where other MK leaders are captured and incriminating documents seized.

October 9. Mandela and comrades are charged with sabotage, promotion of guerrilla warfare, and planning an armed invasion.

Ninety-day Detention Act is passed, permitting interrogations and detentions without trial.

1964   April 20. Mandela delivers his famous speech from the dock.

June 12. Is sentenced to life in prison along with eight co-defendants and taken to Robben Island.

November. Receives a visit from *Daily Telegraph* reporter, who takes the sole published photograph of Mandela as prisoner.

1965   Along with other Section B prisoners, Mandela begins work at Robben Island lime quarry.

Is visited by representatives of American Bar Association and International Red Cross (IRC).

Section B prisoners establish Communications Committee and High Organ, on which Mandela serves.

1966   African prisoners in Section B are given permission to wear long trousers. Mandela participates in hunger strike.

Verwoerd is assassinated; John Vorster becomes prime minister.

SWAPO clashes with South African forces in Ovamboland; "Border War" begins.

1967   Terrorism Act is passed, legalizing detention without trial.

1968   Section B prisoners are allowed to subscribe to select magazines after intervention by IRC.

Mandela's mother dies; request to attend funeral is denied.

Founding of South African Students Organization with Steve Biko as president.

1969   Mandela's son Thembi dies in car accident; request to attend funeral denied.

Winnie Mandela is arrested and held for 491 days under Terrorism Act.

1970   January. Mandela sends letter of complaint to commissioner of prisons.

Protests against behavior of Colonel Badenhorst, the prison's commanding officer to visiting judges; Badenhorst is replaced.

Black Homeland Citizenship Act is passed.

Winnie Mandela is released from prison.

1972   Black People's Convention is launched; Biko banned.

1973   Strikes take place in Durban; independent trade unions formed.

UN declares apartheid a crime against humanity.

1975   Mandela begins writing his autobiography.

Inkatha, Zulu cultural and political movement led by Chief Mangosuthu Buthelezi, is launched.

Portuguese colonies of Angola and Mozambique become independent.

1976   South African forces initiate covert operations in Angola.

June 16. Schoolchildren's uprising starts in Soweto and spreads across country.

Transkei becomes first "independent" homeland, with Matanzima as leader.

Mandela refuses conditional reduction of sentence offered by Jimmy Kruger, minister of justice.

Television is introduced in South Africa.

1977   Prison authorities end daily manual labor on Robben Island.

Winnie Mandela is banished to Brandfort in Orange Free State; Biko killed in detention.

UN Security Council imposes arms embargo on South Africa.

1978   Vorster resigns; P.W. Botha becomes prime minister.

1979   Azanian People's Organization is founded.

Industrial Relations Act legalizes black trade unions.

1980   *Sunday Post* launches nationwide Release Mandela Campaign; worldwide campaign is launched by AAM.

Zimbabwe becomes independent.

Student boycotts, strikes, and community protests break out across South Africa and continue throughout decade.

SASOL oil refinery is bombed by MK.

Mandela is awarded Jawaharlal Nehru Award for International Understanding, the first of numerous major international prizes, awards, and honorary degrees.

1982 Mandela is transferred to Pollsmoor Prison, along with Walter Sisulu, Raymond Mhlaba, Andrew Mlangeni, and Ahmed Kathrada.

1983 Botha implements his constitutional reforms: a tricameral parliament without representation for black majority.

In response, United Democratic Front (UDF) is formed.

1984 Mandela rejects offer pushed by Matanzima that he be released to Transkei Bantustan. Has first contact visit with Winnie.

Nkomati Non-aggression Pact is signed by South Africa and Mozambique, intended to prevent the latter from supporting MK and ANC.

Bishop Desmond Tutu receives Nobel Peace Prize.

1985 January 31. Botha offers Mandela freedom, conditional on renunciation of violence; his rejection is read by Zindzi Mandela to crowd at Jabulani Stadium, Soweto.

National insurrection continues, especially in black townships, and state of emergency is declared.

Winnie Mandela gives militant speech endorsing violence, even necklacing.

COSATU trade union federation is formed.

Mandela requests meeting with Minister of Justice Kobie Coetsee.

Is treated in hospital for prostate condition; receives visit from Coetsee.

December. Mandela is incarcerated separately to facilitate meetings with government officials; notifies Tambo of this initiative via his lawyer, George Bizos.

1986 Meets with members of Commonwealth Eminent Persons' Group and has further meetings with Minister Coetsee; is driven around Cape Town area and even has a chance to escape.

State of emergency is renewed.

1987 Eminent Afrikaners meet with ANC leaders in Dakar, Senegal, and England. Govan Mbeki is released from Robben Island.

1988 February. UDF is banned.

March. South African forces are defeated at Cuito Cuanavale in Angola.

Mandela begins secret meetings with Botha's intelligence chief, Niel Barnard.

Is hospitalized for tuberculosis; transferred upon release to head warder's house at Victor Verster Prison, where meetings continue.

June 11. Mandela's seventieth birthday is celebrated with pop concert at Wembley Stadium, London, broadcast to international audience of 600 million.

Graduates with LLB degree from University of South Africa.

Winnie Mandela's home is burned down in Soweto by residents angered at activities of her bodyguards, the United Mandela Football Club.

December 29. Stompie Seipei is kidnapped by Football Club members; he dies on January 1.

1989 Mandela meets Botha for tea at his residence; requests Sisulu's release.

August 14. F. W. de Klerk replaces Botha as president.

Harare Declaration articulates ANC's position on negotiations; Tambo suffers a stroke.

Walter Sisulu and five other political leaders are released from prison.

Soviet Bloc collapses in Eastern Europe; Berlin Wall falls.

December. Mandela meets De Klerk.

1990 February 2. De Klerk announces release of Mandela and unbanning of ANC, PAC, SACP, and other political organizations.

February 11. Mandela walks out of Victor Verster Prison a free man; is celebrated at mass rallies across South Africa.

Is reappointed ANC deputy president and effectively assumes leadership of ANC.

Namibia becomes independent.

ANC and government leaders sign Groote Schuur Minute, charting way to negotiations; agreement is reached on release of prisoners and indemnities for returning exiles.

Mandela undertakes fourteen-nation tour, including visits to eight US cities; addresses US Congress and joint Houses of Parliament in UK.

ANC announces suspension of armed struggle.

MK leader Chris Hani, still in exile, speaks of need to combat HIV-AIDS.

1991   July 5. Mandela is elected ANC president.

December. Congress for a Democratic South Africa (CODESA) begins negotiations; De Klerk and Mandela clash over MK activities during opening session.

Remaining apartheid laws are rescinded; international sanctions against South Africa lifted.

Winnie Madikizela-Mandela is tried for kidnapping and accessory to assault; receives six-year sentence.

Soviet Union dissolves.

1992   Mandela makes first visit to Davos Economic Summit.

March. Whites-only referendum endorses negotiations.

CODESA talks reconvene, then break down.

June 16. ANC and alliance partners begin "rolling mass action."

Violence erupts at Boipatong (between Zulu hostel dwellers and ANC-supporting township residents) and Bisho, Ciskei (between bantustan military and ANC marchers); talks resume as only alternative to further violence.

Mandela publicly announces his separation from Winnie.

1993   April 10. Chris Hani is assassinated. Mandela appears on television and calls for calm; with this he effectively becomes leader of South Africa.

Oliver Tambo dies.

Winnie Mandela's prison sentence is reduced to fine on appeal.

Mandela is awarded Nobel Peace Prize, jointly with F. W. de Klerk.

Interim constitution is adopted; Transitional Executive Council formed.

1994   April 26–29. South Africa's first democratic election is held. ANC wins 62.6 percent of vote.

May 10. Mandela is inaugurated as president of South Africa.

Restitution of Land Rights Act is passed.

1995   Rugby World Cup is hosted and won by South Africa. Mandela appears at Ellis Park Stadium to acclaim of largely white crowd.

Nelson Mandela Children's Fund is founded.

Nigerian writer-activist Ken Saro-Wiwa is executed despite Mandela's diplomacy; Mandela denounces General Sani Abacha for this deed.

1996   March. Mandela is divorced from Winnie.

Truth and Reconciliation Commission (TRC), chaired by Desmond Tutu, begins hearings on human rights violations during apartheid era.

Parliament adopts new non-discriminatory constitution.

F. W. de Klerk and NP withdraw from Government of National Unity (GNU).

1997   Winnie Madikizela-Mandela appears before TRC; does not acknowledge personal wrongdoing or request amnesty.

1998   Mandela marries Graça Machel on his eightieth birthday.

TRC Report is published; Mandela accepts it, but ANC President Thabo Mbeki challenges it for criticizing ANC's human rights record.

Treatment Action Campaign (TAC) is launched by Zachie Achmat to protest ANC government's failure to provide drugs to victims of HIV-AIDS.

1999   ANC wins 66.36 percent of poll in second general election.

July 14. Mandela ends term as president; is succeeded by Mbeki.

Nelson Mandela Foundation is established.

Mandela opposes NATO intervention in Kosovo; serves as facilitator in Burundian peace negotiations.

2000   Land invasions of white farms begin in Zimbabwe.

Mbeki sends letter to US President Bill Clinton questioning applicability of scientific AIDS research to African conditions.

Mandela calls Zimbabwean President Robert Mugabe a tyrant, yet claims to support Mbeki's "silent diplomacy."

Mandela formally retires from public life.

13th International AIDS conference is held in Durban.

2001   Scandal erupts over kickbacks for ANC leaders in 1998 arms deal.

Mandela is treated for prostate cancer.

AIDS becomes leading cause of death in sub-Saharan Africa.

High court rules that pregnant women must be given AIDS drugs to prevent transmission to babies.

2002   Mandela backs TAC protests against Mbeki government's AIDS policies.

2003   Criticizes US invasion of Iraq and the UK's acquiescent involvement.
Nelson Mandela Award for Health and Human Rights is awarded to Zachie Achmat.
Walter Sisulu dies.
South African government finally approves program to treat HIV-AIDS.

2004   Mandela announces retirement from public life.
Statue of Mandela is installed in Sandton Square, renamed Nelson Mandela Square.

2005   Mandela announces his son Makgatho's death from AIDS.
Mbeki fires his vice president, Jacob Zuma.

2006   Mandela receives Amnesty International's Ambassador of Conscience Award.

2007   Announces formation of The Elders, a group of global leaders working for peace.
Attends conference in New Delhi to mark hundredth anniversary of Gandhi's *satyagraha* campaign.
Statue of Mandela in Parliament Square, London, is unveiled.
Mbeki is deposed as ANC president; Zuma elected.

2008   Xenophobic attacks on immigrants from other African countries are carried out in several South African townships.
Mandela's ninetieth birthday is marked across South Africa; birthday tribute concert held in Hyde Park, London.
Mandela publically criticizes Mugabe after election violence in Zimbabwe.
Mbeki is forced to resign as president of South Africa; succeeded by Kgalema Mothlante.
Barack Obama is elected US president.

2009   ANC wins general election; Jacob Zuma becomes president of South Africa.

Mandela's birthday, July 18, is endorsed by UN as International Nelson Mandela Day.

2010   His great-granddaughter Zenani is killed in car accident.
Mandela appears at closing ceremony of FIFA World Cup hosted by South Africa – his last public event.

2011   Is hospitalized for two days in Johannesburg with respiratory infection.
Arab Spring revolutions break out in North Africa and Middle East.
Mandla Mandela moves the graves of Mandela's children Makaziwe, Thembikile, and Makgatho from Qunu to his homestead and tourist site in Mvezo.

2012   August. Police open fire on striking workers at Lonmin Platinum Mine in Marikana, killing thirty-four; judicial commission of inquiry is set up after public outcry.
Mandela's image is put on all South African banknotes.
Mandela statue is unveiled in Bloemfontein.
Mandela is treated in hospital for lung infection and gallstones; later released.
Zuma is re-elected ANC president, with Cyril Ramaphosa as vice president.

2013   March–April. Mandela is admitted to hospital and later released.
June 8. Is readmitted for recurring lung infection; remains in critical condition for several weeks, as well-wishers offer tributes and prayers.
June 28. Obama visits South Africa; views Mandela's Robben Island cell and pays tribute to his legacy.
July 3. Graves of Mandela's children are exhumed after successful court challenge to 2011 removal; reinterred at Qunu.
July 18. Mandela spends birthday and fifteenth wedding anniversary in hospital; admirers worldwide celebrate his legacy with charitable acts.
After nearly three months, he returns home.
December 5. Nelson Mandela dies.

RITA BARNARD

Introduction

Nelson Rolihlahla Mandela was one of the most revered figures of our time, and rightly so. A "life-loving man" by his own description, he committed himself to a compelling political struggle, faced the death penalty, and endured a prison sentence that entailed the sacrifice of a third of his life to his cause.[1] During these long years, he became not only the world's best-known prisoner, but a symbol of his people's demand for liberation from racial injustice and a galvanizing icon for millions of others all around the world who cherished the principle of equality and yearned for a politics of moral conviction in their own national spheres. He became a name (rather than a face, for it was forbidden in South Africa to circulate his picture) that encouraged many who otherwise might have remained apathetic to identify with the struggle against apartheid. He emerged from prison unbowed and, despite impossibly high expectations, did not disappoint. Gracious but steely, he steered a country in turmoil toward a negotiated settlement: a country that days before its first democratic election remained violent, riven by divisive views and personalities. He endorsed national reconciliation, an idea he did not merely foster in the abstract, but performed with panache and conviction in reaching out to former adversaries. He initiated an era of hope that, while not long-lasting, was nevertheless decisive, and he garnered the highest international recognition and affection. He won the Nobel Peace Prize (along with F. W. de Klerk, the man who agreed to his release and to the unbanning of his organization, the African National Congress, or ANC) and remained in the global public eye thanks to many other awards and celebrations, including a series of AIDS benefit concerts. As a statesman who was in no one's pocket, Mandela remained loyal to friends who were unpopular with the Western superpowers; he opened his speeches with lists of predecessors in whose footsteps he saw himself as following; and he boldly condemned injustices perpetrated in many parts of the world. Unlike many leaders who buy into their own image and overstay their welcome, Mandela chose to step down from the presidency of South Africa after only one term, thereby asserting the importance of the democratic process over his own personal prestige. Of course, as Mark Gevisser has noted, Mandela did not cease to be a global icon after his retirement – a fact that often made things difficult for his successor, Thabo Mbeki.[2] As a private citizen, Mandela continued to exert influence, both nationally, through his various foundations, and internationally, through organizations like The Elders group, a collective of distinguished senior political figures working together for world peace and human rights.

His record, especially viewed from within South Africa, has never been entirely without controversy. There were times during the prison years when he was considered by some in his organization to be a sellout, and his solitary decision to initiate talks with apartheid government officials was likewise faulted. He presided over the adoption of a macroeconomic dispensation that many still consider a raw deal for the poor, and he failed to address HIV-AIDS at a time when the scope of the pandemic might still have been be curbed. There is also a sense in which his chiefly bearing and mode of conduct, the very respect and authority he accrued in representing his nation in his own person, went against the spirit of democracy and, while he constantly insisted that he was a servant of the people and a loyal member of the ANC, his popularity nevertheless generated something of a cult of personality.[3] The effects of his earlier brave and flamboyant actions are also open to debate. The decision to embark on the armed struggle, as well as his conduct of it before his arrest in 1962, was not beyond dispute, even among other activists at the time, and the effects were enduring. As a revolutionary, he displayed a romantic recklessness that led to his capture and thereby, arguably, damaged the anti-apartheid cause. While the trials of the 1960s, in which his appearances were electrifying, enhanced the drama and international visibility of the struggle, they also set it back organizationally. This said, the hope that Mandela inspired, the dignity he embodied, and the moral authority with which he restored South Africa's standing in the eyes of the world were of incalculable benefit to the country and its citizens, as was the model constitution adopted in the second year of his presidency: a constitution that bans all forms of discrimination, including discrimination on the basis of sexual preference. For a while, Nelson Mandela made it possible "to think an aesthetics of innovation, an ethics of conversion, a politics of revolution" – but a revolution that, as he liked to put it, turned out to be a legal, not a bloody, one.[4]

On Transcendence and Disjuncture

Former US President Bill Clinton's remark that "every time Nelson Mandela walks into a room, we all feel a little bigger" can be seen as a down-home way of getting at the politics of the sublime: something that exceeds and transcends the structures, constraints, and ordinariness of the present.[5] Such a politics – or ethics – is articulated in a more philosophical and arresting way in Mandela's own reflections on freedom in the final pages of his autobiography.[6] He describes how his concept of freedom evolved from the callow belief of a country boy that he was born free – free to run in the fields, to swim, to roast mealies under the stars – as long as he obeyed his father and abided by the "customs of his tribe." As a young man, he tells us, he started to feel hemmed in, but merely by rules and circumstances that hampered his individualistic pleasures, like the desire to go out every night or read entirely what he pleased. It was only as an adult that he came to understand that he was living in a country where freedom was systematically denied to people who looked like him. He realized, as he puts it, that "not only was [he] not free, but [his] brothers and sisters were not free." The moment he joined the ANC thus represents for him the moment when "the hunger for [his] own freedom, becomes the hunger of the freedom of [his] people." This realization is based on the perception that "freedom is indivisible": "the chains on all of my people were the chains on me." In prison, paradoxically, his understanding of freedom grew even more capacious: it becomes, in his description, a hunger for the freedom of all people, white and black. This expansion is inseparable from a more profound understanding of the meaning of confinement. As Mandela puts it, the "man who takes away another man's freedom is a prisoner of hatred, he is locked behind the bars of prejudice and narrow-mindedness." Thus, "the oppressed and the oppressor alike are robbed of their humanity." Mandela's retrospective meditation culminates in a remarkable assertion: "When I walked out of prison, that was my mission, to liberate the oppressed and the oppressor both." It offers, also, a call to future action. Even though the struggle for a democratic South Africa has been accomplished, he declares, freedom has not yet been achieved: "The truth is that we are not yet free; we have merely achieved the freedom to be free. The right not to be oppressed."

These inspiring reflections, coming as the climax of a life story as arresting as Mandela's, go some distance toward explaining his national and international appeal. On the most obvious level, one can see how such a story of liberation would speak to colonized people and those who have been denied their civil rights – to those for whom the metaphorics of chains and prison have painful historical resonances. One can also see how this narrative draws on and extends a profoundly African understanding of the obligations of kinship, of humanity-in-reciprocity, as captured in the term *ubuntu*. But we should remember that there are also resonant memories in Europe and the Americas of the dream of liberty and the exultation of release, from the sack of the Bastille, to the Emancipation Proclamation, to the collapse of the Berlin Wall. And while the worldview expressed here is not strictly speaking a Christian one, it is clearly open to Christian projections: Mandela's life can and has been read in terms of a forgiveness of enemies and the possibility of messianic redemption. For people of conscience, who are tainted nevertheless by privileges enjoyed at the expense of others, these reflections are also deeply moving. White South Africans, in particular, can find in these words a release from the shame of being international pariahs and a generous invitation to transcend the prison house of prejudice. It is also quite characteristic of the way Mandela has functioned as a national and global icon that the conclusion to his autobiography is future-oriented and pedagogical. Freedom is not won for once and for all, or by one individual, but must be claimed and lived out by others. These meditations, in other words, are not addressed merely to Mandela's contemporaries. They also issue a challenge to those who have yet to shape their world. Such are the universal resonances of Mandela's conception of freedom, and they are made all the more powerful by his own story of suffering and overcoming. At stake in Mandela's summary of his life's achievement is a call to imagine "the totality of the possible, the infinity of the Maybe," something that goes beyond the present and extends into the past and the future.[7]

While offering us this sublime dare, Mandela insisted again and again that he was a man of his movement and of his moment, "an ordinary man who had become a leader because of extraordinary circumstances."[8] But what was Mandela's historical moment? It has often been observed that the global imaginary tends to fix South African politics in a kind of freeze-frame: the anti-apartheid struggle seems eternally captured in the photograph of Hector Pieterson, shot by the police in the 1976 Soweto Uprising, while Mandela often seems to be fixed at the moment of his release in 1990, when he first lifted his fist in a power salute to greet the crowd.[9] Even if this were the only Mandela scrutinized in this collection, it would be impossible to understand him at that moment without also bringing in the history of his organization, of the years of collective resistance inside South Africa, and of the end of the Cold War and its Manichaean geopolitical system, which made change in South Africa seem so intractable. The South African transition to democracy and Mandela's rise to power occurred at a moment when, however briefly, the winds of change were felt in many parts of the world.

But even this is far too narrow a historical contextualization to properly frame the wide-ranging chapters in this collection, which certainly do not succumb to the temptation of being mesmerized by one victorious moment. A more useful way of framing these essays is suggested at the conclusion to Anthony Sampson's authorized biography of Mandela, where he describes his subject as both premodern and postmodern. The former designation underscores Mandela's formation in the rural spheres of Xhosa tradition, and the latter addresses the ease with which he, in later years, rose to the role of media celebrity, becoming a "master of the photo-opportunity," capable of "mixing politics with showbiz."[10] While it is easy to see what Sampson means, it seems to me that the very disparity he identifies compels us to describe Mandela, quite simply, as *modern*. Mandela, I would suggest, is a man of the twentieth century, viewed in its global complexity as an era of a radically incomplete and uneven modernity. Grasped in this way, the modern world cannot be understood solely as Euro-American, as only a matter of the global North, and it certainly cannot be understood unless we also take account of the history of colonialism – and, for that matter, of anti-colonialism, which has often involved a re-energizing and redeployment of local traditions.

The Marxist theorist Fredric Jameson reminds us that the protagonists and shapers of modernism in the arts and philosophy were often people whose experiences straddled very different worlds: "born in those agricul-tural villages we still sometimes characterize as … premodern, they devel-oped their vocations in the new urban agglomerations with their radically distinct and 'modern' spaces and temporalities."[11] His point is that, even in Europe, the modern experience was one of disjuncture, of living in many worlds and marching to many different beats. Those who grasped this best were people with a sensitivity to temporal lags and accelerations, people with a heightened comparative capacity: with an understanding of both tra-dition and innovation, stagnation and progress. It is therefore not fanciful to propose that the quintessential modern subject might well be someone like Mandela: a black South African, born in a rural and tribal world, coming into manhood and political consciousness in a vibrant, materialistic colonial city, and ending up as a citizen of the world, a deft participant in the contem-porary cultures of the media spectacle.[12] The fact that the white Nationalists who instituted an anachronistic regime of racial segregation were set on denying such subjects a place in modernity, that they refused to see their black compatriots as persons and contemporaries, that they tried, as it were, to turn back the clock is deeply ironic from the perspective I am putting forward. For the system of apartheid only served to exacerbate the sense of disjuncture and discontinuity that was the very hallmark of modernity for so many individuals worldwide.

Mandela was possessed of an unusual flexibility, a "shape-shifting" quality, which enabled him to bridge the different worlds he inhabited in the course of his life with extraordinary courage and grace.[13] As Sampson points out, he was able to find common ground with very different communities and people: "he could relate personally ... to rural tribesmen, to mine workers and streetwise city slickers, to African nationalists and freedom fighters, to Indian and white comrades, to Afrikaner warders, to international business-men or to heads of state."[14] But it is important not to smooth over what Rob Nixon describes as the ambiguities and contradictions of Mandela's relationship to place and time – which was particularly complex during his imprisonment.[15] In these years, Mandela was physically absent from the world at large, alive only in memory and in collective dreams of a trans-formed future. While he was engaged in the dreary, inflexible routines of prison life on Robben Island, he occupied, in the imaginations of others, a kind of messianic time of suspended hope. When he was finally released, Mandela presented something of a puzzle to the international media person-alities who interviewed him: they could not make up their minds, as Nixon puts it, "whether he was a maker or a misser of history."[16] His manners seemed quaint and formal. If, during the 1950s, he seemed to be following the style of the African nationalist leaders like Nkrumah and Kenyatta, he seemed, in the United States of the 1990s, to be reanimating the promise of the long-deceased Martin Luther King and Malcolm X, of whom he was a contemporary.[17] And if, in the eyes of the world, Mandela had what Nixon calls a "marvelous, disconnected, time-machine aura," the sudden acceler-ation of experience – indeed, of South African history – that followed his release was certainly equally strange for the man himself. Mandela's fellow prisoner Ahmed Kathrada has described himself and his comrades as Rip van Winkle figures, for whom the world into which they were released was a kind of science fiction world: strange and unfamiliar. The first microwave oven they ever saw, in the kitchen of Mandela's house at Victor Verster Prison, made a big impression on them; they had not yet encountered com-puters or fax machines, or even things like multi-lane highways, overhead bypasses, and so forth.[18]

If Mandela adapted brilliantly to the brave new world of the mass media and, even more importantly, to the anachronistic task of shaping a feeling of nation-ness at the very moment when various global forces were combining to undermine the sovereignty of nation-states, that does not mean that his personal experience was without strange jolts and surprises.[19] In *Long Walk to Freedom*, he reveals, for example, that he did not immediately under-stand that the woolly objects members of the press held out to him were microphones, and he recalls how surprised he was that a group of young Inuit well-wishers in frigid Goose Bay had watched his release on television and were able to greet him on his arrival at the airport with authentic strug-gle slogans like "Viva ANC!" His comments beautifully register his aston-ishment at the complexities of space and time, the rapidity of change, the incongruities of cultural contact, and the transformational possibilities of technology. "In my seventy-two years on earth," Mandela muses,

> I had never met an Innuit [*sic*] and never imagined that I would.... What struck me so forcefully was how small the planet had become during my decades in prison; it was amazing to me that a teenaged Innuit living at the roof of the world could watch the release of a political prison on the southern tip of Africa. Television had shrunk the world, and had in the process become a great weapon for eradicating ignorance and promoting democracy.[20]

This is Mandela, not just as modern subject, but as modernizer. And the incident is particularly striking to him, the passage makes clear, because he identifies with the Inuit as colonized subjects, about whose "backwardness" he once read as a pupil in English mission schools and who are still carelessly referred to by the Canadian official who accompanies him as "Eskimos." Mandela's interest in culture and "tradition," in other words, is part of his alertness to the possibilities of modernity and part, also, of what Elleke Boehmer describes as his postcolonial assertion – in his life, writing, and thought alike – that humanness and African-ness (or Inuit-ness for that matter) are not oppositional, but coextensive.[21]

If, then, we must reflect on Mandela's historical circumstances, it is also important that we reflect on our own: on the present moment that surely drives and shapes the collective inquiry of this volume. This collection was produced at a time both auspicious and difficult for such an enterprise. The contributors, while often noting the creative and multivalent qualities of their subject in his heyday, worked with the aged and frail Mandela in mind: Tata Mandela with his silver hair and cane, whose recurrent hospitalizations had all South Africans deeply concerned, already pondering the loss occasioned by his death. We were also aware that South Africa and the world have changed since Mandela's presidency. While some parts of the world have been transformed in positive and uplifting ways (one thinks of the election of Barack Obama as US president and the Arab Spring revolutions), South Africa has evolved in a rather more sobering direction. By the time that readers hold this book in their hands or peruse it on their computer screens, the brave new democracy, initiated with the inauguration of Nelson Mandela in front of Sir Herbert Baker's grandly terraced Union Buildings in Pretoria, will have reached is maturity: twenty, twenty-one years old. The astonishing changes from the apartheid era, which may still strike the older ones among us as news, are simply quotidian realities for the young. And those realities are not always happy ones. The economic statistics capture something of the situation: the Gini coefficient, the standard measure of inequality, rose from .57 in 1995 to .63 in 2009. The income share of the top 10 percent of the population grew from 45 to 52 percent. The income share of the poorest 20 percent shrank from 3.6 to 2.7 percent, and the share of the next-poorest 20 percent shrank from 6 to 4.6 percent.[22] On the more human and psychological level, too, there has been a palpable shift from the structure of feeling of the Mandela years to something different, darker – or perhaps merely ordinary.

But this ordinariness clearly means something different from what it meant back in the mid-1980s, when Njabulo Ndebele called for the "rediscovery of the ordinary" as a much-needed change from the "spectacular" but simplistic adversarial rhetoric of the anti-apartheid struggle.[23] "Despite the many radical and real manifestations of social transformation," writes Gareth Cornwell, "it would seem that South Africans have lost that sense of exceptionalism that the more or less peaceful transition of power in the early 1990s conferred upon them, in the eyes of the world, as well as their own." This has meant an adaptation to a number of harsh facts:

> [South Africans] are getting used to the inflated promises of politicians and the disappointment of non-delivery; they are getting used to the idea that their well-being depends upon the vagaries of international economic trends; they are getting used to the fact that they will be governed, like everyone else in the world, by unimaginative self-serving bureaucrats, and that what "freedom" means for the poor is little more than the freedom to assume personal responsibility for their poverty.[24]

What is most striking in these reflections (which arise in an essay subtitled "Long Walk to Ordinariness") is, of course, that final thought on the contemporary connotations of "freedom." The word seems today to have lost something of the quality of hope and transcendence with which it was infused in Mandela's autobiography. It has been narrowed down and hollowed out by neoliberal constraints: by the inequities of capitalism and the market rather than those of race. This change is something that many of the writers included in this volume have tried to assess. They have felt compelled to ponder the pervasive perception that "the Mandela years had been the era of the dream," the Mbeki presidency the years "of the dream deferred," and that South Africa has now awakened, for good and ill, to "a time beyond dreams."[25]

To write about an icon is never easy, especially when one's aim is not the crudely reactive one of iconoclasm. (It is remarkable that not a single essay in this book is interested in debunking its subject, but rather in complicating, recontextualizing, and renaming him.)[26] The problem is beautifully evoked by Jeremy Cronin, a former political prisoner himself and now deputy minister of public works, in his 1997 "Poem for Mandela":

8

It's impossible to make small talk with an icon
Which is why, to find my tongue,
I stare down at those crunched-up
One-time boxer's knuckles.
In their flattened pudginess I find
Something partly reassuring,
Something slightly troubling,
Something, at least, not transcendent.[27]

None of the contributors to this collection, writing at their desks in the United States and South Africa, were close enough to stare at the one-time boxer's knuckles; and, besides, metaphor is for poets. Drawing on the resources of many disciplines – history, anthropology, jurisprudence, political theory, sociology, literature, cinema, and gender and visual studies – the writers included here have had to come up with more than eight lyric lines. Yet they have followed Cronin's example in their efforts not to see their subject's meanings as fixed or inaccessibly "transcendent," but to remain alert to the processes whereby he shaped himself, his country, his continent, and the world. In so doing, all the contributors have had to confront the fact that narrative, the revisiting of a biography that has assumed the character of a sanctified national allegory, can hinder as much as help the discovery of new insights. For narrative, as Tom Lodge, one of Mandela's best biographers, puts it, is the very medium in which Mandela operated. "For Mandela," he notes, "politics has always been primarily about enacting stories, about making narratives, primarily about morally exemplary conduct, and only secondarily about ideological vision, more about means rather than ends."[28] To understand Mandela anew, then, is not to deny that his was, as Lodge puts it, a "politics of grace and honour," but to consider also how it came to be that he was able to embody such high things. The chapters in this volume, while they do cumulatively reveal a great deal about Mandela's life, are therefore best seen as interrupting and interrogating that linear narrative, stirring though it be. Given the range of methodologies and points of view represented here, this collection is the first academic investigation of Mandela that matches the shape-shifting qualities of its subject.

Political and Personal Life

The first part of this book is entitled "The Man, the Movement, and the Nation." Read in sequence, the chapters of which it is composed provide an overview of Mandela's youth, the beginnings of his political career, his imprisonment, his release, the dramatic years of the transition, and the glory days following his inauguration. They also probe the most compelling relationships in his life: with his political organization, the ANC, and with his second wife, Winnie Madikizela-Mandela. But these chapters are analytical and argumentative as well. The last three in particular are marked by an interest in the ethics and politics of affect: in structures of feeling, emotional styles, and national sentiments. This is a new way of approaching Mandela and one that addresses an arresting paradox: that a man who has not been prone to reveal his emotions should have generated such intense public feelings.

Chapter 1, by Philip Bonner, is one of the most narrative and historically capacious essays in this volume, ranging as it does from the years of Mandela's rural upbringing in the 1920s to the final years of his imprisonment in the late 1980s. The main focus, however, is on the period of Mandela's early political activity, from the moment he became a resident of Alexandra township to the moment of his removal to Robben Island – an eventful twenty-year span. Bonner's concern is to trace out what he calls the "antinomies" that define Mandela: tensions between rural and urban influences, familial and political commitments, submission to party discipline and individual assertion, and between antithetical but deeply ingrained personal traits. Whereas the tendency in most biographical and autobiographical writing – a tendency scrutinized in the final section of this book – is to subsume all contradictions into a linear, developmental narrative, Bonner perceives Mandela's greatness not as something achieved by an overcoming or resolution of his antinomies. He suggests, rather, that it may be precisely these unresolved tensions that made Mandela a great man. Bonner's method, therefore, is not to have us see Mandela's rise to prominence as natural or predictable, but to pinpoint moments where that ascent seems unlikely: moments where the contradictions in his character seemed to precipitate new directions.

One of Bonner's most thought-provoking observations is that the veering between Africanist and non-racial positions evident in Mandela's early career also characterizes South African politics more broadly. The history of the resistance struggle, he proposes, has involved a constant seesawing between these two poles, with neither tradition ever disappearing; one always occupies the ascendant position, while the other is temporarily submerged. It is an idea that readers could profitably bear in mind as they engage with other chapters in this book (especially those of Ngwane, Ndlovu, and Van Robbroeck). It is also worth noting how readily the key arguments of this opening chapter can be extended beyond the point at which it ends: with Mandela's decision to begin talks with government officials. This is a momentous instance of individual assertion and, Bonner suggests, one by which Mandela's legacy will be judged. But one also sometimes hears the claim, compelling in its utter reductiveness, that Mandela's legacy, in practical terms, comes down to the anointing of Thabo Mbeki as his successor: a party decision, in other words, to which Mandela – bowing once more to collective discipline – acquiesced. And one of the defining aspects of the Mbeki presidency was surely a re-energizing of Africanist political and philosophical traditions, with results that are still unfolding. The old oscillations and antinomies, in other words, persist – and they are visible in this book as well.

Chapter 2 is concerned with the harsh years of Mandela's incarceration. This period is not easy to write about, as biographers have observed.[29] These were, after all, decades of grinding routine without many notable events; yet they are felt to be decisive – not least because they constitute the sacrifice out of which Mandela's moral capital could be drawn.[30] The most obvious and appealing way of narrating these years is as a story of small cumulative victories, of collective resistance against oppression in its most soul-destroying form. David Schalkwyk, however, takes a different approach here, which is to ask what imprisonment meant for Mandela as a person and how it shaped "the myth into which the man transformed." The answer lies in Mandela's acquisition of a stunning level of control over his emotions, which Schalkwyk chooses to read through the lens of classical Stoicism. Some readers may balk at this heuristic gesture, but we must remember that prisoners needed to draw on all possible cultural resources to survive with dignity. Lodge reminds us, for instance, that the mission-educated men on Robben Island in the early 1960s would recite lines from Macaulay's *Lays of Ancient Rome* to honor their fallen comrades:

> And how can man die better
> Than facing fearful odds
> For the ashes of his fathers
> And the temples of his Gods.[31]

Schalkwyk's interpretive gesture, then, is not as counterintuitive as it may seem. And it is certainly productive in underscoring the disciplinary continuities between prison and the Victorian education Mandela received at Clarkebury and Healdtown schools, as well as the literary sources of inspiration at "Robben Island University." These included, not coincidentally, the meditations of Marcus Aurelius, which Ahmed Kathrada owned, and the plays of Shakespeare, which many of the prisoners read and in which stoicism is a consistent thread.

The conclusion of Schalkwyk's chapter, with its evocation of a struggle in Mandela between the brain and the blood, resonates with Bonner's judgment that Mandela's greatness is not a matter of a resolution of tensions. But we must note a difference too: while Bonner probes aspects of Mandela's character, he does so in a thoroughly political framework, while Schalkwyk does so in a framework that is, in the first instance, ethical. And yet it also limns a certain kind of politics – for, as Schalkwyk points out, Stoicism is also a political philosophy, and one that is concerned with the equality and fellowship of all human beings. If it is focused on inwardness – indeed, on a detachment of the emotions from anything exterior – it is not merely individualistic. On Robben Island Mandela came to realize, as Schalkwyk puts it, that "the burden of selfhood in prison is not only a weight to be carried, but a refrain to be sung in unison." At stake here is an understanding of selfhood that informs not only the passages from *Long Walk to Freedom* discussed earlier, but also one of Mandela's most moving political statements, the defiant declaration read by his daughter Zindzi in 1985 to a crowd in Jabulani Stadium: "Your freedom and mine cannot be separated."

If Mandela emerges from this chapter as a man belonging, ethically and psychologically, to an earlier era (the very word "fortitude," Schalkwyk points out, has an archaic ring), he appears in the next two chapters as a modern personality and as a crucial figure in the forging of a national imaginary in the post–Cold War era. Indeed, these two chapters initiate a concern that surfaces at various points throughout this collection: how to define, through reflections on Mandela, the nature of a South African and, by extension, global modernity.

Insofar as her essay is narrative, Deborah Posel (Chapter 3) continues Mandela's life story where Schalkwyk ends, with the moment of his release from prison: a moment of exuberance and elation, often described as "miraculous" or "magical." Without debunking these feelings, Posel meticulously historicizes them. She offers an account of how "Madiba magic" was constructed – not only by the ANC (which needed Mandela to loom large and mythic to internationalize its cause), but also by the National Party (which, in order to break an ugly political stalemate, needed to transform Mandela from a figure of dread to a figure of hope). The magic, as she shows, was also Mandela's own creation; it was an effect of his elegant, imposing appearance and well-calculated symbolic actions: his performance of the very possibility of reconciliation.

But the chief contribution of this chapter is ultimately theoretical. Its concern is not to plumb Mandela's psychological makeup, but rather the politics of national sentiment that shaped the transition and its legacy. Countering the familiar Weberian account of modernity as rational disenchantment, Posel concludes with a meditation on the modernity of enchantment and its many manifestations in present-day South Africa, from religion, spirituality, and witchcraft right down to the secular magic of the commodity, whose elusive promises are pervasive in the brashly materialistic society that arose out the utopian moments of the transition. Schooled, perhaps, by the ostensibly miraculous founding of the Mandela republic, South Africans today are no strangers to contemporary forms of wishful thinking, to what Jean and John Comaroff have described as the peculiar occultism of our neoliberal world, with its prosperity churches, voodoo economics, and "casino capitalism."[32] The fact that Mandela's smiling visage now appears on all denominations of the South African currency, therefore, raises profound questions about what "Madiba magic" has metamorphosed into – what it has been exchanged for.

While Posel considers Mandela's performances of statesmanship in the context of the transition to democracy, Brenna Munro's wide-ranging essay (Chapter 4) attends specifically to his performance of gender: to his forging, over the years, of distinctively modern ways of being a black South African man. Many writers on Mandela have noted that it is impossible to separate the personal from the political in assessing this life and that any attempt to do so seems particularly futile when we consider Mandela's connection with his former wife Winnie.[33] In Munro's chapter the idea that "the personal is political" crystallizes into a meditation on the ways in which national dreams are gendered, imagined not only as a matter of kinship, but as figured by the heterosexual family – by fathers and mothers, brothers and sisters, sons and daughters. While this observation is generally applicable to the modern nation, it is particularly thought-provoking in the case of South Africa. Apartheid, after all, was in so many ways an assault on the family, distorting relations between parents and children and men and women in countless painful ways. To imagine the new democratic nation thus required a reimagining of the national family.

This chapter, then, takes on the task of showing how Mandela's personal sacrifice of intimate relationships served to enhance his performance of the symbolic role of father of the nation. In the process, it also tells the story of Winnie Madikizela-Mandela: a troubling, larger-than-life figure and a global icon in her own right. In so doing, it reminds us that we cannot fully understand Mandela's political meaning without also attending to the unfolding of the anti-apartheid struggle outside the confines of Robben Island – a struggle in which Winnie, for good and ill, loomed large. It reminds us, too, that Mandela's experiences in the years after his release cannot be grasped as solely triumphant. They coincided also with the dissolution of this marriage, which he clearly treasured but which threatened to tarnish his reputation and thereby damage the chances of a negotiated settlement. In her account of how Winnie's revolutionary motherhood became authoritarian, Munro raises profound questions about gender and sexuality, race and power – about such crucial matters as the right to use violence and the persistent effects, on personal lives, of multiple histories of oppression. While unflinchingly presenting the details of Winnie's misrule in the late 1980s, she also dares ask to what extent the spectacle of female indiscipline that Winnie came to embody – in contrast to Nelson's masculine deliberation and even saintliness – was inflated by a patriarchal vision of gender politics that has proved difficult to dislodge.

Mandela's Thought

The next four chapters, organized under the rubric "Reinterpreting Mandela," offer a re-examination of various aspects of Mandela's thought, both political and legal. To speak of Mandela's thought is not as straightforward a matter as it may sound. For Mandela was a practical politician, not a scholar or theorist. To tease out his thinking requires not only careful attention to his speeches, autobiography, and symbolic actions, but also an understanding of the cultural, conceptual, and philosophical frameworks in which he operated. A certain methodological ingenuity, as well as insight from a variety of disciplines, is required – and that is precisely what we have here. Each of these chapters contemplates aspects of Mandela's life not just in their immediate historical context, but in the *longue durée* of the customs and vernacular literature of the Eastern Cape, colonial and apartheid jurisprudence, the political traditions of the ANC since its inception in 1912, and the evolution of modern warfare. These essays also place Mandela's life in a global context, viewing it in relation to the emergence of human rights discourse in the wake of World War II, to Cold War politics, and to the ANC's long-standing internationalism, which, as Sifiso Ndlovu argues in Chapter 8, profoundly affected Mandela's foreign policy.

An important line of inquiry that comes into view here concerns Mandela's relation to "tradition," a term that raises no fewer questions than "modernity." Ndlovu's contribution, with its emphasis on spiritual and cultural continuities that have persisted in the "new" South Africa, is therefore a good place to start an overview of this part of the book. The aim of this chapter is to offer an account of the presidential years: its challenges and accomplishments, and also its informing vision. Since Mandela was a hands-off president, more resembling a chief of state than a party leader, often not even presiding over cabinet meetings, his own work in those years is not so easy to adjudicate. The more positive assessments tend to focus on the achievement of democracy and reconciliation, through such institutions as the (fairly short-lived) Government of National Unity and the Truth and Reconciliation Commission. The more negative assessments tend to focus on economic policy, on the decision to shift from a developmental macroeconomic plan (as promised in the ANC's election platform of 1994, the Reconstruction and Development Programme, or RDP) to a more neo-liberal World Bank–friendly one (as initiated by the Growth, Employment, and Redistribution Programme, or GEAR, adopted by the Department of Finance in 1996). Ndlovu's modus operandi is not that of either of these two camps. He strives, instead, to focus on Mandela's achievements as shaped by African traditions, including a graciousness in victory and a broadly human-ist ethic that, while devoted to rights, is in no way race-blind. His chapter, therefore, issues a challenge to those who subsume Mandela too easily into Western and Christian narratives of forgiveness, who translate the African traditions of *ubuntu*, of reciprocal recognition and obligation, into some sort of vague, exportable niceness, and who view Mandela (to use Thabo Mbeki's ironic phrase) as "the one good native" who stands out against the ranks of those African tyrants that, in the media stereotype, have come to define the norm for the "dark continent."[34]

Ndlovu's approach is not only to draw from Mandela's speeches and sym-bolic actions a series of moments where he affirms ancestral connections and honors his political predecessors, but to assess several of his achieve-ments (in the domains of gender, politics and economics, and diplomacy) in relation to traditions that, Ndlovu reminds us, are still very much alive in the experience of the majority of South Africans. This is not, however, an approach that neglects the difficult practicalities of governance. Drawing on interviews with participants, Ndlovu makes it clear that the change of gov-ernment in 1994 was a far more challenging task than that confronting a new ruling party in an established democracy: not only did a slew of racist laws require revision, but the entire edifice of a civil service bureaucracy that would actually serve the entire population needed to be built from scratch.

In Ndlovu's chapter tradition is conceptualized as a resource that operates not locally so much as nationally and transnationally. The many moving passages from Mandela's public statements that he brings to our attention encompass a kind of Africanist poetics: a rhetoric of inclusiveness that may extend across national boundaries and may yoke – also in the practice of the historian – the present and the past, the living and the dead. By contrast, Zolani Ngwane (Chapter 5) deals with the concept of tradition in the more locally grounded but also more distanced and dispassionate mode of the anthropologist. Tradition, he reminds us, entails not only cultural resources, but also intimate obligations, which affect different categories of subjects quite differently. This is to say that "tradition" is quite a different thing depending on whether one is a child or an adult, a woman or a man, lowly or socially prominent. It is, moreover, not simply opposed to modernity, but is best understood (especially when we are seeking to understand its deployment by elite men) as a critique of modernity. Ngwane reminds us that for indigenous people in colonial situations, the most alluring promise of modernity, the right to selfhood – to being a subject of history – is denied, and in such contexts of exclusion, tradition is often mobilized and recast in politically potent ways. Viewed from the grass roots (a perspective often adopted in this chapter), Mandela and other nationalist leaders thus assumed something of the role of default elders, entrusted with the perpetuation but also the creative transformation of "tradition" – at least in its more symbolic and less place-bound modalities.

This theoretical meditation becomes the ground for reinvestigating the two aspects of Mandela's life that are most often cited as demonstrating his connection to Thembu and Xhosa culture. The first is his upbringing at the Great Place of Chief Jongintaba Dalindyebo, where Mandela claims to have absorbed the principles of consensual democracy, and his circumcision, an experience he describes as formative in his autobiography and interviews. The second is his 1962 appearance in court, dressed in the regalia of the Thembu royal line: beads and a leopard skin kaross. It is a scene to which several of the contributors to this volume are drawn – and understandably so, since it is such a dramatic example of Mandela's performative politics and is legible from a variety of disciplinary optics. Ngwane's discussion is distinctive in that it demonstrates not only how Mandela's "body-in-tradition" was symbolically overdetermined in this instance, but also how it was able to re-enter tradition in the form of oral narratives and song. When Mandela writes in his autobiography about returning to his family home at Qunu in 1990, he notes his surprise at how all the children sang songs celebrating Umkhonto we Sizwe and how "the knowledge of the struggle had seeped into every corner of African society."[35] Ngwane's meditations reveal something of the vernacular processes through which this happened. His chapter, in sum, is an account of how Mandela, as national leader, did not refuse tradition but redeployed it in a different register and how he articulated a mode of modern self-affirmation that nevertheless involved a strong sense of collective obligation: the kind of gesture also captured at various moments in Ndlovu's chapter.

In the course of tracing out this process, Ngwane introduces us to a figure that looms even larger in the next chapter: that of the court interpreter, who stood "in a hermeneutic relationship between custom and colonial law." It is worth bearing in mind that, when he entered Fort Hare University, Mandela planned to pursue this vocation. And Ngwane's chapter permits us to say that Mandela did so, in a way: that he became a translator of sorts and on a larger scale than as a young man he could ever have imagined.

Adam Sitze's essay, "Mandela and the Law" (Chapter 6), also revisits the figure of the court interpreter and meditates on the trope of translation. But here translation assumes the more radical character of betrayal (*tradutore, tradditore*): an undermining of the structures of South African jurisprudence from within. Sitze considers Mandela within two institutional contexts: that of the university (for Mandela, he reminds us, was a law student for no fewer than fifty years) and that of the courtroom. He invites us, as it were, to read over Mandela's shoulder as he studied his law books, by attending closely to the academic work of a number of key teachers Mandela encountered. These include, at Fort Hare University, Professors J. B. Matthews and D. D. T. Jabavu and, at the University of the Witwatersrand, the notorious Professor Herman Robert Hahlo, whose remark that "women and Africans were not disciplined enough to master the intricacies of the law" is often cited as the sign of his racism and unpleasant personality.[36] Sitze, however, grasps Hahlo's statements as something more than that: as revealing of his view of the law of persons, the very subject in which he instructed Mandela. This view, Sitze demonstrates, has its origins in both Roman law and British common law, where not all humans were "persons," but some were excluded from that category as "minors" and, in colonial jurisprudence, as "nonages," whose "backwardness" disqualified them from the exercise of liberty. It is, of course, a view that was rendered increasingly untenable in the period after World War II, when the concept of the rights-bearing person became universalized. While Mandela himself, then, considered his failure in Hahlo's courses to be his own fault, Sitze suggests instead that Mandela may have been the student who understood Hahlo best: that Mandela grasped the incoherence of Hahlo's conception and was able to articulate a powerful counterview to it in the ANC Youth League Manifesto, with its denunciation of a system in which the African would be "a perpetual minor," indeed, a "criminal still out of prison." Mandela's court performances and speeches from the dock are of a piece with this understanding: they become, in Sitze's reading, not just theater, but, from a jurisprudential view, experimental redefinitions of the concept of the "person." Or to put it differently, Mandela's self-(re)presentation in court simultaneously dramatized the legality of the organization he personified and the illegality of the apartheid state.

In his biography of Mandela, Tom Lodge observes that historians of anticolonial movements have paid insufficient attention to the influence of colonial legal ideas on African nationalist leaders. Sitze's highly original research fills this lacuna brilliantly, but it also complicates Lodge's premise. For, as Sitze shows, Mandela both learned and unlearned colonial law: the discipline of South African jurisprudence did not merely influence him, but moved him to expose its cruel contradictions.

In Chapter 7 Jonathan Hyslop also considers the implications of post–World War II developments for Mandela's political thought and career: the Cold War and the decision of the Soviet Union to support Third World insurgencies, as well as certain crucial changes in the political-legal framework of warfare. As Hyslop argues, the participation of partisans and civilian combatants in the fight against Hitler led, in 1949, to a revision of the Geneva Convention, which made it possible for national liberation organizations to demand legal protections for their fighters. Because of this newly revised conception of the legalities of warfare, guerrilla forces (especially in the decolonizing world) were able to claim something of the status of national armies for themselves and something akin to statelike authority for their organizations. At stake here, of course, are the gray areas between war, revolution, and politics – of which Mandela was acutely aware.

It is no accident, then, that the title of this chapter, "Mandela on War," should echo Carl von Clausewitz, whom Mandela read with great care during his time underground. By tracing out Mandela's understanding of the Prussian general (whose experience dates back to the Napoleonic wars, the historical moment when those gray areas became visible and problematic), Hyslop probes the contentious question of Mandela's thinking about military power and political violence. To envision Mandela as an "instinctive Clausewitzean" is to take issue with interpretations that have begun to emerge, in scholarly and popular domains, of Mandela as a Gandhian figure of non-violence or as a Fanonian figure: a kind of postcolonial theorist-in-action of violent resistance.[37] Neither characterization, Hyslop argues, is accurate. For Mandela's thinking, about passive resistance and warfare alike, was always strategic rather than theoretical or dogmatic. He understood the complex interrelationship between military means, long-term aims, and popular support and always kept his eye on political outcomes. This balanced outlook, Hyslop observes, was not shared by all in the ANC. Many exiles, seduced by the polarities of Cold War thinking, began to identify the party with its military wing, Umkhonto we Sizwe. This tendency not only diminished the ANC's interest, during its time in exile, in fostering aboveground organizational structures, but has also had lasting effects in the "new" South Africa. For the allure of militarism clearly continues today. One need only think of the footage of militants in ANC training camps that was screened at the climax of the party's historic meeting at Polokwane in 2009 when Jacob Zuma was elected ANC president. Against this tendency, the main lessons Mandela learned from Clausewitz – that war is politics by other means and that one can recognize the validity of resorting to arms without romanticizing violence – seem well worth remembering.

Mandela's Image

The chapters that make up the final section of the book, entitled "Representing Mandela," all reflect on the processes and media that have made Mandela a national and global icon. Together these chapters explore his image in literature and print culture, film, and other visual forms, like portraits, photographs, and even a comic book. But they also bring a dimension of self-reflexive inquiry to this volume, which is, after all, yet another attempt to represent Mandela – albeit in multidisciplinary, prismatic, and critical ways. In their meditations on the difficulties that beset such efforts (not least the way in which Mandela always seems to signify some larger concept like justice, forgiveness, reconciliation, or the nation), these contributions alert us to the danger that the myth of Mandela, as Daniel Roux puts it, "hampers our ability to reach more complex understandings of the genealogy of the present." Such concerns can be traced in all of the contributions to this section, culminating in the final pages of the closing chapter, which offer something quite daring: a "pre-mortem" reflection on the rhetoric that is likely to accompany Mandela's death. By way of a proleptic eulogy (the essay was written in late 2012), Sarah Nuttall and Achille Mbembe invite us to wonder how the dead, depoliticized discourses of stereotype and official verbiage could be avoided at the end of Mandela's life and how a limber language that truly honors and emulates him might be forged.

This section opens with Daniel Roux's "Mandela Writing / Writing Mandela" (Chapter 9). On one level, we could see this piece as a sophisticated reading of Mandela's best-selling autobiography, *Long Walk to Freedom*, a work often described as the founding text of the "new" South Africa. Roux ponders the autobiography's overarching narrative pattern, which, he argues, conforms precisely to that of the bildungsroman. Two aspects of the genre are particularly relevant in his view. The first is its temporality – a paradoxical temporality, since we have here a narrative of progress and development, but a development to which the conclusion is on the cards from the beginning. The protagonist, in other words, becomes the very person he always already was. The second characteristic is the bildungsroman's typically harmonious resolution, in which the self-affirmation of the protagonist turns out to be simultaneously an affirmation of the demands of society. These effects of coherence and concord in *Long Walk to Freedom* are enhanced, Roux argues, by the work's characteristic figurative structure: that of chiasmus, or metaphorical inversion. Tracing out the various instances of gardening scattered across the autobiography, Roux demonstrates how, in each case, Mandela's narration seems to transform the garden from a private space of solitary retreat to a public and political space. This recurrent motif becomes a way of yoking together very different moments in Mandela's life story; the schoolboy, the prisoner, and the statesman are all metaphorically merged as gardeners of sorts. Two formal aspects of the work, then, one synchronic (the plot) and one diachronic (the figuration), have the effect of making those antinomies and contradictions that emerge in the critical historian's analysis recede. *Long Walk to Freedom* thus creates the effect of an admirably unified subject, whose life story is not only an allegory of the liberated nation, but also – since it narrates the acquisition of fundamental human rights – a universal tale of vast appeal.

Now, some readers might find this elegant commentary all too literary. But that is to miss the point. For, as Roux puts it, the coherence and stability of Mandela as political icon are, in good measure, a matter of literary form. The chapter demonstrates this claim by surveying the difficulties that a variety of commentators on Mandela have encountered in their efforts to get around the powerfully pre-scripted story of Mandela's life. Writings that claim to reveal the subject's hidden truth end up revealing what has always been on the surface; efforts at demythologizing Mandela unwittingly remythologize him, while attempts to humanize him – to make him more ordinary and flawed – end up making him seem all the more exceptional.

A related argument arises in Litheko Modisane's essay on Mandela and film (Chapter 10), which draws our attention to the ways in which Mandela's life has been packaged for international movie audiences. He suggests that made-for-export films, like *Mandela* (directed by Philip Saville in 1987) and *Invictus* (directed by Clint Eastwood in 2009), are particularly inclined to flatten out any contradiction in Mandela's character in order to make him fit into received Western master narratives – most notably the messianic myth of the savior who will return (as in *Mandela*) or the savior who *has* returned to forgive and forget and erase the past (as in *Invictus*). For all their attempts at providing historical background and credibility (voice-overs, quasi-documentary footage, and the like), these films end up inventing a Mandela who not only is unrealistically virtuous, but operates in ways that actually contradict his emancipatory role.

This chapter fills a curious lacuna. Although Mandela has often been represented in film (both feature films and documentaries) and has been played by a long list of famous African-American movie stars, there has been relatively little scholarly commentary to date on the extent to which his status as international icon has been shaped through this medium. (Modisane rightly notes that the only book on Mandela to provide readers with a filmography is the journalist Max du Preez's popular biography for the *Rough Guide* series; more weighty treatments seem to consider the cinematic Mandela unworthy of attention.) If, therefore, we wish not just to admire Mandela, but to understand what Elleke Boehmer terms "the processes of meaning-making" that have elicited this admiration, we certainly need to consider the ways in which Mandela's personal and public life has been mediated – and indeed distorted – by films that, for the sake of international marketing and accessibility, have tended to recast his story in individualistic, romantic, and religiously redemptive terms.[38]

Lize van Robbroeck's essay (Chapter 11), like Modisane's, turns to the indispensable, yet often ignored visual aspects of Mandela's iconic status. Her meditation could be seen as picking up from Roux's observation that Mandela's life story, as captured in *Long Walk to Freedom*, is not just a depiction or description, but has a performative dimension: it calls something into being. For Van Robbroeck, that something is a particular kind of subject: the individual as model citizen. In her thinking, moreover, representation – both in the sense of depiction and in the sense of standing for or speaking for – comes to assume a specifically pedagogical character. This is evident both in her analysis of the South African–born artist Paul Emsley's monumental portrait of Mandela, which appears on the cover of this book, and in her reading of a work for children: the authorized comic book version of *Long Walk to Freedom*. Both of these works, she suggests, set up Mandela as the ideal responsible citizen and exhort the viewer/reader to emulate him in this achievement. Van Robbroeck theorizes a similar terrain to Roux in her discussion of the comic book's bildungsroman plot. But she captures its workings more philosophically, psychoanalytically, and visually in her discussion of a number of complex images: static representations, as graphic images inevitably are, and yet able to encompass time and impose a certain ideological and pedagogic form on it.

One of Van Robbroeck's major concerns in this essay is to show that, while Mandela is legible in relation to Western ideas about the model subject-as-citizen, he also resisted their Eurocentric character by performing them in a distinctively African manner. In this Van Robbroeck finds common ground with the work of Sitze and Ngwane. Indeed, she also returns to that compelling moment, discussed by both of them – and nicely illustrated in the comic book – when Mandela appeared in court in his famous leopard skin kaross. In her closing reflections, however, she takes the matter of Mandela's flexible embodiment of black masculinity into the present. She notes that US President Barack Obama, like Mandela, seems to have crafted a performance of self that yokes signifiers of blackness and signifiers of responsible citizenship in ways that are somehow reassuring to his white compatriots. Yet this performance is vulnerable to charges – and jokes – about his not being black enough. The same is certainly not true of South Africa's current president, Jacob Zuma. The anxieties he has elicited, Van Robbroeck shows,

are powerfully registered in the visual field: cartoonists and artists have sub-
jected Zuma to cutting satire – at the very same moment that Mandela's
beneficent image has come to be sacralized on the nation's currency. But
his image, she warns, has also been commodified in the most banal forms:
a banalization that threatens to undo Mandela's powerful exemplarity. The
pedagogical power of his visual representation of ideal citizenship, in other
words, may be sliding quite simply into the power of profit.

This danger is articulated in somewhat different terms in the final essay
of this book, Sarah Nuttall and Achille Mbembe's meditation on Mandela
and mortality (Chapter 12). Their strategy here is not to avoid the powerful,
pre-scripted narratives of Mandela's autobiographical writings, but rather
to read them against the grain. The results are striking. While the chapter
is ultimately a celebration of Mandela as a twentieth-century hero, it does
not retrace the familiar triumphal outlines of his life story. What Mbembe
and Nuttall tease out from *Long Walk to Freedom* and *Conversations with
Myself* are the darker threads: a long series of deaths and losses, painful separations, and remarkably powerful descriptions of Mandela's feelings and
thoughts about these experiences over the years. That Mandela heroically
faced the possibility of a death sentence and that he preferred not to express
his hurt and fear in public does not diminish the fact that he suffered the
deaths of many people close to him and often felt the pain of his inability
to meet his obligations to the dead. In sketching this history, Mbembe and
Nuttall force us to rethink the idea of Mandela's exceptionalism. In the fragility of his family life, he comes to seem much more of a typical black South
African man of his generation: a person whose adversities cannot solely be
attributed to his choice of the struggle above family; they also form part of a
much broader racialized and gendered condition that speaks volumes about
the quotidian oppression of colonialism and apartheid.

The aim of this chapter is not, in the end, to demythologize Mandela or
to deny his capacity to allegorize the nation. Indeed, Mbembe and Nuttall
suggest that the image of the frail and faltering Mandela may be available as
an objective correlative of the decline of the hopes that were so alive in the
heyday of his presidency. Like many other authors in this book, they seek,
in conclusion, to cast a light on the present day – on what has happened to
the promises of justice, reconciliation, and proud nationality that Mandela
inaugurated. It is fair to say that this chapter presents the most epochal
assessment of these matters. Turning to the work of the political theorist
Susan Buck-Morss, they associate Mandela with the utopian dreamworld
of the twentieth century: the dream of mass democracy, of a social order
created to sustain and further individual happiness. Mandela is for them
the hero of such a vision in his fight for social arrangements that would

transcend existing forms. But it is helpful to bring to mind here Deborah Posel's meditations on the more commercial modes of enchantment that have succeeded the transformative era of "Madiba magic." In our time, the transformative and promissory dimensions of modernity seem to have retreated into the commodity, the most global of all cultural forms – and one that, Nuttall and Mbembe note, retains a certain magical, even utopian power in individual lives. But divested of its political dimension, this individualized utopia can fall prey to cynicism – to the venality and corruption that seem to be the current order of the day.

We are left, at the end of their chapter, with a sense that this need not remain the case; yet we nevertheless seem to be situated at the end of an era. What is the meaning of Mandela at this moment, when his political ideas are honored more in their breach than their realization? Nuttall and Mbembe exhort us to think of new languages in which to honor Mandela, but that invention must surely entail a recognition that, as Daniel Roux puts it, we still stand at "the very edge of the persuasive and influential national [and perhaps global] imaginary of Nelson Mandela." Moving beyond this, beginning to talk and think outside Mandela's understanding of his time, is a possibility that is still to come. What is clear at this moment is that Mandela continues to issue a call to conscience, to South Africans and the world at large. That is what makes this volume's cover image, Paul Emsley's grave portrait of Mandela, with its unavoidable, direct gaze, so terrifying. The columnist Justice Malala formulated this call simply but eloquently on the occasion of Albertina Sisulu's death in 2011:

> What about us, though? The adversity of apartheid blessed us with men and women whose moral courage and commitment to values is unparalleled. Can we claim to be worthy successors of these people? Soon there will be no Sisulus, Mandelas and Tutus among us. They will be gone. We will look around and realize that it is now up to us to protect the gains they lived – and many died – fighting for. Will we be up to the challenge?[39]

Nelson Mandela died on December 5th, 2013: the very day that the final proofs of this book were due at the press.

NOTES

1 Nelson Mandela, *Long Walk to Freedom: The Autobiography of Nelson Mandela* (New York: Little, Brown, 1995), 624.

2 Mark Gevisser, *A Legacy of Liberation: Thabo Mbeki and the Future of the South African Dream* (New York: Palgrave Macmillan, 2009), ix.

3 On the difference between a kind of "tribal" or "consensual democracy" and "ordinary democracy," both of which inspired Mandela, see Tom Lodge, *Mandela: A*

Critical Life (Oxford: Oxford University Press, 2006), xi–xii, and Andrew Nash, "Mandela's Democracy," *Monthly Review* 50.11 (April 1999), monthlyreview. org/1999/04/01/mandelas-democracy (accessed February 6, 2013).

4   Jacob Rogozinski, "The Gift of the World," in *Of the Sublime: Presence in Question*, ed. Jeffrey S. Librett (Albany, NY: SUNY Press, 1993), 146; Lodge, *Mandela*, viii.

5   Quoted in Mac Maharaj, Ahmed Kathrada, et al., *Mandela: The Authorised Portrait* (Kansas City, MO: Andrews McMeel, 2006), 3.

6   Mandela, *Long Walk*, 623–24.

7   Rogozinski, "Gift of the World," 146.

8   Mandela, *Long Walk*, 556.

9   See Loren Kruger, "Apartheid on Display: South Africa Performs for New York," *Diaspora* 1.2 (1991): 194, and Rob Nixon, "Cry White Season: Anti-Apartheid Heroism and the American Screen," in *Homelands, Harlem, Hollywood: South Africa and the World Beyond* (New York: Routledge, 1994), 77–100.

10 Anthony Sampson, *Mandela: The Authorized Biography* (New York: Knopf, 1999), 574–75.

11 Fredric Jameson, "The End of Temporality," *Critical Inquiry* 29.4 (Summer 2003): 699.

12 For two further accounts of Mandela's relation to modernity, see Jonathan Hyslop, "Gandhi, Mandela, and the African Modern," in *Johannesburg: The Elusive Metropolis*, ed. Sarah Nuttall and Achille Mbembe (Durham, NC: Duke University Press, 2008), 119–36, and Elleke Boehmer, *Nelson Mandela: A Brief Insight* (New York: Sterling, 2010), 11–12, 117–30.

13 Boehmer, *Nelson Mandela*, 5.

14 Sampson, *Mandela*, 576.

15 Nixon, "Mandela, Messianism, and the Media," in *Homelands, Harlem, Hollywood*, esp. 175–79.

16 Ibid., 179.

17 Sampson, *Mandela*, 571–72; Nixon, "Mandela," 179.

18 Ahmed Kathrada, Interview for *Reconciliation: Mandela's Miracle*, dir. Michael Henry Wilson, 2011.

19 On the anachronism of nationalism in the second postcolonial epoch (after the fall of the Soviet Union), see Jean Comaroff and John L. Comaroff, "Millennial Capitalism: First Thoughts on a Second Coming," *Public Culture* 12.2 (2000): 318–26.

20 Mandela, *Long Walk*, 584.

21 Boehmer, *Nelson Mandela*, 17.

22 See data.worldbank.org/country/south-africa. I am grateful to Michael MacDonald for an interpretation of these figures.

23 Njabulo S. Ndebele, "The Rediscovery of the Ordinary: Some New Writings in South Africa," *Journal of Southern African Studies* 12.2 (April 1986): 144–57.

24 Gareth Cornwell, "South African Literature in English since 1945: Long Walk to Ordinariness," in Gareth Cornwell, Dirk Klopper, and Craig Mackenzie, *The Columbia Guide to South African Literature* (New York: Columbia University Press, 2009), 6–7.

25 Gevisser, *Legacy of Liberation*, 320.

26 For critical renamings of Mandela, see Chapter 6 by Sitze, who focuses on the name Rolihlahla, and Chapter 8 by Ndlovu, who focuses on the name Dalibunga, given to Mandela on the occasion of his circumcision, as well as "Nelisile" (the fulfilled one): the mispronunciation, or rather, Ndlovu suggests, the creative anti-colonial reclamation of the name "Nelson" by Mandela's mother.

27 Jeremy Cronin, *Even the Dead* (Belville: Mayibuye Books, 1997), 29–30.

28 Lodge, *Mandela*, ix. Several serious biographies of Mandela have appeared to date; all are valuable and are listed at the end of this volume. For canny assessments of how these biographies reflect their own historical moments and offer different assessments of Mandela's political career, see Lodge's preface and Boehmer, *Nelson Mandela*, 5–9.

29 See, e.g., Lodge, *Mandela*, 120.

30 John Kane, *The Politics of Moral Capital* (Cambridge: Cambridge University Press, 2001).

31 Lodge, *Mandela*, 4.

32 Comaroff and Comaroff, "Millennial Capitalism," 310–18.

33 See, e.g., Lodge, *Mandela*, xi.

34 Gevisser, *Legacy of Liberation*, 264.

35 Mandela, *Long Walk*, 580.

36 Ibid., 90.

37 See, e.g., Boehmer, *Nelson Mandela*, 87–125.

38 Ibid., 9.

39 Justice Malala, "Are We Worthy Successors?" *Sunday Times*, June 8, 2011; www.timeslive.co.za/politics/2011/06/08/are-we-worthy-successors (accessed February 6, 2011).

PART I

The Man, the Movement, and the Nation

I

PHILIP BONNER

The Antinomies of Nelson Mandela

This chapter explores the relationship between Nelson Mandela and the political movement that he ultimately headed: the African National Congress (ANC) and the Congress Alliance. At stake is the story of a man and of a long association marked by a number of striking antinomies and contradictions. The first of these is between Mandela's early rural socialization at Mvezo and Mqhekezweni in the Umtata district of the Transkei and the urban, modern, and – for blacks – less hierarchical world he entered in his twenties. How far, in reality, did he shed the former influences in his later life, and how?

A second antinomy, well known to readers of Mandela's biographies, is between the familial and political in his life. Mandela repeatedly sacrificed family to wider interests – interests that, at first, were not necessarily political, but later wholly so – and he was repeatedly filled with remorse for what he had done. The first instance was his disrespectful treatment of his guardian, who died before Mandela could fully make amends. It set a pattern: in practically all of the subsequent cases where he neglected personal relationships, his attempts at reconciliation came too late and, whatever his regrets about the personal betrayals, he tended to make the same kind of choice again and again. This created an internal tension in Mandela, which one suspects he never really resolved: it is a core and contradictory part of the man.

A third antinomy is evident in the much less frequently discussed tension between Mandela's submission to party discipline and his individualistic tendencies. For most of his political life Mandela observed the principle of collective leadership of the ANC established by Walter Sisulu in 1950. This observance stood firm, despite moments of profound disagreement on his part with what was happening in the movement generally (as, for example, during the acrimonious debate within the ANC in the late 1940s and 1950s over the appropriate relationship with the Communist Party of South Africa [CPSA] and the Transvaal and Natal Indian Congresses). Yet, at other times,

Mandela simply bucked collective discipline and took initiatives that were profoundly controversial in the upper ranks of the ANC and had never been collectively approved. These include Mandela's initiative to ditch passive resistance and move to armed struggle in 1961 and his solitary decision in the late 1980s to enter into discussions with the white South African government over a negotiated settlement between the National Party and the ANC. This contradictory behavior points to a largely unexplained ambivalence in Mandela's thinking and character that remains uncharted territory in the existing literature.

A fourth and related antinomy is evident in a tension between Mandela's consistency and his impetuosity. For long periods of his life, his political thinking and attitudes would remain unchanged, but he could also suddenly lurch forward or away from his established principles to adopt an entirely new political philosophy and persona. This leaves us with puzzling questions. What explains the switch from the one position to the other? And under what circumstances did it occur?

A final antinomy lies in Mandela's antithetical qualities of flexibility and intransigence. Though he was generally ready to recognize his own limitations and mistakes, he could also, at times, adopt an attitude of absolute and unshakable certitude.

In the reflections that follow, I elucidate some of these contradictions. I rehearse some biographical details that are well known, but I do so in order to refresh and complicate our sense of the abiding patterns, as well as the decisive moments of change and the key relationships and influences that shaped Mandela's life. My account focuses most intensively on the years between Mandela's arrival in Johannesburg and his removal to Robben Island, but it extends to include some reflections on his prison years up to the moment of the transition. In probing these antinomies I do not intend to resolve or settle them; nor do I wish to suggest that they diminish Mandela. Indeed, I would argue that these contradictory and complementary parts of Mandela's character are quite possibly and ironically what made him the great man he was.

Moving to the City: Rural Roots and Modern Influences

A tension between rural, traditional roots and modern, cosmopolitan lifestyles and philosophies has not been unusual among black South African political leaders of the twentieth century. What is arguably different in the case of Nelson Mandela is his close association with a chiefly lineage. He grew up – from the age of seven at least – at the village and court of the regent of the Thembu royal house at Mqhekezweni in Transkei. The regent,

Jongintaba Dalindyebo, acted as guardian to Mandela after the death of his natural father, Gadla Henry Mphakanyiswa. Mandela's identity and ambitions were narrowly circumscribed at this point in his life and for many years later: his identity was Thembu more than Xhosa, the broader ethnic designation. He saw himself as destined and equipped for a future as an adviser to the Thembu royal house, like his father, and as a future interpreter at the magistrate's court.[1] Though Jongintaba sent Mandela to Methodist mission schools in the Eastern Cape and ultimately to the University of Fort Hare, Mandela's mental and political horizons were still confined during these years to this home area of Thembuland. He writes in his autobiography that he had not heard of the ANC until he enrolled as an undergraduate at Fort Hare, and at that point he was not particularly interested or impressed. He certainly didn't join. His interests, like those of most young men of similar age, centered on sport (his hero was the African-American boxer Joe Louis), on leisure (his passion was ballroom dancing), on his personal appearance, and on girls. At Fort Hare he struck up a close friendship with the later president of the Transkei, Kaiser Daliwonga Matanzima. Both young men were stylish and good-looking and, as Matanzima remembers, "all the women wanted [them]."[2] But beyond that, Mandela didn't particularly stand out. He didn't excel in soccer or rugby, the popular sports of the place and time (the reason he took up boxing), and he was not particularly intellectually accomplished. In his studies he was competent, even capable, but not outstanding. What was more, and perhaps more significant, he knew it and was prepared to acknowledge it. One might surmise that his subsequent flexibility and openness to criticism derive from this capacity to recognize his limitations.

What transformed Mandela from this quite shy, aloof, and rather unassuming man and set him on an entirely new course was an accident, one that revealed an antithetical, yet equally fundamental character trait: his deep-seated stubbornness. At Fort Hare he became embroiled in a dispute with the university authorities from which he would not back down and for which he was punished by being sent down from the university. His guardian was furious, as he was paying Mandela's fees and had gone deep into debt, partly as a result. He demanded that Mandela return to Fort Hare and, to settle him down, insisted that he and Justice Dalindyebo, Jongintaba's son and Mandela's close friend, enter into arranged marriages. Both rejected the idea of a forced marriage. Mandela was appalled by the appearance of his bride-to-be. Here too Mandela's streak of stubbornness, combined with a streak of vanity, showed itself once again. He and Justice simply absconded to Johannesburg, stealing – to add insult to injury – two of Jongintaba's cows to finance the journey. In doing so Mandela ripped up his life's script. The safe, predictable, expected course of his life was radically changed by one precipitous, impetuous act. The "long walk" had begun, but as a lurch forward rather than a planned, disciplined, ever-ascending progress.

Mandela's early perception of himself and his outward demeanor was powerfully influenced by his sense of his chiefly origins, and he modeled himself on the proud unbowed royals that he imagined both his father, Gadla, and his guardian, Jongintaba, to have been: hence his aloof, distant, dignified pose. In the early part of his autobiography, *Long Walk to Freedom*, Mandela describes his father's principled refusal to attend the court of a local magistrate when summoned to defend himself in a case for which he was stripped of his headmanship. "My father possessed a proud rebelliousness," he writes. "This defiance was not a fit of pique, but a matter of principle. He was asserting his traditional prerogative as chief and was challenging the authority of the magistrate."[3] Chief Jongintaba's behavior and demeanor, which Mandela closely observed as a boy, would also exercise a massive influence over him for the rest of his life. In particular, the regent's manner at court, where he would listen with regal impassivity to all sides of the argument, reflecting, weighing the points, before finally deciding and pronouncing a decision, left an enduring impression on Mandela. In both of these instances, however, he was at least partly modeling himself on a myth. Jongintaba was, in fact, a spendthrift and notorious drunkard for much of his life, something that Mandela apparently chose to forget. His account of his father's dismissal from the headmanship of Mveso is also simply untrue, although Mandela probably did not know this himself. Instead of assuming a defiant posture and refusing to attend a magistrate's hearing about his conduct with the ringing words "Andizi, ndisaqula" (I will not come, I am still girding for war), Mandela's father, as a recently discovered court record shows, did in fact attend the hearing, following which he was dismissed.[4] If Mandela's legacy has frequently been interpreted and narrated as nationalist myth, his own sense of self – the story he told himself – was no less shaped by romantic misperception, by myths that, in his case, may have changed the course of historical events.

Mandela arrived in Johannesburg still very much a scion of the Thembu royal line. Like most new African migrants he headed straight for a person of his own ethnic group. In Mandela's case this was a fellow Xhosa, Walter Sisulu, who helped the new arrival adjust to his new environment. Sisulu himself evinced a curious, though not unusual split consciousness; he had a white father and was an emerging African nationalist, but he nevertheless had a strong sense of Xhosa identity. "Many people from Transkei often went to Walter's office," observes Elinor Sisulu. "In one way or another he was connected with people in the royal house."[5] Sisulu was also secretary of the Orlando Brotherly Society, a Xhosa cultural association connected to the Hintsa branch of the royal family ("a tribal affair," as he once disarmingly and dismissively described it to me), and he introduced Mandela to its ranks.[6] Sisulu found Mandela (or Madiba, as he called him throughout his life) to be an impressive personality: agreeable and likeable, too. He thought Mandela would go places and, even in those early days, thought that his future lay in politics.[7] This perception may now strike us as obvious and inevitable, but we should remember that when Mandela arrived in Johannesburg he was still green and circumscribed in outlook; Sisulu's assessment of Mandela as a promising individual was therefore, in all likelihood, not based solely on the younger man's individual talents and intelligence, but on his chiefly connections and bearing. Such respect for chieftainship on the part of a thoroughly urban man like Sisulu might strike readers as surprising, but it has been a powerful and enduring element in South African politics. This is increasingly evident today, as legislation is passed strengthening the power of chiefs.

Sisulu found Mandela (who was then studying part time at the University of the Witwatersrand (Wits) to complete his BA) his first and not especially illustrious job as a rent collector, working on a commission basis for African landlords in Johannesburg's Alexandra township. Later Sisulu also secured him articles with the legal firm Witkin, Sidelsky, and Eidelmann and, for a period, Mandela even moved in with Sisulu and his wife, Albertina.[8] Sisulu was, in fact, to be the most formative and enduring influence in Nelson Mandela's life. (One former Robben Island colleague once told me, in a conversation following a 1993 interview, that Mandela always consulted Sisulu on everything, "and the one time he didn't, he got it wrong.") Little in Mandela's life could have been more important than the circumstances that brought them together, and these were – at first, certainly – matters of ethnic affiliation. It is out of such traditional, local connections that Mandela's political future as a national and world leader with an extraordinarily ecumenical appeal was established.[9]

Once Mandela was in Johannesburg, his horizons steadily widened. He writes that it was there, in this cosmopolitan, multiethnic environment that he cast off or grew out of the prejudices of his previous existence. Mandela's initial sojourn in Alexandra involved new influences and orientations. Alexandra was one of a handful of mixed African townships on the Rand where Africans could own freehold land. Such freehold rights were a key index of their right to take a place in the modern world and in the ranks of "civilization." Allied to freehold rights, in this definition, were Christianity and education. There is every reason to believe that Mandela shared these attitudes, as his job as rent collector for freehold landlords suggests. What caused a shift in perspective was Alexandra's cosmopolitanism. Both the landlords and tenants were drawn from every kind of ethnic background in South Africa into the ever-growing urban melting pot of Alexandra. The metaphor of melting pot can, indeed, be given a further valence – of heat and turbulence, for this was an environment that gave birth to a variety of internal conflicts and violent gangs. The place left an indelible imprint on Mandela's attitudes and life. As he writes in *Long Walk to Freedom*: "In spite of the hellish aspects of life in Alexandra, the township was also a kind of heaven.... Instead of being Xhosas or Sothos or Zulus or Shangaans, we were Alexandrans. This created a sense of solidarity ... [as] differences were being erased."[10]

Mandela arrived in Alexandra shortly before the bus boycott of August 1943, during which, for nine consecutive days, tens of thousands of township residents walked more than ten kilometers to work in Johannesburg. This protest action transformed Mandela from observer to participant: "This campaign had a great effect on me," he recalled. "I found that to march with one's people was exhilarating and inspiring. But I was also impressed by the boycott's effectiveness: after nine days, during which the buses ran empty, the company returned the fare to fourpence."[11] This last comment hints at a less commonly recognized aspect of the boycott's impact on Mandela's political thinking: namely, his evolving understanding of the role and potential of the general populace. The 1943–44 bus boycotts in Alexandra were seminal events in the history of African resistance in South Africa because they were supported mostly by sub-tenants and were driven from the bottom up. They were movements of extraordinary and unprecedented unity and mass mobilization, subject to the will of the broad community, which mandated and then ratified the actions of the leadership at mass meetings held in Second Square, Alexandra. As the CPSA activist Eddie Roux observed, the boycott was the most significant act of African resistance since World War I. It broke the previous mold and thrust Alexandra to the forefront of nationalist politics.[12] Alexandra was thus a heady mixture: it was quintessentially urban; it was cosmopolitan; it was both bourgeois and proletarian at the same time. It was a living, dynamic contradiction – and one that exercised a lasting influence on Mandela.

Another important influence was the youthful black political elite of his generation, who lived around him in Johannesburg. "Walter's house in Orlando," Mandela writes, "was a Mecca for activists and ANC members."[13] It was here that he met Anton Lembede and A. P. Mda, founding members of the ANC Youth League. The impact of Lembede's militant African nationalism on Mandela's thinking was decisive. As he puts it:

Lembede's views struck a chord in me. I, too, had been susceptible to paternalistic British colonialism and the appeal of being perceived by whites as "cultured" and "progressive" and "civilized." I was already on my way to being drawn into the black elite that Britain sought to create in Africa. That is what everyone from the regent to Mr. Sidelsky wanted for me. But it was an illusion.[14]

Lembede gave intellectual definition to Mandela's multifaceted experience of Alexandra, highlighting the political antimony that it represented but without as yet effecting a resolution.

Mandela was, at this point, no obvious leader. Though he was a founding member of the ANC Youth League when it was formed in 1944, he was not one of its architects or even one of its executive figures like Sisulu, Lembede, Mda, and J. Congress Mbata. Mandela's relative political immaturity is expressed in *Conversations with Myself*. Here, describing these early Youth League meetings, he confesses:

I never spoke. The only thing I took part in was the debates – not in political meetings, but just academic debates.... [Those] I participated in, but meetings I never did, until I joined the [ANC] Youth League. Even then I was very nervous.... I didn't know politics, you see. I was backward politically and I was dealing with chaps ... who knew politics, who could discuss what was happening in South Africa and outside South Africa.[15]

The idea of forming a ginger group within the ANC, however, had been in the air for most of 1942, and this was the air Mandela breathed. A formal decision to move ahead with this idea was taken at the ANC National Conference in December 1943, once the sanction of President-General A. B. Xuma had been given. That conference, Sisulu recalls, was "one of the most important and busiest conferences in years, approving a new constitution, the African Claims, and discussing the question of the emergence of the African Democratic Party [ADP]."[16] The ADP had been launched in October 1943, largely because of disillusionment with the "stagnant and disorganized" character of the ANC.[17] A critical impulse behind this launch was the way in which Xuma, as well as the ANC more generally, had opted to stand aloof that August from the Alexandra bus boycott. According to Robert Edgar and Luyanda ka Msumza, the formation and actions of this rival party were a critical factor in persuading Xuma to support the formation of the ANC Youth League. He feared that the ADP would "siphon off" younger ANC members and therefore was inclined to give these young Turks some leeway.[18]

The two influences that drove the formation of the Youth League correspond to the pressures that were pushing Mandela himself in a more decisive and radical political direction: the swirl of nationalist intellectual ideas and the pressure of popular anger from below. The latter is not usually credited with having much more than a token and abstract influence on the Youth League and its leaders, who are often described as loftily distinct from the grass roots. With Sisulu and Mandela, at least, this was not the case. Both men played a significant and largely unrecognized part, not only in the Alexandra bus boycott, but in the 1944 and 1946 land invasions, initiated by a group of squatters under James Mpanza – a protest often thought to have led to the founding of Soweto. Both of these events, as Mandela and Sisulu sensed, registered a new force in South African politics: the demand by urban Africans to be recognized as urban.[19]

Mandela's political ideas up to 1951 were unremittingly Africanist, as were those that the Youth League expressed at its formation. Its highly racialized program, as well as its more dynamic organization, enabled the League to seize control of the mother body at the ANC's National Conference in December 1949, in something close to a coup d'état. This dramatic initiative can be understood in the broader context of a seesawing debate between non-racialism and Africanism, which has been a recurrent trope in South African resistance history. The takeover by younger activists was replicated again with the rise of Black Consciousness in the 1970s. At stake in both cases was a perceived psychological and political need to break with the tradition of deference and tolerance in order to move the struggle into a new gear. The mechanism by which this break was achieved was, in both instances, the assertion of a dogmatic, polemical racialism. It required going to extremes to make the break; but as is evident from the history of both movements (and, indeed, from the story of Mandela's own life), a multiracial ethos could once again reassert itself, if in considerably amended form.[20] This tension will probably always be with us: even when the one political tradition gains the ascendency, the other lurks with less public profile below.

In any event, Mandela proved to be a much more unyielding Africanist than many of his colleagues in the Youth League, most notably Sisulu. Examples abound of his anti-communism, anti-Indianism, and anti-whiteism – and the qualities he found repugnant were, of course, all synthesized in the Communist Party. How and why he changed has never been adequately questioned. Part of the answer is that Africanism was important to Mandela during the years when he was still inexperienced: its rather dogmatic framework provided him with a sense of assurance as he was finding his political feet and contemplating an ascent up the political ladder. In *Conversations with Myself*, Mandela observes:

There is a stage in the life of every social reformer when he will thunder on platforms primarily to relieve himself of the scraps of undigested information he has accumulated in his head; an attempt to impress the crowds rather than to start a calm and simple exposition of principles and ideas whose universal truth is made evident by personal experience and deeper study. In this regard I am no exception and I have been victim of the weakness of my own generation not once but a hundred times. I must be frank and tell you that when I look back at some of my early writings and speeches I am appalled by their pedantry, artificiality and lack of originality. The urge to impress and advertise is clearly noticeable.[21]

These reflections in hindsight accurately describe Nelson Mandela's role in the Youth League in the mid-1940s.

The combination of intellectual caution and self-promotion seemed to work, however. Mandela soon began to climb the political ladder, first to the executive of the Transvaal province of the ANC in 1947, then to the Youth League's national secretary, then to national president of the Youth League in 1950, then to "volunteer-in-chief" of the Defiance Campaign, then to Transvaal provincial president of the ANC, and finally to deputy national president under Albert Luthuli in December 1952. It was a meteoric rise – and it, too, has never been adequately explained; it is somehow always taken for granted. One reason for his ascent was unquestionably Mandela's staunch and vocal Africanism, which remained dominant in his circle until well after Lembede's death in April 1947. A second was the gradual cohering of a new political network, with Sisulu, Oliver Tambo, and Mandela at the core. This bloc was given concrete expression when the three called on Xuma just before the 1949 National Conference to demand support for the Youth League's radical Programme of Action or otherwise forfeit the group's support for his election to a new term as president general. A third reason for his new prominence was Mandela's undoubted zeal and commitment, which earned him a reputation as a bit of a firebrand. A fourth and related reason was his inner steel, a trait inseparable from that quality of deep-seated stubbornness, which had already been in evidence at Fort Hare. And a fifth and final reason was once again Mandela's chiefly lineage and demeanor: the traditional aspects of the man, in other words, that one might not have expected to play much of a part in the ascent of a modern, national, and, ultimately, international political leader.

What is most significant here, however, is the moment and the circumstances of Mandela's emergence on the national political stage. This elevation occurred when he was appointed volunteer-in-chief of the Defiance Campaign in 1952. From this point on he assumed the mantle of a national leader and was catapulted to the forefront of the political struggle. Nowhere in any autobiography, biography, or memoir is Mandela's appointment considered to be something that requires explanation. This is a quite remarkable omission. Part of the reason – I suspect a large part – was the volte-face that Mandela had executed on the issue of multiracialism in late 1951 or early 1952. From his leading position in the Youth League, Mandela had maintained an unflinching opposition to any semi-structured alliance with either the CPSA or the Indian Congresses up until late 1951. However, he was becoming an increasingly isolated voice in this. Sisulu and much of the activist sector of the ANC had drifted in the opposite direction ever since the 1950 May Day strike in protest against the Suppression of Communism Act and, later that year, the June 26th National Day of Protest and Mourning. In keeping with his earlier anti-communist stance, Mandela was not in favor of joint participation in the former event and he was equally opposed to the second; but when a national conference held in May resolved to call the June 26 work stoppage, Mandela submitted to the collective decision. Walter Sisulu records in his autobiographical notes that "despite hostility, once the decision was taken, Madiba worked all out to implement the decision."[22] This is a notable instance of Mandela's willingness to toe the collective line.

Nevertheless, he maintained his opposition to a joint platform of action between the Indian and African Congresses right up to the decision to launch the multiracial Defiance Campaign in 1951. He had insisted, in fact, that the campaign, which was Sisulu's brainchild, be exclusively African. "I still feared the influence of Indians," he confesses in *Long Walk to Freedom*, even though "I had made progress in terms of my opposition to communism."[23] The issue was taken to a meeting of the National Executive Committee (NEC) of the ANC, where Mandela's position was voted down in favor of cooperation with Coloureds and Indians, and then to the National Conference in December 1951, where Mandela's opposing speech as president of the Youth League received a lukewarm reception.[24] He found himself in a difficult position. Popular hostility to Indians still ran high in many of the Rand's African locations. Indeed, one of the first actions of the Youth League in Mandela's former home of Alexandra (one in which Oliver Tambo, a resident, played a part) was to organize a campaign in 1948 against Indian traders in the township.[25] In 1952 and 1953 a full-scale attack on Indian shops in Benoni location was led by future ANC stalwart "AB" (Elias Monare), while a parallel campaign against Indian taxi drivers was taking place in Germiston.[26] Moreover, the Natal ANC as a whole, led by Albert Luthuli, was unremittingly hostile to a formal pact with the Indian Congresses.[27] At the same time, however, the ANC's highest decision-making bodies had voted in favor of cooperation. What made the situation especially difficult for Mandela was that Sisulu, who was elected general secretary of the ANC at the National Conference of December 1949, had firmly cemented the principle of collective leadership into place. The general secretary's report to the Conference, which he first gave to the National Conference of December 1950, no longer represented the views of the general secretary alone; it was not *his* report, but a report drawn up by the entire NEC.[28] Mandela, moreover, had joined the NEC once Xuma resigned in early 1950, and this meant that he had to relinquish what he himself described as "the role of the gadfly within the organization."[29]

In a sense, then, Mandela was trapped by collective discipline. However, he moved several steps beyond mere acquiescence when he made a further contribution to the Conference, pledging his and the Youth League's wholehearted support for the Defiance Campaign. This represented a much more radical shift than was strictly necessary and again requires explanation. One obvious answer is that Mandela could discern that a political earthquake was happening, creating a new political terrain on which he had to move forward or be left behind. Another important factor, certainly, was the effect of his diverse social contacts. While studying at the University of the Witwatersrand, Mandela became friends with fellow students Ismail Meer, J. N. Singh, Ahmed Bhoola, and Ramlal Bhoola and engaged in lengthy debates with them at their residence in Fordsburg, Flat 13, Kholvad House.[30] Several of their initials repeatedly crop up in Sisulu's autobiographical notes, indicating that they interacted with Mandela in the late 1940s.[31] At Wits Mandela also met members of the South African Communist Party (SACP), Joe Slovo and Ruth First, and established lifelong friendships with George Bizos, Bram Fischer, and other white activists.[32] In addition, Mandela was often invited to multiracial parties. "That mixing was extraordinary," Mandela writes, and it provided a different and stimulating context in which his political evolution took place.[33] In the 1940s Mandela feared that in a situation of close collaboration with Indians and Communists they would exercise too much influence over the ANC; but one gets the feeling that by 1951, because of the social milieu in which he often moved, Mandela's political attitudes were turning. He could not keep the political and the personal hermetically sealed. The ANC National Conference of December that year was perhaps, then, the moment when these boundaries broke down, in a second of Mandela's volte-faces.

Another way of explaining Mandela's change has to do with his elevation to the critical position of national volunteer-in-chief of the Defiance Campaign. This appointment should perhaps be understood as an exercise in co-option on the part of the organization rather than solely the result of a deep change of heart in Mandela himself. In 1952, the Benoni ANC responded to an attack on Indian shops by placing "AB," the instigator of these actions, in a leading position on the branch executive, and it is possible that the National Action Committee was following a similar strategy with regard to Mandela. In the context of the Defiance Campaign, Mandela's steeliness would constitute a prized asset; but, perhaps as important, the leadership position would indelibly affix Mandela's name to joint action and racial collaboration, thereby, in effect, extinguishing the Africanism by which the Youth League had previously been marked. If this was the case, it was a remarkably skillful and successful operation on the part of the NEC. One can only guess whose hand orchestrated the whole thing, but it was, of course, Walter Sisulu who understood Mandela's curiously contradictory nature the best.

Assuming Leadership: Party Discipline and Individual Assertion

Throughout the 1950s Mandela's lifestyle changed and his political thinking continued to evolve. In August 1952 he established a legal practice with his friend and fellow ANC executive member Oliver Tambo. The practice flourished and Mandela's personal confidence grew enormously from his performances and successes in court.[34] He also used his new affluence to adopt the style of a township big shot. He bought a huge Oldsmobile sedan, a make of car that was much beloved by township gangsters of his day, and drove it to work and to political meetings. He cavorted with countless beautiful women. Ellen Kuzwayo echoes the views of many women at the time when she writes in her autobiography, *Call Me Woman*: "I cannot forget the glamorous Nelson Mandela. The beautiful white silk scarf he wore stands out in my mind to this day."[35]

The contradictory pulls of social eminence and political leadership were, however, not so easy to contain, and nowhere was this clearer than in the treason trial that began in 1956 and dragged on until 1961. The alleged treason centered mainly on the Congress of the People, held in July 1955, and the Freedom Charter they adopted. The Congress was explicitly intended to be a fully representative gathering, racially and otherwise, and to stand in direct contrast to the racially exclusive National Convention of 1909, which had agreed on the principal features of the Act of Union of 1910. (It was, in fact, in response to this that the South African Native National Congress, later the ANC, was formed.) To the extent that the Congress of the People was intended to displace or supplant the National Convention, it was considered treasonous, and it was on this rather shaky basis that Mandela and the other trialists were arraigned. The proceedings again showed up significant contradictions in Mandela's political personality. At the trial, he was elected spokesman of the 156 accused, partly because of his legal experience; but in the course of the protracted court proceedings, the nature of his politics – or, more exactly, his political character – changed. Sidney Kentridge, legal counsel for the defense, observed the growth that occurred in Mandela: "It was then," Kentridge remarks, "that I first realized that he was a natural leader of men. He was firm, courteous, always based on thought and reason. His real political intellect emerged from his answers to questions; for the first time he was learning to temper his impatience, to pause and reflect."[36] It was here, in a moment of serious threat, that Mandela developed some of his characteristic leadership traits and strengths. Yet this seriousness was tempered by an element of somewhat vain and frivolous stylishness. The night before the trial was due to resume in February 1959, Mandela accompanied his new wife, Winnie, to Todd Matshikiza's musical, *King Kong*, about a black boxer who tragically murders his girlfriend. It was performed at Wits's Great Hall, the largest non-racial venue in Johannesburg. Mandela particularly liked the song "Good Times, Bad Times," perhaps because it captured something of the strange contradictions of his personal experience at the time. The treason trial, with its absurdly protracted legal proceedings and its happy outcome for the accused, was in a certain sense a new theater for the boxer-lawyer-politician.

The next irrevocable turning point in Mandela's political life followed the Sharpeville Massacre in March 1960, when nearly a hundred African demonstrators were shot and killed, and the subsequent banning of the ANC and Pan-African Congress (PAC). When Oliver Tambo was sent overseas to lead a mission in exile, Mandela took the fateful decision to go underground and clandestinely organize the ANC. Sisulu later wrote in his own autobiography that this was a huge moment of decision. He observes: "[W]e realized we needed a leader in gaol inside more than a leader outside."[37] This was the moment when Mandela decided to sacrifice himself to the political struggle. What this amounted to was a decision to reconstruct his personality and both his personal and public life. In a pamphlet he wrote in 1961, he spelled out quite clearly what this meant: "I have had to separate myself from my dear wife and children, and my brothers and sisters, to live as an outlaw in my own land. I have had to abandon my business, to abandon my profession, and to live in poverty and misery."[38] Mandela compensated for his personal sacrifices by taking on the aura and persona of an ascetic, if romantic revolutionary: a Fidel Castro or Che Guevara. To express this new personality he grew a beard. Throughout 1961 he kept popping up from the underground to telephone the offices of white newspaper editors and became celebrated as the "Black Pimpernel." He became, as his biographer

Sampson puts it, "more famous in the shadows" than in the "daylight" of legal activity.[39]

These personal changes and dashing activities are well known from the biographies and from *Long Walk to Freedom*. But at the same time that they were taking place, Mandela was committing himself to yet another, even more secret self-transformation and one that in many senses dwarfed all the others. He joined the underground Communist Party of South Africa, which had reconstituted itself clandestinely in 1953. Walter Sisulu had previously joined the CPSA in 1955, just before the Congress of the People, and he was soon elevated to the National Executive Committee.[40] A considerable body of evidence now exists to show that Mandela joined the reconstituted and renamed South African Communist Party, probably sometime in 1960. According to party veteran Ben Turok, he was present at SACP meetings as early as December 1960.[41] Mandela had been growing more and more tolerant of South Africa's Communists throughout the 1950s and more sympathetic to Marxism as a political creed.[42] The Sharpeville Massacre, mass detentions, and the banning of the ANC and PAC persuaded both him and Sisulu, as well as many members of the NEC and the SACP, of the need for armed struggle, which was initially discussed by detainees in prison. After the state of emergency was partially eased in July 1960, a top SACP delegation led by Yusuf Dadoo, Mike Harmel, and Joe Matthews visited Russia and China, and the political leadership of both countries apparently sanctioned armed struggle.[43] The first SACP trainees were sent out of South Africa for military training in September of the same year.[44] Already the SACP was moving toward armed struggle. Mandela duly attempted to persuade first Moses Kotane, general secretary of the SACP, and ultimately Chief Luthuli and the Natal Indian Congress of its utility. After the failed three-day workers' stay-away of May 1961 had been crushed, Mandela was prompted to give a clandestine television interview with a reporter from Britain's ITV, in which he gave an early hint of his, Sisulu's, and the Communist Party's thinking when he uttered the prophetic words: "If the government reaction is to crush by naked force our non-violent struggle, we will have to reconsider our tactics. In my mind we are closing a chapter on this question of a non-violent policy."[45] This was a statement that was wholly unauthorized and for which Mandela was rebuked by the ANC's National Executive Committee. Collective leadership had, in effect, been ditched. The question, in retrospect, is whose discipline Mandela was observing. The answer is probably not entirely that of the SACP. With the ANC leadership in disarray and popular anger running high, Mandela evidently concluded that he was on the side of history. It seems, once again, that the man's steeliness and proud rebelliousness, if somewhat more tempered, had broken through his latterly more disciplined, reflective stance.

Much the same pattern persisted through 1961. Mandela intensified his efforts to win over Kotane, Luthuli, much of the ANC, and the Natal Indian Congress to permit a move toward armed struggle. They eventually agreed, provided that it was undertaken by a separate body and not by the ANC. The leadership of the body that was ultimately formed, Umkhonto we Sizwe (Spear of the Nation), or MK, was, it now emerges, wholly Communist in composition; we can no longer confidently single Mandela out as the sole exception.[46] Indeed, he was in this period quite literally changing his personality, though without abandoning its old romantic flair. In October 1961, some while after MK was formed but before it publicly announced its existence and conducted its first sabotage attacks, Mandela moved to a new underground hideout at Liliesleaf Farm, situated on the outskirts of Johannesburg. It was here that he began to live out his new role fully.

In 2005, I visited Liliesleaf as a guest of the Liliesleaf Trust, where I interviewed and videoed several of those arrested in 1963, including Arthur Goldreich. He took us on a tour of the buildings and explained how the Farm had previously been. Still largely intact were outhouses and servants quarters. One of these rooms had housed Mandela. Goldreich described the austere, spartan, unadorned, minimally furnished character of the room, as well as the ascetic, almost monastic life that Mandela lived. His only comforts and companions at that time, Goldreich recalled, were numerous books on revolution and warfare, which he read voraciously in order to equip himself for revolutionary struggle.[47] Among those detailed in *Conversations with Myself* are two books on Malaysia, a book on the Hukbalahap in the Philippines (*Born of the People* by Luis Taruc), and Carl von Clausewitz's *On War*.[48]

We must remember here that the Congress Alliance executive committees had agreed to the formation of MK on condition that it limit itself to sabotage attacks and avoid, to the best of its ability, any loss of life. The fairly futile idea was to bring the government to its senses. Mandela and the core of MK never privately subscribed to this position, believing always, or so Mandela's Liliesleaf reading list suggests, that a popular armed insurrection and guerrilla war were necessary and unavoidable. Here again one sees evidence of the inner steel of Mandela, along with a whiff of the romance of revolution: the antinomies remain. From this perspective, the sabotage campaign was merely a point of entry (or departure) or a ruse.[49] Evidently the collective leadership to which Mandela was prepared to subordinate himself at this stage was not that of the ANC. This registers a deep contradiction, one that, in my view, Mandela papered over in his own mind but with which he could never fully come to terms: a tension between party discipline and individual leadership.

In December 1961 the ANC received an invitation from the African Freedom Movement in East Central and Southern Africa (later the OAU) to attend a conference in Addis Ababa the following February. The underground executive of the ANC instructed Mandela to attend. As Mandela confesses in *Long Walk to Freedom*: "My mission in Africa was broader than simply attending the conference. I was to arrange political and economic support for our new military force, and more important, military training for our men in as many places on the continent as possible."[50] The issue here again is, whose mission was he carrying out? Mandela's Africa diary and his 1962 notebook, uncovered by the Special Branch at Liliesleaf and used in the state's case against him, amply testify to the direction of Mandela's thinking about armed struggle at this point. It was totally at variance with that of the NEC of the ANC. In the course of this trip, he received guerrilla training both in Ethiopia and with the National Liberation Front in Algeria at its bases in Morocco. The insights he gained into waging a successful guerrilla struggle in Algeria seemed to him particularly applicable; they provided, as he puts it, "information on which we could work out our own tactics."[51] Besides consolidating his views on guerrilla warfare, Mandela's Africa trip had a quite different kind of policy repercussion. The combined exposure to both the Chinese view of the ANC and to those of neighboring African states, especially Zambia and Tanganyika, convinced him of the need for a new strategy to redirect the armed struggle along a more African national- ist line, with whites, Indians, and Coloureds retreating into the background and becoming less visible and more supportive.[52] We should bear in mind that most African statesmen had, at this time, only just emerged from the thrall of colonial rule and were highly antipathetic to whites, as well as hos- tile to any kind of external influence, including communism and the Soviet Union. It was for this reason that the PAC often elicited a more supportive and enthusiastic response from these ranks. Thus, at a meeting of a working committee of the ANC's National Executive Committee immediately after his return to South Africa, Mandela "proposed re-shaping the Congress Alliance so that the ANC would clearly be seen as the leader, especially on issues directly affecting Africans."[53] As former SAPC chairman Yusuf Dadoo remarked in March 1962, when Mandela raised the issue with him during an interview in London, this was a major policy shift or deviation. Mandela, it appears, was determined to take a leadership role in an organizationally inchoate situation. When he went to Groutville in Natal the next day "to explain the situation to the chief at some length," Luthuli replied that "he did not like the idea of foreign politicians dictating policy to the ANC. He said we had evolved a policy of non-racialism for good reasons and that he did not think we should alter our policy because it did not suit a few foreign leaders."[54] Here was the authentic voice of the Congress Alliance, deeply disturbed by Mandela's unilateral revisionism; the persistent antinomy of submission and individual assertion was once again surfacing.

Mandela's new, hard, revolutionary orientation remained tinged by another persistent feature of his character and life: his rather romantic and theatrical flair. This quality had been manifest on his Africa trip when he flew from Botswana to Dar-es-Salaam. Despite the fact that he was supposed to be traveling incognito, he arrived – to the dismay of Frene Ginwala, who was arranging this leg of his trip – dressed in thigh-high mosquito boots and a Basotho hat. His return from his Africa trip was equally melodramatic, with Mandela clothed in guerrilla fatigues and bearing a gun. And this was how he was dressed when he went to communicate his new thinking to Luthuli. Here Mandela's legendary stubbornness was again clearly displayed. Despite being counseled by almost everybody about the danger of making the trip, he insisted on going. More careless, impetuous, and romantic still, he attended a Congress Alliance party in Durban, where it seems likely he was spotted by some kind of agent or informer. It was quite possibly this lapse that led to his arrest at Howick on the road from Durban to Johannesburg while he was making his way back.[55] Mandela was now incarcerated, charged, and sentenced to five years' imprisonment. While he was in prison, the Rivonia raid occurred and papers incriminating him were discovered. In the ensuing trial, as is well known, he was sentenced to life imprisonment, of which he served twenty-seven years, mostly on Robben Island.

Acquiring Moral Authority: From Prison to the Negotiated Settlement

It was, of course, on the prison-island that Mandela underwent his final self-reconstruction and metamorphosis. This took place in the inner man. Mandela, as I have noted, was imperious and strong-willed; he found it difficult to bow to the views of others, especially when he strongly disagreed. It was only on Robben Island that he was able to subdue his willfulness. In addition, jail provided the opportunity for reflection. As he wrote himself: "My present circumstances give advantages my compatriots outside gaol rarely have. Here the past literally rushes to memory and there is plenty of time for reflection. One is able to stand back and look at the entire movement from a distance."[56] Mandela developed his intellectual powers in these years, as well as a sense of balance and proportion and a respect for opinions of those other than himself or his comrades. As Fikile Bam puts it, "From year to year he was revising his views. He didn't have ideological depth before he came in. He got that in prison."[57] The daily humiliations Mandela suffered when he first got to the Island taught him self-control. The political prisoners' collective culture and their highly disciplined modes of interaction with the warders gave them the strength to insist on their principles, a practice that was eventually also embraced by the other prison sections. Mandela began to believe, as Anthony Sampson records, that the "occupation of the moral high ground could make it possible to turn some of the thug warders around." He realized that they were not all homogeneous.[58]

The moral authority that Mandela and his fellow prisoners acquired or fashioned in jail also made them, paradoxically, more predisposed to negotiation. Ultimately this hard-gained attribute prepared Mandela to take the risk of entering negotiations with the white government in the late 1980s. He was already seeing prison as a microcosm of a future South Africa where reconciliation was essential for survival.[59] He learned to read and speak Afrikaans and took a special interest in Afrikaners' history and their struggle against British imperialism (including the story of General Koos de la Rey, who, rather than fight in World War I, led a rebellion against the British in 1914). As former MK member Ronnie Kasrils rightly notes, Mandela "knew more about the Afrikaner than we [in exile] who were fighting him."[60] This thorough knowledge about the culture and history of the opponent proved to be an essential tool of negotiation. At his first meeting with government officials, including the minister of prisons, Kobie Coetsee, Mandela disarmed them with his grasp and understanding of the Afrikaner people. "Mandela knew more about the Afrikaners' history than many Afrikaners themselves," recalled Coetsee.[61] Looking back on this period, Walter Sisulu perceived the discussions with the warders and the humanization of the prisoners' relations with them as the precursor of later negotiations with the government: "The negotiations themselves were a process that started from that source."[62]

In 1982 Mandela and several senior ANC prisoners were transferred from Robben Island to the mainland prison of Pollsmoor. From here, in 1986, he began to send out feelers to the Afrikaner Nationalist government about a negotiated settlement. Mandela did so entirely on his own initiative. Neither his prison colleagues nor the leadership of the ANC in exile were aware of the steps he had taken. In a classic expression of his views about collective and individual leadership he writes: "Sometimes it is necessary to present one's colleagues with a policy that is already a *fait accompli*."[63] Elsewhere he records that he had never felt so solitary.[64] Only in 1987 did he communicate his actions, first to Sisulu, Raymond Mhlaba, and Ahmed Kathrada, all of whom had also been shifted from Robben Island, and then to Tambo, head of the exiled ANC. Mandela had moved full circle. Despite his metamorphosis in prison, where his old antinomies appeared to have been subdued, they returned with a vengeance once again in the late 1980s when he initiated these conversations with his adversaries. It is on this final issue of the negotiated settlement that Mandela will ultimately be judged.

NOTES

1 This fixation on courts and the law would be an enduring feature of Mandela's life, as demonstrated in Chapter 6.

2 Fatima Meer, *Higher Than Hope: The Authorized Biography of Nelson Mandela* (New York: Harper & Row, 1988), 9.

3 Nelson Mandela, *Long Walk to Freedom: The Autobiography of Nelson Mandela* (Boston: Little, Brown, 1994), 6–7.

4 Ibid., 6–7; MTATA Archives, Box 1993/24/3, 15 MVESO, vol. 2. J. M. Young, Acting Chief Magistrate to SNA. Acting Resident Magistrate, Umtata. G. F. Owen to Chief Magistrate Transkeian Territories. Proceedings of an Enquiry into Conduct of Headman Mandela of MVESO Location, Umtata Held on 9 July 1926. See also Philip Bonner, "The Headman, the Regent, and the Long Walk to Freedom" (unpublished paper, 2011), 1–3.

5 Elinor Sisulu, *In Our Lifetime: Walter and Albertina Sisulu* (Cape Town: David Philip, 2002), 52, and Walter Sisulu's autobiographical notes.

6 Walter Sisulu, Interview with Philip Bonner and Barbara Harmel, July 10 1993, Shell House, Johannesburg.

7 W. Sisulu, "Prison Biography" (unpublished autobiographical notes, n.d.), 50; E. Sisulu, *In Our Lifetime*, 64.

8 W. Sisulu, "Prison Biography," 32; Mandela, *Long Walk*, 101.

9 Mandela, *Long Walk*, 95.

10 Ibid., 76–77.

11 Ibid., 87.

12 Eddie Roux, "Alexandra Bus Boycott," *Trek* 21 (1945): 12.

13 Mandela, *Long Walk*, 96.

14 Ibid., 97.

15 Nelson Mandela, *Conversations with Myself* (London: Macmillan, 2010), 43.

16 W. Sisulu, "Prison Biography," 36–37; E. Sisulu, *In Our Lifetime*, 64.

17 H. M. Basner, quoted in Philip Bonner and Noor Nieftagodien, *Alexandra: A History* (Johannesburg: Wits University Press, 2000), 81. See also "Africans' Claims in South Africa," www.marxists.org/subject/africa/anc/1943/claims.htm.

18 Robert R. Edgar and Luyanda ka Msumza, Introduction to *Freedom in Our Lifetime: The Collected Works of Anton Muzibakhe Lembede* (Braamfontein: Skotaville, 1996), 16.

19 W. Sisulu, "Prison Biography," 38–39; E. Sisulu, *In Our Lifetime*, 74.

20 See, e.g., Thabo Mbeki's 2002 "I Am an African" speech.

21 Mandela, *Long Walk*, 45.

22 W. Sisulu, "Prison Biography," 54.

23 Mandela, *Long Walk*, 123.

24 Ibid.

25 Bonner and Nieftagodien, *Alexandra*, 129.

26 Philip Bonner, "Family Crime and Political Consciousness," *Journal of Southern African Studies* 14.3 (1988): 413.

27 Jon Soske, "'Wash Me Black Again': African Nationalism, the Indian Diaspora, and Kwa-Zulu Natal, 1944–1960," PhD dissertation (University of Toronto, 2009), 225.

28 E. Sisulu, *In Our Lifetime*, 92.

29 Mandela, *Long Walk*, 118.

30 Ibid., 91.

31 W. Sisulu, "Prison Biography," 40, 46–47.

32 Mandela, *Long Walk*, 91.

33 Mandela, *Conversations*, 42–44, 54–55.

34 Anthony Sampson, *Mandela: The Authorised Biography* (London: HarperCollins, 1999), 77–78; David James Smith, *Young Mandela: The Revolutionary Years* (London: Weidenfeld & Nicolson, 2010), 112–14.

35 Ellen Kuzwayo, *Call Me Woman* (Johannesburg: Raven Press, 1985), 139.

36 Sampson, *Mandela*, 135.

37 W. Sisulu, "Prison Biography."

38 Mandela, *Long Walk*, 276.

39 Sampson, *Mandela*, 144.

40 E. Sisulu, *In Our Lifetime*, 121–22.

41 Stephen Ellis, "The Genesis of the ANC's Armed Struggle in South Africa, 1948–1961," *Journal of Southern African Studies* 37.4 (2011): 657–76; Paul S. Landau, "The ANC, MK, and 'The Turn to Violence' (1960–1962)," *South African Historical Journal* 64.3 (2012): 543–44.

42 Mandela, *Long Walk*, 120–21.

43 Philip Bonner et al., "The Turn to Armed Struggle," *SADET* 1 (2004): 81; Landau, "The ANC," 544.

44 Bonner et al., "The Turn to Armed Struggle," 91.

45 Mandela, *Long Walk*, 270.

46 Bonner et al., "The Turn to Armed Struggle," 89.

47 Arthur Goldreich, in discussion with the author, Liliesleaf Farm, Rivonia, 2005.

48 Mandela, *Conversations*, 107.

49 Jonathan Hyslop's offers a somewhat different perspective in Chapter 7.

50 Mandela, *Long Walk*, 287.

51 Mandela, *Conversations*, 87–103.

52 Mandela, *Long Walk*, 296; Landau, "The ANC," 560.

53 Mandela, *Long Walk*, 311.

54 Ibid., 312.

55 Sampson, *Mandela*, 169–70.

56 Nelson Mandela, "National Liberation," quoted in ibid., 272.

57 Sampson, *Mandela*, 239.

58 Mandela, *Long Walk*, 216.

59 Ibid., 225.
60 Ibid., 229.
61 Martin Meredith, *Mandela: A Biography* (New York: Public Affairs), 368.
62 Sisulu, "Prison Biography."
63 Mandela, *Long Walk*, 531.
64 Meredith, *Mandela*, ch. 17: "Talking with the Enemy," 353–70.

2

DAVID SCHALKWYK

Mandela, the Emotions, and the Lessons of Prison

Suppose your next of kin has passed away and you fail to contain yourself; your enemy will get a chance and strike at you. But if you can contain your emotions, then he won't be able to do that.

Thembu Chief Anderson Joyi, *Frontline* interview, 1996

People say Mandela's not bitter; he's terribly bitter, but he's learned to control it. It's not an absence of bitterness or anger. Nobody gets rid of these things, but some people learn how to harness and control them.

Richard Stengel, in Mac Maharaj, Ahmed Kathrada, et al.,
Mandela: The Authorized Portrait

In *Long Walk to Freedom*, the autobiography he published the year he was elected president of South Africa, Nelson Mandela describes a confusing moment, just after his release from prison and before his appearance on the Grand Parade in Cape Town. Trying to reach the city hall, from which he would deliver his first speech, Mandela and his entourage found their way barred by the mass of people who had been waiting for him for hours. He was "imprisoned," as he puts it, "by thousands of our own supporters ... who might very well kill us with their love."[1] If we were to encounter this sentence in a novel, we would no doubt reflect on the irony of this experience: the newly released hero is entrapped by the very people in whose cause he was incarcerated. In an autobiography, however, it is less clear if such a symbolically resonant close reading is justified; Mandela's detention by his jubilant supporters is, after all, a historical fact. The thought that he could be killed by their love – after the signal failure of the regime to kill him with their hatred – is his own gloss on the event. This mixing of history and symbol, narrative and interpretation captures the difficulties of writing with any certainty about Nelson Mandela the man.

This difficulty is only compounded by the fact that Mandela has tended to be reticent about his emotions. History has left us, for better or worse, with Nelson Mandela the myth, a myth that is not dispelled by the biographical or even the autobiographical writings available to date. Richard Stengel, with whom he wrote *Long Walk to Freedom*, comments on the difficulty of finding the inner Mandela: "Mandela has a wonderful memory but he's not very introspective. You have to interpret what he says through narratives or stories. I was constantly probing for some psychological detail or insight."[2] Tom Lodge, one of Mandela's biographers, observes similarly that Mandela's account of his childhood "emphasizes his experiences rather than his feelings."[3] This remark is generally true of the whole autobiography: it is not in *Long Walk to Freedom* but rather, as we will see, in some of the letters Mandela wrote to his family from prison that we find clues to his emotional life – or, more exactly, to his rigorous strategies for managing his feelings.

There is something of a paradox here. To find the "inner man," we need to turn to prison: the very place where Mandela's subjectivity, his space for personal expression, was most stringently curtailed. Such a critical turn to Mandela's years of incarceration is the project of this chapter. While I will detail some of the conditions of life on Robben Island, my interest, ultimately, does not lie in reiterating these well-documented horrors, but in asking what prison meant to Mandela as a person, what life lessons he learned there, and how these lessons shaped the myth into which the man transformed. In pursuing these ostensibly subjective and personal questions, I do not intend to bracket off the political meanings of Mandela's life or his commitments. On the contrary, I will not only consider his generally stoic attitude toward suffering, but also try to cast new light on the affective, interpersonal, and ethical aspects of his political legacy by reflecting on certain intersections between Mandela's thought and conduct and classical Stoicism – Stoicism with a capital *S*. In doing so, I do not intend to argue any direct influence or to deny other shaping forces, which I will also detail, but precisely to stress the complexity of Mandela's character and the sources of his global legibility and appeal.

This kind of inquiry into the personal lessons of prison has not yet been undertaken – and for various reasons, not least because the prison years were years of routine, in which the most notable, narratable events were small, gradual, and collective victories over the inhuman conditions of incarceration. While it is often remarked that Mandela was absent from public view for twenty-seven years, few scholars have questioned what this forced removal from the bodily, visible, and performative aspects of political life (in which Mandela, both young and old, excelled) meant in terms of the development of his personality and conduct of self. In most third-person accounts, the Mandela who emerged from Victor Verster Prison to lead South Africa into democracy and freedom was a man fully in control of himself – and for this very reason somewhat opaque as a personality. One of his biographers, Martin Meredith, presents this perspective succinctly:

> Behind the façade of fame, Mandela remained at times an enigmatic figure. Prison colleagues who were his companions for years on end sometimes felt they did not really know him. He emerged from prison an intensely private person, accustomed to concealing his feelings behind a mask. He confided in few people. He disliked familiarity. The grip of self-control he acquired in prison rarely left him. His habits remained austere.[4]

Two things are striking about Meredith's observations. The first is the implication that there is something rather detached, alien, and inhuman about a man who was so eminently capable of eliciting intense feelings in others. The second is the perception that it was in prison that Mandela acquired such austere self-control. In his authorized biography, Anthony Sampson also insists that the prison years were formative, but he nevertheless represents this period as something of a hiatus – a relatively empty interlude between his activism, first, as an Africanist firebrand and, later, as a commanding international statesman. Even Mandela's own narrative of these years underplays his self-transformation. He appears in *Long Walk to Freedom* to have entered prison fully formed. Few experiences in prison are explicitly singled out as moments of learning. Yet, despite these accounts and the suggestion by Tom Lodge that Mandela "learned early to repress outward shows of emotion" and that the ability "to control pain and its accompaniment, fear, was one of the defining qualities of manhood he learned as a child," it is hard not to believe that the long, harsh years in prison were decisive in this regard.[5] Indeed, this supposition is confirmed, as we will see, by some of those closest to Mandela.

Robben Island Revisited

It may be helpful, at this point, to recall the conditions of prison life and the bodily and psychological disciplines they enforced. Robben Island, where Mandela spent eighteen years before being transferred to Pollsmoor Prison in 1982, was a bleak and forbidding penitentiary, located within view of Cape Town's beautiful Atlantic seaboard. The first political prisoners, who arrived in 1962, encountered a particularly brutal prison regime under the almost unchecked authority of the white prison guards. In his autobiography, *Island in Chains*, Indres Naidoo, an African National Congress (ANC) activist imprisoned for sabotage in 1963, describes being greeted by the warders as he set foot on its shore for the first time: "This is the Island. Here you are going to die."[6] D. M. Zwelonke recalls how these early prisoners were subject to various tortures, like being tied down on demolished ant-hills.[7] He also recounts the infamous treatment of Johnson Mlambo, who was buried up to his neck, urinated on by one of the guards, and then savagely beaten: "When the warder had finished, his face was covered with piss. Then vicious blows of fists and boots rained around the defenseless head sticking out of the ground."[8] Assaults on prisoners were common during the period 1962–66 – an especially brutal "carry on" occurred one night in 1964 – and were recorded as late as 1971.[9] The practice of holding political prisoners together with criminal convicts, which persisted until 1965, was also intended to demean and terrorize the former.[10] Robben Island, in sum, was a place that taxed men's physical and psychological endurance to the utmost.

Conditions in prison improved after 1966 as a direct consequence of relentless and disciplined action by prisoners themselves, who waged a day-to-day campaign for respect and basic rights and managed under extremely restrictive conditions to alert the outside world to their plight.[11] The political prisoners' background as activists and their familiarity with legal procedures prepared them to organize around particular issues and to enlist prison regulations to check some of the worst abuses. They also gradually succeeded in their deliberate efforts to compel respect from warders through their own dignified behavior (as in their insistence on walking slowly to their worksite at the Island's lime quarry, to prevent the guards from demeaning them by scurrying them along like underlings). Such small victories, pertaining to the daily banalities of bodily and verbal conduct, were important for morale, especially to those who entered prison as accomplished and educated men in mid-career.

In *Long Walk to Freedom*, Mandela recounts his attitude toward the prison, in ways that reveal something of how he was able to continue to think of his conduct of self as performative:

> I was in a different and smaller arena, an arena for whom the only audience was ourselves and our oppressors. We regarded the struggle in prison as a microcosm of the struggle as a whole. We would fight inside as we had fought outside. The racism and repression were the same; I would simply have to fight on different terms.[12]

Those terms included things as small as not responding to verbal abuse, standing tall, and striding at one's own pace. In the special Section B, where leaders of the resistance movement were held in single cells, Mandela was sheltered from some of the worst conflicts and abuse that characterized life in the general cells. Although communication between sections could be conducted only by ingenious subterfuge, he was certainly not unaware of the plight of his fellow prisoners. His situation was not as harsh as that of Robert Sobukwe of the Pan-Africanist Congress (PAC), who was kept in a completely separate bungalow, from which he could exchange only fleeting salutes with others as they passed him on their way to work. Mandela's personal struggle in prison revolved principally around the debilitating psychological effects of imprisonment, his removal from his loved ones, his sense of helplessness, and the erratic trickle of information between the world inside the prison and the world outside.

Emotional Education

The effect of this kind of deprivation on Mandela, by all accounts a flamboyant and flirtatious man, who enjoyed life as a township celebrity and reveled in his travels as an activist, must have been very painful. We can understand his response to it only if we bear in mind that he was educated in fairly spartan conditions in the English mission schools of Healdtown and Clarkebury and even at the University of Fort Hare, where, as a country boy, he was something of an outsider. Missionary boarding schools practiced forms of discipline and deprivation that, as Michel Foucault has argued, bear a family resemblance to the stricter disciplinary machinery of the penitentiary – in the poor food, the strict regimentation, and what Sampson terms "an uncompromising British education."[13] Clarkebury's headmaster, the Reverend Cecil Harris, "ruled ... with an iron hand, more like a field commander than a school head," while Healdtown's governor, the Reverend Arthur Wellington, "was a hard-driven autocrat." Sampson remarks that Mandela "would always be influenced by the schools' puritanical atmosphere, the strict discipline and mental training, the Wesleyan emphasis on paring ideas to their bare essentials ... and the self-reliance in these boarding-school surroundings would add to his fortitude."[14] This last concept, with its quaintly old-fashioned ring, is one I will return to toward the end of this chapter.

For now, let me simply note that Mandela, predisposed perhaps by his prior affective education, developed in prison what Stengel describes as a "very rigorous control over the emotions": a trait that was not yet in evidence in the "passionate young man" of the Rivonia trial.[15] The comments of Mac Maharaj, who had a close relationship with Mandela in the single cells of Robben Island, are particularly intriguing because they enable us to attach a date to what must have been a gradual transformation. "By 1976," he declares, "Mandela had developed an immense capacity for self-control," adding pointedly, "This did not come naturally to him; his self-control was consciously cultivated and nurtured."[16]

The date is significant, because that was the year when a new influx of prisoners – a generation of insurgents who had experienced nothing like Mandela's austere but somewhat genteel, late-Victorian schooling – arrived at Robben Island. These were members of the Black Consciousness (BC) Movement, convicted in large numbers after the countrywide uprisings in the wake of the June 1976 protests against Bantu education. Their very different political style and conduct of self were noted by Natoo Babenia, an Umkhonto we Sizwe (MK) saboteur and fellow prisoner of Mandela's generation, who excoriated the young firebrands as the "TV generation," corrupted by US culture.[17] They demonstrated what Babenia considered undisciplined behavior, but what we might retrospectively see as the personal and affective dimensions of a politics of ungovernability – an expression of relentless insubordination and rage. The BC men "shook the prison to its core," antagonized authorities, and directly challenged the methods, aims, and revolutionary credentials of their elders in the ANC.[18] Their "acting up" was an unsettling experience for the older prisoners, who feared that the gradual, hard-won improvements in their living conditions were threatened by the uncompromising belligerence of the new prisoners. Mandela writes: "It was obvious they regarded us, the Rivonia Trialists, as moderates. After so many years of being branded a radical revolutionary, to be perceived as a moderate was a novel and not altogether pleasant feeling. I could scold them for their impertinence or I could listen to what they were saying. I chose the latter."[19]

This patient, respectful strategy was successful: Mandela was able to use the steely self-control he had apparently developed by 1976 to good effect. In his dealings with the BC prisoners, he could counter rage with reason, incessant confrontation with constructive conversation, and uncontrolled opposition with self-possessed conversion. Mandela's stance was not merely a personal but also a political achievement: what was at stake were different ways of performing militancy. He eventually won over many of the younger comrades to his way, persuading them that the prison guards represented a group of people that the resistance movement would eventually need to negotiate with and govern when they came into power. Maharaj tells the story of his own conversion to Mandela's calculated, long-term strategy:

> There was a period when I became 'ratty'. Any provocation by a warder would incite me to backchat. I began to accumulate prison charges for cutting remarks and intemperate language.... Patiently [Mandela] advised me to maintain my stance; but instead of erupting spontaneously I should ... measure my response, and choose my words. That way I would be in control; my anger would not control me.... Never again did a warder succeed in pinning

charges against me. The advice stuck. My problem is that I am often not sure when I am simulating anger![20]

A BC prisoner, Sonny Venkatrathnam, likewise remarked, "I came out a different person: totally philosophical about things.... What amazed me about Nelson and Sisulu ... was the calmness, the equanimity with which they led their prison lives.... They showed me how to laugh at the tortures we went through."[21]

Mandela, it is evident, taught others, but when repeatedly pressed by Richard Stengel about the lessons he had learned in these years, the difference prison had made, he gave only a terse answer: "I came out mature."[22] To understand what he might have meant by this remark, we might recall a rare and therefore particularly memorable moment in which Mandela did recount a learning experience: a moment of growth in prison and one that did lead to introspection. In Pretoria Central Prison, right at the beginning of his first term of incarceration, Mandela faced the prospect of having to wear the regulation uniform for African prisoners, which included shorts and sandals rather than long trousers and shoes. He protested that it was an affront to his dignity to have to wear clothing appropriate for a boy rather than a man. The commanding officer relented, but only in part; Mandela would be issued long trousers on condition that he be put into isolation: "I assured him that solitary confinement would be fine so long as I could wear and eat what I chose."[23] Although understandable, Mandela's response is naive. Faced with the "tak[ing] away of [his] identity," he feels that he can restore a sense of himself only through individual resistance and by preserving his freedom of choice.[24] But isolation proves to be much worse than not being able to wear trousers or eat what he likes:

> For the next few weeks, I was completely and utterly isolated. I did not see the face or hear the voice of another prisoner. I was locked up for twenty-three hours a day.... I had never been in isolation before, and every hour seemed like a year. There was no natural light in my cell; a single bulb burned overhead twenty-four hours a day.... I had nothing to read, nothing to write on or with, no-one to talk to. The mind begins to turn in on itself, and one desperately wants something outside oneself on which to fix one's attention.[25]

Mandela quickly comes to discover an absolute truth of imprisonment – that solitary confinement is the worst torture of all: instead of enabling one to recover oneself, it splits and alienates subjectivity.[26] He ultimately relents and is reintegrated with the other prisoners. There he readily reconciles himself to sharing the indignity of shorts and the deprivation of cold mealie pap. When he is offered long trousers at the beginning of his second term on Robben Island, he refuses the offer unless everyone is issued a pair.

This incident is a transitional point in Mandela's conception of himself in relation to others – including his jailers. Although he doesn't explicitly register it as such, reflecting instead in somewhat banal terms on the political loss of his incarceration ("the place of a freedom fighter is beside his people, not behind bars"), the moment marks a recognition of the communal burden of selfhood in prison.[27] It is a weight to be carried, but also a refrain to be sung in unison with others.

The Values of Stoicism

There is, however, a later text, written in 1975 (around the time that Maharaj marveled at Mandela's achieved self-control), which suggests that his modes of coping with the isolation of incarceration evolved beyond this point. It is a letter written to his wife, Winnie, then incarcerated in Kroonstad Prison. Mandela advises Winnie (whom he considered "impulsive, quick-tempered and inclined to lose control")[28] about the ways in which imprisonment may foster not self-alienation but greater self-understanding:

> The cell is an ideal place to learn to know yourself, to search realistically and regularly the process of your own mind and feelings. In judging our progress as individuals we tend to concentrate on external factors such as one's social position, influence and popularity, wealth and standard of education ... internal factors may be even more crucial in assessing one's development as a human being. Honesty, sincerity, simplicity, humility, pure generosity, absence of vanity, readiness to serve others – qualities that are within the reach of every soul – are the foundation of one's spiritual life. Development in matters of this nature is inconceivable without serious introspection, without knowing yourself, your weaknesses and mistakes. At least, if nothing else, the cell gives you the opportunity to look daily into your entire conduct, to overcome the bad and develop whatever is good in you.[29]

The letter registers a decisive move away from the terrors of being alone with oneself in the wastes of limitless time toward a sober acceptance of the solitary cell as a space for introspective growth. With its emphasis on self-development, it is ethical rather than political and, in a way that may seem old-fashioned, even archaic in its sentiments – so archaic, perhaps, that it can be seen as corresponding in key respects to the views of another, much earlier politician: Marcus Aurelius, the Stoic philosopher and emperor of Rome from 161 to 180 AD. The advice to eschew what Mandela calls "external factors" in favor of "internal" virtue through "serious introspection" resonates in quite striking ways with the following passage from Aurelius's *Meditations*:

> This then remains: Remember to retire into this little territory of thy own ... Right into thyself. The rational principle which rules has this nature, that it is content with itself when it does what is just, and so secures tranquility.... If thou findest in human life anything better than justice, truth, fortitude, and, in a word, anything better than thy own mind's satisfaction in the things which it enables thee to do according to right reason ... turn to it.... But if nothing appears to be better than the deity which is planted in thee, which has subjected to itself all thy appetites, and carefully examines all the impressions, and ... has detached itself from the persuasions of sense ... and cares for mankind ... give place to nothing else ... for it is not right that anything of any other kind, such as praise from the many, or power, or enjoyment of pleasure, should come into competition with that which is rationally and politically and practically good.[30]

The sentiments expressed here have little to do with the ethos of the liberation struggle, where political intensity seemed to guarantee ethical probity, and even less with twenty-first-century South Africa, where both politics and ethics have been reduced to a scramble for power, wealth, and conspicuous consumption. Even in the tradition of South African prison writing, incarceration is seldom represented as an opportunity for ethical development. In Mandela's letter, the cell, far from being isolating and uncomfortable, is transformed into an ideal place in which to pursue self-knowledge – assessing one's "development as a human being," searching the depths of the soul, and ensuring that one emerges every day as a better person: all pursuits recommended in the *Meditations*.

To suggest that Mandela has something in him of the classical Stoic is not as counterintuitive as it may seem. (A similar argument, we might note, has been made in relation to Gandhi, another austere giant of the twentieth century's struggles for decolonization.)[31] In fact, the connection between Mandela and Aurelius has already been made – if rather tentatively. In the introduction to *Conversations with Myself* – a collection drawn from Mandela's conversations, autobiographical notes, letters, and diary and calendar entries – Verne Harris declares that the "book's form is inspired most directly by Marcus Aurelius's *Meditations*." "While not, perhaps, a great philosopher or writer," Harris observes, "Mandela knew the benefits of meditation, record-making and daily discipline."[32] And, even though the argument I wish to make does not rely on proving any direct influence, it is interesting to know that a copy of the *Meditations* may have circulated on Robben Island.[33] Ahmed Kathrada, a fellow Rivonia trialist and close friend of Mandela's, uses a quotation from Aurelius as an epigraph in his memoir, *No Bread for Mandela*, and it is an entry in volume 4 of his prison notebooks. Given how intensively all available intellectual fodder was mined and shared by the prisoners, it is possible that Kathrada talked about the *Meditations* to Mandela, or even passed on the book to him.

This is, of course, speculation. But other better-documented aspects of the prisoners' reading habits on Robben Island are relevant here.[34] It is clear from several accounts that Greek tragedy made a strong impression on Mandela (especially after the performance of Jean Anouilh's version of *Antigone*, in which Mandela played the tyrant, Creon). In a letter to Adie Joseph written in 1985, he notes, "We are still fascinated by Greek literature of ancient times."[35] Certainly, the plays of Sophocles and Euripides were read and even performed on the Island, and Shakespeare was known, especially in the single-cell section when, at about the time that Mandela wrote his autobiography and his letter to Winnie, Sonny Venkatrathnam passed his copy of the *Complete Works* among his comrades, asking them to sign their names against their favorite passages. Mandela chose a speech from *Julius Caesar*:

> Cowards die many times before their deaths;
> The valiant never taste of death but once.
> Of all the wonders that I yet have heard,
> It seems to me most strange that men should fear;
> Seeing that death, a necessary end,
> Will come when it will come.[36]

The sentiment is close to another Shakespearean epigram, from *Measure for Measure*, which, Mandela tells us, came to his mind on the eve of the sentencing in the Rivonia trial, when he and his comrades faced the death penalty as a real possibility: "I was prepared for the death penalty. To be truly prepared for something, one must actually expect it.... We were all prepared, not because we were brave but because we were realistic. I thought of the line from Shakespeare: 'Be absolute for death: for either death or life will be the sweeter.'"[37] So, even if Mandela had no direct access to the Stoic philosophers, he would have encountered a philosophy that urged the strictest control over one's emotions – indeed, the cultivation of an attitude of absolute self-sufficiency with regard to the exigencies of the world – in Shakespeare, where it is a defining mark of characters like Brutus in *Julius Caesar* and Horatio in *Hamlet*.

It is hardly polemical to say that Mandela's self-control, courage, and endurance are stoical in the ordinary sense of the term. But, in order to grasp certain continuities between this austere management of the emotions and the ethical and political aspects of Mandela's thought and conduct, it might be useful to recall some of the broader ramifications of classical Stoicism as a political philosophy. Stoicism posited the fundamental equality of all human beings as rational animals – male and female, freeman and slave.[38] Its "guiding principle is respect for humanity wherever it is found."[39] In Seneca's words:

> There is no such thing as good or bad fortune for the individual; we live in common. And no one can live happily who has regard to himself alone and transformed everything into a question of his own utility; you must live for your neighbor if you would live for yourself. This fellowship, maintained with scrupulous care ... makes us mingle as men with our fellow men and holds that the human race have certain rights in common.[40]

Mandela's political beliefs were also premised on an essential commonality of human existence (and the resonance between this way of thinking and the African humanism of *ubuntu* is worth probing). Robben Island life was made tolerable precisely by a sense of communality between prisoners and by the insistence of Mandela – and other comrades – that the maintenance of their intrinsic human dignity was dependent on recognizing the dignity of others. Before he entered prison, Mandela had already abandoned his sense of the racial or tribal superiority of the Xhosa nation and his own special status within it, escaping, as he puts it, "the tribalism that still imprisoned me."[41] In prison Mandela would show himself free not only from "tribalism," but also, to the chagrin of some of his comrades, the exclusive group identities that formed part of membership of political parties and movements on the Island. He went out of his way to befriend Eddie Daniels, who was not only "Coloured," but the only member of the Liberal Party on the Island; he was open to discussions with the PAC, as well as often extremely antagonistic groups like Neville Alexander's radical Yi Chi Chan Club and the National Liberation Movement, and was, as we have seen, willing to engage with the radical young members of the Black Consciousness Movement.

According to Anthony Sampson, "[M]any of [Mandela's] basic principles – his capacity for seeing the best in people, his belief in the dignity of man, his forgiveness – were essentially religious."[42] However, if we follow instead Richard Stengel's view that Mandela's apparent lack of bitterness should be seen as the effect not so much of Christian forgiveness as of his control over his emotions, we may be more inclined to bring to mind another key principle of Stoicism here: namely, that people are not intrinsically evil; the evil person is merely misguided and can be brought to virtue through the patient use of reason.[43] Mandela's openness to others was not limited to his opponents among the prisoners. He was one of the few who took an active interest in the history and the lives of the callow and often brutal Afrikaner wardens, always treating them as human beings, going out of his way to accord them appropriate respect, inquiring after their families, and encouraging them to improve themselves through study. One of the wardens, James Gregory, recounts the gradual process whereby, through rational conversation and mutual respect, Mandela won him over to a different point of view: "It was not as if I had some 'road to Damascus' conversion, it was more a simple fact that my preconceptions were wrong.... And once I'd accepted that my preconceptions were wrong, I had to replace them with ideas which were realistic."[44] Mandela's method of leading his interlocutors through a process of rational growth resembles the old Stoic philosophers' belief that "prejudice, error, and bad conduct result from incorrect reasoning, not from original evil" and that careful attention to the "pupil's particular history, experiences, and immediate situation" will lead him or her from prejudice and error to truth.[45] "He never once told me I was wrong," Gregory observed. "Instead he directed his conversation to the process which had led me to those feelings."[46]

If this non-coercive ethical therapy is resonant with Stoic principles, so too is Mandela's inclination (evident in the 1975 letter to Winnie) to distinguish between the "internal" and "external" factors in one's life. For the ancient Stoics, ties to anything outside oneself were without intrinsic value. Whatever is not fully under the control of the self – health, freedom from pain, indeed, all the "external" factors enumerated in Mandela's letter, "social position, influence and popularity, wealth and standard of education" – should have no hold over one. But certain "internal" aspects of human life, especially passion or emotion – fear, anger, and even love – bind us to these external forces. They subject us to change and uncertainty, and should therefore be extirpated or brought under strict control. The solution proposed by the Stoics was, therefore, what Martha Nussbaum calls a "radical detachment," which "greets slavery and even torture with equanimity" and even "receives the news of a child's death with the remarkable words: 'I was already aware that I had begotten a mortal.'"[47] We might bring to mind again Sonny Venkatrathnam's comment on Mandela and Sisulu, who "showed [him] to laugh at the tortures we went through." What this suggests quite powerfully is that the Stoic attitude is one of two options available to political men who are subject to harsh imprisonment, and perhaps the most appropriate and effective one of the two. When control over external conditions is reduced to almost zero, one response is to give oneself over to excessive emotional reactions: fear, anger, resentment, humiliation, and hatred. The response Mandela adopted and inculcated involved, instead, what I have called "fortitude." "Fortitude" – that old-fashioned English Victorian virtue – is given popular expression in Mandela's favorite poem, "Invictus" by William Ernest Henley:

> Out of the night that covers me,
> Black as the pit from pole to pole,
> I thank whatever gods may be
> For my unconquerable soul.
>
> In the fell clutch of circumstance
> I have not winced nor cried aloud.
> Under the bludgeonings of chance
> My head is bloody, but unbowed.
>
> Beyond this place of wrath and tears
> Looms but the Horror of the shade,
> And yet the menace of the years
> Finds and shall find me unafraid.
>
> It matters not how strait the gate,
> How charged with punishments the scroll,
> I am the master of my fate:
> I am the captain of my soul.

Henley's sentiments encompass more than the traditional cliché of the Englishman's "stiff upper lip." They express – in somewhat overblown, Victorian terms, to be sure – an older Stoic faith in the integrity of the "unconquerable soul": an indifference to the vicissitudes of fortune, suffering, or pain; a fearless attitude to death; and, most important, complete control of the self as a stable center in a harsh and unreliable world and before the uncertainties of "fate." Mandela expresses such an attitude especially forcefully in a letter to the Swazi senator Douglas Lukhele: "Spiritual weapons can be dynamic and often have an impact difficult to appreciate except in the light of actual experience in given situations. In a way they make prisoners free men ... to put it quite bluntly, Duggie, it is only my flesh and blood that are shut up behind these tight walls."[48] Mandela remained "master of his fate" and "captain of his soul" by refusing to allow the conditions of prison or the actions of the wardens to control his sense of personal identity or dignity and his emotional responses to their behavior or his situation. He did not confine such control to his own behavior; he also advised his comrades to exercise similar restraint. "Significant progress is always possible," Mandela once declared, "if we ourselves try to plan every detail of our lives and actions and allow the intervention of fate only on our own terms" and "what matters is not so much what happens to a person than the way the person takes it."[49]

Prisoner Resistance and the Politics of Affect

This brings us to the role of emotion – anger in particular – in response to injustice: in other words, the question of resistance. This question is treated at length in Fran Buntman's *Robben Island and Prisoner Resistance to Apartheid*, and I recommend that readers engage with her extensive analysis of both the philosophical dimensions of resistance and its material and psychological conditions on the Island. I shall confine myself, however, to a problem about the appropriateness of the emotions in revolutionary politics that can be formulated as a tension between Aristotelian and Stoic ethics. Aristotelians regard anger as a necessary ingredient of and propulsive force toward appropriate action in the face of oppression or exploitation. Not to be angry before certain events or behavior is, from this point of view, to show an immoral indifference to the situation or acquiescence in the injustice. Stoics, by contrast, believe emotions to be fundamentally dangerous and, therefore, in need of strict control, if not elimination.

Mandela's position and conduct probably lie between these two positions: he neither insists on avoiding emotion altogether, nor proposes that anger is the proper ethical response to injustice. His stance could be described as a moderate Stoicism, in which, in Maharaj's words, "the anger would still charge [his] response, but [he] would be in control."[50] With this in mind we can approach the question of resistance in prison from a fresh angle. Buntman writes of the tension between categorical resistance, in which resistance is pursued relentlessly and without exception for its own sake, and strategic resistance, in which moments of intransigence or opposition are carefully chosen for their maximum contribution to the whole cause. The members of the 1976 generation, who accused the older prisoners of acquiescing in their own oppression, pursued the categorical resistance of pure anger. They made it a point to defy the authorities at every opportunity – thereby upsetting a carefully negotiated set of concessions and compromises that had taken years to forge. Many prisoners of Mandela's generation reacted angrily and dismissively to this behavior, but, as we have seen, Mandela's response was more measured. Refusing to intercede with the angry young men on behalf of the authorities, Mandela sought to win them over to a more thoughtful, controlled, strategic mode of resistance through rational discourse rather than angry denunciation. It is probably true to say that the ability of the prisoners to gradually make the Island their own – reclaiming it in the words of Shakespeare's Caliban (which Billy Nair marked as his own in Venkatrathnam's *Complete Works* on December 14, 1977): "This island's mine, by Sycorax my mother, / Which thou tak'st from me" – was due to the meticulous accommodations of strategic forms of resistance, which depended on strict self-discipline and a continued respect for the humanity and rationality of one's enemy, which in turn was based on an implacable commitment to justice and the equality of all human beings. Mandela did not have a monopoly of such a view (and it would be a mistake to assume that he enjoyed uncontested leadership on Robben Island), but he certainly exemplified in word and action such strategic and long-term modes of resistance.[51]

The myth of Robben Island as a unified community, without serious personal or political division, exemplified by its later title, "our University," is badly in need of deflation and further examination. Buntman's study contains many examples of bitter, indeed violent, conflict and intrigue, but she concludes, correctly, that "the men or the organizations who were forced to live on Robben Island did create a social order that was consistent with many or most of their goals and intentions ... they were able to transform its place in history and its meaning in space and even geography."[52] The question is what role Mandela played in this process. To answer this question we have to face a problem. The immense symbolic power of the man since his release – amounting to the creation of a myth – has released the force of a double metonymy: Nelson Mandela has come to stand for Robben Island as a whole, and Robben Island has displaced the many other concrete places and metaphorical spaces in which resistance to apartheid was forged and in which its hardships were suffered. In the single cells of Section B, as I have noted, Mandela was kept apart from the vast majority of the prisoners on the Island. It is true that Mandela was generally chosen as the spokesperson for the others on the various occasions when representatives of foreign bodies, the International Red Cross, the local and international press, members of the judiciary, and the single, dogged MP, Helen Suzman, visited the Island. It is also true that, by forcing the authorities to recognize him as a representative, Mandela and his comrades were able to negate one of the most fundamental and canny philosophical impositions by the apartheid regime: the refusal to recognize any complaint or request other than one made in the first person singular – "I." By forcing them to accept his right to speak as "we," Mandela could reduce, if not negate entirely, this attempted hegemony over grammar that refused to enable the prisoners to articulate themselves as a community: to speak, suffer, intervene, and make claims on behalf of each other.

This form of grammatical resistance is very important, but it remains unclear whether Mandela was in fact speaking on behalf of all the prisoners on the Island when he used the pronoun "we." Here we confront a paradox, one of those "antinomies" that Philip Bonner describes in Chapter 1. While Mandela could, in the face of the authorities, turn the isolated "I" into a communal "we," he was also able to embark on negotiations with the Nationalist government largely through the force of an individual subjectivity that was forged by his ability to concentrate on the resources of the inner man – an ability I have chosen to call Stoic. Early in his autobiography he describes his admiration for the model of tribal leadership by which the chief "stays behind the flock, letting the most nimble go out ahead," but when he decides to pursue talks without consulting his fellows, he declares, in his "splendid isolation" after his transfer to Pollsmoor Prison, that "there are times when a leader must move out ahead of the flock, go off in a new direction, confident that he is leading his people the right way."[53] The enigma that many – including his closest comrades – find in Mandela is due to a focused concentration on and control of the "inner man," a capacity that was, I would argue, a direct response to the conditions of imprisonment that he encountered on Robben Island. It combined a need to forge a space for the self under conditions that constantly threatened to subordinate and overwhelm the experiencing subjectivity. That space was occupied by, on the one hand, a commitment to the equality of all human beings and, on the other, a belief in their essential rationality and goodness. Combined, these commitments offered a strategy that began with the preservation of personal dignity in prison and ended in an openness to the negotiations that abolished apartheid. The political resistance that characterized Mandela's career as an organizational figure was extended through a set of personal, ethical precepts that were communally distributed. Those lived precepts contribute to the enigma of the man, but they also underlie the immensity of the myth.

The question that remains is at what cost Mandela achieved this extraordinary ethical mode of political engagement and survival. The self-sufficiency of the wise and stoic man, his "radical detachment" from matters that lie beyond his control, can seem, as I remarked earlier, to border on the inhuman.[54] To respond to the news of one's son's death with the remark "I was already aware that I had begotten a mortal," as the ancient Stoic philosophers praised Anaxagoras for doing, seems extreme: it seems to deny a fundamental attachment to human life that is the very basis for ethics and politics.

One of the most wrenching events in Mandela's prison experience is undoubtedly the death of his son Thembi in a car accident in 1969. Handed a telegram by the commanding officer reporting the death, Mandela retreats to his cell: "I returned to my cell and lay on my bed. I do not know how long I stayed there. Some of the men looked in, but I said nothing. Finally, Walter [Sisulu] came to me and knelt beside my bed, and I handed him the telegram. He said nothing but only held my hand. I do not know how long he remained with me. There is nothing one man can say to another at such a time."[55] If Anaxagoras's response is an exemplum of Stoicism, Mandela's is very different. But his incapacity to share his feelings – "I do not have words to express the sorry, or the loss I felt. It left a hole in my heart" – indicates less a philosophical determination to treat emotion as a beast to be tamed than a failure to live with emotion and to engage it as an essential part of one's being.[56]

The passage from Marcus Aurelius that Kathrada culled from his notebooks for his memoir is actually an uncharacteristic one. The Stoic who declared that "the mind that is free from passion is a citadel" also wrote: "If I could live my life over – I think I would have pondered more on the human heart, the emotions, feelings, and those strange perplexing guests who come uninvited to live with us, and who sometimes take control. And I would have pondered on love."[57] There is an extraordinary poignancy in this confession of regret at having paid insufficient attention to the "human heart" (as a subject of inquiry and value rather than an object of control) and to those "strange perplexing guests," the emotions that reside within us – especially love. These words could just as well have been written by Mandela, who often expressed regret at his failure to live up to the affective obligations of family: "Perhaps I was blinded to certain things because of the pain I felt for not being able to fulfill my role as a husband to my wife and a father to my children.... To be the father of a nation is a great honour, but to be the father of a family is a greater joy. But it was a joy I had far too little of."[58]

Saths Cooper, another of the younger generation of prisoners, has lamented the Robben Island prisoners' denial of fundamental aspects of humanity, such as sexuality: a denial that arose from a rigid dichotomy imposed between the personal and the political.[59] Mandela's stoic management of the emotions had many advantages. It was an ideal way of refusing the vicissitudes of fate and impositions from outside; it formed an indispensable platform for turning the enemy into a negotiating partner. But it also brought with it an immense loss of humanity. That loss, regretted by Mandela, Kathrada, and Marcus Aurelius alike, remains unacknowledged in most accounts of the suffering and triumph of the Robben Island experience. Mandela's astonishing self-control masked a constant struggle between "brain" and "blood." This antagonism was one Mandela does not seem to have been able to transcend: "Even as I scribble these hurried lines, the heart and the head, the blood and the brain are fighting each other, the one pining idealistically for all the good things we miss in life, the head resisting and guided by the concrete realities in which we live our lives."[60] Marcus Aurelius's sadness at having pondered too little "those strange perplexing guests who come uninvited to live with us" signals both the poignancy and the flaw in Mandela's faith in the "concrete realities in which we live our lives."

With this tension in mind, we can now return to the confusing moment immediately after his release, in which Mandela was confronted with love and still imagined himself somehow "imprisoned." What Mandela perhaps does not fully grasp here is that love – the dangerous love, in this instance, of the crowds of South Africans for whose sake he had disciplined himself – is, in fact, a concrete reality; it is not just a regrettable, unreachable ideal to pine for.

NOTES

1 Nelson Mandela, *Long Walk to Freedom* (London: Abacus, 1995), 674–75.
2 Mac Maharaj, Ahmed Kathrada, et al., *Mandela: The Authorized Portrait* (Kansas City, MO: Andrews McMeel, 2006), 172.
3 Tom Lodge, *Mandela: A Critical Life* (Oxford: Oxford University Press, 2006), 16.
4 Martin Meredith, *Nelson Mandela: A Biography* (New York: St. Martin's Press, 1998), xv–xvi.
5 Lodge, *Mandela*, 16–17.
6 Indres Naidoo, *Island in Chains: Ten Years on Robben Island by Prisoner 885/63* (Harmondsworth: Penguin, 1982), 18.
7 D. M. Zwelonke, *Robben Island* (Oxford: Heinemann, 1989), 14.
8 Ibid., 14.
9 Neville Alexander, *Robben Island Dossier, 1964–1974: Report to the International Community* (Cape Town: University of Cape Town Press, 1994), 21.
10 Fran Buntman, "Resistance on Robben Island, 1963–1976," in *The Island: A History of Robben Island*, ed. Harriet Deacon (Cape Town: David Philip, 1996), 98.
11 Alexander, *Dossier*, 23.
12 Mandela, *Long Walk*, 464.
13 Michel Foucault, *Discipline & Punish: The Birth of the Prison*, 2d ed. (New York: Vintage, 1995).
14 Anthony Sampson, *Mandela: The Authorized Biography* (New York: Knopf, 1999), 19–21.
15 Richard Stengel, in Maharaj and Kathrada, *Portrait*, 172.
16 Mac Maharaj (ed.), *Reflections in Prison*, Robben Island Memories Series No. 4 (Cape Town: Zebra and the Robben Island Museum, 2001), 5.
17 Natoo Babenia and Iain Edwards, *Memoirs of a Saboteur: Reflections on My Political Activity in India and South Africa* (Belville: Mayibuye Books, 1995), 194.
18 Meredith, *Mandela*, 326.
19 Mandela, *Long Walk*, 577.
20 Maharaj (ed.), *Reflections*, 5. I will return later to the problem regarding the authenticity of emotion that Maharaj raises here.

21 Sampson, *Mandela*, 227.
22 Stengel, in Maharaj and Kathrada, *Portrait*, 172.
23 Mandela, *Long Walk*, 396.
24 Ibid.
25 Ibid., 397.
26 We see this in the way the narrative voice, in the earlier quotation, distances "the mind" as something other than the "one" who speaks – now no longer secure as the "I" that inhabits the first part of the passage – and that now "desperately" seeks an external anchor: "something outside oneself."
27 Mandela, *Long Walk*, 397.
28 Sampson, *Mandela*, 248–49.
29 Nelson Mandela, *Conversations with Myself* (New York: Farrar, Straus and Giroux, 2010), vii. Winnie Mandela had earlier been arrested, in May 1969, and kept in solitary confinement for thirteen months (Sampson, *Mandela*, 248).
30 Marcus Aurelius, *Thoughts of Marcus Aurelius Antoninus*, trans. George Long (Philadelphia: H. Altemus, 1880), 94–95.
31 Richard Sorabji, *Gandhi and the Stoics: Modern Experiments on Ancient Values* (Oxford: Oxford University Press, 2012).
32 Mandela, *Conversations*, xxi.
33 As will become clear, I want to deploy the Stoic philosophers' precepts more as a heuristic device to articulate something about Mandela's political thought and conduct.
34 For more on Shakespeare on Robben Island, see David Schalkwyk, *Hamlet's Dream: The Robben Island Shakespeare* (London: Bloomsbury, 2013).
35 Quoted in Sampson, *Mandela*, 324.
36 *Julius Caesar*, 2.2.32–37, in *William Shakespeare: The Complete Works*, ed. Peter Alexander (London: Collins, 1951).
37 Mandela, *Long Walk*, 445.
38 See Martha Craven Nussbaum, *The Therapy of Desire: Theory and Practice in Hellenistic Ethics* (Princeton, NJ: Princeton University Press, 1994), 324.
39 Ibid., 331.
40 Lucius Anneaus Seneca, *Letters from a Stoic*, trans. Richard Mott Gummere (Lexico, 2011), 48 (Kindle loc. 2989).
41 Mandela, *Long Walk*, 45.
42 Sampson, *Mandela*, 250.
43 See Mandela, *Conversations*, 234: "The realist, however shocked and disappointed by the frailties of those he adores, will look at human behavior from all sides and objectively and will concentrate on those qualities in a person which are edifying, which lift your spirit [and] kindle one's enthusiasm to live."
44 James Gregory, *Goodbye Bafana: Nelson Mandela, My Prisoner, My Friend* (London: Headline, 1995), 117.
45 Nussbaum, *Therapy*, 335.
46 Gregory, *Goodbye Bafana*, 117.
47 Nussbaum, *Therapy*, 363.
48 Mandela, *Conversations*, 182.
49 Ibid., 233, 195.
50 Maharaj (ed.), *Reflections*, 5.

51 But see Buntman's description of Harry Gwala, usually regarded as a firebrand, who followed the same precepts of strict self-discipline (*Resistance*, 237).

52 Ibid., 241, 264.

53 Mandela, *Long Walk*, 25–26, 626–27.

54 Nussbaum, *Therapy*, 363.

55 Mandela, *Long Walk*, 531.

56 Ibid.

57 Marcus Aurelius, *Meditations*, bk. 8.

58 Mandela, *Long Walk*, 720.

59 Buntman, *Resistance*, 246.

60 Mandela, *Conversations*, 222.

3

DEBORAH POSEL

"Madiba Magic": Politics as Enchantment

> The moment we think of the world as disenchanted … we set limits to
> the ways the past can be narrated.
>
> Dipesh Chakrabarty, *Provincializing Europe*[1]

If a small minority despaired that the end of the world was upon them, most
South Africans embraced the country's first democratic election on April
27, 1994, as a euphoric and spectacularly memorable moment. Few will
forget the extraordinary surprise of the long, contented queues of voters
(some people standing patiently in line for more than ten hours); the joyous
exclamations of black people voting for the first time; the rushes of relief
and goodwill from those white people excited to be part of it; the feeling
of a national rebirth happening in the here and now. Many personal recollections capture the heady energy and poignant drama of an act in which
centuries of un-freedom seemed to be dismantled, triumphantly unmade.
As Njabulo Ndebele put it, "When the voting moment came, it was fast
and disarmingly simple, but profoundly intense. It was really happening."[1]
When Nelson Mandela was installed as the country's first democratically
elected president, the national mood was similarly one of elation. In Achmat
Dangor's words, this was "a fleeting moment when history became utterly
important, inescapable and compelling. Nelson Mandela became President
and the word 'freedom' took on an almost childlike meaning, so magical
was its effect."[2]

South Africans are inclined to regard their history as exceptional, but in
fact their mood resonated with what Rob Nixon recognized as the "passion
for abandonment, a desire to be rid of the past" that the end of the Cold War
had unleashed in many parts of the world.[3] And it was linked to a rhetoric
of – and aspirations to – new beginnings, as though the post-authoritarian
era (wherever it occurred) would be a wholesale break rather than merely a
gradual, uneven change. Discarding the mantle of global pariah, South Africa
rapidly became the global exemplar of this new post-authoritarian will to

transcendence, all the more exhilarating for the fact that the transition to "freedom" was negotiated in a spirit of "reconciliation" – and all the more remarkable for the fact that this was happening at the tip of Africa, the "dark" continent. As Nelson Mandela put it, "Together with the people of the world we celebrated a victory that belonged to the world."[4]

In retrospect, it is difficult not to respond incredulously to these declarations of a redemptive rupture with the past or to think of the soaring hopefulness for a new way of being in South Africa as naive. At the time, too, there were frequent exhortations for more sober expectations, pragmatic strategizing, and incremental planning – not least among those who were closely involved in the negotiation process and who were mindful of the abiding fragility of the emerging consensus. Of course, eradicating the imprint of apartheid was going to be a fraught, contested, and protracted process. Yet it would be a mistake, in my view, to discount the surge of euphoria within South African society as insignificant or ephemeral. The onset of democracy was perhaps the closest South Africa has – or ever will – come to a utopian moment, and its optimism and energy bear further scrutiny. Rita Barnard has made a similar point, reflecting on "the elation of national liberation – an experience that metropolitan academics should not presume to treat dismissively."[5]

The euphoria was inextricable from a discourse of "magic" and "miracle," in turn inseparable from the extraordinary persona and presence of Nelson Mandela. It was Mandela, preeminently, who inspired conventionally sober people to speak and write with unfamiliar hyperbole. Many agreed with Archbishop Tutu that without Mandela the "whole country would have gone up in flames."[6] Far more than anyone else, it was Mandela who performed the breach with the past and the "national reconciliation" that went with it. That Mandela stepped out of prison after twenty-seven dark years willing to negotiate with his oppressors became a metonym of the wider national "miracle" of a peaceful transition to democracy, with Mandela acclaimed as the miracle maker. He rapidly came to personify the "new" South Africa in ways that made the project not merely plausible, but persuasive. He also made it appear proximate, even intimate. Affectionately embraced as Madiba, his clan name, connoting simultaneously his elevated station and popular accessibility, he was the avuncular elder whose appeal breached the sedimented South African divides of race, class, gender, and ethnicity. And with that, the notion of "Madiba magic" also entered the vocabulary of the "new" South Africa, as a name for Mandela's singular powers of surprise, of breaking the political mold of the past to enact the impossible, and to do so with captivating charisma and charm.

Such talk of the miracle of the new South Africa and Madiba's magic in bringing it about did more than circulate popular metaphors of the ecstatic exception of South Africa's negotiated transition. These turns of phrase and their repetition across many sites and sightings of politics in this country contributed to the production of a distinctive emotional style (to use Eva Illouz's term): a matrix of thought and sentiment governed by the imaginary of Mandela.[7] This chapter considers how this emotional style was produced and how it worked: its internal symbolic and discursive features, its resonances with more global political sentiments, and its wider political and cultural conditions within South Africa. "Miracle" and "'magic" were the driving tropes of an unprecedented habitus of hopefulness that spanned the old chasms of race. If the elation among black citizens was animated by the incredulity of liberation in the here and now and the "magical" cessation of the horrific political violence that preceded it, for whites the "miracle" promised a release from the telos of brutal revenge for nearly four decades of apartheid domination. The euphoria of averting a violent conflagration was both more powerful and fragile for the horizon of incipient dread that the negotiated transition never wholly vanquished. Albie Sachs points out that "the South African 'miracle' [was] … the most consciously and rationally worked-for happening one could ever have imagined."[8] Prodigious effort and hard-nosed calculation went into the constitutional negotiations, producing first the interim and later the final constitution: a robustly reasoned bedrock of the transition and symbol in itself of the reassuring – and sanctifying – power of law in the new South Africa. But the work of eliciting popular consent went much further, in suffusing the process with a politics of sentiment or, better yet, a politics of enchantment, facilitated by concomitant economic and cultural changes that animated the power of Mandela's image. If Madiba magic was an enabling elixir of the transition from apartheid, this was in turn the sign of a wider landscape of enchantment, the consequences of which should be reckoned with as Mandela's brand of magic fades and others take hold.

Making the Mythic Mandela

If sentiment is defined as "an attitude, thought, or judgment prompted by feeling," it is uncontroversial to claim that the practice of politics is always lubricated by sentiment. Rulers win followers by inspiring trust, hope, and confidence, as much as through rational persuasion; dissension grows in popular feelings of anger, disappointment, mistrust, or dejection, infused into rational assessments of misguided policies or ill-conceived principles;

political mobilization is never an appeal to the resources of reason alone. To think of politics as involving the regulation of popular sentiment is to draw attention to the affective wiring of power, always intertwined with the instrumentalities of ideas, interests, and deliberative calculation.

In the case of the "new" South Africa, the early ingredients of Madiba magic were distilled during Mandela's years in prison, when he began to craft a role for himself as principal magician. The critical period, for the purposes of my account, began in 1980, which saw the beginnings of sustained efforts to mobilize international support for the anti-apartheid struggle by focusing on the injustice of Mandela's interminable incarceration.[9] In March 1980, the South African *Sunday Post* newspaper launched a local Release Mandela Campaign (RMC) in tandem with the international initiative of the African National Congress (ANC). All told, the RMC produced a remarkable 15 million signatures and began to create a heightened international awareness of the man who would soon become "the world's most famous political prisoner."[10] As Tom Lodge points out, this campaign also launched an avowedly reverential, redemptive version of Mandela's political and ethical significance (different in tone from more deliberative renditions of previous years)[11] – as a man of extraordinary and special qualities, uniquely positioned to champion the cause of freedom in South Africa and the world at large. Aubrey Mokoena, the RMC's Transvaal chairman, described him as "the pivotal factor in the struggle for liberation."[12] It was a description that would gain political purchase as the decade wore on, with the momentum and power of the symbolic Mandela an increasingly significant factor in shaping what was strategically possible and ultimately necessary.

In 1986, a visit of the Commonwealth Eminent Persons Group to Pollsmoor Prison drew attention directly and assertively to Mandela's "special qualities" and potentially pivotal role in the country's future, their report giving definition and vitality to a man hitherto existing indeterminately in the invisible inside of a perpetual prison. His visitors memorably declared themselves "struck by his immaculate appearance, his apparent good health, and his commanding presence"[13] – not a description of a victim, but rather an image of one ready and waiting to lead. I recall, as a young adult, the surprise of this text, which gave clarity and energy to a figure that until then had been vague, even inscrutable.

Also in 1986, a book of international tributes to Mandela included that of Susan Sontag, who reflected on Mandela's unique symbolic power as not only the "exemplary" political prisoner, but also the "exemplary human being," having sacrificed himself for the greater human good.[14] Sontag understood that a strategic political project was under way: the making of a Mandela myth, to which she too was actively party:

> It is often said that this man is a "symbol". But no one is inherently a symbol. Someone is made a symbol, as this man has been. The few moral heroes – and this man is a moral hero – who become celebrated (as distinct from the many heroes who do not) do so under the pressure of historical need. The practice of singling out as exemplary one person – specifically, one prisoner or victim – illustrates the way in which all affections and attachments must inevitably become institutionalized, acquire titles, engender hierarchies, in order to have historical weight: in order to be political.... When the struggle is just and the behaviour of the prisoner really exemplary, such singling out is not only ineluctable but positive. It is right that this man has been made a symbol.[15]

Much of the symbolic work, however, was yet to be done – a project to which many influential people and organizations were part, not least Mandela himself, and beginning while he was still in prison.[16] As Achmat Dangor, head of the Nelson Mandela Foundation, put it to me, "Mandela was above all a master politician, even to the extent of managing his iconic image."[17] His own symbolic work began in preparation for his taking a leading role in discussions about negotiations between the ANC and the Nationalist government: "he came to realize the value of his image in prison" as a key resource – potentially a decisive one – in shaping the prospect and outcome of these discussions. Mandela was purported to have told one of his foreign visitors in the late 1980s, before his release: "I am not a God or a prophet but I have to act like one."[18] There are many ways of shaping and wearing a mantle of godlike leadership, of course. Part of Mandela's authority and appeal would be his self-presentation as one who served, whose power was popularly mandated, and who refused deification as an elevated colossus. He clearly understood the prophetic qualities in that persona.

Key leaders of the ANC too were party to Mandela's symbolic choreography, not least in accommodating the salient role assigned to him by his jailers.[19] Mandela's individual prominence in early discussions with the Nationalists provoked some uncertainty and suspicion within the ranks of the ANC in prison and beyond.[20] After all, it was Oliver Tambo who headed the ANC, not Mandela. Mandela was aware of this and had to manage the situation with care.[21] According to Dangor, he acted with Tambo's endorsement: "knowing he [Tambo] wasn't well and knowing the then divisions in the ANC, he thought that Mandela would have the greatest power and leverage."[22] With the possibility of negotiations with the National Party on the horizon, senior strategists within the ANC recognized too that elevating Mandela as the iconic metonym of the anti-apartheid struggle, legitimately standing in for the ANC as a whole, would be one of the necessary conditions of his power to bring the ranks of the ANC and the United Democratic Front (UDF) to the negotiating table after his release.

Perhaps what was less obvious at the time was the extent to which the National Party negotiators would themselves become party to the production of the mythic Mandela, having recognized his symbolic capital as a critical tool in their hands too. Mandela's talks with Justice Minister Kobie Coetsee had begun in December 1985. Following the launch of the RMC, Coetsee had asked Mandela's jailers for a "detailed analysis of his personality" and received an account of a man poised to take charge: "exceptionally motivated," "harbouring no bitterness towards whites ... with an unflinching belief in his own cause," and "certain of eventual victory."[23] The report concluded that Mandela "commands all the qualities to be the number one black leader in South Africa," with all the requisite charisma and "psychopolitical posture."[24] By 1985, Mandela had himself resolved to play a leading role in shaping talks with his jailers and wrote to Coetsee requesting a meeting.[25] Coetsee did not reply but paid Mandela a surprise visit in December while he was recuperating from surgery in hospital – in retrospect a clear signal of Coetsee's recognition that discussion with this one man would be decisive in determining the prospects for a negotiated settlement with the ANC. The first step was taken immediately: on his return to prison, Mandela was relocated to a new (and significantly larger) cell, separating him from his fellow political prisoners, so as to create the space for regular and informal meetings. Coetsee began crafting a relationship that would give rein to Mandela's particular skills and powers – by now recognized as useful, if grudgingly so, by those members of the regime seeking to initiate negotiations with the ANC.

But if the Nationalists aspired to authorship, they soon recognized that there could be no script without the leading dramatis persona of Nelson Mandela. By the end of 1989, "it was obvious to South Africa's rulers that only their most famous captive could render any settlement legitimate."[26] And the only way of doing this was to partake actively in an astounding symbolic reversal: refiguring the man who had been incarcerated as white South Africa's iconic terrorist, public enemy number one, as an "exemplary human being." To understand why, it is necessary to locate Mandela's symbolic powers within the affective wirings of the apartheid project.

The apartheid regime produced its own emotional style, which permeated the horizon within which the "new" South Africa was symbolically scripted, as both its condition and counterpoint. Elements of apartheid's emotional style shifted over time, but – at the risk of simplifying these complexities – I suggest that fundamental ingredients endured throughout the variegated life of the regime.[27] The expectation of a violent telos to its political project was deeply etched into the white polity from the very outset of apartheid. From its pragmatically tempered first phase in the 1950s, followed by the more avowedly ambitious and hubristic bluster of "grand apartheid" in the 1960s, then the strategic "reform" of the 1970s, and its more aggressive and militaristic turn in the 1980s, a fundamental animating impulse was fear of *die swart gevaar* (the black menace), the rallying cry of the National Party in the 1948 election, which had brought it to power. The *kragdaadigheid* (forcefulness) of apartheid would insinuate fear into the lives of black South Africans too: a fear intertwined with resignation, anger, and bravado, borne of the milieu of "social danger" (to use Veena Das's phrase) that molded the apartheid project.[28] The bluster of white power went hand in hand with a deep sense of white insecurity – in anticipation of the prospect of angry revenge for the humiliating predicament of ongoing racial subjection. Paradoxically, apartheid statecraft deliberately kept this threat alive, repeatedly resorting to variants of *die swart gevaar* to justify its efforts to bolster the coercive edifice of white supremacy. The power to prevail never vanquished the anxiety of defeat.

By the 1980s, there were several indicators of a lingering and widespread dread of incipient black insurrection within various sectors of the white population – a symbolic residue of apartheid's tenacity. If some versions of the pending nightmare imagined the spectacle of inchoate violence on the part of the black mob, others were cast within the dominant ideological rhetoric of the 1980s as the culmination of a coordinated "Communist" onslaught mounted against the apartheid regime. Surveys by the Human Sciences Research Council at the time registered the impact within white society of these notions of the enemy, in the overwhelming support for repressive measures against suspected agents of "terror."[29] Vincent Crapanzano's 1985 ethnography of everyday life among middle-class whites in a small town in the Western Cape demonstrated the effects of this kind of mindset in a micro-politics of suspense. Their existential predicament, he argued, was the anxiety of waiting: waiting for a future that was indeterminate in detail but foreboding in outline, its contours shaped by "the dread black cloud hanging over us."[30] He noted different inflections of waiting for English and Afrikaans speakers: if both were equally preoccupied with an ominous future, the former were more inclined to cast themselves in the role of victims, passive and fatalistic.[31] Three years later, a study of "elite Afrikaner attitudes to social and political change," conducted alongside the crescendo of popular uprisings against apartheid, concluded that "fear and despair" were uppermost in well-to-do Afrikaners' expectations of their immediate future.[32] When they were asked to rate a series of "internal threats to South African security," their responses indicated "first of all, [that] everything [that they were asked to rate was] a threat to between 81.2 and 99.8% of prominent Afrikaners."[33] Beyond that, it was the threat to "physical safety ... and the sanctity of their property" that loomed the largest in their hierarchies of fear.[34] It is not surprising, then, that the late 1980s saw the early growth of the private security sector, illustrating an increasingly embattled version of white middle-class life.[35] Boundary walls on residential properties grew higher; sophisticated house alarms were becoming de rigueur.

By the late 1980s, with the country edging to the brink of a civil war, the more pragmatic leadership of the National Party saw in Mandela the key to a more stable future, on condition that he became nothing short of the nation's hero to whom all South Africans could turn for moral succor.[36] How else, symbolically, could the Nationalist vanguard manage the long-standing circuitry of white fear and black suspicion and anger? In his study of middle-class whites cited earlier, Crapanzano mused that

> waiting is infused with desire. In its positive modality, it is directed towards something that is desired: it is longing. In its negative modality, it is directed towards something that is not desired: it is dread.... *Waiting's desire is magical since there is nothing in pure waiting that we can do but wait, have faith, hope for the best, as the saying goes, and prepare for the worst.*[37]

On the terrain of symbolic politics, the challenge of a negotiated settlement with the ANC for the Nationalist leadership would be to persuade South Africa's whites that Mandela's influence was exactly what they had been longing for all along: a longing to be spared the dreaded brunt of black rage.

There was much work to be done, symbolic as much as in the realm of realpolitik – on the understanding that these were powerfully intertwined. "Madiba magic" was yet to be adumbrated and unleashed. I don't wish to overstate the degree of strategic deliberation or overt investment in the emergent meanings of Mandela; no doubt, symbolic capital accretes more syncretically, with uneven degrees of planning and intention, and strategies take shape and effect within a world only partially amenable to deliberate control. Still, perhaps the most striking – and distinguishing – feature of the mythic Mandela was the extent of the national and international consensus that went into his making: the shared recognition of the desirability of the myth, as well as key elements of its content, across racial lines and political divisions (a recognition, to be sure, that was at times granted far more grudgingly and ungenerously than at others).

The production of what would become known as Madiba magic emerged through a series of high- and low-profile performances of statesmanship and their widely (even if not uniformly) ecstatic reception within the polity. The first was the global spectacle of Mandela's release from Victor Verster Prison on February 11, 1990. Other scholars have underlined the importance of Mandela's incarceration as the symbolic origin of his subsequent magic. His spectrality – shrouded in the darkness of the jail, without a voice, his face unseen – had not only enhanced his moral stature, but fueled intense "media fascination"; he was, as Rob Nixon put it, "a gigantic photo opportunity in reverse. Mandela became an off-camera phenomenon, and his silence grew more eloquent than words."[38] On the eve of his release, the frenzy of interest – national and international – was heightened by the sheer curiosity of seeing the real human being in real time.

De Klerk and his team understood perfectly well the political import of a heroic release: "the release of Mandela, we knew from a newsworthy point of view, from the point of view of world attention, was the crucial thing."[39] And newsworthy it was, watched by a global television audience of more than 1 billion. Mandela's exit from prison would thus signify the beginnings of a symbolically powerful realignment between South Africa and the wider world, away from the prevailing rendition of global racist pariah toward greater international recognition and applause – itself an element of De Klerk's own symbolic capital as a leader attempting to marshal his constituency in support of negotiations with the ANC.

As it turned out, the occasion was only partly choreographed, with far bigger crowds than originally anticipated and unexpected delays, necessitating ad hoc changes to carefully hatched plans. Mandela took center stage – cameras flashing, people cheering, huge crowds jostling – with spontaneous joy, though he seemed a little overwhelmed. His speech was somewhat wooden, its delivery stiff. But his sometimes quizzical spontaneity humanized him; there he was, a live human presence, hand in hand with his wife, Winnie – both extraordinary and ordinary. It was a combination that configured his symbolic capital from that moment on.

The early months of Mandela's freedom were peppered with angry outbursts at De Klerk and his cohort, provoking reassertions of a determined militancy. Initially, Mandela also reiterated his commitment to armed struggle. In the mythic retelling, however, he is recalled as having emerged from prison a wholly changed man, without bitterness or anger and with a newfound willingness to "reconcile" with the enemy in the name of the mutual commitment to human rights. Mythically, Mandela walked to his eventual freedom "healed" by his own suffering in prison: the template for what would become one of the major tropes of the "new" South Africa, central to the repertoire of the Truth and Reconciliation Commission and the project of "national reconciliation" at large.

All those party to the constitutional negotiations under way in the early 1990s were acutely mindful of the salience of a discourse of human rights, as the glue that could cement previously ideologically disparate positions and as a way of inserting South Africa's transition into the international project of post-authoritarian democratization.[40] The mythic Mandela contributed a particular valence to the idea of human rights, hitching it to a narrative of suffering and vulnerability, and then the courage and wisdom to transcend it. So Mandela's "long walk to freedom" was also retrieved as a journey from revolutionary militancy to a robustly peaceable commitment to human rights – similarly signposted by the fall of the Berlin Wall in 1989 and, with it, the collapse of the Soviet communist version of freedom. The massacres in Tiananmen Square, on one hand, and the Iranian *fatwah* against Salman Rushdie, on the other, had provided resonant counterpoints to the Berlin celebration. In many global media, events in Iran in particular reconstituted the symbolism of revolution as fundamentalist rather than emancipatory – and inimical to the idea of human rights. This was a juxtaposition symbolically figured in Mandela's own "journey," from his "revolutionary" activism of old, to dialogue and "reconciliation," watchwords of the international human rights project.

In announcing Mandela's release in parliament on February 2, President De Klerk declared that "the season of violence is over. The time for reconstruction and reconciliation has arrived." This was premature, to say the least. The years following Mandela's release, and preceding the first democratic elections in 1994, were the most violent in South Africa's history.[41] If Mandela's release and the constitutional negotiations had put South Africa in the frame of the global media, the concomitant escalation of political violence became a media spectacle in itself. National media too gave sustained coverage of the raging conflict, focusing on the battle between the ANC-aligned UDF and Inkatha, which produced a daily diet of what had become known as "black-on-black violence." So the dominant images of the imminent threat to the negotiation process were of angry and dangerous black men brandishing weapons at each other. Within some sections of white South Africa this was, once again, the *swart gevaar* writ large: images of black savagery, in this instance wreaking havoc within black communities but portending the kind of bloodlust that had long been imagined as the revenge wrought for white supremacy. Radio talk shows gave vent to expressions of anxiety: "I tried to get into New Zealand because I tend to see chaos in this country"[42] was not an unusual line. At its most extreme, the anxiety produced panic buying of tinned goods, dried fruits and milk, gas cylinders, and generators following rumors of electricity cuts, and a run on weapons and ammunition in gun shops.[43]

Critical to the production of Madiba magic, then, was the rendition of a different version of Mandela's blackness: as a locus of his personal transformation from anger and aggression to a more controlled, if still commanding, presence – without forgoing any of his stature as a heroic and forceful black leader. Careful attention was paid to the appropriate imagery in the ANC's election campaign in the early months of 1994. As Eve Bertelson has pointed out, the images that were chosen for the final and culminating phase of the ANC's election campaign foregrounded the "new" Mandela: the wise, yet vulnerable sage; the strong, visionary statesman with appropriate gravitas and experience, rather than younger firebrand:

> The photo of Mandela chosen to conclude the campaign is not the most glamorous or youthful one available, but all its signs have been carefully chosen. It is side-lit; it exposes facial flaws; it stresses age (the grey hair), determination (the set of the mouth and jaw) and vision (the piercing off-camera gaze). These selections are "anchored" by the words: "Sekunjalo" and "the dawn of freedom."[44]

Further decisive symbolic work took place in a series of huge and effusive gatherings leading up to his inauguration as president. It had begun four years before when, two days after his release from prison, Mandela was feted at mass rallies, in Soweto, Durban, Bloemfontein, and Port Elizabeth, drawing monumental crowds – the largest, of 200,000 people, attending the gathering in the province where Mandela was born and the crucible of ANC support. These audiences were primarily black, and as John Carlin puts it, they enacted "Mandela's coronation as king of black South Africa" – unassailable in his power to command popular support.[45] The first was a "National Service of Thanksgiving" that preceded the inauguration. It was held at the FNB Stadium in Soweto – itself symbolically rich, redeeming Soweto from its history as black labor reservoir, invisible and residual to the "real" city of Johannesburg, reassigning it to the political and ethical heartland of the "new" South Africa. Brigalia Bam, representing the South African Council of Churches, welcomed the assembled crowds to the country's "miracle" – "a word that I would hear over and over again in the extraordinary days that followed," according to one of the journalists who covered the proceedings.[46] The meeting was suffused with an overtly religious sensibility. The crowd was asked to rise to "pray together in thanks for the miracle." A joyous Archbishop Desmond Tutu was unrestrained: "We are the rainbow people of God! We are free!" Mandela too addressed the multitude, in remembrance of those who had died in the struggle – his message also cast in a rhetoric of redemption, declaring that life for South Africans would never be the same again:

Nothing I can say can fully describe the misery of our people as a result of that oppression, but the day we have been fighting for and waiting for has come. We are saying, let us forget the past, let us hold hands, it is time now to begin anew. The time has come for men and women, African, coloured, Indian, white, Afrikaans- and English-speaking to say we are one country, we are one people.[47]

Then came the inauguration itself – hyperbolic in so many respects – installing Mandela as the first black president of the newly liberated South Africa. It was an occasion that triumphantly returned South Africa to an imagined global community of respected nations. More heads of state than had been together for any occasion since the funeral of J. F. Kennedy attended Mandela's inauguration. Mandela's former jailers were also present, as his special guests, an enactment of his willingness to transcend his and, metonymically, the country's combative past. The grounds of the Union Buildings, previously a symbol of white Afrikaner hegemony, were packed with people of all ages and hues – itself an astoundingly new occurrence, given South Africa's distant and immediate past, and powerfully performative, as if enacting the "rainbow nation" that had come into being then and there. The giant television screen covering the proceedings showed the crowd to itself, in giant confirmation of its newfound diversity – an image that was still unfamiliar to South Africans, so that these huge visuals were powerful vectors of the new sensations of racially mixed gatherings. And their breathtaking fragility, in turn, underscored their emotional dependence on Mandela, as the presence without whom this could all just as easily fall away.

Mandela's speech invoked a "rainbow covenant" to bind "all South Africans, black and white." "The time for the healing of wounds has come," he intoned; "the moment to bridge the chasms that divide us has come. The time to rebuild is upon us." It was a message reiterated by a litany of the conventional icons of national unity – only now newly constituted: along with a new national flag, a national anthem that conjoined the long-standing anthem of the anti-apartheid struggle, "Nkosi Sikilela" – for many white South Africans, "synonymous with the *swart gevaar*"[48] – and "Die Stem," the anthem of old. Many people regarded the most powerful moment as the dramatic flyover of military jet fighters, suddenly symbols of national pride rather than white predation and aggression. In his autobiography, Mandela made it clear that the symbolic reaches of the flyover were carefully planned: "not only a display of pinpoint precision and military force" (useful iconography in and of itself for a new and uncertain regime), "but a demonstration of the military's loyalty to democracy, to a new government that has been freely and fairly elected."[49]

Many who were there, including seasoned journalists, produced uncharacteristically effusive accounts of the occasion. According to one of the journalists in attendance, "Never have I seen such a large crowd so incredibly orderly, dignified, disciplined, co-operative, graceful, and united: never have I been with so many happy and joyous people....The miraculous events in South Africa made hope possible for me again. I ... will never be the same again. Never again can I say that anything is impossible."[50]

Another of these high-profile, symbolically extravagant occasions was the 1995 Rugby World Cup, in which South Africa emerged victorious – as if in confirmation of its newfound victory at the helm of the global community of nations. Jacqueline Maingard has given detailed accounts of the opening and closing ceremonies, revealing the range of symbolic work that went into enacting the country's cultural "rainbow" during these events.[51] The tournament features center stage in John Carlin's account of the "miraculousness of the miracle."[52] As he documents, ANC leaders, including Minister of Sport Steve Tshwete (a rugby enthusiast) and Mandela himself, paid close attention to the symbolic nuances as much as to the headline framing of the event, acutely aware of the centrality of the game of rugby in the cultural and political imagination of white Afrikanerdom. When Mandela emerged on the field wearing the team's rugby jersey emblazoned with a springbok, the effect was electrifying, as the crowd – largely white – began chanting, "Nel-son! Nel-son!" The captain, François Pienaar, described it as "a moment of magic, a moment of wonder." As Carlin puts it, "The symbolism was mind-boggling."[53] The springbok had been the official emblem of the apartheid regime; as the emblem of the national rugby team, it exuded an aggressive white machismo, integral to the game of rugby but equally iconic of apartheid's nationalist chauvinism. The springbok on Mandela's heart was all the more powerful, then, for its tacit doubleness: simultaneously signifying the newfound embrace of the enemy, with a reminder of what it had been, thus also registering the (repressed) possibility of its return.

Throughout Mandela's tenure as president and beyond, his extraordinary persona was also scripted through a series of more ordinary encounters, equally replete with symbolic meaning and traction. Once he was president, one of Mandela's more startling gestures was to travel to Orania, bastion of an unreconstructed Afrikaner nationalism, to have tea with Betsie Verwoerd, widow of Hendrik Verwoerd, notorious as the leading architect of the apartheid project. The generosity of the occasion and others like it contributed to Mandela's powers of conversion, of bringing disbelievers on-side, as he performed the willingness to "reconcile" on behalf of a fledgling nation. There were other ways too in which Mandela was able to draw ordinary

South Africans, perhaps unexpectedly, into a sense of a collective, defined by his presence as its convener. He would be spotted – and reported – walking the streets near his house in Houghton, dropping into neighbors' houses for tea; he accepted an invitation from a family he hadn't known to attend their son's bar mitzvah. He was purported to have answered letters from adults and children, personally. Many South Africans have photographs of themselves and/or their children with Mandela during these years – opportunities that arose as a consequence of his commitment to frequent low-profile public appearances, in a myriad of venues and places. Many have recounted their personal interactions with him with a mixture of incredulity and awe. The "Have You Met Madiba?" blog, for example, begins with the claim: "I had an interesting debate with some friends a few days back. Out of five of us present, four of us had met Nelson Mandela." Responses from others who also met Mandela are invited and make for fascinating reading, showing how a plethora of minor encounters elevated him into a position of extraordinariness:

"I met him too. Bumped into him in a toyshop in Sandton.... he was gracious and charming to me and my two little boys. I felt as though I had met a supreme being and walked on air for the next week."

"Met the great man when i was in my teens, just after he got released, at the joburg city hall. My dads friends arranged a meet the great man evening. Awesome human being. If only we could all be more like him."

"yup met him too. Whilst Mandela was president, I was friends with a minister's son. Won't mention which ... but I was chilling at their house when madiba walked in."

"the most amazing thing is that a world icon, who was locked away for so long, is so accessible. I was privileged to meet him twice and both times I was struck by how tall he is and how gentle he seems."

"I met Madiba in 1998 while he was still president. Our debating team was in Pretoria and we drove past his home as he drove in. We "debated" with the gate man until he let us leave a note, which we did, with our phone number on. We had hardly driven off when we received a call and an invitation for tea. He had some time before meeting Kofi Annan and spent 47 minutes talking with us and signing personalized notes for us, on the presidential stationery. Amazing stuff. He was HUGE and gentle and extremely perceptive and kind."

"I shook Madiba's hand (after pretending to be someone else and getting past the securities. I do not know if that counts as a meeting. I remember thinking: "he is huge!" I looked up at the legend in front of me as in a dreamworld, especially when the legend said: 'How are you my dear?' Until today I cannot recall what I answered."[54]

An Enchanted Polity

So much for the rationally orchestrated modalities of "the miracle." Equally significant in making sense of "the Mandela moment" is the political-cultural landscape that gave the myth its popular traction: the enabling conditions within and beyond South Africa that were rooted in a wider genealogy of enchantment.

The concept of enchantment has attracted renewed interest of late, as a revealing lens held to notions of modernity or modernities.[55] If enchantment refers to the experience of intense and alluring wonder, it straddles an emotional spectrum, encompassing uncertainty, dread, and anxiety as much as elation, surprise, and exhilaration, either in tandem or co-productively. A mix of mystery and certainty surrounds the enchanted occurrence: its origins are somewhat inscrutable or invisible, while the occurrence itself is manifest. Enchantment is therefore also closely associated with conviction: a feeling of being in the midst of truth, but one that is revelatory rather than discursive, blindingly evident rather than produced on the strength of rationally assembled evidence. In fact, we are enchanted, in part, by the absence of any need for further explication, as if the occurrence that produces our feelings of conviction is self-explanatory, tautologically obvious through the sheer fact of what occurs, even if it is impossible to fathom fully how and why it occurred. So enchantment is elicited by wondrous outcomes that efface the processes that brought them into being. Enchantment also suggests a particular relationship to time, as if its normal flux is temporarily suspended, in a moment or period of being transfixed or spellbound.

It was Max Weber who classically declared modernity disenchanted, as a consequence of the ascendancy of scientific modes of knowledge and the evacuation of a metaphysics of experience from the realm of power and its effects. In Weber's words, "The increasing rationalization and intellectualization ... means that principally there are no mysterious incalculable forces that come into play, but rather that one can, in principle, master all things by calculation. This means that the world is disenchanted."[56] In modern societies, he argued, political legitimacy hinged largely on the scrutability of decision making, the binding power of law, and the advent of rigorously impersonal mechanisms of bureaucratic regulation. Disenchanted governance dispensed with sacred logics of power and mysterious claims to expertise; rather, in the midst of a complex division of labor, tasks were ideally assigned to those appropriately expert in undertaking them, with processes of decision making discernibly rational and informed.

Weber's critics typically extend, rather than supplant, his diagnosis of modern disenchantment, pointing to modes and sites of enchantment that have either coexisted with and/or informed the rigors of reason and rational governance.[57] It is not only that God has remained alive and well in many modern polities, alongside the lingering – and sometimes resurgent – purchase of religious institutions and beliefs in the micro-politics of everyday life; nor is it merely that a cast of ghosts, witches, and other occult characters have often inhabited the interstices of more rationalist versions of power and experience. There is an element of enchantment in *all* the affective performances of modern nationhood, in which symbols and rituals evoke strong emotional bonds to a community of strangers, in excess of a merely rational interpellation. And this attests to the magic in the work of nation building, with repertoires of ceremony and spectacle to conjure "imagined community" – impossible within the disenchanted strictures of bureaucracy and law alone.

If anything, late modernity has surely enhanced, rather than diminished, the enchanting repertoires of statecraft. There is very little that is transparent and scrutable in the workings of global financial markets – perhaps the quintessential site of late modern enchantment – even if the rationality of markets is exactly the rhetoric of their regulation. And a sense of mysterious forces afoot is affirmed in the proliferation of efforts to get rich through various strategies of spiritual investment, enlisting the services of any number of spiritual brokers who advertise their services on- or offline. For ailing states in which the apparatuses of law and bureaucracy have long been something of a charade – as in the many African regimes that navigate the booms and busts of their political markets – "quotidian ceremonial, extravagant in its dramaturgy and improvisational content alike," has become the prevailing currency of statecraft. Peter Geschiere and others have written too about a long-standing history of witchcraft in Africa that shows no signs of abating.[58] "On a global scale," write Jean and John Comaroff, "enchantment abounds."[59]

The enchantment of the post-apartheid order builds on a long-standing history blending disenchanted and enchanted modes of governance. If apartheid was in some ways the epitome of a modernist enthusiasm for rational planning and proactive regulation, this was coupled with the active promotion of Christian nationalism, as an equally explicit objective of the apartheid project – with Afrikaner nationalists claiming to have been elected by their God to the cause of white supremacy. The colonial "civilizing mission" had long enlisted many black South Africans into the ambit of the church. And indigenous African faiths posited their own supernatural actors, including witches, producing what Adam Ashforth has called a milieu of "spiritual insecurity" that flourished in the midst of the country's modernizing project.[60]

It is salutary, then, to be reminded of the metaphysics of daily life that persisted through the country's democratic transition. The 1996 census, the first to produce nationally comprehensive data on religious affiliations, revealed that only 11.5 percent of the population said they had "no religion." Of the remainder, the vast majority – 74 percent of the population – identified themselves as Christian, spanning many varieties thereof, including African Independent and charismatic churches.[61] The rhetoric of South Africa's "miraculous" transition was seldom explicitly religious, but as the preceding section revealed, there were key moments in the orchestration of the mythical Mandela when his leadership was rendered as a blissful gift from God. Whether explicit or not, the idea of the hand of God revealing itself in shepherding the transition – particularly given the extremity of its surprises – would have resonated within a polity long accustomed to a religious metaphysics of social and political life and a version of political leadership as divinely ordained.

Likewise, for those who lived alongside the ancestors, Madiba magic was itself a sign of the supernatural forces enabling his powers. As one of the respondents in a 1992 survey put it, "When Mr. Nelson Mandela was released from prison, he went back to his birth place to tell the ancestors that he was released from prison, and was now on a mission to liberate the country. All the blessings and the changes which are coming to us with him [Mandela] are because the ancestors are backing him and helping him."[62] The *sangomas* (healers) sharing the stage with Mandela at various mass rallies in the early 1990s made a similar point, "calling down ... the blessings of the ancestors ... in a procedure that has become commonplace in post-apartheid pageantry."[63]

South Africans also partook of a wider global milieu of secularized enchantment, in the "beguiling effects of mass culture,"[64] which grew more prominent as apartheid censorship atrophied, allowing widening popular access to television shows, magazines, images, and sentiments circulating in late-modern Western societies. Many South Africans with access to these media – across racial divides – were as taken with the lives and loves of global celebrities as was the case elsewhere and were growing accustomed to the spectacles of wonderment in the face of "special people" that global television and popular magazines made possible. Elements of Mandela's symbolic crafting drew actively, perhaps deliberately, on these emerging predilections. He played magical media moments with flair, as in his widely publicized meetings with the Spice Girls and Princess Diana, both in 1997. After his encounter with Victoria Beckham, he didn't disappoint the assembled horde of journalists. Deploying the kind of hyperbole typical of celebrity culture, he declared it – improbably – "one of the greatest moments of my life." After spending time with Princess Diana at his house in Houghton, he confessed to the media, "I am still trembling."[65] Mandela was, in many ways, a consummate, and self-styled, celebrity.

If the popular willingness to *love* Mandela – to allow him to work his magic – drew upon such old and new habits of enchanted thought and feeling (uneven though they no doubt were), it was the conundrum of the transition that surely gave immediate relevance and purchase to such predilections. In his astute rendition of the tense history of nationalism and its imprint post-1994, Ivor Chipkin underlines the paradox of summoning a "new" nation of South Africans into being: "The South African people lacked national marks. It was really only clear who they were not. They were not the South Africans of old: those who had perpetrated and endured the injustices of the past.... They had neither a common culture, nor race. Despite this, the first democratic elections proceeded as if they had; as if, nonetheless, it made sense to include them in a single demos."[66] As I see it, Mandela's metonymic power – to stand in for and enact this "new" people as if it had already come into being – provided a resolution to the paradox: South Africans were now a people in his image and what it stood for, already made new.

There was another element of the paradox too: the need to summon "the people" into a shared future with little prior sense of what that future would hold. Political life was at its most violent just before the elections, creating a situation of heightened fragility and impending disaster, on the very cusp of democracy's triumph. The country was poised for unprecedented orders of change, which would sound the death knell of white supremacy and institutionalized racial discrimination; the vision was ambitious, the promise of a democratic constitution enshrining a bill of rights was reassuringly robust, but the detail on how to accomplish all of this was scant, the realm of "policy" uncertain. The remarkably inclusive election signified an emerging national consensus on the idea of a "new" South Africa, despite little clarity as to what form this would take and how the still-palpable breaches of the past would be "healed." Indeed, it wasn't possible to work all of this out without a national affirmation of the need for it to occur. The escalating political violence added a sense of urgency to the need to begin a process without knowing in detail where it was headed. A conviction of living in miraculous times provided an enabling way of thinking, a structure of belief. The idea of a miracle effaces process and renders discussion and analysis thereof unnecessary. A miracle simply *is*, and is compelling and captivating for that revelatory certitude. In his blog, "The Madiba Magic to Look a Racist Straight in the Eye," Sandile Memela writes, "There is some mysterious madiba magic in being able to open your heart to forget the dreadful consequences of almost 400 years of brutal dehumanisation to melt away just like that."[67] "Melting away just like the that" aptly captures how the tropes of enchantment worked. In Mandela's presence and following his interventions, the violence disappeared, "just like that." It wasn't clear where it had gone or why; it also wasn't clear if and when it would return – an uncertainty that renewed popular conviction in the salience of Mandela's presence. And in the dramatic spectacles of "the rainbow nation" – in 1994 and 1995 – the old South African sclerosis of race and class had likewise seemed to "melt away just like that" in the euphoric moment, as if self-evidently possible and, in fact, already emergent.

Of course, the arteries of the post-apartheid body have not been free-flowing, occluded as they are by old and new trajectories of difference, inequality, and exclusion. Still, it may well be that for these very reasons, the beginnings of a radical rupture with the past constituted in the early 1990s could have been effected only by an expression of faith – be it in secular or religious register – in a new vision that hadn't yet taken shape: a willingness to suspend disbelief and to trust in the integrity of the process with the conviction of those enchanted by it without absolutely rational guarantees.

Coda: The Magic of Money

Mandela stepped down from the presidency in 1999, a time of unprecedented economic prosperity. The majority of white South Africans were better off than they had been under apartheid. A surge of accumulation within the upwardly mobile black population produced a small but conspicuously affluent elite and a larger, assertively aspirant middle class.[68] The major enchantment of these times has been with the commodity, exuberantly – fiendishly – embraced, as the advent of freedom has been, for many, the freedom to consume.[69] So it is no accident that charismatic churches have flourished – including prosperity churches whose God blesses the wealthy and admonishes the poor.[70] And witches have had a field day among those envious of the successes of others.[71] Those at the bottom of the economic heap have not fared as well: between 1993 and 2000, the proportion of those defined as poor continued to grow. Since then, the system of social grants has allowed a modest amelioration.[72] But overall, the high levels of economic inequality produced by apartheid have gotten worse: South Africa is now one of the most unequal societies in the world.

In November 2012, the South African Reserve Bank minted new banknotes bearing the face of Nelson Mandela, "to honour South Africa's struggle icon." "Our currency is our unique symbol of our nationhood, with many of us handling banknotes every day," said the bank's governor, Gill Marcus.[73] So the abiding everyday encounter with Madiba for present and future generations of South Africans will be with the literal currency of his iconic image. It risks another astounding symbolic reversal, this time from the spectacle of "reconciliation" to the divisive magic of the cash nexus. The unwitting irony – as compared with the earlier project of alert symbolic choreography – is itself a sign of the times.

NOTES

1. Njabulo Ndebele, *Fine Lines from the Box* (Cape Town: Umuzi, 2007), 51.
2. Achmat Dangor, *Forbidden Fruit* (Cape Town: Kwela Books, 2001), 37.
3. Rob Nixon, "'An Everybody Claim Dem Democratic': Notes on the 'New' South Africa," *Transition* 54 (1991): 21.
4. Farewell speech as president, June 16, 1999, mycapetown.co.za/news/2012/07/in-celebration-of-nelson-mandela's-birthday.
5. Rita Barnard, "Speaking Places: Prison, Poetry and the South African Nation," *Research in African Literatures* 32.3 (2001): 155.
6. Cited in Mark Gevisser, "Strange Bedfellows: Mandela, de Klerk and the New South Africa," *Foreign Affairs* 79.1 (2000): 177.
7. Eva Illouz, *Cold Intimacies: The Making of Emotional Capitalism* (Cambridge: Polity Press, 2007), 7.
8. Albie Sachs, cited in Gevisser, "Strange Bedfellows," 174.
9. See Genevieve Klein, "The British Anti-Apartheid Movement and Political Prisoner Campaigns, 1973–1980," *Journal of Southern African Studies* 35.2 (2009): 465–67, for the origins of this campaign.
10. www.sahistory.org.za/topic/nelson-mandela-timeline-1980–1989.
11. Tom Lodge, *Mandela: A Critical Life* (Oxford: Oxford University Press, 2006), 196.
12. Ibid.
13. Commonwealth Group of Eminent Persons, *Mission to South Africa: The Commonwealth Report* (Harmondsworth: Penguin, 1986); extract cited on www.nytimes.com/1986/06/13/world/excerpts-from-report-on-south-africa-issued-by-commonwealth-mission.html.
14. Susan Sontag, "For Nelson Mandela," *Threepenny Review* 28 (1987): 27.
15. Ibid.
16. See also Lodge's *Mandela*, an excellent account on which I draw extensively.
17. Achmat Dangor, Interview by author, September 12, 2009.
18. Ibid.
19. See, e.g., John Carlin's interview with Walter Sisulu, www.pbs.org/wgbh/pages/frontline/shows/mandela/interviews/sisulu.html.
20. Ibid.
21. As in his call for the continuation of the armed struggle on his release – perhaps to deflect any accusations of a secret pact between him and his jailers.
22. Dangor, Interview.
23. Colin Bundy, "Messianic Icon of Steely Grace," *Times Higher Education*, September 9, 2006; www.timeshighereducation.co.uk/story.asp?storyCode=205533&sectioncode=22.
24. Ibid.

25 Nelson Mandela, *Long Walk to Freedom* (London: Abacus, 2009), ch. 89.

26 Ibid., 166.

27 For a more extended analysis see Deborah Posel, "The Apartheid Project, 1948–1973," in *The Cambridge History of South Africa*, vol. 2, ed. Anne Mager, Bill Nasson, and Robert Ross (Cambridge: Cambridge University Press, 2012), 319–68.

28 Ibid.

29 Gunnar Theissen, "Between Acknowledgement and Ignorance: How White South Africans Have Dealt with the Apartheid Past" (Johannesburg: Center for the Study of Violence and Reconciliation, 1997), Sec. 3.4.

30 Vincent Crapanzano, *Waiting: The Whites of South Africa* (New York: Random House, 1985), 248.

31 Ibid., 204.

32 Kate Manzo and Pat McGowan, "Afrikaner Fears and the Politics of Despair: Understanding Change in South Africa," *International Studies Quarterly* 36 (1992): 4.

33 Ibid., 11.

34 Ibid., 12.

35 Julie Berg, "The Accountability of South Africa's Private Security Sector," Criminal Justice Initiative of the Open Society Foundation of South Africa (2007), 4.

36 See Lodge, *Mandela*, 166; also John Kane, *The Politics of Moral Capital* (Cambridge: Cambridge University Press, 2001), 140.

37 Crapanzano, *Waiting*, 46 (my emphasis).

38 Rob Nixon, "Mandela, Messianism, and the Media," *Transition* 51 (1991): 44.

39 F. W. de Klerk, Interview by John Carlin, *Frontline*, PBS, n.d., www.pbs.org/wgbh/pages/frontline/shows/mandela/.

40 Hugh Corder, personal communication; see also Annie Leatt, "The State of Secularism: Constituting Religion and Tradition Towards a Post-Apartheid South Africa," PhD thesis (University of the Witwatersrand, 2011).

41 See www.justice.gov.za/trc/media/1997/9705/s970527e.htm.

42 Donatella Lorch, "South Africa Is Hoarding as Fear Rises," *New York Times*, April 4, 1994.

43 Ibid.

44 Eve Bertelson, "Selling Change: Advertisements for the 1994 South African Election," Paper presented to the Wits History Workshop conference "Democracy: Popular Precedents, Practice, Culture," July 1994, 9.

45 John Carlin, *Playing the Enemy: Nelson Mandela and the Game That Made a Nation* (Harmondsworth: Penguin, 2008), 91.

46 Jim Wallis, "Hearts and Minds: The Miracle of South Africa," *Sojourners* (July 1994); www.sojo.net/index.cfm?action=magazine.article&issue=soj9407&article=940.

47 Quoted in ibid.

48 Springbok rugby player Kobus Wiese, quoted in Carlin, *Playing the Enemy*, 176.

49 Mandela, *Long Walk*, 747.

50 Wallis, "Hearts and Minds."

51 Jacqueline Maingard, "Imag(in)ing the South African Nation: Representations of Identity in the Rugby World Cup 1995," *Theatre Journal* 49.1 (1997): 15–28.

52 Carlin, *Playing the Enemy*, 3.

53 Ibid., 221–23.

54 sarocks.co.za/2008/03/10/have-you-met-madiba/.

55 See Michael Saler, "Modernity and Enchantment: A Historiographic Review," *American Historical Review* 111.3 (June 2006): 692–716.

56 Max Weber, "Science as a Vocation," in *From Max Weber: Essays in Sociology*, ed. Hans Gerth and C. Wright Mills (New York; Routledge, 1968), 155.

57 See Saler, "Modernity and Enchantment," 695–702.

58 Peter Geschiere, *The Modernity of Witchcraft: Politics and the Occult in Postcolonial Africa* (Charlottesville: University of Virginia Press, 1997).

59 John L. Comaroff and Jean Comaroff, "Millennial Capitalism, Occult Economies and the Crisis of Reproduction in South Africa," in *Religion and Sexuality in Cross-Cultural Perspective*, ed. Stephen Ellingson and M. Christian Green (London: Routledge, 2002), 228.

60 Adam Ashforth, *Witchcraft, Violence and Democracy in South Africa* (Chicago: University of Chicago Press, 2005).

61 Leatt, "The State of Secularism," 164–65.

62 Cited in Ashforth, *Witchcraft*, 220–21.

63 Ibid., 221.

64 Saler, "Modernity and Enchantment," 707.

65 www.washingtonpost.com/wp-srv/inatl/longterm/s_africa/stories/star072598.htm.

66 Ivor Chipkin, *Do South Africans Exist? Nationalism, Democracy and the Identity of "the People"* (Johannesburg: Wits University Press, 2007), 174.

67 www.thoughtleader.co.za/sandilememela/2008/01/24/the-madiba-magic-to-look.

68 Jeremy Seekings and Nicoli Nattrass, *Class, Race and Inequality in South Africa* (University of KwaZulu–Natal Press, 2006), ch. 9.

69 Deborah Posel, "Races to Consume: Revisiting South Africa's History of Race, Consumption and the Struggle for Freedom," *Ethnic and Racial Studies* 33.2 (February 2010): 157–75.

70 Ilana van Wyk, *A Church of Strangers: Sociality, Ritual and the Universal Church of the Kingdom of God in South Africa* (Cambridge: Cambridge University Press, 2013), 10–11.

71 Ashforth, *Witchcraft*.

72 Dori Posel and Michael Rogan, "Gendered Trends in Poverty in the Post-Apartheid Period, 1997–2006," *Development Southern Africa* 29.1 (2012): 98.

73 www.timeslive.co.za/local/2012/10/31/mandela-bank-note-to-begin-circulation-next-week.

4

BRENNA MUNRO

Nelson, Winnie, and the Politics of Gender

Nations are not born, they are made; in Benedict Anderson's phrase, they are "imagined communities." Summoning up a sense of belonging among people who are strangers to each other is no easy task, and it is even more fraught in countries emerging from histories of settler colonialism, where fellow citizens are former enemies. The fantasy of the nation as a *family* has often been used to make strangers imagine themselves as something like kin, and it is no surprise, then, that in South Africa Nelson Mandela has been cast in the role of "father of the nation." The project of building the post-apartheid "rainbow" nation depended a good deal on how his authoritative, yet emotive masculinity made very different kinds of people feel included in his adoptive embrace. Iconic in her own right, Winnie Madikizela-Mandela is a far more contradictory and tragic figure: the "mother" of the struggle who fell from grace. Both Nelson and Winnie are to some extent the creations of our collective imagination, screens onto which dreams and night-mares have been projected. The drama of their intertwined lives has been an unusual founding-family romance and has affected not only how South Africans have thought about race and nation, but how gender, sexuality, and family have been envisioned.

The unfolding public saga of Nelson Mandela's "private" life, with its marriages, divorces, separations, reunions, and bereavements, has been emblematic of the South African experience during apartheid and its after-math. The personal is political for an icon, and gender performance is an integral part of the theater of politics. All of us perform our gender in an intricate, mysterious mix of the innate, the habitual, and the deliberate, but Mandela's self-fashioning also has an element of the strategic. While his per-sona has always had an assured, Old World, gentlemanly quality – perhaps because of his aristocratic youth in the Thembu royal court and his mis-sionary education, or perhaps because he was blessed with height, strength, and grace – he has also forged a series of distinctively modern ways to be a black South African man throughout his political career, departing from convention in significant ways. Contrast, for example, current South African President Jacob Zuma's unabashedly patriarchal deployment of the politics of ethnicity, through his much-publicized polygamy, with Mandela's preference for companionate marriage throughout his life. While he was hardly an egalitarian husband, particularly in the early years, his embrace of secular humanism is visible in his approach to marriage as a freely chosen partnership; and he has always chosen women with strong personalities.

His first wife, Evelyn Mase, was a Jehovah's Witness, and in his autobiography, *Long Walk to Freedom*, Mandela presents their divorce in terms of the conflict between religious and political convictions: "A man and woman who hold such different views of their respective roles in life cannot remain close.... When I would tell her that I was serving the nation, she would reply that serving God was above serving the nation."[1] When he met Winnie Madikizela, he was already a well-known political figure and a man of nearly forty, while she was twenty-three, new to the city, and not part of his political circle; but she was educated, ambitious, and civic-minded, having taken a post as a social worker at Johannesburg's mammoth Baragwanath Hospital. She was also strikingly beautiful and, like him, always stylishly dressed. Both transplants from the rural sphere, they shared a taste for the city as a space of self-invention.

Their marriage coincided with the apex of a form of black urban South African public culture known as the "Sophiatown Renaissance," in reference to a lively township in which blacks owned property, racial boundaries were crossed, and sexual mores were often more bohemian than respectable. Sophiatown itself was demolished by the apartheid regime, as blacks were cast out of the cities into the townships and bantustans, and this lost city life became an emblem of a potential democratic future. The Sophiatown Renaissance was marked by a defiant cosmopolitan modernity that refused identification with the "tribal culture" to which apartheid assigned "Bantus," taking its cues from Hollywood and African-American jazz culture instead. The most emblematic black popular publication of the period, *Drum* magazine, gave the African National Congress (ANC) and the Defiance Campaign of the 1950s a high profile, amidst its coverage of musicians, gangsters, pin-ups, and drag queens. Before Winnie and Nelson met, the young photographers at *Drum* often asked her to pose for them, and news photographer Peter Magubane became a loyal friend of the couple.[2] The visual image was important in an era when mass print media were becoming ubiquitous in South Africa, and the way their images were embedded in popular print culture brought the ANC a higher profile.

Mandela excelled in the performative spaces of the courtroom and the political rally and was clearly as aware of the spectacle he presented as he was of the words he was using. For the first five years of his working life in Johannesburg, Mandela wore the same borrowed suit, painstakingly keeping it neat; he worked hard to become the dashing, well-dressed man in the arresting black-and-white photographs that became so talismanic after his imprisonment. His sartorial style of this period suggests that he wanted to project a masculinity that underscored the ability of black men to be "civilized." Mandela had to de-emphasize his actual body in order to align black masculinity with the intellect, but with Winnie by his side, he was not de-sexed.[3] Their evident intense mutual attraction fit right in with the discourse of heterosexual romantic love that was being cultivated by magazines like *Drum*, and Winnie was in many ways the perfect prop for Nelson's production of a debonair masculinity. The way they were "doing gender" thus had a range of political meanings. Decades before "black is beautiful," the two of them were a visible celebration of black African glamour and desirability, and enacted a model of companionate heterosexual marriage that signified as both respectable and modern.

The couple had only two years of married life together. In the wake of the Sharpeville Massacre in 1960 and the ensuing escalation of state repression, Mandela persuaded the now-banned ANC to take up arms, and went underground. His brief life on the run brought him into the public eye more than ever before.[4] For the eager readers of newspaper stories about the "Black Pimpernel," as he was dubbed, Mandela had become like a fictional character in a serialized adventure story.[5] In 1961, he gave his first television interview, for a British journalist, and he looks very much the outlaw and militant; in a dark workingman's jacket, he is bearded, unsmiling, slightly unkempt. This version of Mandela, at his most macho, was to be used on posters, pamphlets, badges, and T-shirts throughout the long period of his imprisonment, both by those cultivating a Che Guevara–like revolutionary aura around Mandela and, conversely, by supporters of apartheid presenting him as a "terrorist."

When Mandela was finally caught and put on trial for treason in 1963, he used the occasion as an opportunity for political theater. His final speech from the dock condemning apartheid forcefully made the case for black people's liberation, and when he first appeared in court, he was wearing beads and a leopard skin kaross. As we can see from Wolfie Kodesh's description of Mandela's staring contest in court with the magistrate (who was "transfixed like a mongoose looking at a snake"), this performance was (along with the many other significations discussed elsewhere in this book) an assertion of an unashamed black masculinity; Mandela's racialized body was on display, aligned now with verbal eloquence. Mandela was not alone in wearing this style of dress, though; Madikizela-Mandela, too, came to court in traditional Xhosa clothing, making an equally dramatic entrance. After the minister of justice banned her from wearing this incendiary garb, she wore clothes in the colors of the ANC or ensembles from other African countries that Mandela had sent her during his clandestine travels. Interestingly, hundreds of other women came to court wearing the traditional clothing she had been forbidden; this collective act of mimicry and solidarity tells us a great deal about the influence her performance of political wifehood was beginning to have.

Robben Island was one of the most important sites for the incubation of a democratic political culture and an exclusively male cadre of future power brokers. However, the imprisonment of so many of the anti-apartheid movement's activists in the 1960s brought the struggle temporarily to a halt outside, and Mandela was not able to "lead" in the usual way. As the poet Breyten Breytenbach put it, Robben Island was "like a ship of ghosts patrolling just offshore" for those left behind.[6] It took the work and imagination of countless people to keep Mandela alive in the public mind as a symbol of the anti-apartheid movement, and Madikizela-Mandela's role in this regard was crucial. Her "conjugal rights," albeit whittled away by the authorities, made her an important link between Robben Island and the outside world. A British television interview with her just after Mandela's sentencing sets the tone for the coming years; luminously beautiful, she deals with the journalist's questions with dignity, speaking softly, simply, and gravely.[7] Magubane suggests:

> Without Winnie, Nelson wouldn't have been what he is.... When newspapers could not write about him, she could have his problems publicized. Without her, the ANC would have been forgotten. She was the only person who stood by the ANC and said, "I dare you to stop me."[8]

Like many female political figures before and since, her outspokenness in the public sphere was authorized by the very conventionality of her position as the loyal wife. Paradoxically, being her husband's spokesperson enabled her to become a leader in her own right.

Njabulo Ndebele's novel, *The Cry of Winnie Mandela*, takes the figure of Penelope, waiting for the return of Ulysses, as the starting point for a reflection on Madikizela-Mandela's life.[9] If Penelope stands for female virtue defined as passivity, then Winnie, of course, was no Penelope. Suddenly a single mother of two small daughters when Mandela was imprisoned – Zenani (Zeni) and Zindziswa (Zindzi) – Madikizela-Mandela had to deal with two and a half decades of almost daily police harassment, friends that turned out to be spies working for the state, banning orders, arrests, spells of imprisonment, and the impossibility of keeping a job under these circumstances. Throughout all of this she remained an unbowed critic of apartheid, who had the world's ear. In *Part of My Soul Went with Him*, the admiring, collaborative "autobiography" adapted from interviews with Winnie, she projects a toughness, experience, and defiance of white male power that is more Steve Biko than Nelson Mandela:

> Then they tried to interrogate me, but if you have been inside as long as I have, you cannot go through that worthless exercise again. No policeman can come to me today at my age and think that he can still interrogate me. In my younger days it was different, but any squeak of a little policeman who came to question me today would just be wasting his time.[10]

Winnie's fierce, solo resistance made her a global feminist icon, not least for Nadine Gordimer, who cast her as the stylish, beautiful, and resolute wife of a jailed political leader in *Burger's Daughter*: a character who provides the ambivalent female protagonist a model of emphatically feminine political commitment.[11]

Madikizela-Mandela turned her symbolic position as "mother of the nation" into an active, revolutionary role; in doing so she was following the lead of many other women involved in the struggle. Elleke Boehmer has analyzed how nationalisms have tended to cast women in the role of idealized mothers rather than as warriors or strategists, effectively removing them from the sphere of public engagement. As she puts it, "The new postcolonial nation is historically a male-constructed space, narrated into modern self-consciousness by male leaders, activists, and writers, in which women are more often than not cast as symbols or totems, as the bearers of tradition."[12] Yet, as Anne McClintock observes, women involved in African nationalist movements remade the concept of motherhood:

> Over the decades, African women nationalists ... have transformed and infused the ideology of motherhood with an increasingly insurrectionary cast, identifying themselves more and more as the "mothers of the revolution." ... Even under the State of Emergency, women have everywhere enlarged their militancy, insisting not only on their right to political agency but also on their right of access to the technologies of violence.[13]

Emma Mashinini, for example, who was an important anti-apartheid union organizer, presents political commitment as driven by the desire to nurture. She vividly evokes the horror of torture at the hands of the apartheid security forces by describing how it made her forget her beloved daughter's name.[14]

The Soweto Uprising of the 1970s was a political conflict in which the apartheid state ruthlessly pitted itself against children. Young people had collectively refused the imposition of education in Afrikaans, and thirteen-year-old Hector Pieterson, shot and killed by police, became an emblem of the many children-turned-activists imprisoned, tortured, and killed by the regime right up until the end of apartheid. The "mother of the nation" stepped in, helping to form the Black Parents Association (BPA). Sheila Meintjes describes the protective, yet collaborative role the "adults" played in the ongoing unrest in the townships:

> The BPA raised funds, organized burials, and mediated between students and authorities in schools. Winnie visited police stations, and harangued the police. She helped organize meetings and she spent hours with bereaved parents. She also recruited students into the ANC and helped them to leave the country. But her activities were cut short by arrest and detention.[15]

The state tried and failed to prove that Madikizela-Mandela had played a role in fomenting the uprising, but she was effectively exiled to the bleak rural town of Brandfort in 1977, whose local languages, Afrikaans and Sotho, she did not speak. In a beautifully written letter to a friend, she describes the difficulties of her experience there, dumped in a house without water or electricity, in terms that echo Mashinini's emphasis on motherhood lost:

> Being with Zindzi in the past two years sort of cushioned the impact of the pain; now she is gone.... It is the first time that I truly feel what my little Siberia is all about. The empty long days drag on, one like the other, no matter how hard I try to study. The solitude is deadly, the grey matchbox shacks so desolate simply stare at you as lifeless as the occupants, who form a human chain of frustration as they pass next to my window.[16]

The Mandelas had sent Zindzi, their youngest daughter, to stay with a family friend in Johannesburg because the isolation and police harassment had caused her to become dangerously depressed.[17] Historians and biographers have asserted that this was a period in which Madikizela-Mandela began drinking excessively. Nonetheless, she managed to triumph over Brandfort, politicizing her initially hostile neighbors, once again through "motherly" means: setting up a crèche and a clinic for children.

We get a glimpse of the image of her husband that was meanwhile being constructed across the postcolonial world (particularly after the ANC kicked off its Release Mandela Campaign in 1980) through Nigerian writer Wole Soyinka's 1988 poem "'No,' He Said." The poem presents the imprisoned Mandela as a paragon of heroic masculinity, resistance itself personified and distilled in the refrain of refusal throughout the poem: "no, he said." He is mythicized as Ogun, the Yoruba god of iron and war, as Prometheus, and as a Christ-like fisher of men:

> And they saw his hands were clenched.
> Blood oozed from a thousand pores. A lonely
> Fisher tensed against the oilcloth of new dawns,
> Hand over hand he hauled. The harvest strained.
> Cords turned writhing hawsers in his hands. "Let go!"
> The tempters cried, but – no, he said.[18]

In this vision of Mandela, he is both keeping the struggle alive and hauling the "new dawn" or future "harvest" of the democratic nation into being. He is a salt-of-the-earth colossus who embodies the nation: "Blood oozed from a thousand pores," as if all of those suffering under apartheid are bleeding through his hands. This corporeal, yet abstract figure presents an impossibly stoic masculinity that is stripped of personality. As Mandela says at the end of the poem when he is finally given voice: "I am that rock / in the black hole of the sky." The imagery used throughout the poem evokes the seascape of Robben Island, and there is no trace of Winnie in this all-male world. Interestingly, however, the language of oozing, tensing, straining, and hauling in the stanza referenced here calls childbirth to mind; it is part of the queerness of myths of nation, perhaps, that masculinist fantasies of nation making invoke male pregnancy.

The man who became the country's leader during the transition to democracy was not, however, made of rock or iron. When Mandela walked out of Victor Verster Prison into the awaiting crowds with his wife by his side in 1990, like Lazarus emerging from his tomb, the fact that he was now a white-haired old man was a shock to the global audience, who had seen almost no new images of him in nearly thirty years. The unique masculine persona that subsequently emerged seems deeply bound up with his particular vision of nation building. Although Mandela had initiated the armed struggle, he was not a military leader coming out of a war of national liberation, like the patriarchal and homophobic Robert Mugabe in neighboring Zimbabwe. He stood for a negotiated peace, for forgiveness and reconciliation. These values are not usually coded as masculine. As Ndebele puts it in his novel, "When we gave up the AK-47 for negotiation, we opted for intimacy. In the choice we had between negotiation and revolutionary violence we opted for feelings and the intellect."[19] This is not to say that Mandela did not exert authority; a crucial moment in which he did so was in the wake of the assassination of the popular young ANC activist Chris Hani by a right-wing white extremist in 1993, when the country was enduring an unstable interregnum between apartheid and democracy. Although Mandela was not yet officially the president, De Klerk conceded that Mandela should be the one to address the nation on television, and he successfully called for calm rather than revenge:

> This is a watershed moment for all of us. Our decisions and actions will determine whether we use our pain, our grief and our outrage to move forward to what is the only lasting solution for our country – an elected government of the people, by the people and for the people. We must not let the men who worship war, and who lust after blood, precipitate actions that will plunge our country into another Angola.[20]

Mandela brings emotion into the public sphere in this speech, appealing to his audience by acknowledging their "pain," "grief," and "outrage." He is not particularly emotionally expressive himself in public; his years of working in the dust of the quarry on Robben Island damaged his eyes, so that crying is physically difficult for him.[21] Nonetheless, he seems able to magnetically draw feeling out in other people. The Truth and Reconciliation Commission (TRC), a project that is emblematic of Mandela's "rainbow" era, was all about public and indeed political emotion, as people who had experienced trauma and loss wrestled with their sorrow and anger in front of a national and global audience, and the expression of authentic remorse was sought from perpetrators of violence.

At the end of a speech Mandela made while running for president in the first multiracial elections of 1994, he departed from his usual formal and deliberate oratorical style, saying: "My last word is that I love each and every one of you. I surely wish the pockets of my shirt were big enough to fit you all in. There is a grandfather here who regards each and every one of you as my children, as my grandchildren."[22] It is hard to imagine many other political figures saying such a thing and being taken seriously, but it is striking how often people turn to the word "love" when they are talking about Mandela. As Mark Gevisser puts it, "People obeyed Mandela because they loved him."[23] This public feeling is possible in part, of course, because of Mandela's moral integrity. His long years of imprisonment and his forgiveness of his enemies on his emergence give his life story the quality of a spiritual fable. Saintliness is not necessarily gendered; in terms of contemporary global figures who stand for *goodness*, Mandela is akin to both the Dalai Lama and Burma's long-imprisoned democracy activist, Aung San Suu Kyi. But Mandela has himself eschewed the idea that he is a saint, and indeed his humanness is as important to his appeal, as we can see in the image of the protective grandfather.[24]

There is a difference, of course, between the real Mandela and the imagined Mandela. The beloved "father of the nation" was what Sampson calls a "Victorian paterfamilias" with his own children – authoritarian, distant, easily disappointed.[25] He expresses strong regrets about not being able to be a "real" father to his children in his autobiography:

> When your life is the struggle, as mine was, there is little room left for family. That has always been my greatest regret, and the most painful aspect of the choice I made.... My children said, "We thought we had a father and one day he'd come back. But to our dismay, our father came back and he left us alone because he has now become the father of the nation."[26]

The sacrifice of personal family life, however, is part of Mandela's appeal as an imagined national father. The famous pleasure he takes in holding other people's babies, that staple of the political photo op, comes across as authentic rather than rehearsed because his audience knows that he was deprived of them for so long in prison.

A minor, yet much-reported episode from the transition years gives one a sense of how the public Mandela reconfigured ideas about family, masculinity, and race during this time. In 1995, Mandela invited the wives and widows of both ANC and Nationalist Party leaders for a luncheon; tellingly, the one woman who was excluded was Winnie, from whom he was by then separated. Ninety-four-year-old Betsie Verwoerd, the widow of H. F. Verwoerd, the Afrikaner prime minister who had masterminded apartheid, was the one woman who declined. She sent a polite but frosty note saying that he was always welcome to visit her. So he promptly set out, in his state helicopter, for her little rural town of Orania – a place, not coincidentally, that right-wingers fantasized would be the center of an all-white *volkstaat* independent of the new South Africa – to take her up on her invitation. In photographs of the event, this tiny woman with her hair in an old-fashioned bun, beams up at Mandela; she had found that the "terrorist" was a "gentleman." The image of a tall, patrician black man with his arm placed protectively around a frail white grandmother is emblematic of how Mandela's public persona transfigured notions of black masculinity once again; this is a long way from images of black men as a threat to white womanhood or as emasculated "boys." It also summons up the idea of an interracial "family" that is not defined by blood connection.

During the same period, Mandela had another meeting that signaled his inclusive, adoptive embrace in a very different way, with the effervescent young activist Simon Tseko Nkoli. Nkoli was South Africa's best-known black gay man in the 1990s, having emerged as a leading voice for gay rights from within the anti-apartheid movement. Nkoli was part of the most famous political trial of the 1980s, the Delmas treason trial, and while in prison, he came out to his fellow defendants, initiating an internal debate that laid the groundwork for the inclusion of gay rights in the 1996 Constitution – the first in the world to protect people from discrimination on the grounds of sexual orientation. As ANC and United Democratic Front (UDF) stalwart Mosiuoa "Terror" Lekota said: "How could we say that men and women like Simon, who had put their shoulders to the wheel to end apartheid, how could we say that they should now be discriminated against?"[27] Most forms of modern nationalism have excluded gay people from citizenship, and the fantasy of the nation as a *heterosexual* family has been a conceptual mechanism of exclusion. What was it about the new South Africa's family romance of nation, then, that allowed, for at least a brief period, gay people to be imagined as belonging? Perhaps it has to do with the "rainbow" dream of an inter-racial national family of choice rather than a "natural" kinship based on the heterosexual couple.

During the years of transition to democracy, the founding family itself was not living up to the heteronormative ideal it had long projected. If Madiba was the saintly grandfather who fused power with sentiment, for many onlookers Winnie came to embody a monstrous motherhood and the unruly, unfaithful wife. After returning to Soweto from Brandfort in 1985, she famously declared that "together, hand in hand, with our boxes of matches and our necklaces we shall liberate this country," referencing the brutal, strangely feminized form of vigilante justice sometimes used against suspected collaborators.[28] This statement reinforced racist associations between blackness and "barbaric" violence and was therefore one of very few made by Madikizela-Mandela that the apartheid authorities were happy to allow the press to quote.[29] There has been much speculation about what pushed her to embrace violence, just as Mandela was coming to be associated with peacemaking. What she suffered during apartheid was arguably worse than the ordeals the men on Robben Island withstood, because she was so much more alone. The relentlessness of the police toward her was extraordinary, and she was effectively imprisoned in the home.

> Once, woken at four in the morning and told that she was being arrested, she closed her bedroom door while dressing. A white policeman ... pushed open the door and grabbed Winnie by the shoulder. Incensed by the intrusion, and without stopping to think of the consequences, she grabbed him and threw him to the floor.... Six of his colleagues waiting outside carried her bodily to a police vehicle, wearing only one stocking and one shoe, and took her to prison.[30]

In this *unheimlich* scene of state terror, domestic space is violated along with bodily dignity, Winnie's self-fashioning and femininity torn from her. In 1969, she was kept in solitary confinement for thirteen months, far longer than most human beings can endure without psychic damage, and, "as Helen Suzman put it, 'they turned her from a warmhearted person into a mad creature.'"[31] In *The Cry of Winnie Mandela*, Ndebele describes her as the "daughter" of Major Theunis Swanepoel, the notorious apartheid state security agent who was determined to break her, and imagines her describing the impact of that experience in reproductive terms: when Swanepoel "let us leave his citadel of torture, I carried inside of me like a pregnancy, this terrible weight of loneliness and the embers of rage."[32] For many interpreters, then, Winnie is the tragic product of the apartheid state, transformed into the offspring of suffering and inflicting it in turn on the children of the nation. That her story reads as Greek tragedy speaks to the horror and sadness of what apartheid wrought in a very different way than the parable of forgiveness and grace that Mandela's life provides.

The household she established when she returned to Soweto in the mid-1980s was not the refuge for waifs and strays that her previous homes had often been. She formed the infamous Mandela United Football Club (MUFC), a group of about thirty young men she housed, who were her entourage, bodyguards, and adopted wards all at once – along with their "coach," Jerry Richardson. While the MUFC wielded power in the township like a militia, internally it was run as if it were a family; everyone involved, no matter his age, called Winnie "mummy."[33] Revolutionary motherhood had become authoritarian:

> Members were subject to her own strict rules. They were required to return home by a certain time each night, signing in and out of the house in a special register. Failure to sign the register meant a whipping, from Winnie as well as from the other youths. Looking for more recruits, club members roamed the township, accusing those who did not want to join them of being police informers or 'sell-outs.' Many who were coerced into joining subsequently found it difficult to leave. No one could resign voluntarily from the club. Stories began to circulate of youths being taken to Winnie's house and never seen again.[34]

The emotionally vulnerable Zindzi – globally visible as the "daughter of the nation" when she read out a message of defiance from her imprisoned father to Jabulani Stadium in 1985 – became embroiled in her mother's fiefdom. She was in a relationship with a club member who freely confessed to involvement in a killing – storing the guns underneath Zindzi's bed – in order to prevent Madikizela-Mandela and Zindzi from being involved in the police investigation.[35] She had a child with another, Sizwe Sithole, the head of the MUFC's "disciplinary committee," who killed himself in a police station in 1990, allegedly out of remorse for having implicated both the mother of the nation and her daughter in serious crimes.[36]

The MUFC gained a reputation in Soweto for the brutal treatment of those it deemed collaborators and enemies. Sampson describes the context:

> The township was coming close to civil war as young people took up weapons. As Azhar Cachalia, the Treasurer of the UDF, later described the problem: "By mid-1985, thousands of unaffiliated youths lacking direction or cohesion, many of them badly affected by their experience of detention, saw themselves as soldiers in the liberation struggle." They formed their own armed gangs, staking out territories.... The UDF leaders, undermined by mass arrests and detentions, could not control them.... And the police clearly had their own agenda. They had penetrated some gangs with informers and agents provocateurs, playing them against each other, provoking suspicion, betrayal and reprisals, while not intervening against Winnie.[37]

When the UDF, representing the on-the-ground anti-apartheid movement of the 1980s, publicly repudiated Madikizela-Mandela in 1989, it used the phrase "reign of terror" to describe the complex tangle of misdeeds perpetrated by the MUFC.[38] She has been implicated in the deaths of at least sixteen people, most of them teenagers.[39] As one of Ndebele's characters puts it to Winnie, "There is a long list of lives that in one way or another appear to have intersected with yours. They rise out of the TRC records like vapor."[40] Although Madikizela-Mandela's possible crimes are dwarfed by the scale of violence unleashed by the apartheid state across the region over the course of her lifetime, they provided a drama, played out in serial form from the late 1980s to the late 1990s through media reporting, multiple trials, and the TRC, that epitomized important issues for the nation then in the throes of being born. Who had the right to use violence, what kind of rule of law would be built on the ruins of apartheid, and how would the psychic and social effects of histories of violence be managed? Questions of gender, sexuality, race, and power were also, of course, very much at stake.

In July 1988, a group of pupils from a nearby school burned down the Mandelas' house as retribution for a beating some of them had received there; no one in the crowd of neighbors silently watching the blaze intervened.[41] When Mandela learned about this, he decided not to press charges and asked Winnie to disband the MUFC. He also formed the Mandela Crisis Committee, made up of community leaders involved with the anti-apartheid movement, such as Frank Chikane of the South African Council of Churches, the trade unionist Cyril Ramaphosa, and Dr. Nthato Mothlana of the BPA, to try to limit her behavior and the damage it was causing to the movement's reputation; the only woman on the committee was Sister Bernard Ncube. Madikizela-Mandela, no longer willing to play the role of obedient wife, did not comply. In December of that year, the MUFC kidnapped four youths, physically assaulted them, and killed the youngest, Stompie Moeketsi Seipei, in the tragic affair that became symbolic of her transformation, for many, into malevolent mother of the nation.

The kidnapped youths – who were fourteen, eighteen, nineteen, and twenty-nine – were living in a house run by a liberal priest, Paul Verryn, one of very few whites working to help people in the townships; his was a sanctuary for lost "boys" that rivaled Winnie's. There were rumors that Verryn was gay and that he was sexually abusing the youths in his care, although these rumors seem mostly to have come from Madikizela-Mandela and a follower of hers named Xoliswa Falati. In the "interrogation" that the youths described suffering in her home after they were kidnapped – a mirroring of the police torture so many of them had experienced – accusations that they were having sex with each other and with Verryn and that they were sellouts were intermixed. In this welter of suspicions, homosexuality was understood to be a form of racial and political betrayal, while sexual abuse and homosexuality became synonymous. Madikizela-Mandela has always maintained that she was merely rescuing the youths, but this assertion glosses over the important fact that they were not claiming to have been abused when they were taken and have consistently testified since the kidnappings that there was no abuse; in fact, when one of them escaped from her house, he ran to Verryn for help. When the story first broke in 1989, she gave an interview to NBC in which she said of him, "I don't understand how a man of his standing continues to sodomise black children … my responsibility as a mother is to draw attention to this problem."[42] In her parliamentary address on the topic in 1994, she asserted, "I unhesitatingly fell in with a plan to rescue them and gave them refuge in my house."[43] The idea that one is protecting a sexually abused child by inflicting "disciplinary" violence on the child is, of course, deeply problematic, and offers a chillingly similar logic to the contemporary phenomenon of the "corrective rape" of lesbians. In Madikizela-Mandela's 1991 trial for kidnapping and accessory to assault, which followed the conviction of Jerry Richardson for Seipei's killing, a prominent line of her defense was to continue to slander Verryn and to make homosexuality and race the subject of the trial. A photograph of one of her supporters outside the court holding a homemade sign saying that "homosex is not in black culture" became an iconic media image. In her astute analysis of the discourses at work in these events, Rachel Holmes suggests that the presentation of these young men as children in need of Winnie's protection undermined their sexual and political agency.[44] She points out that Seipei was not just a child, but a well-known activist, who had been one of the youngest detainees in South Africa under the state of emergency, the "Little General," who had once declared to the *Sunday Times*, "We are braver than the adults."[45] Although he was the particular object of the MUFC's attentions because there were rumors that he had become an informant, Seipei also represented a youth rebellion that challenged the authority of adult leaders like Madikizela-Mandela – a politicized youth culture that generated anti-apartheid activists like Simon Nkoli and Zackie Achmat, who were subsequently outspoken about gay rights and government inaction on AIDS. The historical meaning of this episode, as Holmes argues, is bound up with the question of gay rights:

> In 1991 the ANC Constitutional Committee included a clause in the draft bill of rights that outlawed discrimination and harassment on the basis of sexual orientation. In the same year, the Winnie Mandela trial became the occasion for widely disseminated public statements that discriminated against homosexuality and precipitated anxieties about the status of lesbian and gay rights in the ANC, whatever the official policy commitments.[46]

A repudiation of homosexuality couched in the terms of African nationalism – one that very much lives on today – thus gained public articulation through this event, but it was also galvanizing for South African gay rights activists. As Madikizela-Mandela's reputation was being damaged, the constituency within the ANC that was in favor of gay rights gained the upper hand during this crucial period of nation formation.

The UDF publicly condemned Madikizela-Mandela in the wake of Seipei's killing. During the kidnappings, Mandela had joined the local attempts to intervene, urgently sending instructions to release the youths, but after his release from prison, he defended his wife. He told a reporter that the intention of the police in relation to Winnie was "not to investigate the commission of any crime, but ... to destroy the image of the family."[47] Mandela also arranged for her to be made the ANC head of social welfare, and she was elected leader of the newly re-formed ANC Women's League in 1990, despite strenuous opposition in both cases; the party became deeply riven over her. Mandela stood by her throughout her 1991 trial, in which the judge found her guilty of kidnapping and being an accessory to assault, sentencing her to five years in prison. This sentence, however, was reduced to a fine in her 1993 appeal, and Madikizela-Mandela never served any time. In a 1994 speech to parliament, she blamed her conviction on "those apartheid courts which are a disgrace to the judicial system."[48] However, police and prosecutors appeared to be unwilling to make a case against her as apartheid waned and the transition began. There were several MUFC crimes for which she was never interviewed, let alone charged, while key witnesses and material evidence went missing in her trial. In her 1993 appeal, no new evidence was introduced, despite several witnesses who had previously protected her having publicly recanted their stories. The appeal court's lenience may have reflected a pragmatic desire to prevent Winnie from becoming a martyr at a moment of national instability in the wake of Hani's assassination.[49]

A different form of public accountability came with the 1997 TRC hearing examining her role in eight murders and ten other serious crimes. "As a South African media event," Krog declares in her TRC memoir, it was comparable to "the release of Nelson Mandela from prison."[50] Max du Preez describes how Madikizela-Mandela's "approach to the hearing was simple: she denied everything and expressed her outrage that anyone could accuse her of anything unbecoming."[51] Krog notes how she used the words "ridiculous" and "ludicrous" so often that the victims' relatives started to "anticipate her answers with their own sneering versions of 'ridiculous' and 'ludicrous'."[52] The hearing did provide the occasion, however, for Nicodemus Sono to finally speak publicly about his long-missing son, Lolo, whom he last saw, badly beaten, in a van with Madikizela-Mandela, who informed him that his son was a sellout and drove away with him. When two former UDF leaders, Murphy Morobe and Azhar Cachalia, took the stand and explained why the movement had repudiated her, they received a standing ovation. Archbishop Desmond Tutu begged her to acknowledge wrongdoing, appealing to her sense of her own status: "you don't know how your greatness would be enhanced if you would say sorry." Madikizela-Mandela finally made this concession: "I am saying it is true: things went horribly wrong and we were aware that there were factors that led to that. For that I am deeply sorry."[53]

Divorcing Winnie, then, saved Mandela's reputation. In 1992 he publicly separated from her. She had been having a relationship with a much younger man, a lawyer called Dali Mpofu, who had worked on her case and whom she had made her deputy in the Social Welfare Department, and the ANC was investigating their fiscal affairs. The *Sunday Times* printed a painfully intimate and irate letter she wrote to Mpofu, which someone in the ANC had found and leaked. In the letter, she referred to Mandela as *tata* – turning the notion of him as a father into a form of disparagement – and made damning admissions about her financial dealings. Madikizela-Mandela's political career had been dealt a body blow, and she was not included in the pageantry of the first free South African elections in 1994, the goal of so much of her life's work. She refused to settle when Mandela asked for a divorce, and at the trial his candid, quiet testimony that "I was the loneliest man during the period I stayed with her" consolidated sympathetic onlookers' sense that his failure to hold his wife to account for the MUFC was not an ethical lapse but an emotional one.

It may have been the public revelation of Madikizela-Mandela's sexual transgression that finally made her accept temporary defeat. Global media coverage of Winnie during this period repeatedly referred to her as "mugger of the nation." Desiree Lewis argues that these kinds of vilification "consolidated conventional stereotypes of black woman as other: sexual promiscuity, excess, immorality and imperviousness to codes of social decency and morality."[54] Krog, similarly, asks: "Why is it that ... a black woman from a long-isolated country, creates such an unprecedented media frenzy? Is it because Winnie Madikizela-Mandela answers to the archetype black and beautiful? Or ... the stereotype Black and Evil?"[55] The intertwined racism and sexism at play in the media response to Winnie's transgressions themselves produce an unease about critiquing her. As Holmes puts it:

> In the oversimplifications of ... global media ... Winnie Mandela was either demonized as the imperfect mother and wife of a couple represented as "parenting" an emergent nation or complacently exonerated by liberal commentators anxious that to question her use of power was to somehow be implicated in her vilification by the white state.[56]

The spectacle of Winnie's female misrule, inevitably contrasted to Mandela's saintliness, rather than the steadfast integrity of so many other black South African women who fought apartheid, may well have exacerbated a patriarchal vision of gender and politics. The lesson all too easily appeared to be that women cannot handle power and that a woman without a husband to guide and contain her would go wrong – rather than, say, the dangers of maverick political leaders, male or female, who operate outside structures of democratic accountability.

Madikizela-Mandela's self-serving leadership of the ANC Women's League and the long struggle to oust her had a more tangible negative impact on feminist organizing in post-apartheid South Africa.[57] Shireen Hassim argues that the 1980s, like the 1950s, were an extraordinary period for women's participation in politics in South Africa, because the anti-apartheid movement was focused on grassroots organizing around everyday local issues through community groups. Women were rightly seen as crucial to this project; they "reconfigured the universe of political discourse to include ... gendered concerns," thus providing an opening for feminist politics in the transition.[58] Although the post-apartheid ANC subsequently took gender equality far more seriously than it had in the past, producing a uniquely progressive constitution, there has been disappointment about the achievement of broad social change for women. Helen Moffatt highlights the paradox of post-apartheid South Africa consistently boasting "the most enviable rate of female political participation in the world," while also experiencing "the worst rates of violence, particularly sexual violence, against women anywhere in the world not at war."[59]

The dissolution of the Mandela marriage, however, may have allowed more unorthodox versions of "the family" to thrive in the collective imagination. In 1990s South Africa, the nation saw itself reflected in a messy first-family *soapie*, just as South African culture was euphorically rejecting the puritanism of apartheid. The pop singer Brenda Fassie – black, bisexual, and much beloved – played the role of queer prodigal "daughter" during this era; Winnie took her in when she was struggling with addiction, and both Winnie and Nelson visited her deathbed, separately. Gay Jewish Afrikaner Pieter-Dirk Uys, meanwhile, sometimes dubbed *tannie* (aunt) of the nation, performed as Winnie in his 1996 play *Truth Omissions*, with "tyre bangles and matchbox earrings,"[60] in a kind of barbed camp homage that echoed the many township drag show renditions of the "mother of the nation."[61] Madikizela-Mandela's implosion of the figure of the virtuous mother might have in some way released women from this particular confining script, allowing them to create other narratives for themselves. The legacy she leaves for gender politics in South Africa is thus complex and contradictory.

Mandela's third wife, Graça Machel, brought a kind of grace to his final years with her easy warmth, dedication to human rights, and courage in the fight against AIDS; indeed, she had qualms about giving up her independent identity as an activist to become "Mrs. Mandela." Machel's mode of modern femininity evades the good wife/fallen woman dichotomy of Winnie's mythic life story, but as the widow of Samora Machel, the leader of Mozambique's anti-colonial struggle, her 1998 marriage to Mandela was also a dynastic alliance of sorts. It was, in another sense, the reassertion of conjugal respectability. Unlike Graça, Winnie is, as Lewis puts it, "a symbol of contradiction, of subversion, of disrespect, of impatience, an anarchic symbol, a symbol that appeals to those who have nothing at stake in the available status quo."

Madikizela-Mandela has somehow survived all her political, tabloid, and legal trials, and perhaps this defiant outsiderdom – as well as the memory of the sheer grit she displayed in her prime – is what appeals to the many South Africans who have continued to defend and admire her. It feels wrong, perhaps, to give up on the woman who never gave up on the struggle. Her continuing magnetism may be counterintuitively tied, too, to her history of pain and mistakes. In her moving reflections on gender and the TRC, Nthabiseng Motsemme notes the habits of silence with which many women in particular bear and contain the trauma of the past half-century of South African history:

> Silence may have been used by mothers to create illusions of stability, of constancy and of matter-of-factness ... to maintain some kind of moral order in their homes. Many of us who grew up during the years of the State of Emergency in the 1980s in urban ghettos are familiar with this form of shielding silence by mothers to carve an imaginary calmness amid constant violence.... These are the women we have seen walking along South Africa's streets who are cloaked in a silence that is grief and loss. For some of these women ... "grief" and "suffering" become linked and associated with "being woman."[62]

Perhaps Winnie's refusal to be silent, to be a *good woman*, offers psychic relief in this context; many of her supporters are women.

Her periods of exile from the inner circle of power have also positioned her as a voice of dissent. The post-apartheid neoliberal policies of the ANC have not brought shared prosperity, and Madikizela-Mandela has insistently spoken up about poverty. While her critiques of the ANC often hit the mark, she is a problematic advocate for the poor; a brief, telling sketch in Zakes Mda's novel *Ways of Dying* presents her as a "bejeweled" and opportunistic visitor to the slums.[63] She has aligned herself with Julius Malema, the controversial, expelled leader of the ANC Youth League, who combines left-wing politics with anti-white rhetoric, authoritarian hostility to press freedoms, and sexism: he received a hate crime conviction for declaring that the woman accusing Zuma of rape in 2005 had had a "nice time." Malema styles himself as Winnie's "son" and she as his "grandmother," deploying the iconography of nation-as-family once more, while his hectoring performance of masculinity is arguably the polar opposite of Mandela's.[64] At a 2011 party thrown by one of South Africa's new millionaires, Kenny Kunene, at which Malema was an honored guest, sushi was eaten off the prone bodies of scantily clad young women. This image, which caused an uproar in the press, encapsulates the class and gender politics of the new South African elite.[65] Ironically, it is hard to imagine Winnie herself accepting relegation to that kind of subservient role.

Perhaps Mandela's forging of new black masculinities and Winnie's refusal to be an obedient black female subject will ultimately be seen as part of a historical era of both trauma and transformation, in which norms of gender and sexuality were being widely challenged and remade. The state of contemporary sexual politics in South Africa, exemplified by the ANC's Constitutional Review Committee's recent agreement to consider repealing the gay rights clause in the Constitution, might indicate that the era of "transition" is shifting into a period of socially conservative reconsolidation.

NOTES

1 Nelson Mandela, *Long Walk to Freedom: The Autobiography of Nelson Mandela* (Boston: Little, Brown, 1994), 240.

2 Anné Mariè du Preez Bezdrob, *Winnie Mandela: A Life* (Cape Town: Zebra, 2003), 46.

3 Elleke Boehmer, *Nelson Mandela: A Brief Insight* (New York: Sterling, 2008), 128, 136–38.

4 Mandela, *Long Walk*, 316.

5 Bezdrob, *Winnie Mandela*, 98.

6 Breyten Breytenbach, *The True Confessions of an Albino Terrorist* (London: Faber & Faber, 1984), 100.

7 John Thynne (producer), *The Real Winnie Mandela* (BBC4, 2010).

8 Anthony Sampson, *Mandela: The Authorized Biography* (New York: Vintage, 2000), 253.

9 Njabulo Ndebele, *The Cry of Winnie Mandela* (Claremont: David Philip, 2003).

10 Winnie Madikizela-Mandela, *Part of My Soul Went with Him*, ed. Anne Benjamin (New York: W. W. Norton, 1984), 24.

11 Nadine Gordimer, *Burger's Daughter* (New York: Viking Press, 1979).

12 Elleke Boehmer, *Stories of Women: Gender and Narrative in the Postcolonial Nation* (New York: Palgrave, 2005), 22.

13 Anne McClintock, *Imperial Leather: Race, Gender, and Sexuality in the Postcolonial Contest* (London: Routledge, 1995), 381–82.

14 Emma Mashinini, *Strikes Have Followed Me All My Life* (London: Women's Press, 1989), 86.

15 Sheila Meintjes, "Winnie Madikizela-Mandela: Tragic Figure, Populist Tribune, Township Tough?" *Southern Africa Report* 13.4 (1998): 14.

16 Madikizela-Mandela, *Part of My Soul*, 44.

17 Emma Gilbey, *The Lady: The Life and Times of Winnie Mandela* (London: Cape, 1993), 122.

18 Wole Soyinka, "'No,' He Said," in *Mandela's Earth and Other Poems* (New York: Random House, 1988), 21–23.

19 Ndebele, *Cry*, 85.

20 Nelson Mandela, *Conversations with Myself* (New York: Farrar, Straus and Giroux, 2010), 338.

21 Boehmer, *Nelson Mandela*, 155.

22 *The Speeches of Nelson Mandela* (MPI Home Video, 1995).

23 Mark Gevisser, *A Legacy of Liberation: Thabo Mbeki and the Future of the South African Dream* (New York: Palgrave Macmillan, 2009), 262.

24 Boehmer, *Nelson Mandela*, 140.

25 Sampson, *Mandela*, 243.

26 Mandela, *Long Walk*, 719–20.

27 Ken Davis, "Hamba Kahle (Farewell) Simon Nkoli," *Green Left Weekly*, January 20, 1999), www.greenleft.org.au/1999/345/19684.

28 Sampson, *Mandela*, 344.

29 Gilbey, *Lady*, 146.

30 Bezdrob, *Winnie Mandela*, 134.

31 Sampson, *Mandela*, 248.

32 Ndebele, *Cry*, 121.

33 Gilbey, *Lady*, 154.

34 Martin Meredith, *Nelson Mandela: A Biography* (New York: St Martin's Press, 1997), 376.

35 Gilbey, *Lady*, 167–73.

36 Ibid., 226–29.

37 Sampson, *Mandela*, 368.

38 Meredith, *Nelson Mandela*, 385.

39 Ibid., 385, 377.

40 Ndebele, *Cry*, 76–77.

41 Meredith, *Nelson Mandela*, 378–79.

42 Gilbey, *Lady*, 205–206. We might note that Verryn was cleared of all accusations by a local community inquiry, a formal church investigation, and the 1990 trial of Jerry Richardson for Seipei's killing.

43 Rachel Holmes, "Queer Comrades: Winnie Mandela and the Moffies," *Social Text* 52/53 (Autumn–Winter, 1997): 161–80.

44 Ibid., 169.

45 Ibid.,164.

46 Ibid., 163.

47 Meredith, *Nelson Mandela*, 437.

48 Holmes, "Queer Comrades," 177.

49 John Carlin, "South Africa Sighs with Relief as Winnie Avoids Jail," *Independent*, June 3, 1993, www.independent.co.uk/news/world/sa-sighs-with-relief-as-winnie-avoids-jail-an-appeal-judges-decision-not-to-imprison-mrs-mandela-has-removed-a-serious-threat-to-the-peace-talks-writes-john-carlin-from-johannesburg-1489320.html.

50 Antjie Krog, *Country of My Skull: Guilt, Sorrow, and the Limits of Forgiveness in the New South Africa* (Johannesburg: Random House, 1998), 319.

51 Max du Preez, *The Rough Guide to Nelson Mandela* (London: Rough Guides, 2011), 216.

52 Krog, *Country*, 336.

53 Ibid., 339.

54 Desiree Lewis, "Mother of the Nation," *Chimurenga Online*, December 22, 2003, agentsix.co.za/Dev/chimurenga/archives/1430.

55 Krog, *Country*,.319.

56 Holmes, "Queer Comrades," 175.

57 Gilbey, *Lady*, 285–87.

58 Shireen Hassim, *Women's Organizations and Democracy in South Africa: Contesting Authority* (Madison: University of Wisconsin Press, 2006), 14.

59 Helen Moffett, "Gender," in *New South African Keywords*, ed. Nick Shepherd and Steven Robins (Johannesburg: *Jacana*, 2008), 104.

60 Pieter-Dirk Uys, *Elections and Erections: A Memoir of Fear and Fun* (London: New Holland, 2003), 45.

61 Mark Gevisser, "*The Lady: The Life and Times of Winnie Mandela*, by Emma Gilbey," *Guardian*, December 7, 1993.

62 Nthabiseng Motsemme, "The Mute Always Speak: On Women's Silences at the Truth and Reconciliation Commission," *Current Sociology* 52.5 (September 2004): 909–32, esp. 920–25.

63 Zakes Mda, *Ways of Dying* (Oxford: Oxford University Press, 1995), 173.

64 "Malema Defends His 'Mama,' Winnie Madikizela-Mandela," *Mail & Guardian*, July 21, 2012, mg.co.za/article/2012–07–21-julius-defends-his-mama-winnie-madikizela-mandela.

65 Celia Dugger, "Partying Amid Poverty Stirs South Africa Debate," *New York Times*, February 14, 2011, www.nytimes.com/2011/02/15/world/africa/15southafrica.html?pagewanted=all.

PART II

Reinterpreting Mandela

5

ZOLANI NGWANE

Mandela and Tradition

I would like to start by juxtaposing two statements by Nelson Mandela that reveal strikingly different attitudes toward "tradition," the tricky concept that is the focus of this chapter. The first is from the opening section of his autobiography, *Long Walk to Freedom*, and concerns what Mandela calls his "country childhood." "My life, and that of most Xhosas at the time," he says, "was shaped by custom, ritual and taboo. This was the alpha and omega of our existence and went unquestioned."[1] The second is from his testimony at his 1996 divorce trial, which was contested by Winnie Madikizela-Mandela on the grounds that he ignored the Thembu custom of having tribal elders mediate their dispute. "I respect custom," he declared in court, "but I am not a tribalist. I fought as an African nationalist and I have no commitment to the custom of any particular tribe."[2]

These contrasting remarks highlight an abiding tension that seems to haunt the speaking subject of black South African nationalist self-narratives. It stems from the subject's consciousness of *his* (for this subject is characteristically male) insecure claim to those generic features of modern self-making by which he would be the sole author(ity) of his "own existence ... own individuality ... own personality."[3] The source of this insecurity is evident in the first statement, where Mandela refers to "*our* existence" and registers the pervasive power of the collective and the customary. The second statement, with its assertive series of first-person pronouns ("I" as opposed to "us" and our"), expresses Mandela's reclamation of individual agency and volition from those modes of structural affiliation to which he was totally surrendered as a child. At first glance this second statement seems to be the complete negation of the first. But the individualist assertion is, in fact, ambivalent, for Mandela appears to have liberated himself from one set of commitments (involving tribalism and custom), only to commit himself to another (involving the liberation struggle and African nationalism).

The tension between individual consciousness and commensal obligations that we see in these juxtaposed remarks is common across the entire spectrum of black South African writing. But what is distinctive about elite narratives like Mandela's is the way in which this tension is resolved – almost always in favor of individuality, but through the mediation of a higher commitment to the struggle or the nation. At this higher level the subject need neither surrender to tradition uncritically, nor reject it outright (the only options open, as we will see, to women and others of low social status). Instead, through the higher authority of a nationalist discourse, elite autobiographies like *Long Walk to Freedom* tend to relegate obligations arising from commensal relations to the ethnic peripheries where their protagonists' stories begin. Tradition can then be celebrated and memorialized from a distance (as we see in Mandela's recollection of his childhood in Qunu) as the humble, often forbidding beginnings of the now-national subject. The winning secret in this masculinist discourse is that the subject is able to negotiate himself out of tradition without making the politically and culturally unpopular choice of "modernity," but by embedding tradition (or, rather, certain modalities of tradition) in the very expression of African nationalism itself.

In this chapter I want to consider Mandela's early life in order to show how elite narratives tend to divide the world of the hero's childhood between a female-dominated, self-sufficient, and tradition-bound domestic environment and a more complex, male-dominated public environment, with possibilities for learning and independent growth. I would like to suggest that nationalist narratives like Mandela's tend to recount childhood exploits quite nostalgically and to memorialize intimate relationships within the household, rather than broader social connections. Not only do they thereby relegate "tradition" to a particular place, but they are also able to deflect attention away from the public space of male subjectivities, the institution of chieftaincy in particular, highlighting it only as the seedbed for the narrator's subsequent political consciousness. I will also comment on Mandela's initiation experience, which looms large in his recollections of his youth. If his life in the Thembu court of Chief Dalindyebo, along with his schooling at Clarkebury, Healdtown, and Fort Hare, sets Mandela apart from most boys his age, as some of his biographers suggest, the way he handled his initiation seems to me to make him even more distinctive.

I will also consider Mandela's dramatic use of traditional Thembu costume and oral heroic narrative during his trial in October 1962. This famous incident, I will argue, brings to light a different expression or modality of tradition: one that is not place-based, but becomes instead part and parcel of the discourse of resistance at a national level. I will demonstrate how, in his court performance, Mandela invoked his traditional heritage, very broadly conceived, both as a metonym for histories and struggles of "the entire African nation" and as a critique of the exclusionary politics of colonial and apartheid modernity. My analysis of the trial will show that at this pan-African level Mandela's body became overdetermined, multiply inscribed by images derived from a shared and hybrid colonial experience (which included Western education and Christianity) – thereby intensifying and diversifying the reach and possibilities for meaning of his body-in-tradition.

Tradition and African Nationalism

Before I turn to these two aspects of Mandela's life narrative, however, some definitional work is necessary. In order to frame the discussion that follows, and as a way of highlighting the point that "tradition" means different things for different categories of social subjects, I would like to sketch out briefly how different kinds of people negotiate the conventional obligations that come along with those sometimes murky moral relationships in which, by custom, one stands to others in one's kin group. We should note immediately that these relations and obligations are often quite practical and appropriative. They can include anything from an ancestor's request for a new blanket, to the expectation that one will raise the child of a relative in need, to the presumption that one will not unilaterally alter one's position in the order of relations without consulting those who by custom bear the responsibility to keep it stable – as Winnie alleges (opportunistically, in her case) in opposing Mandela's divorce application. Early vernacular literature, radio plays, and other oral narratives in the Eastern Cape, Mandela's region of origin, as well as black South African autobiographical writing, seem to stage four possible types of response.[4] These four are codified and conventionalized around particular categories of persons in ways that not only reveal how relations of power are embedded in gender and generational difference, but also betray anxieties about the impact of larger social changes on these power relations and the rural economies they sustain. From these narrative stereotypes, I will suggest, we may glean some insights about how tradition features in the cultural management of power relations embodied in class, gender, and generational differences.

The first type of response to tradition is simply to surrender to it. This submissive course of action is associated with women and children, the management of whose productive and reproductive capacities through customs, ritual, and taboo is crucial to the physical continuity of the system. As Mandela observes of his early life, children do not have much say; and young wives, too, must navigate day-to-day affairs under myriad restrictive conventions. It is mostly over these two categories of people that ritual and taboo have that "alpha and omega" power Mandela mentions.

It is for this very reason, however, that people in this category are also the likeliest candidates for the second type of response to tradition. This response is to reject tradition outright, usually in the name of new commitments or affiliations – for example, to religion or education. Subjects in this category are usually young educated women who marry into traditional families and refuse to adapt to the demands of tradition. An example is the character Thembeka, in A. C. Jordan's celebrated Xhosa novel, *Ingqumbo Yeminyanya* (1940), a work that thematizes the problematic relationships between tradition, social change, and individual consciousness. Thembeka, a graduate of Fort Hare, is married, against the custom of arranged and polygamous marriages, to Zwelinzima, the rather disinclining heir to the Mpondomise chiefdom. Both are committed to a "civilized" lifestyle, but it is the woman Thembeka whose revolt against the prescriptions of custom is presented as the most uncompromising and disruptive. She refuses point-blank to oblige her in-laws on matters of decorum and wifely comportment and denies them their customary right to her labor and ability to have children – the two principal things for which women are acquired in the first place. Even more gravely, she kills the family totem, a mole snake called *majola* (after which the clan is named), thereby preventing her newborn child from being "made" a "Majola" and symbolically shutting her womb to the lineage. Her fate raises dire concerns in the novel about how education gets the better of a woman. A real-life example of this mode of response is Winnie Madikizela-Mandela, also a university graduate, who would not let her mother-in-law perform the ritual first bath for her baby and refused to join Mandela's family in a ritual cleansing ceremony in preparation for his trial in 1962. Though we cannot say that these actions had the tragic consequences of Thembeka's fictional ones, they would certainly have elicited that same sort of anxiety and censure. My point here is not only that women and education have not always been thought to go very well together in traditional societies, but that traditional claims on women are much more hands-on than those on men. This is because such claims have to do with women's bodies and are directly related to the daily upkeep and long-term reproduction of the physical plant, if you will, through the production of people and food. Their refusals are thus more threatening to the system than are those of men, even though there certainly are men whose behavior might arguably have similar effects.

The third possible response to the demands of tradition is associated in black South African writing with elite male figures like household heads, male professionals, and progressive chiefs (Jordan's Zwelinzima immediately comes to mind), who are structurally positioned to adapt rituals and customs to contemporary circumstances. The thinking behind such adaptations is that, like white people, women, and children, "ancestors are fools" (*abaphansi zizilima*); they have a poor sense of temporality, context, and complexity and make demands as if things like *uNongqawuse* (the nineteenth-century Cattle Killing), *ubende* (lung sickness), *itrust* (betterment schemes), *idiphu* (dipping tanks), *ijoyini* (migrant labor), and *nomaziphathe* (the homeland system) had not already undermined the social relations of traditional economies that customary obligations both presuppose and seek to reinforce. In times of such uncertainty, when the structural vulnerability of the system objectified in traditional practices is brought to consciousness, clan elders and household heads have often had to play the part of enlightened believers with one foot outside the system, if only in order to help keep everyone else's two feet in. In this position they are able to bring the normative ideal closer to the experiential level by virtue of their authority to, say, substitute a chicken for the traditional offering of a goat or to declare a sacrificial beast acceptable to the ancestors even if it does not bellow and so forth. This *interpretive* authority in relation to tradition gives the elders a conventionalized agency that women and young people do not have. It makes sense, therefore, that while both women and men might theoretically agree to the idea that tradition should be dynamic, it is mostly men who experience it as such.

A. C. Jordan provides a good illustration of this category of person in the figure of the fictional chief Zwelinzima, husband of the doomed Thembeka. Zwelinzima introduces reforms in his tribal court and royal lifestyle that provoke opposition from traditionalists. He is able to survive and to make some progress, however, because he can adapt his foreign developmentalist discourse to the local ideology of peasant economies. As a man, he can work with others to isolate and embarrass his opponents, while also appealing to the needs of tradition itself to make the case for reforms. In the minds of his people, Zwelinzima, as an enlightened chief, occupies a space made popular by court interpreters. A profession sought after by many young black men (including, as we shall see in the next chapter, the young Mandela), court interpreters had, until quite recent times, the privilege of standing in a hermeneutical relation to the institution of customary law, just as individual household heads stand, at the homestead level, in relation to tradition. Because their jurisdiction is the white magistrates' court, beyond the local tribal court of the chief, court interpreters like Sol Plaatje and Bud'Mbelle might be seen as forerunners of a generation of political activists like Mandela who helped revive and popularize the African National Congress (ANC) in the 1940s and 1950s. However, where court interpreters were still institutionally restricted to ethnically specific regional courts, the new generation of political elites operated at a national level.

This group of male national political elites constitutes the fourth category of response to tradition. It is the response I have already associated in my opening remarks with Mandela, who seems able to cast a devotion to the anti-colonial and anti-apartheid struggle as a higher expression of traditional obligation. This ability is not an individual achievement, but must be grasped historically. By the time of Mandela's meteoric rise in the ranks of the ANC (detailed in Chapter 1), political leaders had assumed interpretive authority over people's collective experiences under apartheid that surpassed both that of chiefs at the local level and that of court interpreters at district and regional levels. Indeed, the perception that the category of *iinkokheli zoluntu* (people's leaders) ranked above the level of local chiefs had become pervasive after the movement had regained popularity in the black community following the success of the defiance campaigns of the 1950s. The widely publicized arrests, detentions, and trials enhanced the prestige of the ANC leadership. More important, unlike both chiefs and court interpreters, the nationalists were not perceived as complicit in the politics of the apartheid state. They were custodians of tradition, but they were not subject to it in the same way that chiefs were.

The paradoxical response to customary obligations of individuals in this category – men whose refusals of tradition, in effect, confirm it – does not appear much in fiction, because vernacular literature in South Africa has historically avoided overtly political themes.[5] It can be gleaned, however, from autobiographies of literary men like S. E. K. Mqhayi, Es'kia Mphahlele, and Bloke Modisane and of political figures like Naboth Mokgatle, Albert Luthuli, Z. K. Matthews, and Mandela, as well as from key biographical works on figures like Walter Sisulu, Oliver Tambo, and Sol Plaatje.[6]

To be sure, there are remarkable differences in the manner in which these men position themselves in relation to tradition and even in their use of the concept. But what we can nevertheless glean from this archive is a sense that "tradition" tends to divide into two separate spheres. It can refer, first, to a set of ritual practices that are usually confined to rural areas and to the relatively private sphere of family and kin. Most elites travel to ancestral homes, often in the homelands, for funerals, weddings, and family reunions, and sometimes to celebrate and thank ancestors for promotion, a new car, or the birth of a child. Historically journeys to ancestral homes in the countryside were associated with migrant workers, but the practice has in recent years also been continued by "upmarket migrants," middle-class men who live permanently in cities but travel to places like Umthatha during the December holidays to engage in a diffuse set of rituals with peers.[7] But in both cases, old and new, this version of tradition is place-based: it concerns certain practices that one performs in a particular localized context.

The second sense of "tradition" consists of certain symbols (including dress, forms of address, praises, song, and dance) that can be abstracted from these local and corporeal contexts of ritual practice (where, interestingly, they might have memorialized regional inter-ethnic conflicts) and embedded in a wider discourse of political resistance and nationalism. We can trace this transfer of symbols from local conflicts to a nationalist consciousness in the poetry of Mqhayi, Jolobe, and Vilakazi, where the term "ancestors," for example, incorporates diverse figures like Shaka, Hintsa, Moshoeshoe, and Mzilikazi into a single genealogical register.[8] This incorporation is not, however, a simple or unproblematic matter. Long after the 1930s, when the young Mandela would have paid audience to the nationalist narratives of his traditional elders, figures like Shaka and Dingane (Zulus, in other words) still did not feature very positively in local oral histories in the Eastern Cape.[9] Even Plaatje's *Mhudi*, a novel that stages what we could call a "rainbow nation" spirit of reconciliation, does not do well in creating an understanding, let alone a lasting military alliance, among the contending tribal forces on the Highveld. Right up to the 1960s (to judge by some reactions to the traditional costume Mandela wore during the famous court appearance), there were still doubts about the capacity of these symbols to mobilize beyond their tribal origins. The work of translating these local symbols into nationalist metaphors, however, intensified during the political theater and poetry of the 1970s, leading up to the now-derided slogan "Culture is the weapon of the struggle." Tradition, in this abstracted and symbolic sense, served to mobilize resistance to apartheid at a national level and facilitated the celebration of blackness as a shared experience and heritage.

This is the form of tradition that the elites make public in their narrative practices, and it is this "resistance" version of tradition (rather than tradition as appropriative obligation) that has received most attention in critical work on nationalist texts like Mandela's autobiography. Postcolonial critics insist that the invocation of tradition in such texts should not be understood as simply the antithesis to modernity; rather, it must be seen as highlighting the exclusionary tendencies of modernity as a discourse of power. It is to be grasped, on the one hand, as a critique of forms of modernity that have perpetuated Western domination of the rest of the world and, on the other, as a positive effort to defend and extend the promise of modernity through idioms embedded in local (national) subjective experiences. Like appeals to religion and custom (or what Edward Said sardonically refers to as "native nonsenses" that the African subject was expected to "check at the door with the porter" to gain entry into modernity), tradition has become normalized in this theoretical perspective into a generic attribute for projects about selfhood or nationhood emerging from the postcolonial world.[10] It is a way of "doing" modernity, of giving it a regional or even vernacular inflection.[11] One might highlight here an interesting collusion between theory and elite narrative practice. By accepting at face value the nationalist notion of tradition as political resistance, scholars of nationalist narratives may be reinforcing the elitist tendency to separate tradition from the ritual practices and customs of their upbringing – a gesture that effectively obscures the gender and generational variables of tradition I have tried to bring to mind here.

Tradition, Childhood, and Youth

In elite self-narratives the early life of the subject is shaped by two overlapping formations of tradition – the private sphere of the household and the public sphere centered on the chiefly court. The first encompasses the domain of domestic economies where tradition is concerned with the ideological management of the means and relations of production – both of people and of sustenance. Mandela's life in Qunu, therefore, would have revolved around the hearth – a central icon in the formation of moral subjectivity through the act of cooking and consuming food and the transmission of moral education through folktales and fables. Presided over by the mother or grandmother and consisting of adult women and children (adult males, including the household head, often being out on migrant labor), relationships and roles within the household and among all related households are conventionalized and routinized by custom. Children learned passively by observation, while young wives' capacity to objectify their experiences was limited by the system of *ukuhlonipha*, a normative discourse that stabilizes gender hierarchies through linguistic tropes of deference and obedience prescribed for newly married women. This domain includes within its logic peer socialization practices, such as the celebrated boyhood "free time" that Mandela recalls spending on games and staged fights while collectively shepherding. In many cases the division of labor by gender is loose at this age, with boys participating in the household, and some girls, like Winnie Madikizela, for example, tending to the animals with boys. This is the time of the most intimate relationships the boys will have within the household with siblings and parents, and it is often romanticized in elite narratives like Mandela's autobiography. For most elite nationalist subjects this is also a typical age for a major traumatic experience, particularly related to moving and separation. Mandela was nine when he left his mother to join the royal household at Mqhekezweni. But there are many other similar stories: Plaatje was eight when his parents left him with his uncle, Luthuli was ten when he moved from Zimbabwe to Natal with his mother, Sisulu was thirteen when he left home to find work, Mokgatle was eleven when he first left home, and Mphahlele was all of five when he was separated from his parents to be with his fierce grandmother.

In black South Africa this farming out of children is often naturalized as part of custom or tradition. In fact, Matthews (who himself spent his early childhood with grandparents) calls it "common traditional practice."[12] In general, people tend to view these practices as highlighting the functionality of tradition in adapting people to change in their social environment. Two important issues become elided in this naturalization of the trauma. The first is the relationship between these practices and the structural violence of apartheid and poverty (or, indeed, "modernity"). Calling them traditional practice hides the fact that they are essentially coping mechanisms and makes it easy to leave them outside the category of structural factors that need redressing. The second thing that is elided by attributing these practices to tradition is the reality of the trauma for the individual subject. The cover of tradition makes it sound almost culturally insensitive to raise questions about how the experience of separation must have felt to Mandela and to his mother. Some writers on Mandela's life have, of course, raised this question (and Nuttall and Mbembe reflect on it in Chapter 12), but we are still far from developing a critical understanding of this phenomenon without either simply reducing it to standard psychological constructs or confining it to the Unknown Soldier's tomb of tradition.[13] There is probably a correlation between this early loss and the nostalgic indulgence with which the subject of childhood is treated in most elite narratives.

As the boys get older and move away from simple games, they participate in the more ideologically oriented leisure practices like *imitshotsho* that socialize them into complex social roles and beliefs. Again because most elite subjects like Mandela grew up in Christian households that forbade participation in these "heathen" youth activities or because they spent their youth years in boarding schools away from home, they often missed this latter stage of peer socialization. This is a developmentally significant moment when the boys are big enough to have social lives away from the homestead but are not yet admitted to the male community of initiated men and household heads. Because they are at the stage where their behaviors have social impact, they are often subject to collective corporal punishment at the chiefly court by men or, in cases of very serious infringement, mass circumcision. In his collection of Xhosa stories, *Kwezo Mpindo ZeTsitsa*, A. C. Jordan portrays boys at this stage as generally alienated from public political life and standing in a structurally antagonistic relation to the community of men and the chiefly court.[14] Again, Mandela is an exception here since he grew up in court, where he became exposed to its proceedings and the casual conversations of the men. Even in Mandela's case, however, his education at court was not formal or intentional but more a matter of eavesdropping on conversations from which he was often chased away. Thus the idea of a male pedagogical space around night fires where elders passed on knowledge to boys like Mandela exists more in his biographers' imagination than in reality.[15] It is more likely that Mandela overheard these conversations after the regular courtly meetings, either outside or in the royal dining hall, where Ntombizodwa, the daughter of Mandela's guardian, would have been able to sit as well.[16] These encounters were nonetheless very important for Mandela, as they were for Mphahlele and other nationalists, and constituted the foundations of his political consciousness. Outside of the relations within the homestead, this is another typical formation of tradition that elite nationalist narratives invoke. It is less the structure of chieftaincy itself, or even particulars of its administration, than it is the proto-historical discourses that are generated within it that are the most important in the formation of nationalist self-narratives.

The initiation experience itself comes as a great leveler, as all the initiates – including, at Mqhekezweni of Mandela's day, the chief's son, Justice – go through the grueling rite together. This experience became an important reference point for Mandela's later recollections of his early life. His autobiography contains probably the most explicit published description of the rite, a disclosure that men, by custom, generally refrain from. What stands out the most in Mandela's initiation narrative is the vigil he keeps over the smoldering ashes of his youth following the burning of the enclosure at the end of the rite and after his cohort has returned home. By all counts this was a scandalous act, in that it not only was a violation of tradition on Mandela's part but, even more important, compromised both his fellow initiates and the men who would still have had responsibility over them at this point. Having just returned from seclusion, the new men are not yet out of the woods but are still vulnerable to all sorts of witchcraft, and that is why they are never allowed to separate, go outside alone, or be out of sight of their caretakers. Yet, as he tells it, Mandela managed to slip away from the crowd to be alone with his brief past as a boy. It is not clear what recognitions flooded his mind at this time, except that the speech by one of the chiefs at the ceremony that day had seemed to pronounce the impossibility of the future that was supposed to begin for all the initiates on that same day. For young men like Mandela the rite authorized their entry into the status of household heads (with rights to property, wives, and children) and public political subjects whose "words would be taken seriously."[17] In his speech Chief Meligqili charged that this dignified status would nonetheless be denied them because their soon-to-ensue pursuit of its material conditions (mostly through wage labor) would only cause them to regress to boyhood and relegate them to servitude in white South Africa.

In his reflective moment at the scene of his erstwhile boyhood, Mandela, however, does not seem to be concerned about the impossibility of his manhood in this traditional sense. The speech challenges his readiness for a larger project in service to which he had imagined his own manhood. The recognition of the sheer weight of his destiny forces on him a kind of Christological doubt, and he finds himself wanting. As he puts it: "Looking back, I know that I was not a man that day and would not truly become one for many years."[18] This is one moment in Mandela's life when he seems the most connected with his feelings – pain, fear, self-doubt, frustration, and longing. It is a revealing reaction in that it is at once a radical assertion of individuality and independence and a demonstration of self-doubt or indecisiveness (all of which attest to Mandela's thoughtfulness and a deep reflective capacity), but also of a sense of insecurity.

This emergent subjectivity, self-consciously casting a forbidden gaze on custom, is a good place to recap the main themes covered in this section. By removing himself from the group and taking a step back from his present toward his past, Mandela is authorized by a different regime of objectifying knowledge: one from which standpoint tradition has already become limited, if not altogether disenchanted. From the distance of a nationalist commitment he can retrospectively surrender his youth to tradition, if only with the foreknowledge that it did not then make him a man. The struggle matured him and made him a man with – and not for – tradition. Elite narratives, as I set out to suggest, use the subject's commitment to the struggle to negotiate him out of the obligations of traditional affiliations without appearing to reject tradition.

The Warrior-King, Medicine Man, and Messiah

On October 15, 1962, at the start of his trial for inciting a stay-away and leaving the country without a passport, Nelson Mandela made a dramatic entrance into the court wearing a Thembu royal costume made of leopard skin and beads. In his closing statement Mandela was to reinforce this visual cue with a narrative that drew on his experiences, some of which I have already reflected on in the preceding section, of growing up within a chiefly court in the Transkei where he observed what he called traditional "justice in practice" and heard oral histories of precolonial African polities. As a total event this trial can enrich our understanding of the place of tradition in Mandela's mature political consciousness and, more generally, of the ambiguous ideological import of local ethnic pasts in the construction of larger ideological formations like African nationalism.

Coming between the better-known treason trial (1956–61) and Rivonia trial (1964), both of which have received book-length studies, the 1962 trial was relatively brief, entailed less serious charges, and had only Mandela as defendant. What gives this trial its distinctive significance, however, is precisely the fact that Mandela was the sole defendant, which was accentuated by his decision to act as his own counsel. Mandela always stood out in court, both as an attorney and as the accused during the two other trials. The absence of co-defendants in this case, however, meant that his body would be the dominant icon, decentering the conventions of South African courts of law with an affected ritual elaboration and providing a mnemonic device for oral reconstructions of that event for many years to come. Mandela became both the embodiment of the struggle and a vicarious sacrifice for it. More specifically, his body, defamiliarized in the context of the court by both the exotic costume he had donned and his exhortation of traditional modes of justice and historical consciousness, became the centerpiece in a medley of symbolic references. These references reflect the multiple ideological heritage of a colonial society. In order to understand the valence of this imagery better it is well to summarize what was at stake in this particular trial.

The marathon treason trial had reached its farcical end a little more than a year earlier, mostly as an embarrassing loss for the state. But some important developments that occurred in the intervening period, both organizationally for the ANC and personally for Mandela, gave any shrewd observer reason to expect a less favorable outcome this time around. First, the ANC, banned since April 1960, had taken a decision to form what would be its military wing, Umkhonto we Sizwe (MK), under Mandela's leadership. Limited acts of sabotage had already been taking place in various parts of the country by the time Mandela came to trial. Second, following the treason trial Mandela went into hiding to avoid arrest and to pursue work for the clandestine ANC's National Working Committee, including organizing a national stay-away to coincide with the Republic Day slated for May 31. Third, while still underground Mandela illegally left the country on a tour that included some East and West African countries.

Given all that, Mandela's arrest portended a realistic danger for a wide network of people besides him. The magnitude of that danger would depend on how far the state's intelligence reached into these developments – not far enough, as it turned out. In a sense, though, Winnie Mandela's fear that her husband's arrest would be "an end to a political dream" was prescient in two ways.[19] As a prelude to Rivonia, the 1962 trial helped close a chapter in the struggle for South Africa, spearheading a process that would send Mandela to Robben Island on a life sentence. More personally, though, his capture brought home to him and to Winnie that what had passed for a family life had come to a definite end. During Mandela's life underground, they had lived their fragile marital life often as stolen moments in comrades' apartments, sometimes surreptitiously at Mandela's hideout in Rivonia, and in their own home as unpredictably as the "knock on the window" in the dead of the night that announced his intermittent brief visits.

A picture thus emerges of Mandela progressively disaffiliating from family, as he explained in a press statement in 1961: "I have had to separate myself from my dear wife and children, from my mother and sisters to live as an outlaw in my own land.... The struggle is my life."[20] During this time Mandela was also operating outside the organizational structure of the ANC, a strategic necessity given the ANC's need to distance itself from the new MK that Mandela was building. David Smith is probably going too far when he suggests that the ANC was consciously growing a "fall guy" in Mandela, although it must have been clear to everybody that as long as he remained inside the country his days were numbered.[21]

It is evident from people's interactions with and conversations about Mandela at this time that, as he began to operate mostly on his own, he developed a public image that centered on his body – a corporal icon with phantasmal amplifiers. The mythology around Mandela's body developed sharply during his time in hiding when he would make spectacular unannounced appearances at meetings and rallies around the country. For most people his trial would be the last time they would see Mandela in person, but the mythology would precede his confinement in Robben Island. Before his arrest, reports and rumors of sightings of his phantom-like body had begun to circulate in hushed conspiratorial tones in the townships, and his words (from speeches he delivered, pamphlets, and press statements) were jealously guarded articles of value shared with trusted friends. In oral narratives in the Transkei, for example, "what Mandela said" (called *ukuquza* or *ukugqumza* by high school students) was a compilation of memorized sentences that contained lines from Mandela's press statements, the Freedom Charter, and verses from the Bible. When he walked into that court Mandela had already attained something of a Christological status as a miracle worker, and now the stage was set for the Passion event. Lodge appropriately sees this period as the "making of a Messiah" out of Mandela.[22] The image of a heroic redeemer is indeed reinforced by the song, "*Shosholoza Mandela*," sung by the spectators during the trial. The song paints an image of Mandela as invested with the collective agency of the whole people and propelled by a force of destiny to which he has surrendered his own agency: "uza kuzwa ngathi masekulungile" (you will hear from us when it's over).

Another set of symbols that coalesced on his body derive from the world of his childhood, which Mandela describes in anthropological terms at the beginning of this essay: the almost closed-in world of custom, ritual, and taboo. In nationalist self-narratives, real education often begins, as we have seen, with heroic stories of community elders in the public space, while the hearth-bound mothers' folktales and fables receive a condescending nod. Here I want to raise the fact that during his hiding and trial Mandela's personality (both as cultivated by him and as interpreted by his audiences) draws on the symbolism of power and transformation that forms the basic sociology of Xhosa folktales. While the strong reinforce their power by brute force, the weak often depend on skillful and magical manipulation of the bodily form by way of disguise, defiance of gravity, changing into other life forms, and sheer wit. In his engagement with the law of the state, Mandela exhibits some of these "weapons of the weak," painstakingly, yet wittily defending modernity by shining the light on its shortcomings in context, arguing himself into its purview by using idioms from cultures it excludes. Mandela is well known for his notoriously clumsy disguises, which again enhanced the image of a trickster and magician. Legendary stories of his ability to fool the police by being someone or something else, or by simply evaporating, led to a belief that he had *isilamsi*: basically the ability to change form, but more specifically the criminal practice of magically swopping someone's money with useless paper.

The most important visual inscription of Mandela's body during the trial was his costume. Although some of his biographers, perhaps a reflection of their own fantasies, describe it as either a patchwork of "jackal skins" or, more ambitiously, a "lion skin," it is the leopard that is traditionally considered a Thembu royal symbol of power, majesty, grace, and agility. In that costume Mandela not only reached back, but reached higher in stature than even his father, who was a headman, to the ruling princely line of the Thembu. No longer simply the counselor to kings that he was groomed to be as a young man, he was now, in that witness box, as if on his throne meting out justice on the system that put him on trial. In a classical folktale twist of fate, where the lowly becomes elevated, Mandela the prisoner sits in judgment at the end, particularly with his closing statement.

How did Mandela understand his own use of traditional symbols in this trial? How did he negotiate his individuality in the light of the images of warrior-king, suffering messiah, and magician or medicine man that invested his body? The tensions at stake in this medley of symbolism run deep and were reflected at the time in the reactions of some of the people who were involved in the trial. In the first place Mandela had played into a specifically Xhosa/Thembu traditional symbolism with his costume and oral historical narrative. Second, Mandela pushed a strong pan-African nationalism in his statement, stretching his oral narrative beyond its local Thembu context to embrace traditional heroes from across South Africa and using his account of his trip outside the country to make an almost exhaustive list of leaders of independent African countries with whom he met. Third, this Africanism, reminiscent of his earlier radical nationalism under the influence of Anton Lembede, seemed a belated rebuff of the non-racial Congress Alliance politics toward which he had gravitated in the course of the 1950s. Indeed, non-racial coalition politics had proved effective in the 1950s, and Mandela had wholeheartedly thrown himself behind the Defiance Campaign, which led to important friendships with Indian and white individuals.

The lurking tension in this performance is first highlighted by the reaction of the state itself. For the magistrate and police the fear was that such exhibition of tradition might inflame the already restive black audience in and outside the court, including, as it turns out, those already in prison. This fear was real enough that Mandela was not allowed to wear what they called his "blanket" outside court. This response is a double-edged sword, however, for while it plays into the intended meaning of tradition as resistance, it also reinforces stereotypes of African barbarism and bestial violence. We might recall here, for example, the fact that the spear, a common symbol of anti-colonial resistance across ethnic divisions from which the ANC military wing got its name, was hardly ever a mainstream public symbol of struggle until it came to be embraced as a "cultural" weapon by Inkatha in the late 1980s. From Mandela's autobiography we learn that the poet Mqhayi used a spear, rather awkwardly, in his performances and, while the spear occasionally featured in the theater and poetry performances in the 1970s and 1980s, it remained a marginalized symbol in mainstream politics.[23] The point is that during the era of Luthuli, the Christian chief and Nobel Peace Prize laureate, the kind of symbols that became elevated to represent the image of the movement had to pass an unspoken civility test. Mandela's interpretation of his court performance and perhaps his choice of symbols as well (he probably would not have made it into court with a spear and shield) was not totally arbitrary, but was carefully orchestrated to navigate all these ambiguities.

The second take on the tension embedded in Mandela's performance is reflected in his lawyers' Marxist critique of the traditional costume as a reversion to backward modes of solidarity (tribalism), which, in the context of the 1960s, reinforced the apartheid ideology of separate ethnic-based nationalities. Mandela was definitely aware of this contradictory sense of tradition, and his own reservations are well documented. As I will show, however, the lawyers' criticism missed the point, because Mandela was invoking tradition to forge a different kind of collective identity than the tribalism they sensed lurking in it.

The last response to Mandela's performance came from the spectators, who included his mother, members of his kin, and Winnie, also in her own traditional gear. Mandela describes the impact of his costume on the audience as "electrifying," a word also used by the editor of his collection of essays, *The Struggle Is My Life*, to describe people's reaction to Mandela's speech in Pietermaritzburg a year earlier. Very little else is mentioned about the crowds in *Long Walk to Freedom*, but it is clear from other accounts that it was an active audience. After all, the state's decision to change the site of the trial from Johannesburg to Pretoria was motivated by fear of expected crowds of demonstrators. And, as I have already noted, accounts of this trial lived on in oral narratives.

How did Mandela, then, resolve the seeming contradictions of his invocation of tradition during that trial? As I have already said in regard to the elitist use of traditional symbols, Mandela resolved the problem of tradition by nationalizing its local and regional meanings to stand for the collective experiences of Black South Africans in the first instance and then generally for the people of the African continent. In his hour-long statement in mitigation of sentence, Mandela uses heroic stories he heard as a child growing up in tribal court in the Transkei to paint a much wider picture of precolonial African societies, highlighting common features such as the Council, "Imbizo or Pitso or Kgotla," which limited the powers of the chief or king, and communal ownership of the land and natural resources, calling these "the seeds of a revolutionary democracy."[24] There is reason to believe that his experiences during his African trip in 1961 forced him to rethink the strategic value of some Africanist cultural discourse. On this trip he seems to have been surprised, even alarmed, by the criticism the ANC received from African leaders for its alliance with non-African organizations. There was clear danger that the ANC would lose African support to the openly Africanist Pan-Africanist Congress, which seems to have taken advantage of this situation through its own propaganda machinery. Mandela's concerns about the non-racial stance of the ANC were not a matter of political turnabout on his part, but a strategic concern about the external support for the ANC.

Thus, in addition to celebrating black history in his address, Mandela inserts his Thembu traditional heritage into a wider Africanist discourse. Explaining the costume, he said: "I had chosen traditional dress to emphasize the symbolism that I was a black African walking into a white man's court." The costume showed, he insists, that he was "the inheritor of Africa's difficult but noble past and uncertain future." It is significant that he never uses "Xhosa" or "Thembu" here, but invokes the names of traditional leaders from across South Africa as "the pride and glory of the entire African nation."[25] In short, tradition for Mandela is more a symbol, a resource in a political rhetoric, than a ritual practice. The latter is too restricted to a particular group; and while Mandela, as he says again in the second statement mentioned at the beginning of this chapter, respects it, he does not see himself committed to it. Like most intellectuals Mandela believes he can patronize or pay tribute to tradition (by engaging an *imbongi*, paying *lobola*, or hosting a ritual slaughtering), while retaining his independence from its precepts. But as I pointed out before, his refusal of tradition does not amount to its rejection.[26] At stake is, rather, a strategic redeployment of it, in a discourse of nationalism and a narrative of individual self-affirmation, albeit a self-affirmation that also involves collective obligations. I think, however, that scholars of nationalist narratives ought to be mindful of the fact that tradition as a critical construct in nationalist narratives is of a piece with those customs and rituals (often compulsory for women and children) that nationalist narratives affirm by disavowing. By focusing only on the political work that tradition performs in the struggle for liberation or on its powerful critique of European modernity, we lose the opportunity to pursue continuities between public rhetoric of nationalism and relations of gender inequality in the private sphere of the family.

In the final analysis, Nelson Mandela is today a tradition himself, and a tradition that is far from unchanging. He embodies some of our common dreams and has inspired ways of thinking and acting toward one another as a people. The realization of the rainbow fantasy will always be in a state of deferment, so that future generations will have a chance to reimagine him according to their own lights and for their own purposes.

NOTES

1 Nelson Mandela, *Long Walk to Freedom: The Autobiography of Nelson Mandela* (Boston: Little, Brown, 1994), 11.

2 Martin Meredith, *Mandela: A Biography* (New York: Public Affairs, 2010), 541.

3 Philippe Lejeune, "The Autobiographical Contract," in *French Literary Theory Today*, ed. Tzvetan Todorov (Cambridge: Cambridge University Press, 1982), 193.

4 Xhosa novels in the 1920s and 1930s began using conversion oral narratives to explore the adverse impact of conversion, particularly of women, on traditional lifestyles. Leading examples include G. Sinxo, *UNomsa* (Alice: Lovedale Press, 1922), and H. M. Ndawo, *UNolishwa* (Alice: Lovedale Press, 1932). As the structure of social relations in the church became effectively homologous to those

of the community (the church required of women the same deference to men as tradition did), it was the more individuating experience of education that continued to epitomize modernity as a form of social alienation. See A. C. Jordan, *Ingqumbo Yeminyanya* (Alice: Lovedale, 1940).

5 Vernacular literature in South Africa was first published by missionary presses that imposed moral over political themes on authors. In later years vernacular literature was widely published by the government press for schools, which is how authors made some money in the absence of a reading public. Here too the avoidance of political themes was a requirement. Protest literature in black South Africa is published mostly in English.

6 S. E. K Mqhayi, *Umqhayi WaseNtabozuko* (Alice: Lovedale Press, 1939); Ezekiel Mphahlele, *Down Second Avenue* (London: Faber & Faber, 1959); Bloke Modisane, *Blame Me on History* (New York: Simon & Schuster, 1986); Albert Luthuli, *Let My People Go: The Autobiography of Albert Luthuli* (New York: McGraw-Hill, 1962); Naboth Mokgatle, *The Autobiography of an Unknown South African* (Berkeley: University of California Press, 1971); Z. K. Matthews, *Freedom for My People: The Autobiography of ZK Matthews* (Cape Town: David Philip, 1986); Mandela, *Long Walk to Freedom*; Brian Willan, *Sol Plaatje: South African Nationalist, 1876–1932* (Berkeley: University of California Press, 1984); Elinor Sisulu, *Walter and Albertina Sisulu* (Cape Town: New Africa Books, 2011); Lulli Callinicos, *Oliver Tambo: Beyond the Engeli Mountains* (Cape Town: New Africa Books, 2012).

7 Ayanda Manqoyi, "Upmarket Migrant Labor and Notions of Belonging," Honours Research Proposal, Department of Anthropology, University of Cape Town, 2012.

8 S. E. K. Mqhayi, *Prince of Britain* (1925), in *Voices from Within: Black Poetry from Southern Africa*, ed. Michael Chapman and Achmat Dangor (Johannesburg: A. D. Donker, 1982); J. J. R. Jolobe, *The Making of a Servant*, in *Voices from Within*; B. W. Vilakazi, *The Gold Mines*, in *Voices from Within*.

9 D. Z. Makaula, *UMadzikane okanye Imbali YamaBhaca* (Berkeley: University of California Press, 1966).

10 Edward Said, "Representing the Colonized: Anthropology and Its Interlocutors," *Critical Inquiry* 15.2 (1989).

11 See B. M. Knauft, "Critically Modern: An Introduction," in *Critically Modern: Alternatives, Alterities, Anthropologies*, ed. B. M. Knauft (Bloomington: Indiana University Press, 2002); for a more recent take on modernity and ethnicity see Jean Comaroff and John L. Comaroff, *Ethnicity, Inc.* (Chicago: University of Chicago Press, 2009).

12 Matthews, *Freedom for My People*.

13 E.g., Tom Lodge, *Mandela: A Critical Life* (Oxford: Oxford University Press, 2006).

14 A. C. Jordan, *Kwezo Mpindo ZeTsitsa* (Alice: Lovedale Press, 1975).

15 Mary Benson, *Nelson Mandela: The Man and the Movement* (New York: W. W. Norton, 1986); Anthony Sampson, *Mandela: The Authorized Biography* (New York: Alfred Knopf, 1999). This idea of "a communal fire place" for men and boys is developed more in the biography of Mphahlele (1959), who grew up in the Transvaal, but is not typical in the Eastern Cape.

16 Ntombizodwa gives as much detail about the stories elders like Tat'uJoyi used to tell. See Fatima Meer, *Higher Than Hope: Mandela* (Durban: Madiba, 1989).

17 Mandela, *Long Walk*, 28.

18 Ibid., 31.

19 Winnie Mandela, *Part of My Life Went with Him* (New York: W. W. Norton, 1985).

20 Nelson Mandela, *The Struggle Is My Life* (New York: Pathfinder Press, 1986), 121.

21 David J. Smith, *Young Mandela* (New York: Little, Brown, 2010).

22 Lodge, *Mandela*.

23 In the popular struggles of the 1980s the AK47 (of the controversial *umshini wami* song) took the place of the spear as the symbol of the struggle.

24 Mandela, *The Struggle Is My Life*.

25 Ibid., 141.

26 According to Smith, *Young Mandela*, 7, it was Winnie who decided on Mandela's costume and brought it to him without his knowledge. Although it is remarkable that Mandela seems to have forgotten this detail, what is even more interesting is that while Winnie refused tradition in regard to herself and her children, she recognized its political purchase in relation to the state. This is why she had been wearing her traditional costume in court and why the state forbade her to wear it.

6

ADAM SITZE

Mandela and the Law

For a long time now, it has been impossible to hear the name "Nelson Mandela" without also thinking of the law. For Dumisa Gumede, the protagonist of Lewis Nkosi's novel *Mandela's Ego*, the "Mandela" of the early 1960s was a "big-shot lawyer," who was "single-handedly leading a great fight for the rights of black people" and "talk[ed] back with impunity to white magistrates."[1] For an *imbongi* performing at a rally at Umtata shortly after Mandela's release from prison, the man had become something even greater – "the law of truth" itself:

> Wayigqibezel' imfundo yakhe bayokudibana ngobugqwetha benyaniso,
> Khumbula kaloku amagqwetha ukutheth' ityala lawo engagqwethanga
>   kweliny' igqwetha.
> Asuk' ema amagqweth' azigqwethela,
> Kuba yayingagqweth' inyaniso.

> Once he had finished his education they [the Boers] met the law of truth.
> Imagine, lawyers representing themselves.
> They just stood and defended themselves,
> Because they were lawyers of the truth.[2]

For the philosopher Jacques Derrida, the name "Mandela" signifies "a *man of the law* [*un homme de loi*]": a lawyer who respects the law and inspires respect for the law in any reader who reflects upon his writings.[3] While it is not completely off the mark to link "Mandela" to "the law" in this way, the association nevertheless runs the risk of obscuring another relation between Mandela and the law, one no less decisive for the solitude and silence that even today surrounds it. Between 1939, when Mandela began studying administrative law at the University of Fort Hare, and 1989, when Mandela finally received his LLB degree through correspondence from the University of South Africa (UNISA), Mandela would enroll in no fewer than fifty courses in law at four different universities. For fully half a century, Nelson Mandela was, in a sense we yet have fully to comprehend, a student of law.

Fifty years of legal studies. The first thing that stands out here is the "inhuman patience" of a figure whose profile first became visible while hidden away in prison.[4] Even during this time, when his studies were interrupted by the vindictiveness of his prison guards (who punished him for clandestinely producing an autobiography) and the obstinacy of the UNISA registrar (who did not regard his liver and kidney surgery as any excuse for missing one of his examinations),[5] Mandela persisted in his pursuit of a law degree, giving new meaning to UNISA's Latin motto, *spes in arduis* (hope through adversity). But set off from this familiar silhouette of conviction and courage, as its backdrop or perhaps even as its very condition of possibility, one can discern the outline of a different dynamic. Academic disciplines, albeit in a much different mode than the discipline exerted upon a body obliged to crush rocks or sew mailbags, are apparatuses of power. The concepts they provide for grasping reality, the techniques they offer for intervening into and steering the world, the desires they incite, and the fantasies that underlie them – all of these amount to subtle constraints that limit the very students whose minds and voices they also enable. Nowhere is this truer than with the discipline of jurisprudence. Academic jurisprudence in apartheid South Africa was composed of ostensibly opposed traditions, English common law and Roman-Dutch law, which together provided the state with the vocabulary for its self-justification and allowed it to insist on its adherence to the "rule of law." Although South Africa has seen its share of fine radical lawyers, these were the exception and not the norm, and they typically arrived at their sense of political responsibility despite their training in jurisprudence, not because of it. In the main, academic jurisprudence under apartheid doubled as a form of social discipline: it was a mode of controlling, subjugating, and normalizing thought, a training in obedience and quietism, a point of entry into a regime that used the legal lexicon to reassure itself of its own rectitude and to rage against its adversaries with self-righteous cruelty.

What could Mandela possibly have wanted from his studies in this field? What could he have wanted to think, or perhaps to cease thinking, so that he would return to his law books so regularly? What desire could have driven this figure, the very "personification" of liberation, to devote himself with such dedication to an academic discipline that helped justify the very domination he so passionately hated? And how, if at all, might an inquiry into this will-to-know – not simply as it appears in Mandela's autobiography, biography, and archives, but also as it may be inferred from the concrete institutions such as the university and the courtroom through which

Mandela passed – cause us to rethink the association between Mandela and the law that seems so obvious to us today?

Translation and the Law: Mandela at Fort Hare

Mandela's earliest desire, we read in his autobiography, was to work as a clerk or court interpreter.[6] This position, the highest Africans were permitted to attain in the civil service of the Union of South Africa, involved responsibilities that were as indispensable to the administration of justice as they were impossible to discharge felicitously. The court interpreter, as Sol Plaatje wrote in an unpublished treatise of 1908–1909, was essential for the administration of justice in South Africa, where the colonizer spoke at least two languages, and the colonized at least eleven. In the absence of a court interpreter, as Plaatje explained, it would have been impossible for judge, plaintiff, defendant, counsel, and witnesses even to communicate, much less to weigh evidence, submit testimony, enter pleas, cross-examine, or swear oaths. So, too, would it have been impossible to maintain even the illusion of the fairness, equality, and justice to which Africans were, at least in theory, guaranteed under conditions of Cape liberalism. And yet the presence of a court interpreter by no means provided an antidote to the ailments of colonial legality. Court interpreters were called upon to perform translations not only between linguistic systems that shared little in common, but also between juridical and even theological traditions, which, more often than not, were simply incommensurable. At best, the court interpreter would be able to produce unwieldy and uneconomical equivalents between all of these different languages, discourses, and traditions. At worst, the court interpreter was arrogant, incompetent, or treacherous.[7] The vocation of interpreter involved not only skill, Plaatje would therefore argue, but also a special genre of "conscience," the specific contours of which he does not delineate but the immense demands of which may be inferred from his essay.[8] The "conscience" of the court interpreter would have entailed the impossible but necessary responsibility of producing nothing less than a common language of justice – a language whose signifiers and concepts would have allowed for the participation of Europeans and Africans alike.[9]

Prior to 1910, the chance to invent a language of this sort – much less speak it in any meaningful sense – would have been slim, since jurisprudence of the time justified rather than limited the excesses of colonial administration. Especially after 1927, with the passage of the Native Administration Act, the court interpreter would have been employed under conditions that would have dismayed the Plaatje of 1909. Whereas colonial rule was grounded in a developmental narrative according to which "the native" could be gradually included within "civilization" by means of education and uplift, the bureaucracy of segregation sought to "retribalize the native" by creating out of the patchwork system of pre-Union native administration a unified system of separate courts (the "Chiefs' Courts"), separate jurisprudential traditions ("customary law"), and separate legal procedures ("unrestrained" by European rules of evidence, perjury, or written records).[10] Here the work of the court interpreter would have taken place within the constraints of a vast administrative apparatus whose magistrates and field officers were directed by an authority, the minister of native affairs, who doubled as "supreme chief of all natives" and was vested with an almost unchecked power to legislate by simple proclamation.[11] Under these conditions, translation would have performed the work not of justice but of injustice – of rendering intelligible laws the "root principles" of which, to the extent they were coherent at all, were founded in simple hatred.[12]

Strange though it may sound, it was a profession of this sort that the young Mandela seems to have desired when he began his studies at Fort Hare in 1939. To prepare for it, Mandela majored in native administration, while also taking courses in history, English, social anthropology, native law, and Roman-Dutch law.[13] These topics would not have been presented to Mandela in an uncritical way; nor, however, would they have been revolutionary. The Fort Hare professors from whom Mandela received his earliest legal training spoke the language of Cape liberalism, which affirmed "equal rights for all civilized men, irrespective of race,"[14] while also conceiving civilization as an ongoing task of empire. One of these professors was Z. K. Matthews, a London-trained lawyer and the first black South African to receive an LLB.[15] From Matthews, Mandela would have received the legal training he needed to serve in the Department of Native Affairs. Matthews placed great value on the works of imperial jurisprudence. He cherished the emphasis on the "rule of law" in A. V. Dicey's 1886 lectures, *Law of the Constitution*,[16] and in his course on administrative law, he assigned Lord Hailey's 1938 *African Survey*, a mammoth work of British colonial social science on the "Bantu problem" throughout Africa and the paradigmatic text of twentieth-century British colonial administrative reason. At the same time, however, it seems improbable that Matthews would not also have included in his teachings the substance of the MA thesis he completed at Yale University in 1934. This comprehensive 400-page document criticized the "despotism" of the Native Administration Act No. 38 of 1927, analyzed the differences between dictatorial and democratic chieftainships, and argued for "the development of one system of South African Law to which Native Law may contribute, as well as Roman Dutch Law."[17] For a student whose desire was to become a court interpreter, who may have felt summoned by the call of the peculiar "conscience" implicit in this profession, Matthew's thesis could not but have held special appeal. Even though this argument, like Plaatje's, remained squarely within the horizon of imperial jurisprudence, which aimed at nothing if not "a common language of justice between Europeans and Africans," it also would have brought to the surface the antitheses and even incoherence of that same jurisprudence, as if empire were non-identical not only with the "different" populations it conquered and administered, but also with itself.

Much the same could be said for another of Mandela's Fort Hare professors, D. D. T. Jabavu. Jabavu's mastery of Latin would have enabled him to make sense of British imperialism's constant comparisons to the Roman imperialism from which it sought to differentiate itself.[18] So, too, would he have been able to evaluate, from an "untimely" perspective, the power of the governor-general to legislate by proclamation. He would have been able to see that this unlimited power resembled nothing so much as the power of the "dictator" under Roman law, this extraordinary magistrate who ruled without the intervention of the tribunes during periods of tumult and sedition. In articles published in 1920 and 1934, Jabavu did just that, offering unusually perceptive critiques of the Union of South Africa's hated "pass laws," which obliged Africans to carry and display "reference books" each and every time they sought to move from one declared area to another, or even if they desired to remain in a given area. For Jabavu, these laws resembled the sort of exceptional measures that ordinarily existed only under conditions of martial law (where, exactly as in native administration, occupying armies require civilians to carry "passes" in order to move in and out of "proclaimed areas"). For Jabavu, in other words, it would have been possible to assess from an "ancient" perspective colonial bureaucracy's "modern" claims to set the native on the path toward advancement, uplift, and civilization; in fact, as he wrote, this bureaucracy simply trapped the native in a state of perpetual "martial law."[19] This teaching would have been reinforced by a text that held special importance for Jabavu (whose father was severely criticized in it) and that Mandela can be presumed to have read: Sol Plaatje's *Native Life in South Africa*. With its systematic critique of the Land Act of 1913 and its striking formulations of the cruel absurdities of segregation, Plaatje's text would have offered the young Mandela a crucial ability: to interpret native administration not from within the horizon of its own self-understanding, as a program of incremental development, but rather as a scheme designed to accomplish nothing less than what Plaatje called the "extermination" of African populations.[20]

Mandela's participation in student protests at Fort Hare and his subsequent expulsion from the university are often taken as the beginning of his transition to political militancy.[21] But perhaps Mandela experienced another sort of trouble at Fort Hare, one no less important for being quieter, less public and visible, and more difficult to articulate and name. Perhaps it was there that Mandela encountered, at the root of South African law, a specifically *conceptual* trouble. From Matthews and Jabavu, Mandela would have been left with the realization that the very same colonial administrative apparatus that spoke of itself, using the lexicon of nineteenth-century liberalism, as a "guardian" and "trustee" for native populations, could and did double as an *occupying army*, an apparatus whose normalized exceptions to law – pass laws, above all – resembled nothing so much as perpetual "martial law." To encounter this doubleness would have been a very different matter than realizing that an otherwise theoretically coherent administrative law was, because of the distortions produced by the insertion of racial and ethnic categories, unequally applied in practice. It would have amounted to the recognition that the very theory of colonial administration itself was afflicted by a coincidence of opposites, a coexistence of the rule of law with the anomie and despotism of martial law, and that no amount of improved administration would undo this incoherence. But supposing this were so, it seems unlikely that this conceptual trouble would not also have caused trouble for Mandela's earliest desire, his wish to serve as a court interpreter in the Department of Native Administration. Two alternative views would have presented themselves. The first is the possibility that native administration could not be put aright by the "conscience" of the court interpreter, because, according to the old saying *traduttore, traditore*, the translator here would amount, in a very rigorous sense, to a traitor, a figure who aids and abets an occupying army by explaining, domesticating, or even justifying its violence. The second is the possibility that the "conscience" of a court interpreter could put it aright (because only an unprecedented labor of translation, and not liberal jurisprudence on its own terms, could reintroduce liberal tolerance to the intolerability of its own demand for despotism, and thus prepare the conditions for the emergence of a common language of justice). At Fort Hare, Mandela would have encountered a liberalism defined by its intolerable internal contradictions, a liberalism that was, as Mandela later would say, at one and the same time a brutal imperialism[22] whose most distinctive feature was its coexistence with its own opposite: colonial despotism. If this were the case, it would make sense that, upon moving to Johannesburg in 1942, Mandela would want "to unlearn" some of the lessons he had been taught at Fort Hare.[23]

The Law of the Person: Mandela at Wits

Between 1943 and 1949, Mandela would pursue his LLB degree at the University of the Witwatersrand (Wits). While there, Mandela would take most of his classes from a professor named Herman Robert Hahlo. From the passages devoted to Hahlo in Mandela's *Long Walk to Freedom*, it is clear that this teacher had a lasting influence on Mandela, though in the most negative sense possible. Hahlo was someone who believed that law was a "social science" discipline too rigorous for women and blacks to master.[24] As someone who had "drunk deeply from the cup of apartheid,"[25] Hahlo was a man whose opinions Mandela wanted to "disprove."[26] To understand Mandela's time at Wits and his ongoing "unlearning" of law, it will be necessary to reconstruct what sort of poisonous learning might have been proffered by this curious professor. Born in the United States in 1905, Hahlo was trained as a legal scholar in Germany, where he studied Roman law at the Universities of Berlin and Halle. Forced to leave Germany because of his Jewish heritage, Hahlo emigrated to South Africa in 1934, where he was quickly credentialed in a system of legal education that understood Roman law to be the essence and basis of its claim to European inheritance. However, Hahlo also recognized the contributions made to South African law by English common law. He would propose that the "spirit" of South African law consisted in the unique way that it allowed for a reconciliation of English and Continental juridical traditions that, even within Europe itself, remained separate. This "spirit" (which, according to the Nazi jurist Carl Schmitt, was dead in Europe itself) seemed to Hahlo to live on, in remarkably unified and comprehensive fashion, in South African law. Precisely because of its position exterior to Europe, South Africa (or so this recent arrival thought) allowed European jurisprudence to survive the disintegration it suffered in Europe itself. If ever there were a representative of the Eurocentric jurisprudence to which apartheid laid claim, Hahlo was it.

And yet, precisely here, in the version of European jurisprudence inherited and transmitted by this unusual professor, there stirred a subtle but decisive juridical problem that would have been of special importance to Mandela. During the same years that Mandela was enrolled in Hahlo's "The Laws of Persons and Corporations," Hahlo himself was at work on a comprehensive study that he tentatively titled "The Law of Persons."[27] The "law of the person," which is so essential to law that the law in general may even be said to "live in persons,"[28] nevertheless marked a surprisingly difficult problem for the tradition of jurisprudence in which Hahlo was trained. English liberal thought, like the Roman law from which it is in part derived,[29] is predicated on the notion that "persons" have certain rights and privileges, among which are *dignitas* and *libertas*. But just as every "person" is not necessarily a living being (as is the case with corporations and colleges), so, too, not every living being, not even every member of the species *Homo sapiens*, is necessarily a "person." In the Roman law tradition in which Hahlo was trained, the concept of the "person" was limited only to free Roman citizens, a *fictio legii* that gained its coherence only insofar as it could be opposed to another concept, the slave (understood as a form of living property or "thing"). To make matters more complex, Roman law also recognized numerous "gradients" of a person (pertaining not only to race, nationality, domicile, and age, but also to sex and marriage, senility and minority, age and nonage, competence and incompetence, lunacy and reason, prodigals and absentees, legitimate and illegitimate children, etc.). As a result, the law of the person, this cornerstone of rights as such, never failed to taper off into a manifestly administrative discourse, an evaluative framework that, despite being founded on a fundamental *qualitative* distinction between "persons" and "things," nevertheless also entailed complicated *quantitative* distinctions of "statuses" or "ranks" internal to the concept of the "person." This framework, upon which the entire jurisprudence of the ancient law of the person was founded, would survive, albeit in very different ways, in the modern law of the person. English common law, like the Roman law on which it was in part based, distinguished between "persons" and "minors" (those under the age of twenty-one, who could not be expected to be in full command of their faculties and therefore required a parent, trustee, or guardian to manage their interests). In colonial jurisprudence, particularly in the political thought of J. S. Mill, the concept of the "minor" provided a key rationale and justification for the creation of despotic governments that were vested with the paternal authority to manage the interests of entire "races" whose "backwardness" qualified them as "nonage" and disqualified them from the exercise of liberty.[30] In English colonial jurisprudence, to say nothing of US common law, the law of the person was more than just a cornerstone of modern rights. It was one of the cornerstones of legalized racism.

What held for Roman law and English common law held, as well, for the tradition of Roman-Dutch law transmitted by Hahlo. Writing in 1960, Hahlo would declare South African law of persons to be one of the most conservative areas of South African jurisprudence. "There are few branches of South African law," Hahlo suggested, "where the principles of the original Roman-Dutch law have been so faithfully maintained as in the law of persons and family relations."[31] In terms that cannot have differed markedly from what Mandela encountered in lectures fifteen years earlier, Hahlo defined the law of the person in South Africa by referring to its European origins:

> Following the lines of traditional European jurisprudence, South African law defines a legal *persona* as any being or entity capable of rights or duties, and distinguishes between natural and juristic (or artificial) persons. Every human being is a person in law, having the capacity for rights and duties, but there are considerable differences in status between persons of different class and condition. The main factors determining a person's legal status in South African law are race, nationality, domicile, and age.[32]

Elaborating upon this point, Hahlo then proceeded to summarize the "four main racial groups" between which South African law distinguishes. "The differences in legal status between these four groups are considerable," he reports, "especially as regards the franchise, employment, movement, residence and the capacity to own or occupy immovable property."[33] Only after setting these premises into place did Hahlo describe the aim of the "present policy of 'apartheid'": "to set aside separate areas for residence by members of the different racial groups, and to provide the different Bantu peoples with their own national homes."[34] Today, to be sure, we are inclined to view apartheid as one of the paradigmatic violations of the rights of the person. For Hahlo, however, the very opposite was true. Apartheid was not inconsistent with the law of the person; it was a *subset* of the law of the person.[35] It was an extension, into the division and distribution of land and labor, of the hierarchies of legal status that, in empires both ancient and modern, always had been a part of the law of the person.

Hahlo's writings on the law of the person also provide the proper context for understanding his demeaning remarks about Africans and women. These remarks are presented by Mandela's biographers, following the lead of Mandela's own autobiography, as an example of the classic "authoritarian personality": Hahlo was not only prejudiced, but mean, tidy, and excessively rule-bound. But from the perspective of the jurisprudence that he taught, Hahlo's "personality" has an even greater significance still. Hahlo's claim that blacks and women were not sufficiently "disciplined" to learn law was consistent with, if not outright required by, the very Roman law doctrine Hahlo himself was teaching. Hahlo's insults implied the application of the ancient law of the person to his very pedagogy, as if the ancient law of the person could be taught only to "persons" as defined by the ancient law of the person itself. In form as well as content, therefore, Hahlo would have presented himself as the very personification of the ancient law of the person. Above all, his own personal conduct toward Mandela – which involved *including* Mandela within the classroom while also *excluding* him in advance from the tradition being taught in the classroom – would have personified the strange but consistent way in which the ostensibly admirable qualities of the law of the person (respect, *dignitas*, etc.) always turn out to be underwritten by an administrative discourse that is structured by intricate hierarchies of rank and status. To limit one's interpretation of Hahlo's racism and sexism to psychology, understanding his meanness as the expression of an irrational pathology "internal to" his personality, is thus to miss the sense in which that meanness was the rational and necessary expression of the very doctrine Hahlo himself proffered.

If this is the case, it is significant that the comprehensive book that, in 1944, Hahlo proposed to write on the law of the person never would materialize in a complete and systematic form.[36] To be sure, it is hard to imagine a moment when perplexity over the law of the person would have been more acute than in the years following 1946. In the wake of World War II, the law of the person would be reiterated under conditions defined not only by the 1948 Universal Declaration of Human Rights, but also by the corresponding emergence of secular, scientifically grounded concepts of "anti-racism," which culminated in UNESCO's statements of 1950 and 1951.[37] In the new juridical context defined by these mutually constitutive discourses, the law of the person would no longer function as one of the cornerstones of legalized racism; it now would be mobilized as one of the very metonyms for the universal rights that accrued to the human by virtue of the simple, tautologous fact of being born a human.[38]

Given the difficulty of universalizing such a manifestly exclusionary jurisprudence, it would be reasonable were Hahlo to find himself struggling anew in the post-war period with his own ability to transmit, as an intelligible and systematic doctrine, the law of the person he had learned in Berlin in the 1930s. Hahlo's inability to publish a comprehensive book on this topic is, from this perspective, not simply a "personal" failing; to the contrary, it's a symptom of something incomprehensive, perhaps even newly incomprehensible, in the post-war iteration of the law of the person itself. If this is so, we might suppose as well that Hahlo transmitted that incoherence – despite himself and in a most productive manner – to his most famous student. On Mandela's side, after all, Hahlo's "Law of Persons and Corporations" would be the only intermediate course at the University of the Witwatersrand that Mandela would end up retaking thrice. "I have passed all of the qualifying courses in the Intermediate LL.B.," Mandela would write in a 1946 student loan application, "except the 'Law of Persons' in which I shall write a supplementary examination in February, 1947."[39] In his autobiography, Mandela went out of his way to blame himself, not Hahlo, for what he regarded as his poor performance at Wits, claiming that his failure to disprove Hahlo was his fault alone: "My performance as a law student was dismal."[40] But given Hahlo's own apparent difficulty with the law of the person during these years, Mandela's autobiographical confession might be off the mark; it might personalize a failure that was anything but personal, because it involved an incoherence internal to the very concept of the person. It might be more precise to say that Mandela's repeated failures to comprehend the law of the person as taught by Hahlo were successful comprehensions of a doctrine that, especially during the years of 1943–49, labored under the weight of its own incipient incomprehensibility. In short, if it is true that at Wits one of the courses that Mandela had the most trouble with was Hahlo's "Law of Persons and Corporations," it is also true that this trouble was not at all limited to Mandela, or even for that matter Hahlo. It was, precisely, an epochal trouble: a trouble that attended the birth of universal human rights in the post-war period, inasmuch as these rights emerged through the universalization of a concept, the person, whose own distribution of rights, at least up until that point, always had been starkly anti-universal. It was as if there were something in this reiteration that Mandela simply could not internalize, simply could not abide by, simply could not comprehend. And if Hahlo's unwritten manuscript is any indication, it seems that this lacuna was shared by the professor whose overriding wish seemed to be to share as little as possible with the very student who, it seems, ended up understanding him best.

Mandela & Tambo

In 1949, a year after the Nationalist Party came to power in South Africa, Mandela submitted an application to the Faculty of Law for "supplementary examinations" in jurisprudence, the law of delicts, and the law of evidence, all three of which he needed to pass in order to receive his LLB.[41] Hahlo, who had been dean of the law faculty since 1946, chaired the committee that would reject Mandela's application.[42] This deprived Mandela of the chance to pursue the degree he would have needed in order to practice as an advocate, but it did not deter Mandela from pursuing the profession of law. For Mandela, law would never be simply one among many ways to "make a living." But neither would it be the sort of quasi-theological "calling" described by Max Weber, where daily work acquires the moral significance of a secular attempt to secure the salvation of the soul. Rather, it would provide Mandela with the lexicon, the skills and techniques, and the institutional apparatus that together would allow him to begin rethinking anew the work of the "court interpreter." Under conditions of colonialism and segregation, the interpreter's work of translation was difficult or even impossible: at the same time that imperial liberalism sometimes promised harmony between "European and African ideas on law and justice" as one of the desiderata of colonial rule,[43] its constitutive paternalism simultaneously required it to perpetually defer that promise, so that *in concreto* it remained in a permanently suspended state. Under conditions of apartheid, by contrast, the notion that "European and African ideas on law and justice" could harmonize was the very threat against which the entire edifice of apartheid was braced. Translation, after 1948, was no longer an administrative act necessary for the uplift and civilizing mission of colonial rule; taken to the extreme, the integration, intermixing, or merging of traditions it entailed amounted to the anti-apartheid activity par excellence, the very paradigm of treason against a regime founded on the notion that "separate cultures should develop along separate lines."[44] Mandela's exclusion from the formal study of law in 1949 didn't end up dissuading him from treating the profession of law as a chance to engage in the work of the "court interpreter." Just the opposite: it gave him a new and better perspective from which to renew and reimagine this work – to translate the very work of translation from an instance of colonial administration into the "call" of a new sort of conscience.

Because South African law, like English common law, distinguished between advocates and attorneys, Mandela remained able to practice as an attorney even after his expulsion from Wits. In 1951, Mandela passed his Attorneys' Admission Examination, and on March 27, 1952, four months before he would be formally excluded from Wits for non-payment of fees,[45] Mandela was admitted as an attorney of the Court of the Transvaal Provincial Division.[46] By that point, thanks to Walter Sisulu, Mandela already had been engaged as a clerk since March 8, 1943, in the law firm of Witkin, Sidelsky, and Eidelman for the requisite three years,[47] where, under the guidance of Lazar Sidelsky, he helped draw up real estate contracts for the firm's African clients and where he had the opportunity to work alongside Gaur Radebe, a radical attorney and member of the African National Congress (ANC) and South African Communist Party.[48] In August 1952, after finding employment with a series of white law firms with liberal and communist politics, Mandela finally opened his own firm. Later that year, he would be joined by Oliver Tambo, who had recently passed his Attorneys' Admission Examination and was employed by the law firm Kovalsky and Tuch.[49] Although the 1950 Group Areas Act required all black professionals to acquire formal permission for their activities from the governor-general and even though Mandela and Tambo lacked this permission, they opened their practice anyway,[50] defiantly setting themselves up in a building called Chancellor House, whose chambers were located directly across the street from the Johannesburg magistrate's court.[51]

The new laws and regulations passed by the apartheid government criminalized the very existence of ordinary urban Africans and produced great numbers of clients who were in need of legal representation, who lacked the means to hire lawyers, and to whom the firm of "Mandela & Tambo" offered its services free of charge.[52] Mandela & Tambo, the only law firm in South Africa composed entirely of African lawyers, quickly became known to those who suffered from laws whose absurdities and cruelties were, as Mandela wrote, almost impossible to comprehend.[53] In his autobiography, Mandela describes Chancellor House less as an office building than as a vast, prosthetic ear. In its cramped, overcrowded hallways, Mandela and Tambo would hear in excruciating detail about the suffering produced by apartheid laws and regulations, and between their political activities in the ANC and their increasing inability to remedy racial injustices within the confines of increasingly racist laws, their recognition of the limits of lawful opposition to apartheid would have been acute. But in the Roman law with which both Mandela and Tambo were familiar, *officium* was a word that designated "duty" and "service," with the duty of "justice" being the highest office of all, and from the countless stories of Mandela & Tambo what stands out is just how seriously each partner took his official duties as an advocate.[54] The partners insisted that ordinary Africans have the chance to be represented not according to the informal procedures of the "native courts" the Union of South Africa had established in 1927, but according to the official procedures that characterized "European" courts. Only with reference to this insistence is it possible to understand why Mandela and Tambo alike also insisted upon the observance of even the most minor courtroom procedures, above all when the advocate or client in question was an African.[55] Official courtroom procedure was not, for these advocates, a mere formality or courtesy; nor was its observance simply a reformist technique for including Africans within a system of "European" justice that, exclusion of Africans aside, otherwise was somehow fair. Already in the 1950s, these procedures had for Mandela and Tambo a dialectical significance: their suspension by white judges and policemen were signs not only of racism, but also of the "contempt" in which the all-white legal system held the idea of law itself. Mandela's insistence upon these procedures in his own case likewise was not merely a form of political resistance; it was the earliest iteration – the practical, pre-theoretical iteration – of the argument that Mandela later would present to the all-white courts in his trials of 1962–64: that South African courts were defined by their non-identity with the very tradition of law in which they rooted their "Western" identity.

This, needless to say, was not an argument that apartheid courts or ministries were willing or even able to hear. First Mandela, in December 1952, and later Tambo, in 1954,[56] would suffer one of the strangest and most brutal forms of legal persecution invented by the apartheid government: the "ban" or "banning order." These terms described the discretionary power of the South African executive branch to forbid a person, for a period of up to five years and sometimes longer, from (1) being a member of specific organizations (which were mostly Communist or anti-apartheid in orientation); (2) being in or leaving a specified place or area; (3) receiving visitors (Mandela would be prohibited from speaking with more than one person at a time); (4) performing any act as specified by the minister of justice; and (5) having one's speech or writing quoted.[57] At its most powerful, the banning order produced a deprivation of public space so extreme that it amounted to the wide-open confinement of the banned person at his or her own expense. The South African jurist Anthony Mathews used no metaphor when he argued that banning orders caused "a civil death and to a large extent a personal and social death for the victim of the banning order."[58] Because the definition of human life has, since Aristotle, pivoted on the capacity for speech,[59] the person who suffered the banning of her or his capacity for speech experienced something very close to capital punishment as defined by classical Roman law: to have one's *caput* or *persona* removed was to suffer death without physically dying and to live a life without being fully alive.[60]

The banning orders served on Mandela clearly were intended, as he would later say, to force him to abandon his legal practice.[61] Not only did these bans restrict Mandela from traveling outside of Johannesburg to consult with rural clients and argue cases in other jurisdictions; they also were administered by the minister of justice with strategic ambiguity and studied incompetence, in a secretive manner the opacity and unpredictability of which clearly were designed to increase Mandela's uncertainty, freeze up his ability to plan, and "imprison his spirit."[62] Far from succeeding in their intended purpose, however, the apartheid state's bans simply strengthened his existing convictions and confirmed the dialectical conclusion Mandela had clearly already reached by then. Outlawing him not because of his actions but because of his conscience – "because of what I thought," as Mandela would put in 1962[63] – the apartheid state's bans did not exclude Mandela from the practice of law; rather, they placed apartheid law outside the bounds of the very theory of criminal law itself. By denying Mandela "the right to lead a normal life,"[64] these bans did not force him into "living death"; they prepared him to live the life of an outlaw. To obey the basic principles of Western law, in short, it would be necessary to disobey the laws of the apartheid state, this state that justified its violence by identifying itself as the legatee of the West in darkest Africa.

This dialectic, it should be noted, put Mandela at odds not only with the apartheid state, which was dedicated to persecuting him by any and all means, but also with the influential South African philosopher R. F. A. Hoernlé, whose objections to apartheid were, however grave, nevertheless outweighed in the end by his even stronger opposition to revolutionary violence and civil disobedience alike. For Hoernlé, the law was the law: self-identical with itself and rationally constituted in form if not in content, the law demanded obedience no matter how repugnant to the liberal spirit its particular provisions might be. On this view, any theory of disobedience, whether in the name of Gandhian non-violence or Marxist revolutionary violence, would be an opening to anomie and, for that same reason, illegitimate, unreasonable, and immoral.[65] Mandela's earliest legal studies would have pointed toward a slightly different conclusion. Even prior to the apartheid government's militarized suppression of the general strike of May 1961, which was Mandela's stated reason for changing his mind about the effectiveness of Gandhian non-violence as a "tactic,"[66] Mandela would have learned from his Fort Hare professors that law in the Union of South Africa was defined by an irreducible incoherence: it not only *coexisted with* but also *demanded* the very arbitrary violence that the "rule of law," this concept so treasured by white South African jurists, was supposed to constrain.[67] For Jabavu and Matthews, and for Plaatje as well, South African law was not at all self-identical with itself. Even prior to the dark years of the 1950s, and without any assistance from Gandhian *satyagrahis* or revolutionary Marxists, South African law already hosted within itself the very anomie Hoernlé seemed to fear. Instead of the rule of law, it was governed by dictatorship; instead of peacetime norms, it was ordered according to the exceptions of martial law; instead of health, welfare, and safety, its administrative apparatus produced conditions for the extermination of African populations. But while Jabavu and Matthews may have disagreed with Hoernlé's premise that South African law was self-identical with itself, they did not disagree with the conclusion Hoernlé drew from that premise, namely, that conscience alone provided no warrant for the rebel to undo unjust law through deeds rather than words. Like the leaders of the ANC, many of whom were themselves lawyers, Jabavu and Matthews remained committed to the notion that constitutional change ought to be accomplished within the limits of the existing constitutional order.

On this point, above all, Mandela seems to have unlearned what he was taught at Fort Hare. Writing in 1944, Mandela and a number of fellow Fort Hare graduates produced the Manifesto for the recently formed ANC Youth League (ANCYL). Written the same year that Mandela was enrolled in Professor Hahlo's Roman Law I course at Wits, the Manifesto demonstrates an acute awareness of the inner logic that links the Roman law of the person – the notion that a "minor" or "person of nonage" requires a "guardian," "custodian," or "trustee" to temporarily act on his behalf – with the despotic apparatus of the Department of Native Administration (its thanato-politics, its criminalization of daily life for Africans, the sense in which its pass laws normalize martial law, its dictatorial authority to govern by proclamation). In the Manifesto, Mandela et al. argued that the doctrine of "trusteeship" not only consigned the African to the status of a "perpetual minor" and turned him into a "criminal still out of prison," but also was designed "to drive the African steadily toward extermination."[68]

What differentiated these claims from their iterations by an earlier generation was the ANCYL's critique of the ANC's failure to theorize the genealogy of its own organizational practices. Because the ANC was "obsessed with imperialist forms of organization,"[69] it limited itself to those political demands that could be articulated using the juridical forms already sanctioned in advance by empire (such as the rule of law and the rights of the person). Not only did this uncritical relation to its own modes of administrative reason blind the ANC to the reality of the Department of Native Administration, which was producing the conditions for the extermination of African populations – not despite but precisely because of its loyalty to liberal juridical forms; it also allowed the ANC to be annexed into an apparatus of Native Administration itself, converting it into an "unconscious police" that repressed any grievances against Native Administration that could not be expressed using these same forms.[70] The ANCYL executive, not unlike the ANC itself (co-founded in 1912 by Pixley ka Seme and R. W. Msimang), was dominated by lawyers: along with Mandela, Tambo, and Sisulu, the charismatic ANCYL president Anton Lembede also had legal training. But the ANCYL, as distinct from the ANC, posed as a problem for thought the very idea of "administrative reason" itself. Its position was clear: anything less than the creation of a new and different form of administrative reason, a new and different sort of "organisational machinery,"[71] would not suffice to repeal the legislation and abolish the "differential institutions" that enabled white domination. As a result, the ANCYL would set forth a "programme for action" that would extend well beyond the ANC's traditional demands for "political democracy" to include policies designed to create new relations between Africans and whites in the domains of economics, education, and culture (policies that, in adherence to the classic paradigm of modern administrative reason, would be "modified from time to time to meet new situations and conditions and to cope with the ever-changing circumstances").[72] In *Long Walk to Freedom*, Mandela interprets the ANCYL Manifesto with reference to the generational conflicts within the ANC and to the tension between African nationalism and communism.[73] From a jurisprudential perspective, however, it is host to a different dynamic: it reveals a Mandela troubled by the ANC's unselfconscious replication of the juridical forms of imperial administrative reason.

This has implications, in turn, for the way we think about Mandela and the law. Most readers will have come to identify Mandela with the law because of his heroic speeches from the dock in his 1962 and 1964 trials.[74] Fewer will have formed this association because of Mandela's time as a lawyer in the 1950s. But prior both to his lawyering of the 1950s and to his speeches of the 1960s – and, in many ways, as their common condition of possibility – Mandela had long studied another branch of law, native administration, whose history is much less glorious than public law, much more difficult to explain and to critique as well, and yet much more pertinent to the lives of black South Africans under apartheid.[75] No doubt we are still in the habit of assuming a mutual exclusivity between charismatic and bureaucratic authority, so that we perhaps assume that a figure who is graced with the former could only alienate and weaken himself if immersed in the latter's hair-splitting drudgery. But to understand Mandela's relation to law, we may have to unlearn this habit. In the very years when his fierce cross-examinations, his mastery of South African criminal and civil law, and his command of courtroom procedure combined to give him an authoritative reputation as a "lawyer of truth,"[76] Mandela also was hard at work figuring out how to uproot another branch of law: colonial administration.

On Trial

In 1962, after many months underground, Mandela would be arrested by the apartheid Security Police. Determined not to repeat the mistakes of the treason trial of 1956–61, which ended in the acquittal of Mandela and his 155 co-defendants, the apartheid regime put Mandela on trial in 1962 for inciting a general strike and for leaving South Africa without a passport. In July 1963, while serving his sentence and studying the history of English law through correspondence at the University of London,[77] Mandela would be rearrested and put on trial yet again, this time for retroactively violating a law called the "Sabotage Act" (Act 37 of 1963), which had been passed by the all-white parliament while he had been imprisoned. Mandela would be found guilty for this offense as well, but not before delivering a speech from the dock that involved "the most comprehensive and widely reported critique of the administration of justice ever made in South Africa."[78] On November 7, 1962, Mandela had already delivered a first speech from the dock, in which he declared himself without obligation to obey the laws of the apartheid state, speaking in ringing terms about the "conflict" that "any thinking African in this country" experiences between "his conscience on the one hand and the law on the other."[79] On April 20, 1964, at the very opening of his "Rivonia trial," Mandela would issue his second speech from the dock. In this four-hour-long statement, which came to be known as his "political testament," Mandela not only translated his own "life story" and political convictions into the terms of English legal history, but also demonstrated, in even greater detail than in 1962, the failings of the apartheid state. Covered by all of the leading Anglo-American newspapers, despite Mandela's status as a "banned" person, and reprinted in book form, first by the ANC's Publicity and Information Bureau and then by Heinemann under the Nehruvian title *No Easy Walk to Freedom* (1965), Mandela's courtroom speeches of 1962 and 1964 would introduce him to international readers who, in the preceding years, would have developed an opposition to apartheid because of the Sharpeville Massacre, and also because of consistent motions before the (increasingly decolonized) United Nations, the emergence of the Non-Aligned Movement, and, in the United States, the Civil Rights Movement. If the very name "Nelson Mandela" would come to register as a synonym for the law, it is in no small part thanks to these speeches.

But even and especially here, the identity between "Mandela" and "the law," wound too tight, conceals a more intricate relation. In October 13, 1962, before his first speech from the dock, Mandela entered into the apartheid court wearing not a suit and tie, as he normally did, but a leopard skin "kaross." In *Long Walk to Freedom*, Mandela explains that this was a gesture to show "contempt for the niceties of white justice,"[80] but it was equally a gesture that personified the contempt in which South African justice held law itself.[81] The entire itinerary of Mandela's legal training – from his encounter with Hahlo in Roman law, to his reflections on the "minor" in his ANCYL Manifesto, to the stifling experience of his banning – had prepared him to problematize the legal category of the "person," to understand how his "person" would be represented in the apparatus of the white court, and to think about ways for him to redeploy his "person" so that it would undo that apparatus from within. Understood from this perspective, Mandela's kaross is not simply "theater";[82] it is an experiment with the very concept of the "person" itself. Before Gaius divided Roman law into *actiones*, *res*, and *personae*, ancient Greek philosophers and poets already had spoken in deeply ambiguous ways of the *prosōpon* (πρόσωπον), which designated not only the "mask" donned by actors in order to allow their audiences to glimpse something of their countenance and character, but also the "face" that we present to the gaze of others and that marks us as specifically human. For his part, Thomas Hobbes would inaugurate the epoch of modern sovereign power by explaining that it cannot operate without a representational dimension that he defined precisely as a *prosōpon, persona*, and Person.[83] When Mandela donned his kaross, he was not then simply performing resistance. He was pressing with great precision and force upon one of the most exposed nerves in modern political philosophy. He was treating his position as an outlaw, as a rogue whose exteriority from the law was demanded by the law itself, to position himself precisely as the personification of the sovereign power of the excluded African majority. By the 1980s, as Susan Sontag wrote, it was clear that Mandela was a "*de facto* head-of-state, the president of a democratic country that does not yet exist but will exist."[84] But already in 1952, Mandela began to understand himself as the first black president of South Africa,[85] and by 1955, with the publication of the Freedom Charter, the post-apartheid era had begun in principle if not in fact. By banning Mandela, the apartheid state wanted to outlaw the exemplary figure of the anti-apartheid struggle, reducing him to a voiceless living being. But in the very Western tradition the apartheid state claimed to be defending against Mandela, and above all in the Hobbesian formulation of sovereign power that inaugurates the tradition of British liberalism, *every* sovereign person by definition doubles as an outlaw, a warlike rogue. The sovereign person of Hobbesian political philosophy, as distinct from the juristic person in Roman law, is for this same reason not opposed to the animal; this God-like person is, to the contrary, *itself* an animal, or at least an animal of a very special type, one whose exteriority to the law is at once excessively artificial (marking its exceptional status with explicitly theatrical artifice) and excessively bestial (to be precise, a wolf, an unpredictably predatory and aggressive animal, one bound by no command or responsibility whatsoever).[86] Understood in these terms, the kaross Mandela donned in 1962 – in no less a juridical space than the "dock," so named because of its resemblance to a "cage" for animals – was not simply a costume for representing the opposition between "Africa" and "the West"; it was a cunning way to personify the non-identity of Western law with itself, to deploy the machine of Western sovereignty in order to short-circuit the sovereignty of the very court that claimed to be defending the West from its mortal enemies. The apartheid state's bans tried to depersonalize Mandela, pushing him altogether outside of the field of legality; in so doing, those very same bans ended up inviting Mandela directly into law's most intimate exterior, into the place modern law reserves for the specifically *sovereign* person.

In his 1964 Rivonia trial, Mandela mobilized the same unique place, though now in a different way. That the Rivonia trial was to be prosecuted as an international "show trial" was never in question. Minister of Justice John Vorster saw the trial as a pedagogical opportunity to instruct internal and external publics alike about the existential threat that Communism posed to South Africa's attempt to maintain Western civilization in Africa.[87] To ensure that Mandela would be found guilty on this world stage, he appointed Dr. Percy Yutar as prosecutor. Called the "most qualified legal brain" in all of apartheid South Africa,[88] Yutar earned in 1939 only the second LLD in law to be awarded by the University of Cape Town,[89] where he wrote a dissertation on property law and was trained in Roman-Dutch law, as well as a version of English common law influenced by the positivist jurisprudence of John Austin.[90] In Austinian positivism, which formalized selected precepts from Hobbesian political philosophy into a rigorous science, "law" was a command that was issued by a sovereign to a subject and that obliged that subject's obedience by threat of force.[91] Although positivist jurisprudence certainly was not ignorant of the Thomistic doctrine that unjust laws are not laws at all, it famously granted no legal grounds, only moral ones, for disobeying the law. Yutar could be counted on to prosecute Mandela with uncommonly dogged focus.

Even so, it was precisely also this focus that left Yutar singularly unprepared for the way his legal strategy – his pursuit of a guilty verdict alone – would play directly into the administrative and political strategy of the accused.[92] Much more than Yutar or even the minister of justice, Mandela saw that "the heart and kernel of this case was not in this courtroom, but in the world outside."[93] Whereas Yutar's Hobbesian positivism obliged him to assume unquestioningly the jurisdiction of South Africa's court to apply its sovereignly constituted laws, Mandela threw that same jurisdiction into question from the standpoint of the Hobbesian sovereign itself. The unstated premises and implied audience underlying Mandela's speech from the dock, not to mention his masterful deployment of English legal history in the speech itself, together functioned to reintroduce into the South African courtroom the jurisprudence that gave birth to South African law, yet that, particularly after 1961, South African jurisprudence sought at any cost to disavow. Instead of consenting to a positivist understanding of his trial, on the terms of which his "person" would have an unambiguous juridical signification, Mandela treated the intense attention it focused upon his "person" as a chance to prosecute the apartheid state before the "court of world opinion." Prior to that, as its condition of possibility, was an unusually clear self-consciousness about the limits and uses of the very idea of the person itself. Before Mandela could comprehend his "persona" so impersonally – treating it, in effect, as nothing more than a mask through which a "voice sounds" (per-sonare, "to sound through") – it first would have been necessary for him to estrange himself not only from its doctrinal declension (as a cherished tradition from Roman law), but from its personal sense as well (as the key to his finite and singular existence). Only then could Mandela treat "Nelson Mandela" in the way that he did: as a prosthetic extension of himself, as the persona of a sovereign who, internally excluded within law, remained in a state of war or "open hostility" with the apartheid regime. Not despite but precisely because of his legal training, Dr. Percy Yutar was destined to misunderstand the continuities between the external aim of Mandela's internal sabotage campaign – to scare away the foreign capital upon which the South African economy was dependent[94] – and the external aim of Mandela's militant speech from the dock – to destroy the legality of the apartheid state and to substitute in its place the legality of the insurgent organization he self-consciously personified. If Mandela willfully implicated himself in Umkhonto we Sizwe, admitting the main burden of the state's charge against him, it was not then simply "to save" the organizations of which he was the personification.[95] It was to continue the struggle that motivated those organizations, only now in a way that implied a highly inventive use of the concept of the "person" – its weaponization as a means to the end of "making government impossible."

Uprooting the Law

Writing in 1985, Jacques Derrida offered insightful if misunderstood words of praise for Mandela. For Derrida, all law – and not simply illegitimate legal systems such as that of the apartheid regime – comes into being in and through a "founding violence" whereby it is incommensurable with the juridical order that violence calls into being.[96] Law acquires its foundation through an exceptional, extra-legal act – war, revolution, or, above all, colonization – that, once founded, it cannot then integrate into its norms and procedures and that consequently remains permanently in excess of its own self-understanding as a system. The genius of Mandela's 1962 and 1964 courtroom speeches, according to Derrida, is that Mandela embodied this excess in and for a regime that, precisely in its obsessive emphasis on the rule of law, defined itself by denying it. Mandela's speeches exemplified for the apartheid state both the universality to which it was obliged to aspire to remain consistent with its claims to the rule of law and the excluded trace of law-founding violence – colonization – it needed to forget. To truly inherit the Western legal legacy with which the apartheid state wanted to identify itself, Mandela showed, it would have to admit into its legal order the supplement it excluded – the African majority – through the colonial foundation of South African law itself. By the time Mandela was finished with his exposition, he thus succeeded in placing the apartheid state in an impossible position. Accused of treason, of being a traitor, Mandela treated the charge of treason with the voice of a translator, a court interpreter, translating the charge of treason into its opposite, a charge of excessive loyalty. This was a loyalty to law so extreme that it undid from within the loyalty to law of the very court that tried him, revealing it to have betrayed the same law it brought to bear in its accusations of treason. To let Mandela live, particularly after such an internationally significant show trial, would have been to permit the existence of a painful reminder that apartheid law was non-identical with the very Western tradition to which it liked to trace its roots. But to sentence Mandela to death would have been suicide: by executing Mandela, the apartheid state would have succeeded only in executing the public embodiment of its own highest principles.[97]

Derrida's analysis certainly does imply that Mandela is a figure whose conscience is commensurable with and translatable into the forms of Western law. Although Derrida does not say so explicitly, the history of law in the West, beginning at least with Socrates, is the history of trials that are lost *so that* the truth may be won and *in order for* it to be won. What Plato writes of Socrates' accusers – that they are "injuring the State at its very heart" when they undertake to harm Socrates himself[98] – holds true for what Derrida writes of Mandela as well. But to see in Mandela a mastery of Western law is not the same as viewing him as "the ultimate apostle and interpreter of the rational legal traditions associated with the Western Enlightenment"[99] or as "the ultimate expression of the rationalist legal traditions associated with the Enlightenment."[100] What Derrida perceives in Mandela's speeches is a teaching rather more intricate: that Mandela is *excluded from* the very set – Western law – whose internal unity and coherence he also *expresses*. Or conversely – and more to the point – that in Mandela's person Western law discovers itself to be *structured around the exclusion of its own essence*. Derrida's point is not, then, that there is an identity to Western law that Mandela exemplifies; it is that Western law is constitutively non-identical with itself – that its peculiar force consists in the way that it is always already still on the way toward arriving at itself, that it is continually at work achieving its own potential, that it is its own structural failure and incompletion – and that Mandela personified this non-identity in and for the very regime that most insisted on its suppression – that is, on having a legal system that staked its existence on having, maintaining, and defending a "Western" identity.

Are we mistaken, then, to identify the name "Nelson Mandela" with the very idea of law itself? Yes, if what we see in this name is nothing more than a synthesis of the various models of conscience we've already come to expect from the Western tradition (such as the one that is obedient to a "higher law" than the law of the state or the one that follows the dictates of an "inner voice" more compelling than any external command). But this is not the only way to see Mandela's name; nor, perhaps, is "Nelson Mandela" even the name we should remember when we seek to remember Nelson Mandela. It may even be that fame has been bad for this name, since it has caused first the loss of Mandela's given Xhosa name, Rolihlahla, and then the replacement of Mandela's birth name with a nickname, "Madiba." It is as if everything has transpired to leave in silence Mandela's first name, but no silence could be more misleading. "Rolihlahla" means "pulling the branch of a tree" or "troublemaker" or, as Derrida will slyly note, "uprooting [*déracinement*]."[101] With this name we can remember the genesis of a singular genre of conscience – a conscience that constantly rose above apartheid law, to be sure, but that accomplished this by radicalizing the trouble it found already there within the law, by digging underneath the law, uprooting it. "Rolihlahla," conscience of a troublemaker, name for a vigilance that came into being in response to a set of unprecedented possibilities that define Western law and yet that Western law – tragically divided against itself, fighting itself – neutralizes, restrains, excludes, and denies. Name, as well, for a meticulous labor – a special way of studying the law, one that seized, in particular, on the *impossibilities* that together structured the training for a profession that otherwise promised nothing more than drudgery and oppression. Name for questions posed to jurisprudence that exceeded the answers that jurisprudence was able to offer in response. Name, finally, for the particular mode of self-consciousness that emerges from this excess, a self-consciousness that came into its own by "unlearning" the juridical traditions it encounters. A "South African law" that would include contributions from "native law" and "Roman-Dutch law" alike; a practice of translation that would produce the common language of justice adequate to this "law"; a law of the person that, having become fully impersonal, would no longer exclude any living being, and hence could give life to this justice – these *im*possibilities were the force that pulled Mandela into the profession of law and that spurred him to uproot, from within, the decidedly undesirable possibilities presented to him by the jurisprudence of his time. The possibility, in short, of *the impossibility of apartheid*, with everything the word "apartheid" implies – this was the "calling" that allowed Nelson Mandela to master Western jurisprudence without also being mastered by it and that imprints his conscience upon ours, especially today.

Acknowledgments

I acknowledge that the research assistance provided by the staff of the Nelson Mandela Centre of Memory does not constitute an endorsement of my work, or any of the views contained therein, and should not be construed as such. Any conclusions I have reached are my own. The research for this essay was supported by a grant from the Amherst College Faculty Research Award Program, as funded by the H. Axel Schupf '57 Fund for Intellectual Life.

NOTES

1 Lewis Nkosi, *Mandela's Ego: A Novel* (Umuzi: Roggebaai, South Africa, 2006), 19–20.

2 See Russell Kaschula, "Mandela Comes Home: The Poets' Perspective," *Oral Tradition* 10.1 (1995): 102.

3 Jacques Derrida, "The Laws of Reflection: Nelson Mandela, in Admiration," in *For Nelson Mandela*, ed. Jacques Derrida and Mustapha Tlili (New York: Seaver Books, 1986), 26; Jacques Derrida, "Admiration de Nelson Mandela ou Les lois de la réflexion," in *Pour Nelson Mandela*, ed. Jacques Derrida and Mustapha Tlili (Paris: Éditions Gallimard, 1986), 28.

4 Wole Soyinka, "Your Logic Frightens Me, Mandela," in *Mandela's Earth and Other Poems* (London: Methuen, 1988), 4.

5 See Letter from Registrar of the University of South Africa to Nelson Mandela, January 12, 1987, Archive, Nelson Mandela Centre of Memory, Johannesburg, South Africa.

6 Nelson Mandela, *Long Walk to Freedom: The Autobiography of Nelson Mandela* (Boston: Little, Brown, 1994), 45.

7 Sol Plaatje, "The Essential Interpreter," in *Sol Plaatje: Selected Writings* (Johannesburg: Witwatersrand University Press, 1996), 51, 53–54, 56–57; cf. William Hailey, *An African Survey* (Oxford: Oxford University Press, 1938), 282, 298.

8 Plaatje, "Interpreter," 57.

9 This is not, it should be noted, exterior to colonial rule. "The general aim of legislation in British colonies may be said to be directed towards producing a common body of law which is expressed as applicable both to Europeans and Africans" (Hailey, *African Survey*, 274).

10 Mahmood Mamdani, *Citizen and Subject: Contemporary Africa and the Legacy of Late Colonialism* (Princeton, NJ: Princeton University Press, 1996), 71–72; Ivan Evans, *Bureaucracy and Race: Native Administration in South Africa* (Berkeley: University of California Press, 1998), 168–70. See also Hailey, *African Survey*, 297.

11 See Z. K. Matthews, "Bantu Law and Western Civilization in South Africa: A Study in the Clash of Cultures," MA thesis (Yale University, 1934), 33–35, 341–47.

12 On the "root principles" of the 1913 Land Act, see Sol Plaatje, *Native Life in South Africa, Before and Since the European War and the Boer Rebellion*, 3d ed. (London: P. S. King & Son, 1917), 200, 210.

13 Mandela, *Long Walk*, 44; Nelson Rolihlahla Mandela, Transcript, University of South Africa, issued February 7, 1952, NMFAP 2011/1, Nelson Mandela Foundation, Johannesburg, South Africa.

14 R. F. A. Hoernlé, *South African Native Policy and the Liberal Spirit* (Johannesburg: Witwatersrand University Press, 1945), viii. Matthews thought highly of Hoernlé's lectures. See Z. K. Matthews, "R. F. A. Hoernlé, *South African Native Policy and the Liberal Spirit,*" *Race Relations* 8.2 (1940): 34–7. On Matthews and Cape liberalism, see also Catherine Higgs, *The Ghost of Equality: The Public Lives of D. D. T. Jabavu of South Africa, 1885–1959* (Athens: Ohio University Press, 1997), 48.

15 Z. K. Matthews, *Freedom for My People: The Autobiography of Z. K. Matthews* (Cape Town: David Philip, 1981), 91.

16 Ibid., 230–31.

17 Ibid., 99; cf. Matthews, "Bantu Law," 354. On chieftainship, see also Z. K. Matthews, "An African View of Indirect Rule in Africa," *Journal of the Royal African Society* 36.145 (October 1937): 434–35.

18 See, e.g., Higgs, *The Ghost of Equality,* 9.

19 D. D. T. Jabavu, "Native Unrest" and "Pass Laws," in *The Black Problem: Papers and Addresses on Various Native Problems* (Lovedale: Lovedale Institution Press, 1920), 6, 19; cf. D. D. T. Jabavu, "Bantu Grievances," in *Western Civilization and the Natives of South Africa: Studies in Culture Contact,* ed. I. Schapera (New York: Humanities Press, 1934), 290.

20 On the way that the Land Act of 1913 prepared the conditions for the "extermination of the blacks," see Plaatje, *Native Life,* 213.

21 Tom Lodge, *Mandela: A Critical Life* (Oxford: Oxford University Press, 2006), 11.

22 Mandela, *Long Walk,* 302.

23 Ibid., 69. See also Nelson Mandela, *Conversations with Myself* (New York: Farrar, Straus and Giroux, 2010), 27.

24 Mandela, *Long Walk,* 90; cf. Anthony Sampson, *Mandela: The Authorised Biography* (London: HarperCollins, 1999), 34; David James Smith, *Young Mandela: The Revolutionary Years* (New York: Little, Brown, 2010), 86.

25 Smith, *Young Mandela,* 87.

26 Mandela, *Long Walk,* 90.

27 In his 1946 letter of application to become chair of the Department of Law, Hahlo enclosed the table of contents for a proposed book, "The Law of Persons." Letter from H. R. Hahlo to the Registrar, University of Witwatersrand, June 27, 1946, H. R. Hahlo Papers, University Archives, University of Witwatersrand, Johannesburg.

28 Colin Dayan, *The Law Is a White Dog: How Legal Rituals Make and Unmake Persons* (Princeton, NJ: Princeton University Press, 2011), 25.

29 H. R. Hahlo, "The Genesis of South African Law," in H. R. Hahlo and Ellison Kahn, *The Union of South Africa: The Development of Its Laws and Constitution* (London: Stevens, 1960), 47.

30 Uday Singh Mehta, *Liberalism and Empire: A Study in Nineteenth-Century British Liberal Thought* (Chicago: University of Chicago Press, 1999), 98–103; Antony Anghie, *Imperialism, Sovereignty, and the Making of International Law* (Cambridge: Cambridge University Press, 2005), 32–99.

31 Hahlo, "Law of Persons and Family Relations (Excluding the Law of Husband and Wife)," in *The Union of South Africa,* 345, cf. 41–42.

32 Ibid., 345.

33 Ibid., 346.

34 Ibid. This is, significantly, the first mention of "apartheid" in Hahlo and Kahn's comprehensive volume.

35 See also, on this point, Matthews, "Bantu Law," 215.

36 He would only ever publish Part I of the book, "Husband and Wife." The remaining three sections, "Parent and Child," "Guardian and Ward," and "Juristic Persons" either would be published in fragmentary form elsewhere or, as in the case of the section on the "juristic person," would remain unpublished altogether.

37 On human rights and the law of the person, see Joseph Slaughter, *Human Rights, Inc.: The World Novel, Narrative Form, and International Law* (New York: Columbia University Press, 2007), 17–24. On the emergence of the discourse of anti-racism in the post-war period, see Étienne Balibar, "Racism Revisited: Sources, Relevance, and Aporias of a Modern Concept," *PMLA* 123.5 (2008): 1633.

38 Slaughter, *Human Rights, Inc.*, 55–59.

39 See Letter from Nelson R. Mandela to the Secretary of the Bantu Welfare Trust, December 30, 1946, Papers of the South African Institute of Race Relations, Department of Historical Papers, Cullen Library, University of Witwatersrand, Johannesburg, Ad8431RJ/Pb11.3.9. Mandela would end up passing his 1947 supplementary examination in law of persons. See Nelson Mandela, LLB Transcript, Student #7920, University Archives, University of Witwatersrand, Johannesburg. The "supplementary exam" was an administrative measure, frequently used in the Faculty of Law, allowing students to retake examinations they had failed on a prior occasion. See "Minutes of a Special Meeting of the Board of the Faculty of Law Held at the Dean's Residence on Thursday," December 14, 1944, 8:15 PM, University Archives, University of the Witwatersrand, Johannesburg, FLS/341/44.

40 Mandela, *Long Walk*, 90.

41 Mandela, LLB Transcript. On the requirements for the LLB degree, see University of the Witwatersrand, *Calendar 1949* (Johannesburg: Hortors Limited, 1949), 191–92. On this episode, see Smith, *Young Mandela*, 85–87; Bruce Murray, *Wits: The 'Open' Years: A History of the University of Witwatersrand, Johannesburg, 1939–1959* (Johannesburg: Witwatersrand University Press, 1997), 56.

42 Smith, *Young Mandela*, 87.

43 Hailey, *African Survey*, 294.

44 On the sense in which apartheid excludes "merging" and "integration," see W. W. M. Eiselen, "Harmonious Multi-Community Development," *Optima* 9 (March 1959): 3.

45 Mandela, LLB Transcript, 2.

46 Nelson Rolihlahla Mandela, Certificate of Enrollment as an Attorney, U.D.J. 353a. Signed by the Honourable Justice Steyn, NMAP 2010/10, Nelson Mandela Foundation, Johannesburg, South Africa.

47 Nelson Rolihlahla Mandela, Ex Parte Application for Admission as an Attorney, Supreme Court of South Africa (Transvaal Provincial Division), February 12, 1952, NMFAP 2011/1, Nelson Mandela Foundation, Johannesburg, South Africa.

48 Mandela, *Long Walk*, 71, 73; Sampson, *Mandela*, 37.

49 Mandela, *Long Walk*, 148–49.

50 Nelson Mandela, "Black Man in a White Court," in *The Struggle Is My Life* (New York: Pathfinder Press, 1986), 151.

51 Luli Callinicos, *Oliver Tambo: Beyond the Engeli Mountains* (Cape Town: David Philip, 2004), 173.

52 Ibid., 174–75.

53 Mandela, *Long Walk*, 150.

54 Cicero, *De Officiis*, 1.20.

55 In the text that Mandela would have read in his course on native administrative law with Z. K. Matthews, by contrast, the informal character of "native courts" is described in considerable detail. See Hailey, *African Survey*, 294–315.

56 Callinicos, *Tambo*, 194.

57 Anthony Mathews, *Freedom, State Security, and the Rule of Law: Dilemmas of the Apartheid Society* (Cape Town: Juta, 1986), 101; H. R. Hahlo and I. A. Maisels, "The Rule of Law in South Africa" *Virginia Law Review* 52 (1966): 1, 17.

58 Mathews, *Freedom*, 125.

59 Aristotle, *Politics*, 1253a, 8–15.

60 J. L. Strachan-Davidson, *Problems of the Roman Criminal Law*, vol. II (Oxford: Clarendon Press, 1912), 18.

61 Mandela, "Black Man," 151.

62 Mandela, *Long Walk*, 144.

63 Mandela, "Black Man," 157.

64 Ibid.

65 Hoernlé, *Lectures*, 116, 119–20, 153–55.

66 Mandela, *Long Walk*, 271–74, cf. 127–28.

67 See also, on this point, Matthews, "Bantu Law," 33–34.

68 Nelson Mandela, "ANC Youth League Manifesto," in *The Struggle Is My Life*, 12–15, cf. 157.

69 Ibid., 24.

70 Ibid., 16.

71 Ibid., 24.

72 Ibid., 23.

73 Mandela, *Long Walk*, 98–101.

74 Noel Solani, "The Saint of the Struggle: Deconstructing the Mandela Myth," *Kronos* 26 (2000): 44.

75 As Martin Chanock once put it, "The elaboration of the administrative law seems to me to be at the heart of the legal processes in South Africa." See Chanock, "Writing South African Legal History: A Prospectus," *Journal of African History* 30.2 (1989): 286, cf. 273.

76 See Kaschula, "Mandela Comes Home," 102.

77 Letter from Nelson Mandela to Professor W. J. Hosken, Dean of the Faculty of Law, UNISA, November 25, 1988.

78 See Albie Sachs, *Justice in South Africa* (Berkeley: University of California Press, 1973), 218.

79 Mandela, "Black Man," 152–53.

80 Mandela, *Long Walk*, 325.

81 Mandela, "Black Man," 154.

82 On this point, see Catherine Cole, *Performing South Africa's Truth Commission: Stages of Transition* (Bloomington: Indiana University Press, 2010), 45–51.

83 Thomas Hobbes, *Leviathan*, ed. Richard Tuck (Cambridge: Cambridge University, 1996), 111–15, 120.

84 Susan Sontag, "This Man, This Country," in *For Nelson Mandela*, 50.

85 Smith, *Young Mandela*, 99.

86 Jacques Derrida, *The Sovereign and the Beast*, vol. I, ed. Michel Lisse, Marie-Louise Mallet, and Ginette Michaud, trans. Geoff Bennington (Chicago: University of Chicago Press, 2009), 17–18, 27–30, 32–58.

87 Asked how "the escape of [Arthur] Goldreich would affect the trial of those arrested at Goldreich's house in Rivonia," Minister of Justice John Vorster replied, "It will be more or less like producing Hamlet without the Prince. But the show will go on just the same." Joel Joffe, *The State vs. Nelson Mandela: The Trial That Changed South Africa* (Oxford: Oneworld, 2007), 9.

88 Kenneth Broun, *Saving Nelson Mandela: The Rivonia Trial and the Fate of South Africa* (Oxford: Oxford University Press, 2010), 19.

89 See, on this point, Denis Cowen and Daniel Visser, *The University of Cape Town Law Faculty: A History, 1859–2004* (Cape Town: Siber Ink, 2004), 148; cf. Denis Cowen, "The History of the Faculty of Law in the University of Cape Town, 1859–1959," *Acta Juridica* (1959): 14 n. 48.

90 On the influence of positivism on South African law under apartheid, see John Dugard, "The Jurisprudential Foundations of Apartheid Legal Order," *Philosophical Forum* 18.2–3 (1986–87): 115–18; Anthony Matthews, *Freedom, State Security and the Rule of Law: Dilemmas of the Apartheid Society* (Berkeley: University of California Press, 1986), 297.

91 John Austin, *The Province of Jurisprudence Determined* (Cambridge: Cambridge University Press, 1995), 18–37.

92 Joffe, *State vs. Nelson Mandela*, 44.

93 Ibid., 227.

94 Nelson Mandela, "Rivonia Trial," in *The Struggle Is My Life*, 167.

95 Joffe, *State vs. Nelson Mandela*, 93, 109; 246–47.

96 Derrida, "For Nelson Mandela," 18.

97 Ibid., 21.

98 Plato, *Euthyphro*, a 2. On Mandela and Socrates, see Barbara Harlow, "Speaking from the Dock," *Callaloo* 16.4 (Autumn 1993): 876.

99 Tom Lodge, *Politics in South Africa: From Mandela to Mbeki* (Bloomington: Indiana University Press, 2003), 8.

100 Elleke Boehmer, *Mandela: A Very Short Introduction* (Oxford: Oxford University Press, 2008), 132.

101 Mandela, *Long Walk*, 3; Derrida, "Laws of Reflection," 22, 38; Derrida, "Admiration de Nelson Mandela," 25, 41.

7

JONATHAN HYSLOP

Mandela on War

Nelson Mandela once remarked that "Shaka ... had tactics ... like those of Kutuzov against Napoleon."[1] This invocation of the French emperor and the Russian commander who opposed him, and the association of them with South Africa's most renowned indigenous military figure, may surprise the reader. But it is comprehensible in terms of two of Mandela's long-standing intellectual interests. He was an admirer of Tolstoy, whose novel *War and Peace*, set around the time of the 1812 invasion of Russia, Mandela apparently read in prison. And he was influenced, perhaps profoundly, by his reading of the work of a man who had fought in the Napoleonic Wars, the Prussian soldier and military theorist Carl von Clausewitz.

In mid-1961, Nelson Mandela, working underground to create a guerrilla movement, was hiding from the Security Police in a flat in the Johannesburg suburb of Berea. He spent much of his time reading and taking extensive notes on Clausewitz's magnum opus, *On War*. Mandela had started to read the book at the suggestion of the apartment's owner, Wolfie Kodesh, a Communist from the city's Jewish community. Mandela enjoyed Kodesh's conversation, and Kodesh would have been an interesting interlocutor on the subject of war. He had served in the South African forces in World War II and had been involved in the leadership of a leftist servicemen's organization, the Springbok Legion. Kodesh told Mandela that "Clausewitz was to war what Shakespeare was to literature."[2] Around this time, Mandela also read other books on warfare, including Deneys Reitz's luminous memoir of guerrilla fighting in the Boer War and volumes on the Communist-led insurgencies in the Philippines and Malaya, on Castro's revolution in Cuba, and on the violent Zionist campaign against the British in Palestine.[3] He also read Mao Zedong's work. Kodesh was impressed by Mandela's deep concentration and assiduous note taking.[4]

As the moment in Kodesh's flat suggests, Mandela was a serious student of military doctrine, and one who sought guidance on it from a wide variety of sources. This chapter explores the character and origins of Mandela's thinking on military power and political violence. It contends that Mandela developed his own concept of war and that this had important similarities with that of the long-dead Prussian general. Mandela was to recall in his autobiography that "Clausewitz's central thesis, that war was a continuation of diplomacy by other means, dovetailed with my own instincts."[5] There is a level at which Mandela was, indeed, an instinctive Clausewitzian. I do not mean to suggest that Mandela often consciously referred to Clausewitz. Mandela was an eminently practical political intellectual rather than a theoretically based, exegetically inclined scholar. But Clausewitz did strike a chord with him, because of their common concern with the complicated relationships between military means, military objectives, and popular support. There was an elective affinity between the way Mandela thought about these questions and Clausewitz's text.

Mandela has often been portrayed in international popular imaginations as a leader in the tradition of Gandhi and Martin Luther King, a proponent of principled non-violent resistance. But this is a completely misleading view. Not once in his career did Mandela endorse pacifism as a universal principle. Throughout his life, he believed that there were circumstances in which the use of violence was politically justified. His thought on this question, however, was always informed by a deep ethical concern and a sense of responsibility for the possible unintended consequences of violence. In recent years, an antithetical view has arisen among some writers in the tradition of postcolonial theory: a conception of Mandela as an anti-colonial revolutionary in the lineage of Frantz Fanon, favoring the purifying violence of insurrection by the oppressed. And in some cases, he is portrayed as oscillating between a violent Fanonism and a peaceful Gandhianism.[6] But Mandela was no Fanonian either. Unlike the revolutionary psychoanalyst, he never thought of armed resistance as offering any healing power for the colonized. Mandela's ideas about the use of force were pragmatic and instrumental. He was, indeed, influenced by leaders of the anti-colonial movement in which Fanon participated, the Algerian National Liberation Front (FLN). But their advice pointed him in a very different direction from that suggested by Fanon's theories. And Mandela's ethical approach to the use of force was informed by exactly the kind of humanist ideas that Fanon and postcolonial theorists eschew.

It is also important to recognize that Mandela's thought about warfare was shaped by the historical context of the Cold War. This is a sensitive point because the apartheid government always claimed, simplistically, that the African National Congress (ANC) was a Communist front and alleged that Mandela himself was a Communist. So historians have often avoided placing Mandela in relation to Communism in order to avoid the appearance of retrospectively endorsing this propaganda. But the reality is that many of Mandela's closest political colleagues were pro-Soviet Communists and that his movement did indeed receive material support from the Soviet Union. Given that in the 1960s the confrontation between the West and the Soviet Union in the global periphery was becoming increasingly militarized, it was inevitable that Mandela's ideas about war would also be influenced by the Communist movement. Moreover, good evidence is now emerging that Mandela was, at a crucial moment in his political life, from about 1958 until 1962, a member of the South African Communist Party (SACP).[7]

The Un-Gandhian Mandela

Mandela never seems to have been attracted by pacifism. He recalled in prison the impression made on him in his youth by tales of the historic African champions of military combat against colonialism and spoke of his continued veneration for them: "Heroes like the Khoi leader [Autshumayo], Maqoma of the Rharhabe, Bambatha, Cetswayo of the Zulu, Mampuru of the Pedis, Tshivashe of the Vendas and a host of others were in the forefront of wars of resistance and we speak of them with respect and admiration."[8] Like many of the African elite, Mandela strongly identified with the Allied cause in the early years of World War II. He described how, as a student at Fort Hare, he applauded an address in support of the war effort by Prime Minister Jan Smuts and listened to BBC broadcasts of Churchill's "stirring speeches."[9]

Although the peaceful campaigns of the ANC in the early 1950s were modeled on Indian *satyagraha* principles, Mandela was much more attracted by the pragmatic Nehru (who by then had already led India in a major war) than the utopian Gandhi.[10] And as his radicalization proceeded, he began to contemplate violent resistance. At a 1953 public meeting in Sophiatown, Mandela expressed the view that "non-violence was a useless strategy and could never overthrow a white minority regime bent on retaining its power at any cost.... Violence was the only weapon that would destroy apartheid, and we must be prepared in the near future to use that weapon."[11] Mandela was rapped over the knuckles by the ANC executive for his statement, but it clearly represented his real sentiments. In the same year, Mandela's closest political confidant, Walter Sisulu, had the opportunity to attend a youth congress in Romania and was to go on from there to the Soviet Union and China. Before leaving, he had a discussion with Mandela at which they agreed that Sisulu would raise the possibility of armed revolution with the Chinese leadership. However, when Sisulu broached the question with a high-powered delegation of the Communist Party of China, the idea was firmly rebuffed.[12] Mandela accepted this response, but the incident demonstrates Mandela's independent interest in armed methods and that he always was a believer in the possibility of a just war.

Mandela consistently emphasized that he saw non-violence as a tactic and not a principle: describing the political thinking of the ANC in the 1950s and early 1960s, he said that "[w]e took the attitude that we would stick to non-violence only insofar as the conditions permitted that. Once the conditions were against that, we would automatically abandon non-violence."[13] In 1969 he wrote to the minister of justice that "[w]orld history in general, and South African history in particular, teaches that resort to violence may in certain cases be perfectly legitimate."[14] In the same letter he suggested that those who enjoyed political rights would never be justified in resorting to armed force, but those denied such rights were entitled to do so if peaceful methods of change failed.

When the occasion to turn to armed struggle arrived, Mandela firmly grasped it. The Sharpeville Massacre sparked a political crisis in South Africa in March 1960, a state of emergency was declared, two thousand political activists, including Mandela, were detained, and shortly thereafter the ANC and Pan-African Congress were banned. There was widespread talk among the ANC prisoners about turning to violence. But serious planning for such a contingency began among a very small group who contrived to stay in touch despite being in prison; this group was composed of Mandela, Sisulu, Duma Nokwe, Joe Slovo, and Rusty Bernstein. At this time all five were Communist Party members. When Mandela was released, he remained a defendant in the long-running treason trial, in which he gave extensive evidence on his political thinking. By the end of 1960, Mandela was leading an initiative for an "All-in African Conference" that would call for a national convention to prepare an inclusive constitution. By this time the ANC and Communist Party leadership held out little hope that such a gathering would evoke a positive response from Dr. Verwoerd's government. The purpose, rather, was to show that every attempt had been made to bring about peaceful change before resorting to armed struggle. With the Afrikaner nationalist breakaway from the Commonwealth and the declaration of a republic scheduled for May 31, 1961, Mandela initiated a three-day strike for the period leading up to the ceremony. However, in a still poorly understood decision, Mandela became disheartened by the response to the strike, even though others saw it as fairly successful in the main urban centers, and he took responsibility for calling it off after the first day. On the same day, he told a British television interviewer that "if the government reaction is to crush by naked force our non-violent demonstrations, we will have to seriously reconsider our tactics. In my mind we are closing a chapter on non-violent tactics."[15] A month later, Mandela proposed to the ANC working committee that the movement adopt violent methods and form its own armed wing. At two subsequent meetings in Stanger, Natal, the debate continued. Mandela won his position, over the opposition of the ANC's revered head, Chief Albert Luthuli, who held to a steadfast Christian-Gandhian viewpoint. Mandela liked to claim that he had eventually persuaded Luthuli, but the evidence is overwhelming that the chief never changed his view, although he kept quiet about his opposition for reasons of organizational loyalty.[16]

Mandela now emerged as a military commander. He was appointed leader of the new armed organization, Umkhonto we Sizwe (MK), and was empowered to create its structure. This was eventually centralized around a hideout on Liliesleaf Farm in Rivonia, northern Johannesburg. On December 16, 1961, MK launched a campaign of sabotage. A decision was taken that MK needed to acquire logistical support, equipment, and training from African states, so in January 1962 Mandela left for a political tour of the continent. This took in many countries, but the greatest impression was made on him by his discussions with members of the Algerian FLN, whom he visited at their bases in Morocco and who were about to take power in their own country after years of fighting against French colonial power. He also made a visit to England with his colleague Oliver Tambo, who was busy establishing the ANC's exile organization. The journey concluded with a course of military training in Ethiopia. This was cut short by a call for Mandela to return to South Africa. He came back in late July. Mandela's African travels appear to have marked the end of his membership of the Communist Party; while most of his closest collaborators continued to be among the Communists, his political and military thinking became more independent from this point. After a visit to comrades in Durban, Mandela was arrested on August 5 on the way back to Johannesburg. In November 1962, he was sentenced to five years' imprisonment for incitement and for leaving the country without a passport. On July 11, 1963, Liliesleaf Farm was raided by the police, breaking the MK command structure. Mandela was brought to trial with other arrested leaders, charged with treason. Much of the trial focused on a document for "Operation Mayibuye," a plan for a hugely ambitious guerrilla offensive with foreign support. It remains unclear how much of a hand Mandela had in this. The accused mounted a political defense of their resort to violence, culminating in Mandela's great speech from the dock. The defendants faced the possibility of the death penalty, but in July 1964 they received life sentences.

The Un-Fanonian Mandela

Mandela was attracted to guerrilla warfare as an instrument for bringing about change. But he did not embrace the glorification of insurrection to which this could and did lead in the thought of some of the "Third Worldists" of the time. He believed in the application of the minimum force necessary to bring about his political objectives.

Mandela's military doctrine was deeply influenced by the example of the Algerian FLN, but not in the ways one might expect, given the present-day renown of Frantz Fanon. There is no evidence that Mandela ever read Fanon and, although Fanon had been part of the FLN exile apparatus in North Africa, he had died the year before Mandela visited Morocco. Moreover, Fanon's views were at odds with those of the mainstream of the FLN leadership. He had supported a faction led by Abane Ramdane, which rejected any form of negotiation with the French before the colonial power recognized Algeria's independence. The majority of the FLN leaders, under Belkacem Krim, gave their verdict on this position in 1958, when they had Ramdane executed and placed Fanon on a list of those who would have to be repressed if Ramdane's supporters created trouble.[17]

On his 1962 visit to the FLN, Mandela was especially impressed by Chawki Mostefai, the head of the Algerian mission in Morocco. Mandela recalled many years later that "[v]ery few things inspired me as the briefing from Dr. Mostefai."[18] Mostefai explained to Mandela that the FLN had initially believed that they could defeat the French militarily but had come to see that "a purely military victory was impossible."[19] Instead they had focused on political warfare. Mandela recalled in his biography that Mostefai argued that guerrilla war was not designed to win a military victory so much as to unleash political and economic forces that would bring down the enemy. "[Mostefai] advised us not to neglect the political side of war while planning the military effort. International opinion, he said, is sometimes worth more than a fleet of jet fighters."[20] This analysis has been mostly confirmed by the work of subsequent historians. The FLN had largely been defeated on the battlefield by the French army by 1959, but the political convulsions that they created within the French body politic won them their independence. A crucial role in this process was played by the small but astute FLN delegation at the UN, through their activity in isolating the French diplomatically.[21]

The ANC in exile learned a great deal from the FLN's use of international forums. But large sections of the ANC increasingly developed delusions about their ability to overthrow the regime militarily. Mandela, by contrast, seems always to have believed that military pressure on the regime was designed to create a crisis leading to a negotiated political solution. His discussion with the FLN was to shape his subsequent thinking. Neville Alexander, a politically independent revolutionary and friend of Mandela's on Robben Island during the 1960s, was appalled when Mandela told him that he had learned from the Algerians that "there was no point in trying to overthrow the apartheid regime: the ANC had to force them to the negotiating table."[22] In his draft autobiography, written in prison, Mandela stated that "[t]he ANC never deviated from the principle that the liberation of our country would ultimately be brought about through dialogue and negotiation."[23] This was not strictly true of significant parts of the organization, but it was the case with Mandela himself.

Thus the initial approach to warfare by the ANC was carefully calibrated. In the first round of MK attacks, only property was targeted.[24] Subsequently, military and police personnel were attacked, but not civilians. The policy of the ANC through the 1960s and 1970s was not to attack white civilians; they did not launch any of the types of bombings of civilian venues that the FLN frequently used in Algeria and France. Although this prohibition eroded in practice in the 1980s, it did not do so with Mandela's blessing. Mandela also specifically repudiated the "necklace" killings of the 1980s, in which ANC supporters burned alleged spies to death.[25] His thinking in these cases was highly pragmatic. If the long-term goal was a political deal with the old regime, then excessive forms of violence would make that difficult to achieve.

But this standpoint was also rooted in a universalist set of values that derived both from the liberal Christianity of his missionary education in the Eastern Cape and from humanist elements in the Marxism to which he was exposed in Johannesburg. He adopted a form of humanism that would be scorned by Fanonians. Thus when Fanon dismisses "this Europe where they were never done talking of Man," because "we know the price paid for every one of their triumphs of the mind," he would seem to be a long way from Mandela with his love of the Greek classics and Tolstoy, his self-confessed Anglophilia, and his persistent attempts to win over his Afrikaner prison warders.[26] Though Mandela abandoned formal religion, there are strong signs that he continued to subscribe to a very Protestant set of values (or perhaps a Stoic one, as David Schalkwyk argues in Chapter 2). He wrote to his wife from prison in 1975: "Honesty, sincerity, simplicity, humility, pure generosity, absence of vanity, readiness to serve others – qualities which are within easy reach of every soul – are the foundation of one's spiritual life."[27]

Another aspect of Mandela's vision of military strategy that does not jibe well with radical Third Worldist notions is its non-racialism – a remarkable feature of the ANC in the period between the 1950s and 1990s. Unlike African nationalist movements elsewhere in the continent, it did not envisage the expulsion of the white or Indian minorities after the political transition. Non-racialism implied both the inclusion of sympathetic whites and Indians in political struggles and the inclusion of people of all races in a future political dispensation. Non-racialism became a fixed part of Mandela's personal beliefs. Mandela's personal openness to it was a product of a number of factors, including a relatively non-conflictual relationship with missionary teachers in his early years, his great personal self-confidence, and some of the cosmopolitan influences of daily life in Johannesburg in the 1940s. But there is no doubt that the major factor was Mandela's experience of the friendship and comradeship of white and Indian Communists with whom he began working at the end of the 1940s.[28]

Mandela also differed from Fanonians in that he did not see the peasantry as the "truly" revolutionary class. It would, in any case, have been hard to find classic "peasants" in the South Africa of the early 1960s, as rural communities were by then heavily reliant on incomes derived from migrant labor in the cities. Despite his pride in his traditionalist rural background, Mandela delightedly embraced the cultures of the working class and black intelligentsia of the Rand townships when he arrived there in the 1940s. And his organizing work, aboveground in the 1940s and underground in the early 1960s, was focused on the urban world. Thus during his reading on warfare he was excited to discover Menachem Begin's account of Zionist attacks on the British in Palestine because "it was a movement in a country which had no mountains"; in other words, the book showed that it was not necessary to have a rural base in order to wage guerrilla war. [29]

Mandela as an "Instinctive" Clausewitzian

While I would not want to claim that Mandela often consciously referred to Clausewitz, the long-dead Prussian general's thought has a far closer affinity to Mandela's thinking about war and violence than that of the Mahatma, Martin Luther King, or Fanon. At one point in his interviews with the co-author of his autobiography, the US journalist Richard Stengel, Mandela made the following comments about his early reading of military literature:

> [I]t was to find out firstly, what are the principles of starting a revolution? An armed revolution, armed warfare. That's why I read Clausewitz, because it did not deal with guerrilla warfare; it deals with the rules of war, the principles of war.[30]

Here Mandela is identifying, albeit somewhat inarticulately, the conceptual problem of the gray lines between war, revolution, and politics in the modern world, an issue for which Clausewitz is a crucial starting point. Mandela thought of the struggle on which he embarked as a combination of all three of these phenomena. This reflects not confusion on his part, but the reality that in modern times attempts to draw simple distinctions between war, revolution, and politics frequently come adrift. Mandela's "instinctive" feel for Clausewitz came from an understanding that *On War* addressed this complexity in a very far-sighted way.

Although an influential school of military theory has recently persuaded many that "asymmetrical warfare" in which states confront non-state insurgents is a development of recent decades, the historical picture is considerably more complex than that. In the eighteenth century, Europe was increasingly able to impose on the world a highly ritualized form of war in which, in conflicts between *soi-disant* "civilized" nations, the officer class of different countries observed common conventions – at least in theory. The states of the ancien régime had a common fear of arming their people, often preferring reliable foreign mercenaries for their soldiery. The wars of the French Revolution transformed this situation in two major ways. On the one hand, the revolutionary and Napoleonic military leadership created the idea of a fully mobilized nation in arms, in which the whole people was engaged in war. On the other hand, there were movements of popular, and increasingly nationalist, resistance to the French, characterized by the techniques of what became known, after the Spanish example, as the guerrilla.

Clausewitz, as an officer of the Prussian army, participated actively in the Napoleonic Wars and was especially involved in 1812–13 in organizing a popular armed militia against the French. He was thus on the cutting edge of the breakdown of distinctions between politics, war, and revolution, and it is not surprising that Mandela should have found him an empathetic thinker. Indeed, Mandela had a better grasp of Clausewitz's approach than do scholars who see him only as a proponent of wars between states. Clausewitz was the most political of military thinkers. For him, modern warfare was based on the interaction of three dimensions: political purposes, military instruments, and "popular passions."[31] Mandela, too, saw the tools of war as situated between his political objectives and the political ideas of the populace. He, too, placed political considerations before military ones.

The French Revolution, then, radically destabilized the boundaries between war and revolution, and military lawyers spent much of the next century trying to put the revolutionary genie back in the bottle.[32] The Geneva Conventions tried to establish the rights of uniformed combatants and, although often honored in the breach, the idea that prisoners of war should be fairly treated established considerable international legitimacy for itself. The Hague Conventions tried to lay down the principle that civilian populations should be protected, provided that they did not engage in armed resistance to a foreign army. But a consequence of these attempts to regulate war was that the civilian guerrilla, who was to become an increasingly central figure of modern warfare, had no protection at all. He or she could legitimately be shot as a bandit.

Yet the experience of World War II was to shift the international political-legal framework of warfare again, in a way that had important consequences for Mandela and the ANC. Because both the Soviet Union, on the one hand, and Britain and the United States, on the other, had been strongly supportive of underground armed civilian resistance to Nazi occupation in Europe, there was an impetus to amend international law to recognize and protect civilian combatants. This was put into practice in the 1949 revision of the Geneva Conventions.[33] Thus, as anti-colonial movements developed in Africa and Asia in the post-war years, a new ideological space was opened for national liberation organizations to demand legal protection for their fighters. But even more, by according to guerrillas the status of troops of national armies, the new legal regime helped the movements from which guerrillas came to claim the status of state authority for themselves.

For the ANC this new situation was to open political opportunities, but also to create dilemmas. The framing of the ANC as a statelike organization and MK as its army took effective advantage of the changes in international politico-legal discourse to legitimize the struggle. But in the future, the model of formal warfare with its absolute distinction between friend and enemy was to prove difficult to reconcile with Mandela's aim of a negotiated settlement within a single national political entity.

Many military theorists came to see Clausewitz as the forerunner of the merciless twentieth-century doctrine of total war. Clausewitz's emphasis on the concentration of overwhelming offensive force against the enemy seemed to accord with this view. So did his idea of "absolute war," in which the pure logic of war pushes in the direction of the complete destruction of the enemy. But absolute war is a kind of ideal-typical notion that cannot be realized in the complicated actuality of the world. For Clausewitz, the "friction" of contingency ensures that "real war" is constrained and must, almost necessarily, be conducted in a more limited manner.[34] Clausewitz's approach required a balance between his tripartite division of political objective, military means, and popular support. To set unrealistic objectives – to demand more from the enemy than one's actual military force can extract and to exhaust popular support – is to court defeat. In this sense Clausewitz is an advocate of compromise with reality rather than of total war. Mandela, too, had a strong sense of the limits of the possible. He knew from the beginning that the ANC's military campaign could not be conducted successfully without reference to its political objectives and consideration of its relationship to popular support.

And he also understood that military means are always finite. The standard radical critique of Mandela has been that, in the transition of the early 1990s, he compromised with the old regime, thereby allowing continuity of the old social structures. According to both African nationalist and leftist critics, he should have continued the armed struggle to the point of a revolutionary overthrow of the old regime. But this is advocacy of an abstraction. By 1990 there was absolutely no evidence that the military power of the old regime was crumbling. Although their actions were popular, the guerrillas remained militarily marginal, and there was plenty of evidence that the deadlocked conflict was leading to social fragmentation rather than unified insurgency. Mandela grasped, both in principle and in the specific circumstances of the 1990s, that "absolute" war was neither possible nor desirable.

The Military Politics of the Cold War

Mandela's military thought should also be set in relation to the history of South African Communism and of the international Cold War. In a situation where the Western powers were backing the Pretoria government as a lesser evil than the extension of Soviet influence in South Africa, while Moscow was firmly opposed to Pretoria, the Soviet Union looked attractive to African nationalists. Moreover, Marxism provided a plausible ideological critique of colonialism and imperialism. And the local Communists were certainly indefatigable in their political campaigning against apartheid.

It is not surprising, then, that an ANC–SACP alliance developed apace from around 1950. What is important to understand here is that most in the ANC came to see the world in Cold War terms, with the Soviet Union and the Communist movement as their allies against the Pretoria government and the West. Mandela came to admire some of the key ideas of Marxism – especially the notion of the classless society – and, for nearly a decade before the ANC went underground, Communists of all races were among his closest personal friends and collaborators. Then, around 1958, it appears that Mandela joined the Communist Party. This moment was a crucial one, because his subsequent, approximately four years of party membership coincided with a shift by the Soviet Union toward support for guerrilla insurgencies in Africa, Asia, and Latin America. Although the ANC's turn to the armed struggle was driven primarily by national developments, it took place at the same time as, and was reinforced by, this change in Soviet policy.[35] This policy, which was to continue until the mid-1980s, would contribute to the ANC in exile becoming increasingly caught in a militarized politics.

A number of the key South African Communists of the era were World War II veterans. They tended to see the world through the lens of their participation in the war against Hitler. Thus they identified the National Party regime with Nazism. Given the Nazi analogy, Communists thought in terms of the political models of the Popular Front of the 1930s and the Grand Alliance of the 1940s, in which "democrats" across a broad ideological spectrum would ally against Fascism. This legitimized their alliance with the "nationalist" ANC. Given the World War II framing of the struggle by the Communists, they could easily envisage themselves in the model of the anti-Fascist resistance of the war years. And indeed, World War II–era white ex-servicemen did much of the logistical work for the 1961–62 bombing campaign. There was also a strong tendency to transfuse ideas from Communist experience elsewhere into the movement. Thus the theory of the "National Democratic Revolution," which became the doctrine of the ANC and SACP during the 1960s was not, as is frequently claimed, a uniquely South African creation. Its origins are traceable to the ideology developed in Eastern Europe by the Stalinist parties in the late 1940s to chart the political direction of the new pro-Soviet states.[36]

The Communist understanding of the conflict opened up potential sympathy for ideas of armed struggle and gelled with Mandela's impatience with peaceful methods. The turn to armed struggle in 1960–61 was inspired by the Communist Party and ANC's admiration for Castro's revolution in Cuba and for the Algerian FLN, as well as by their excitement over informal rural insurgency in the Pondoland area of Cape Province. But this policy was also responsive to a shift toward local confrontations with the West in the global politics of the Soviet Union. This is not to say that the Communist Party was following orders from Moscow. Indeed, a minority of the party objected to the turn to violence. Much energy has been expended by ultra-right-wing authors in showing that the South African party took instructions from Moscow and by sympathetic writers in showing that it did not. But this is, in a way, to miss the point. The South African Communists wanted to support the Soviet Union. They did not lack initiative or independent ideas, but their desire was to be aligned with the policies of the USSR, which they saw as the cornerstone of international "progressive" politics. They could be relied on to act accordingly without direction from outside.

The Soviet willingness to support anti-colonial insurgency was new. Once decolonization became a rising reality in the late 1940s, the Soviet approach was not so much to support the movements against colonialism as to build close relationships with those newly independent Asian and African governments that they saw as progressive. Even at the height of the 1950s Cold War, questions of realpolitik made the Soviet Union wary of encouraging local Communists to take radical anti-colonial positions. For example, in the Algerian War during the 1950s, the Soviet Union gave virtually no support to the FLN and the French Communist Party did not call for separation from Algeria, largely because the Soviet Union believed that it was necessary to strengthen the anti-American sentiments of the French political establishment in order to isolate the United States in Europe.

However, the early 1960s saw something of a radicalization of the Soviet stance. In part this was because of China's challenge to the international leadership of the Communist movement, with its rhetoric of global guerrilla militancy. The Soviet Union stood to be outflanked on the left by Mao. In Europe, the success of the FLN had inspired a support movement among political radicals in which Trotskyists, anarchists, and other dissident leftists had taken the lead, again posing problems for mainstream Communists.[37] These factors pushed the Soviet Union and its allied parties toward a more militarist and radical stance on anti-colonial revolution. But there was also a way in which the aging Soviet leadership found itself inspired and reconnected with its historical radicalism by the new revolutionary movements on the periphery. After an early 1960 meeting with Fidel Castro, which took place during a no-frills trip to the Cuban leader's hunting cabin, the senior Soviet leader Anastas Mikoyan exclaimed: "Yes, this is a real revolution. Just like ours. I feel as though I've returned to my youth."[38]

The conjuncture of the early 1960s, with these new confrontations, gave a fresh impetus and radicalism to Soviet strategy in Africa, Asia, and Latin America. Nikita Khrushchev saw the rise of insurgencies and "progressive" governments in the Third World as opening up new political space for the Soviet Union: "The success of the national liberation movement, due in large measure to the victories of socialism, in turn strengthens the international positions of socialism in the struggle against imperialism."[39] Thus, while the turn of the ANC and the SACP to armed struggle was not dictated in any direct way by the Soviet Union, it coincided with and was largely enabled by a shift in Soviet policy toward the colonial and postcolonial world. On the global periphery, the Cold War was about to become hot.

During Mandela's active leadership of MK, links to the Soviet Union expanded. Direct connections between the SACP and the Soviet Communist Party were resumed in 1960, when a delegation led by Yusuf Dadoo visited Moscow and direct subventions to the SACP began. The upgrading of the importance of South Africa in the Soviet mind was reflected in the allocation in November 1961 to Central Committee member Boris Ponomarev of a South African portfolio, a responsibility he held over the next twenty-five years. Following a visit by Mandela's old comrade, Oliver Tambo, to Moscow in 1963, military collaboration between the Soviet Union and the ANC became extremely close: MK members began to be sent to a camp near Odessa for training later that year, and a special facility for training the South Africans was opened at Prevalnoye in the Crimea.[40]

Mandela and the Problem of Militarism

Recalling his days underground in later years Mandela commented that "[w]e wanted to avoid militarism."[41] But with Mandela in prison, the ANC very quickly drifted away from his belief in armed struggle as a means to force the regime to the negotiating table, replacing it with a belief that it was actually possible to overthrow the state by force. This represented in many ways a misunderstanding of the implications of the Cuban and Algerian experiences. The Batista regime in Cuba was socially isolated and crumbling from within at the time of the Fidelist uprising. The French had been able to withdraw from Algeria. By contrast, during the 1960s and 1970s, the white South African regime was constructing a formidable new military machine and honing its bureaucracy, and there was no possibility of its withdrawal to a metropolis. The sociological literature on revolutions strongly suggests that revolutionaries take power not so much by seizing states as by entering the vacuum that is created when coercive power collapses or is withdrawn.[42] The regime in South Africa was powerful and resilient and was to remain so throughout the anti-apartheid struggle.

As the initial attempts to develop guerrilla war failed, the exiles did not draw the conclusion that it was a doomed strategy. Rather, they sought better military models. Following a visit by a leadership delegation to Vietnam in 1978, the ANC adopted a new version of the guerrilla strategy known as "protracted people's war." By the late 1970s, elements of the MK leadership had increasingly come to believe in the possibility of the armed overthrow of the state, and this sense was heightened by the massive upsurges of resistance in the townships in 1984–86. But as the successful repression of the revolt in the 1986 state of emergency showed, the state was nowhere near collapse.

During the prison years, a considerable gap opened up between Mandela and the exile leaders. Although Mandela certainly favored a strong guerrilla campaign, he does not seem, in prison, to have departed from the idea that it was one of a number of measures to force the regime to the negotiating table. And, no longer a member of the Communist Party, he was able to shape his own strategy.

A major factor in this divergence was that in exile the ANC underwent a militarization from which Mandela was largely shielded by his imprisonment. To some extent this was the product of the bureaucratic logic of entanglement with the Soviet bloc and its military apparatus. In exile MK received, between the 1960s and mid-1980s, extensive military training and material support from the USSR, Cuba, East Germany, and other Eastern bloc countries. Mandela certainly favored this connection and was always grateful to these countries for the support they had provided at a time when the West was covertly backing the Vorster and Botha governments. He was, for example, always warm in his admiration for Fidel Castro.[43] But the structure of MK abroad led it to became politically sclerotic in its thinking. Senior ANC leader Mac Maharaj, who had been a friend and comrade of Mandela's in prison, found, when he went into exile in the late 1970s, that "work amongst the masses had been neglected inside the country. There was no political underground. The struggle was being pursued almost exclusively in armed terms, whether armed propaganda or sabotage or clashes with enemy forces. The de facto position now was that only armed struggle was the way forward ... in practice, the Revolutionary Council had tilted the balance between the military and political struggle in favor of the military."[44] Maharaj was not without militarist inclinations himself, but he was horrified at MK chief Joe Modise's lack of understanding of the political dimension of warfare.[45] MK had lost a proper Clausewitzian appreciation of the complexity of the relationship between its limited military means, popular support, and feasible political objectives.

But the militarist position was also to be found on Robben Island, where Mandela and Sisulu constantly had to defend a flexible conception of the relationship between war and politics against a significant faction of prisoners led by the dogmatic Stalinists Govan Mbeki and Harry Gwala, who were constantly attempting to collapse the ANC into the Communist Party and to advocate crude versions of militarism.[46] Mandela and Sisulu's negotiating skills and constant drive for consensus usually gained the upper hand, but the problem reflected how far militarism grew in influence.

Mandela in the Transition

Mandela played a crucial role in leading the ANC out of its impasse of the mid-1980s. It is characteristic of Mandela's public persona that he subordinated himself to the collectivity of the ANC, always portraying himself as just another member of the movement. This was at one level a sincerely held belief and suited the collectivist ethos of the movement. But in reality, he often broke new ground through personal leadership. In an interview with Stengel,

Mandela recalled his decision to initiate negotiations with the regime in 1985: "If I had told my friends that I was going to [negotiate] ... they would have rejected it. So what I decided to do was to start negotiations without telling them, and then confront them with a fait accompli."[47] It is true that a small group in the exiled ANC led by Thabo Mbeki engaged in negotiation from around the same time. But Mandela's initiative was all-important. It signified his understanding that the ANC was in a strong position because of the scope of internal resistance to the regime and apartheid's isolation, but that it was not in a position to seize power by military means or likely to be so at any time in the future.

In the ANC's difficult negotiations with the regime after his release from prison in 1990, Mandela held out the prospect of a reconciliatory peaceful settlement. When he felt it necessary, he confronted his followers in order to break them of their militarism. In a notorious incident, he was booed at a mass rally in Durban when he told the crowd to throw their weapons into the sea. Yet he never took off the table the possibility of a resort to arms if things went wrong. Just months before the democratic elections of 1994, Mandela met with the leaders of the intransigent wing of the Afrikaner nationalists, General Constand Viljoen and Ferdi Hartzenberg. Mandela bluntly asked them if they were planning to stop the poll by violent means. Viljoen answered in the affirmative, threatening civil war. Mandela recalled: "I was shaken but pretended that I was supremely confident of the victory of the liberation movement. I told them that they would give us a hard time.... But in the end they would be crushed."[48] Despite his uncertainty, Mandela made the necessary threat of force. So, while there is no doubt that Mandela underwent a complex process of personal development as a leader in prison, it is clearly mistaken to think that he emerged as Gandhian.

What Mandela's current critics on the left do not understand is that it was the right that wanted and would have benefited from the collapse of the negotiations. The ANC was not in a position to win an armed struggle outright. The alternative was not victory, but collapse into a Yugoslavia-style morass of civil war. Thus Mandela explained the strategy of giving vent to the emotions generated by the 1993 assassination of Communist leader Chris Hani through a series of demonstrations: "If we had not done so the right wing and those sinister elements would have succeeded in drawing the country [in]to a racist war and incalculable loss of human lives and bloodshed.... [W]e frustrated the objective of the people who killed Hani."[49] It is difficult on any sober reckoning of the situation in the early 1990s to dispute Mandela's evaluation of the likely consequences of the failure to reach a negotiated solution.

Conclusion

While the courage of Mandela and his comrades in embarking on the armed struggle remains deeply impressive, the wisdom of it is questionable. Discussions of the decision often blur two very different questions. These are, first, was the turn to armed struggle ethically justified and, second, was it effective? It is entirely possible that the answer to the first question is affirmative but that the answer to the second is still negative. Arguments for complete pacifism have a compelling moral power, but in an imperfect world few would embrace the full logic of Gandhianism. Most would accept that resistance to tyranny does at some point justify the resort to violence; the issue then is at what point that turn comes. Certainly, South Africa in 1960 was a racial tyranny. Certainly, the state had rebuffed calls for peaceful change. And there is no doubt as well that the 1960 emergency marked a qualitative intensification of state repression; detention without trial was introduced and torture of political activists, almost unknown in the 1950s, became common. So there might be a moral case for the resort to force.

But in terms of political effectiveness, the strategy did not work. This cannot be reduced to the contingency of the capture of the ANC leadership at Liliesleaf Farm. The plans for insurrection hatched by the underground leadership were wildly impractical. Despite the intensified repression of the early 1960s, it is far from clear that the possibilities of using aboveground forms of organizing had been exhausted – as quite a number of leading ANC and Communist figures suggested at the time. The decision to abandon aboveground organization diverted the energies of political activists away from sustaining such political initiatives.

Subsequently, the focus on military strategies tended to make the exiled ANC obtuse in its relationship to new aboveground movements that developed in the country. While there is no doubt that bombings of strategic facilities were morale boosters for the movement against the regime, guerrillaism never rose to a level that really threatened the state. In the end, internal revolts by trade unions, civic organizations, and youth movements, international pressures on the regime, economic decline, and socio-political shifts within the white polity were more important than the armed struggle in bringing about the end of apartheid.

And militarism has had unforeseen consequences in undermining the construction of a democratic politics in post-apartheid South Africa. By identifying the ANC primarily with MK, and the ANC and MK with the nation, and by carrying this set of identifications forward into the era of peace, the ANC saddled itself with a symbolism that was hardly compatible with politics in a constitutional democracy. Political opponents were often regarded more as wartime enemies than as democratic competitors. The ANC refused to acknowledge that it was now simply one of several political parties and tended to conflate itself with the state in a way that has undermined the autonomy of independent institutions. Moreover, despite the limited role MK played in the South African conflict and the passage of nearly two decades since the laying down of arms, the imagery of armed struggle still pervades much that the ANC says. There is a kind of celebration of the soldier as the perfect citizen, which casts a pall over attempts to construct a civic and civil discourse. The young populist leader Julius Malema's 2008 call for his supporters to "shoot to kill" for the election of Jacob Zuma as president exemplifies the problem. And when Malema later fell out with Zuma, the association of MK veterans felt called upon to remind him that, in their camps in Angola, he would have been shot for mutiny.

The political philosopher John Keane has pointed to the political dangers inherent in contemporary tendencies to produce an "ontology of conflict" in which attempts to generate ethical discourses are seen as necessarily masking power. In this ontology, violence is aestheticized.[50] Unmediated conflict is seen as somehow authentic and pure, and compromise and conciliation as weakly artificial. Mandela, however, recognized the validity of resort to arms without giving in to the temptation of romanticizing violence. As a military leader he managed to utilize force in a way that was pragmatic and ethically informed. And in constructing peace, he understood that all political arrangements are in a sense artificial: that to establish a constitutional state after civil conflict requires infinitely intricate constructive work that challenges the Manichaean distinctions of friend and enemy the logic of war tends to create. He managed, to use Keane's words, to "think against common sense views of ... conflict ... to see instead that the self and other, the internal and the external, may well not be opposites, but that they are often enough always inside one another."[51] In understanding that South Africa could not avoid violent conflict but that the prosecution of conflict without limit was a danger to any possibility of creating a viable future society, Mandela charted an intelligent and principled course. And this can also be understood as a notably Clausewitzian way of thinking: Mandela grasped that responsible leadership requires a recognition of the conditions of real war, of the limits of what it can achieve, and of the problems that flow from it, rather than the pursuit of the chimera of absolute war.

NOTES

1 Nelson Mandela, *Conversations with Myself* (New York: Farrar, Straus and Giroux, 2010), 259.
2 Anthony Sampson, *Mandela: The Authorised Biography* (Johannesburg: Jonathan Ball, 1999), 153.
3 Mandela, *Conversations*, 107.
4 Interview with Kodesh by John Carlin on PBS, no date given; www.pbs.org/wgbh/pages/frontline/shows/mandela/interviews/kodesh.html.
5 Nelson Mandela, *Long Walk to Freedom* (London: Abacus, 2007), 328.
6 See e.g., Elleke Boehmer, *Nelson Mandela: A Very Short Introduction* (Oxford: Oxford University Press, 2008).
7 On this matter I follow Bonner in Chapter 1.
8 Mandela, *Conversations*, 31.
9 Mandela, *Long Walk*, 58.
10 Mandela, *Conversations*, 53.
11 Ibid., 182.
12 Ibid., 74.
13 Mandela, *Long Walk*, 53.
14 Mandela, *Conversations*, 146.
15 Sampson, *Mandela*, 148.
16 Scott Couper, *Albert Luthuli: Bound by Faith* (Pietermaritzburg: UKZN Press, 2010).
17 David Macey, *Frantz Fanon: A Life* (London: Granta, 2001), 337–38, 355–56.
18 Mandela, *Conversations*, 95.
19 Mandela, *Long Walk*, 355.
20 Ibid.
21 Matthew Connelly, *A Diplomatic Revolution: Algeria's Fight for Freedom and the Origins of the Post-Cold War Era* (New York: Oxford University Press, 2002).
22 Sampson, *Mandela*, 166.
23 Mandela, *Conversations*, 248.
24 Ibid., 147.
25 Ibid., 256.
26 Frantz Fanon, *The Wretched of the Earth* (New York: Penguin, 2001), 312; Mandela, *Conversations*, 113–14.
27 Ibid., 211.
28 Ibid., 44.
29 Ibid., 106.
30 Ibid.
31 There is a vast literature on Clausewitz, but the following are particularly instructive: Peter Paret, "Clausewitz," in *Makers of Modern Strategy*, ed. Peter Paret (Princeton, NJ: Princeton University Press, 1976), 186–213; Ian Roxborough, "Clausewitz and the Sociology of War," *British Journal of Sociology* 45 (1994): 619–36; Hew Strachan, *Carl von Clausewitz's "On War"* (London: Atlantic, 2007).
32 See Carl Schmitt, *Theory of the Partisan* (New York: Telos, 2007).
33 Martin van Creveld, *The Culture of War* (New York: Ballantine, 2008), 299.

34 Hew Strachan, *Clausewitz's "On War,"* 147–90.

35 Odd Arne Westad, *The Global Cold War* (Cambridge: Cambridge University Press, 2007).

36 As was demonstrated by Peter Hudson in a 1986 article "The Freedom Charter and the Theory of National Democratic Revolution," www.transformation. ukzn.ac.za/index.php/transformation/article/view/385/204.

37 Jan Willem Stutje, *Ernest Mandel: Rebel Tussen Droom en Daad, 1923–1995* (Antwerp/Ghent: Houtekiet/Amsab-ISG, 2007), 146–57.

38 Christopher Andrew and Vasili Mitrokhin, *The World Was Going Our Way: The KGB and the Battle for the Third World* (New York: Basic Books, 2005), 36.

39 Westad, *Global Cold War*, 166.

40 Vladimir Shubin, *ANC: A View From Moscow* (Johannesburg: Jacana, 2008), 9–39.

41 Mandela, *Conversations*, 108.

42 Theda Skocpol, *States and Social Revolutions* (Cambridge: Cambridge University Press, 1979).

43 Mandela, *Conversations*, 389; Nelson Mandela and Fidel Castro, *How Far We Slaves Have Come! South Africa and Cuba in Today's World* (New York: Pathfinder, 1991).

44 Padraig O'Malley, *Shades of Difference: Mac Maharaj and the Struggle for South Africa* (New York: Penguin, 2008), 218.

45 Ibid., 224.

46 Mac Maharaj, in ibid., provides a convincingly devastating account of the machinations of Govan Mbeki and Harry Gwala against Mandela, both in prison and after their release.

47 Mandela, *Conversations*, 246.

48 Ibid., 353.

49 Ibid., 339–40.

50 John Keane, *Global Civil Society?* (Cambridge: Cambridge University Press, 2003), 181–82.

51 Ibid., 182.

8

SIFISO MXOLISI NDLOVU

Mandela's Presidential Years:
An Africanist View

When Rolihlahla Nelson Mandela was released from prison in 1990, there were internal dynamics in the liberation movement that might have scuppered his ascendancy to the presidency of both the African National Congress (ANC) and the country. But this did not happen, because Mandela's colleagues in the ANC made it possible for him to reach the pinnacle of politics and assume the presidency. To say this is not to downplay Mandela's personal role in his achievement. His demeanor while in prison, including his loyal and supportive behavior toward his colleagues in the liberation movement, was praiseworthy. He harbored no overt personal ambitions and insisted that not he, but Oliver Tambo, headed the ANC and that all members of the organization should be accountable to Tambo. This was one of the liberation movement's strengths: Mandela, Walter Sisulu, Wilton Mkwayi, and other long-term prisoners bore no personal animosities or jealousies toward Tambo; they respected him profoundly. Tambo, in turn, supported efforts to use Mandela, through the Release Mandela Campaign, as a unifying symbol of the anti-colonial struggle. This was a case of mutual affection that displayed the human side of the liberation struggle in South Africa. It also says a great deal about both men's maturity and level of political consciousness. The collective and consultative traditions of the ANC proved invaluable during Mandela's term as the first president of the democratic Republic of South Africa. These traditions, as much as Mandela's charismatic personality, shaped the style and the achievements of his brief time in office.

Much of what has been written about Mandela's presidency, insofar as it tends to emphasize the man's unique personal agency and iconic stature, is refracted through Western eyes. The focus on Mandela the individual – evident in many assessments of his presidency as a miraculous golden age – is ideologically biased: it deploys, ultimately, an ahistorical theory of humanity and individual agency. At stake is often a kind of feel-good universalism that presumes to pass for objectivity. The Clint Eastwood film *Invictus* (discussed in Chapter 10 by Litheko Modisane) is a good example of this effect: a sentimental story of racial reconciliation, effected by a single saintly man, is yoked to quasi-documentary footage of the struggle and inauguration. The familiar grand narrative of national reconciliation in which Africans are all too often expected to forgive and forget about racism and past injustices by colonizers is one that conforms to a predetermined template of racelessness. In my view, this kind of narrative, with its superficial universalism, is actually covertly racist.[1] Books, films, documentaries, and other publications on Mandela's presidency expressed in African languages and privileging an Afrocentric viewpoint are notably scarce. Frequently, accounts of his efforts at reconciliation, his lack of bitterness, and so forth, confuse *ubuntu* (a spirit of fellowship and humanity) as practiced by Mandela with a universalizing colorblindness; they conflate the man's commitment to internationalism with a vague homogenizing cosmopolitanism. The mythic Mandela thus becomes an exception that proves a racist rule: an African leader who seems all the more admirable against a perceived norm of African tyrants and dictators.

This chapter, while also accounting for the main achievements and conditions of his brief time in office, situates Mandela's presidency within a world shaped, more profoundly than is often realized, by African thought, cosmology, philosophy, oral tradition, and the struggle for liberation. I am adopting this approach to jettison the idea that the emancipatory aspects of Mandela's presidency should be seen solely in terms of a Eurocentrically conceived modernity, in which Africa and "tradition" are always somehow timeless or belated. Though Mandela was in many ways a modern person (it is impossible for readers of *Long Walk to Freedom* not to note the excitement with which he describes his arrival in the big city of Johannesburg), he remained rooted also in tradition. In fact, this antinomy, as Philip Bonner notes in Chapter 1, marks the biographies of many African leaders in the twentieth century. Throughout his life – right up to the present – Mandela, while insisting that he is not a "tribalist," has certainly "respect[ed] custom"[2] and has dug into the emancipatory spiritual world of his African ancestors and political predecessors to discover his humanity and that of the oppressed and downtrodden people. It is telling that in the years of his retirement he eschewed the comfort of urban life in Johannesburg and returned to his birthplace to spend the last period of his life with the poverty-stricken people in the rural areas of the Eastern Cape. Mandela's return to Qunu should urge scholars to make a greater effort to understand the African customs, traditions, language, and idioms that have always defined his world, attachments that, as I will show, go along with rather than contradict his international stature, influence, and vision.

I would remind readers here that Nelson was not Mandela's given name; it was assigned to him by an overzealous primary school teacher, steeped in the Western tradition of dishing out, willy-nilly, "Christian" names to Africans. The popular use of Madiba, his clan name, may therefore be seen as a subversive public protest against the adoption of his "Christian name."[3] The use of the clan name also signifies the relevance of African thought, history, and philosophy in South African society. I am of the view that Mandela's mother, Nosekeni Mandela, was contesting the oppressive European culture when she referred to him, not as Nelson, but as Nelisiwe (the Fulfilled One), a quintessential Nguni name. Her subversive renaming signifies that Africans have their own ethnic identities, indigenous languages, and names that define their world – and these are not necessarily raceless. The implication is that African knowledge and its cosmological world did not come into being through the so-called discovery of Africa by European colonialists. "Mzala" Nxumalo argues that the time has come for both liberal and neo-Marxist writers (including the exponents of theories on cosmopolitanism) to acknowledge the importance of African ethnic identity, not as a fiction of the "civilising mission" or a product of imperial "divide and rule" policies, but rather as a lived historical experience with indigenous linguistic, cultural, and customary norms that predate the advent of European colonialism.[4] This becomes crucial when we analyze the life history of Mandela, who confirms this view by signing himself as Dalibhunga, his prophetic indigenous name – one that emphasizes links with the indigenous leaders who championed the system of consensual governance guided and coordinated by *ibhunga* (councils) during precolonial times.[5]

Rupture and Continuity

When the redoubtable O. R. Tambo, Mandela's colleague in the political battlefield, business partner in the legal fraternity, and closest friend, returned from exile in 1990, he immediately visited the grave of John Langalibalele Dube, the first president of the ANC. Tambo undertook this journey to inform Dube about his return to the country of his birth. He briefed and updated the deceased on the status of the ANC and developments in the years while he, Tambo, had been at the helm. He also solicited Dube's protection and spiritual guidance, because the unbanned ANC was now engaged in a new phase of the liberation struggle; its future was to be determined by substantive negotiations with a formidable enemy: the apartheid regime.

Right before he was officially proclaimed president of the Republic of South Africa, Mandela followed Tambo's footsteps. On April 27, 1994, the second day of the democratic elections in South Africa, Mandela, like Tambo, saluted Dube by visiting his grave at Ohlange, before walking over to the polling station at the school Dube founded and casting his vote. These symbolic gestures affirm a traditional understanding of the continuity of life and death and suggest that the very real rupture that was the "new" democratic South Africa went hand in hand with certain political and cultural continuities. Mandela provided a solemn progress report to Dube: "Mr. President, I am here to report to you that South Africa is today free and your soul may now rest in peace."[6] At this important moment in his career, Mandela formally and publicly acknowledged the presence of ancestral memory (a view also embraced by the majority of South Africans) – and not for the first time in his life. He did so as well at his trial held at the Old Synagogue Court in Pretoria in 1962. On this occasion, Mandela, the combative revolutionary, expressed the following about his ancestors, who graced the land long before the arrival of white colonizers:

> Many years ago, when I was a boy brought up in my village in the Transkei, I listened to the elders of the tribe telling stories about the good old days, before the arrival of the white man. That our people lived peacefully, under the democratic rule of their kings and their "amapakati," and moved freely and confidently up and down without hindrance. Then the country was ours, in our own name and right. We occupied the land, the forest, the rivers; we extracted the mineral wealth beneath the soil and all the riches of this beautiful country. We set up and operated our own government, we controlled our own armies and we organised our own trade and commerce. The elders would tell tales of the wars fought by our ancestors in defense of the fatherland, as well as acts of valour performed by generals and soldiers during those epic days. The names of Dingane and Bambatha, among the Zulus, of Hintsa, Makana, Ndlambe of the amaXhosa, of Sekhukhune and others in the north, were mentioned as the pride and glory of the entire African nation.[7]

As modern revolutionaries involved in the anti-colonial struggle waged by the ANC, Mandela and Tambo still respected an African cosmology and African belief systems, in terms of which a person must aspire to be united, ultimately, with the earth where his or her ancestors (*abaphansi*) reside. In this they shared a common ground with the founders and former presidents of the ANC, who included both educated men and traditional leaders: all participated in a sense of the connection between the living and the deceased.

Ancestral memory is animated by the idea that history is alive; it is always here with us. According to Mazisi Kunene, who was Tambo's right-hand man in the early 1960s, African religion and belief systems postulate that "all members of the family past, present, future must be consolidated to form one continuous family. By family is meant primarily the members who trace their ancestry to one common Ancestor. The concept does not end there. It is extended ideologically to include the whole human society so that society is the sum total of many families and not of individuals."[8] Kunene's articulation of this indigenous South African humanist philosophical tradition not only enables us to understand *ubuntu* in a more culturally specific manner than is often the case. It also reveals the fundamental reason the ANC, in its pursuit of national liberation, officially adopted a vision of international solidarity propelled by resilient members of human society, regardless of race, color, or creed, as one of its unshakable pillars. It is for this reason that the ANC endeavored so persistently in the United Nations to have apartheid proclaimed a crime against humanity – not merely a crime against black South Africans.

The ANC's conception of human society is further explained by Kunene when he writes that each historical era has vast cumulative achievements that represent the social (and political) activities of numerous individuals, known and unknown. Collectively, he asserts,

> these honourable individuals who have made their contribution to human welfare and progress are known and honoured as Ancestors. In this context the lessons of the past become crucial and may decide the fate of a society or societies. Thus, the contributions of the Ancestors are not only laudable in themselves but are also a primary aspect of the survival and continuity of life.

In a passage that recalls the vision of Anton Lembede (a significant influence on the young Mandela), Kunene elaborates: "The achievements of the Ancestors are not isolated acts of individual heroism, but describe the collective efforts of all those who make up our history. What is primary therefore is not the individual heroic act, but heroic actions of all members of the past generations."[9] Tambo and Mandela's investment in honoring ancestral memory must be seen in this light, and it allows us to conceptualize a specifically South African version of a usable past: the experience of those who came before can speak to us about what to do in future situations. At work here (both in the case of the ANC leaders and in my own chapter) is the idea that history is about the past in the present; our present concerns influence what we think about the past. The project that animates my inquiry is, in fact, to underscore how the collective efforts on the part of what Kunene calls the "honourable individuals" of past generations inspired Mandela in his everyday life, particularly when he was the president of South Africa.

His victory speech after his election as president of South Africa in 1994 is revealing in this regard. He acknowledged: "I am personally indebted and pay tribute to some of South Africa's greatest leaders including John

Dube, Josiah Gumede, G. M. Naicker, Dr. Abdurahman, Chief Luthuli, Lilian Ngoyi, Helen Joseph, Yusuf Dadoo, Moses Kotane, Chris Hani, and Oliver Tambo."[10] Mandela was committed to following these predecessors' path, especially in affirming an inclusive, internationalist, political vision of humanity. This vision defines the broad accomplishments of his presidency, as I will suggest in this chapter, and it is in this light that the other often-cited achievements must also be seen. These achievements include, on the international level, Mandela's spectacular success in enabling South Africa, the former pariah state, to reassume its place as part of the world at large. On the national level, his accomplishments include the establishment of democracy and democratic institutions, the fostering of reconciliation through the mechanisms of the Government of National Unity and the Truth and Reconciliation Commission, and, though this legacy is not uncontested, an attempt to redress the economic as well as gendered and cultural iniquities of the past through the development of new policies on justice, equality, health, and education.

Democracy, Reconciliation, and Rights

At its annual conference in Bloemfontein in May 1923, the ANC became the first organization in South Africa to call for the adoption of a bill of rights. The ANC's vision was that human rights should be universal, that all South Africans had a God-given right to ownership of land, that there should be equality before the law and equal political rights, and, finally, that all South Africans, irrespective of race, color, or creed, should have the right to vote for their government of choice. In his recent book, *Human Rights in South Africa*, Saul Dubow argues that ANC's level of support for universal human rights was not consistent throughout the twentieth century, suggesting, for instance, that during the years in exile, ANC members were uncomfortable with liberal and individualistic versions of human rights rhetoric (especially that of the United States, which tended to equate the liberation struggle with the Civil Rights Movement and opposed sanctions against South Africa). But, as Dubow also makes clear, the ANC decisively affirmed its original vision during the final years of the struggle and the transition.[11] The organization, as it were, returned to its roots, to the clarion call that inspired the founders in the early twentieth century. As president, Mandela paid tribute to this groundbreaking step by past generations of ANC leaders when he said in May 1994, "It was their vision which inspired us when we adopted the first ever Bill of Rights in this country. That same vision spurred us to put forward the African Claims in 1946 [sic]. It is also the founding principle of the Freedom Charter." A bill of rights, first envisaged by the ANC in 1923, was duly enacted as part of the country's 1996 constitution.[12]

From consensual governance to diplomacy, dialogue, and the politics of compromise, all practices that had for centuries informed African societies, a united ANC Alliance pursued a negotiated settlement in South Africa through the Convention for a Democratic South Africa (CODESA), which commenced its deliberations on December 20, 1991. After protracted negotiations and a power-sharing political settlement, President Mandela governed the country for two years through the Government of National Unity (GNU). It comprised the ANC, the National Party (NP), and the Inkatha Freedom Party (IFP), with F. W. de Klerk as deputy president and Chief Mangosuthu Buthelezi as a cabinet minister. The concept of a government of national unity, though also propelled by the need for compromise in the wake of political stalemate, must be grasped as expressive of the spirit of *ubuntu* and of long-established African traditions wherein society frowned on extremism of any kind. In a conflict situation, for example, not even the victor could lay claim to the entire fruits of victory; nor could the defeated enemy be completely excluded. This is the spirit in which the GNU and the Truth and Reconciliation Commission were accepted by Mandela's government and the African majority: the political victors.

Addressing this matter, Mandela noted in a parliamentary speech: "Amongst the principles which the liberation movement pursued from the beginning of negotiations is that out of any debate we [as South Africans] must emerge stronger and more united, and that there should be no winners and losers."[13] The future of South Africa and its people was more critical than grabbing all the loot to the exclusion of the white minority. Hence proportional representation in parliament was preferred to the Westminster system. The fact that both the NP and IFP overestimated their role and eventually resigned from the GNU had to do with the complexities of day-to-day multi-party politics. Mandela's relations with De Klerk, moreover, were never warm and trusting; the latter was, after all, the leader of a politically astute minority that would have liked to dictate terms to the majority, and Mandela consistently held De Klerk responsible for fomenting, through "third force" activities, the political violence that plagued several townships on the Rand and areas of KwaZulu-Natal during the years of the transition and even after 1994.[14] In the face of such undemocratic manipulation, Mandela insisted that "our approach to issues of political power should proceed from the premise that it is an expression of popular will, and not a mysterious force wielded by a chosen few."[15]

In recent years, there has been increasingly vociferous criticism of the ANC and of Mandela's presidency by those who maintain that Mandela "sold out" or "betrayed" the masses by including their former oppressors in the GNU after the 1994 elections. This view ignores Mandela's particular view of democracy. Other, more sympathetic commentators also do not fully grasp the spirit that made the GNU possible. Chris Landsberg, for example, explains the GNU solely in contemporary party political terms:

> The ANC compromised on its demand for unfettered majority rule, exchanging majoritarianism for a fixed, five-year 'sunset' arrangement involving a Government of National Unity, which would incorporate minority parties – including the party of the incumbent white minority government – once an adversary. This GNU would govern for at least five years – up to June 1999 – whereafter the 'sunset' clause would become voluntary and optional.[16]

This is not incorrect, but we should note, additionally, that Mandela was always aware that South Africa needed to be united in purpose; this was not the time to score cheap political points. In other words, the decision to accept a government of national unity should not simply be seen in terms of a political compromise made under duress; it also drew on a tradition of generosity toward adversaries, a tradition that does not partake of the "winner-takes-all" mentality – an unpalatable aspect of capitalist democracies.

We should remember, further, that national unity is pursued not just by political parties; Mandela was also accountable to the trade unions and workers – to civil society. His support of the trade union movement is reflected in his address at the fifth national meeting of the Congress of South African Trade Unions (COSATU) on September 7, 1994: "To take part in a gathering of this nature, bringing together part of the core of cadres of the democratic movement," he declared, "is for us, a homecoming.... We stand before you fully conscious of the fact that together, we spared neither life nor limb to ensure that South Africa is where it is today. We shared the trials and tribulations so that South Africa should be free.... Lines of communication should always be open between various government departments and the labour movements."[17] Though the ANC's relationship with COSATU became more difficult in the wake of the adoption of a business-friendly macroeconomic policy in 1996, it is nevertheless the case that South Africa remains one of the few countries in the world to take workers' rights seriously; here trade union movements wield tangible power. It is significant, therefore, that Mandela's first cabinet included not only members of the NP, but also royalists and blood-red Communists – and a historically unprecedented number of women.[18] We might bring to mind, again, the ecumenical list of political ancestors whose names Mandela invoked in his victory speech: they included not only ANC stalwarts like Dube and Tambo, but Indian colleagues like Naicker and Adburahman, Communists like Dadoo, Kotane, and Hani, women like Lilian Ngoyi and Helen Joseph, and a traditional leader, Chief Luthuli. The inclusive spirit Mandela put forward in this crucial address, in other words, had real political effects in the decisions he made as president.

Economic Justice and Cultural Heritage

Nothing is ultimately more contested about Mandela's presidency than its economic legacy, and especially the shift from the Reconstruction and Development Programme (RDP), the ANC's developmentally inclined electoral platform of 1994, to the more "neoliberal" Growth, Employment, and Redistribution Programme (GEAR), which was adopted in 1996. Indeed, it is because of this shift that many of the charges of "selling out" mentioned earlier arise. We must bear in mind, however, that Mandela (and his vice president, Thabo Mbeki, who was an important player in all this) had the unenviable task of "balanc[ing] competing demands for restitution of black rights with pragmatic requirements for economic growth in a globalizing world economy."[19] Despite the growing emphasis on macroeconomic stability over redistribution, it is nevertheless true that during Mandela's presidency the needs of Africans – pressing issues such as education, health, housing, and social welfare – were for the first time prioritized in the national budget.

That these needs were the result of centuries of exploitation Mandela grasped all too well; and he could express their urgency poignantly: "Behind the glitter of city lights, the halo of a relatively advanced technology and smoothness of paved roads," he declared in a 1995 speech, "lies the reality of a rate of illiteracy that is among the highest on the continent, poverty, homelessness, landlessness and malnutrition that beset millions."[20] His views on developmental issues appear in several other speeches he delivered while he was president,[21] and they are reflected also in the two dozen or so "Presidential Lead Projects": special, high-visibility projects initiated with RDP funding in the areas of land reform and rural development, urban housing and infrastructure, education and health. Mandela's attitudes toward rural women, in particular, and his willingness to engage with the realities of their lives are perhaps most strikingly captured in a later speech, "Planet and Humanity" (2002), which describes his experiences visiting his birthplace: a geography, he tells us, that is "not of landscapes and topography," but "of the people." He recalls how he asked three women whether they were going to boil the water they had collected before using it. Perplexed at his ignorance, the women retorted simultaneously: "Boil it with what? Look up, right up to the horizon, there is not a single tree. We have no electricity. How

must we boil it? We use cow dung, and that gives more smoke than heat." [22]
A chastened Mandela promptly set out to raise funds to improve the living
conditions of people in rural areas.

Though the optimistic developmental aims of bringing redress and visibility to those most marginalized were hampered by problems of implementation, the years of the Mandela presidency were nevertheless successful
in opening South Africa up to all its citizens. Education and sport were
desegregated, cultural production was liberated from apartheid's puritanism
and censorship, and South African history and heritage were transformed.
"In the past," as Peter Limb puts it, "museums had depicted the triumphal
march of white settlers; there was little space for the stories of Africans." [23]
This was redressed in the creation of new museums, like the Robben Island
Museum, and in the institution of new public holidays, including Women's
Day, Human Rights Day, Freedom Day, and Workers' Day. The spirit in
which this redress took place was, once again, not one of victorious gloating. This much is evident in a speech Mandela delivered on December 16,
1995, the first-ever Reconciliation Day:

> There are few countries which dedicate a national public holiday to reconcil-
> iation. But then there are few nations with our history of enforced division,
> oppression and sustained conflict. And few still, which have undergone such a
> remarkable transition to reclaim their humanity.... [W]e do know that healing
> the wounds of the past and freeing ourselves of its burden will be a long and
> demanding task. This Day of Reconciliation celebrates the progress we have
> made.... The Government of National Unity chose this day precisely because
> the past had made 16 December a living symbol of bitter division....Today we
> no longer vow our mutual destruction but solemnly acknowledge our interde-
> pendence as free and equal citizens of our common motherland. [24]

President Mandela, in other words, not only highlighted the checkered
history of this date – that of the Battle of iNcome in 1838, celebrated by
Afrikaners as "Bloedrivier" and as proof of divine sanction of their racist
nationalism – as a marker of the bitter historical divisions in South Africa,
but also re-emphasized the meaning of the transition as a reclamation of
humanity and *ubuntu* for all citizens.

It is important to note also that the House of Traditional Leaders,
derived from African history and rooted in consensual democratic governance, was established during Mandela's presidency, in terms of the 1996
constitution. The release of Mandela by the apartheid regime and the acceptance of the principle of democracy as the basis of governance in South
Africa led to considerable reflection on the role of various constituencies –
some were the product of colonial times, while others retained elements

of indigenous origin. Examples include the bantustan governments; the liberation movements, together with their military wings; and traditional leadership as a form of governance. The fate of some of these formations was decided in the political bargaining process, but the ambiguity of the status of traditional leadership has been more problematic because of the combination of historical factors behind its continued existence. To this day there is a lack of resolve on the conflicting need for a broader national democracy (defined in terms of equal opportunities and political power for all) and the call for according legitimacy and clout to indigeneity, thus shoring up the continued existence of traditional leadership. This issue was one that presented a great challenge to Mandela's presidency.[25] Clarity was needed on the core roles and functions of traditional leadership as a form of governance if it were to function alongside a modern democracy. How, for example, was "customary law" to be retained? What kind of ideological orientation should structure the relationship between government and traditional leadership? And, perhaps most important, how does customary law relate to human rights law? These are difficult questions, and it is no wonder that contradictions soon became apparent.[26] Yet the institution of the House of Traditional Leaders must be grasped as an aspect of the "new" South Africa that reaffirms continuities with African cultural heritage and reminds us that, from the start, the ANC included traditional leaders along with professional men in its ranks.

African Nationalism and Internationalism

Like his domestic policies, Mandela's human and social rights–based foreign policies were profoundly influenced by the founding fathers of the ANC. When the Union of South Africa was established in 1910, prominent Africans such as John Dube made diplomatic overtures to resolve the national question peacefully. A multiracial deputation to London failed to get the color bar clauses removed from the Union's constitution.[27] But this setback did not deter the ANC from seeking a negotiated solution and, in 1914, another diplomatic mission to the UK was undertaken. This democratically elected ANC deputation, which included, among other luminaries, the writer Sol T. Plaatje, was also unsuccessful. A third attempt was launched in 1919, when the ANC again appealed to the British government on behalf of black South Africans. But their peaceful mission for social and political rights for all South Africans failed to reach its noble goal.[28] Eventually (especially in the wake of apartheid's violent repressiveness), this well-meaning and non-violent approach – an approach that recognized that the struggle for emancipation was necessarily international – proved unsuccessful. Yet it is noteworthy that the once-radical Mandela, when appointed president of South Africa seven decades later, was prepared to learn from his predecessors and assumed the inclusive, diplomatic, and internationalist posture favored by an earlier generation of ANC leaders.

Arising from the vision and actions of the founding members of the ANC, then, the foreign policy of the ANC was fortified by a belief in *ubuntu* and dialogue; it also encompassed non-violence, anti-racism, anti-colonialism, internationalism, and justice in a non-racial democracy. Further guiding principles were added in the mid-twentieth century; these included international solidarity and the establishment of a strong working relationship with multilateral organizations such as the United Nations and the Organization of African Unity (OAU). It was therefore not surprising that when Mandela assumed the presidency in 1994, South Africa's foreign policy continued the legacy formulated by the older generation and was defined by the notion of "a better Africa and a better world." Mandela prioritized these fundamental, *ubuntu*-inspired values as essential to cultivating a humane foreign policy.[29] In short, internationalism as practiced by Dube and others was the cornerstone of Mandela's foreign policy.

His initiatives in this domain, to be sure, have not been free of criticism. Brendan Vickers, for one, has claimed that Mandela's foreign policy was "penny-pinching" and plagued by ideologically opposed camps he identifies as the "idealist solidarists and the neo-realist free-marketeers."[30] But, viewed in a broader historical framework, it becomes clear that Mandela's diplomacy was not about pinching pennies or dollars, but about building a stable bridge with former opponents and world superpowers, such as the United States, the United Kingdom, France, and (West) Germany, and promoting a "South–North" dialogue through a progressive foreign policy program focused on reconciliation and on forgiving – but not forgetting – past injustices. Most of the Western superpowers were historically loyal allies of white South Africans and the apartheid regime, because they had substantial investments there. They publicly opposed the ANC and willfully undermined the anti-colonial struggle – including the work of the OAU, which was one of the engines that drove the liberation struggle. It is important to bear in mind that France controlled a thriving sanctions-busting business of selling arms to the apartheid regime and that both West Germany and the United States helped develop apartheid South Africa's nuclear weapons program. It fell to the people in the street, as civilians, in these Western countries to support the struggle for national liberation in South Africa.[31] In her quest to protect white minority rule in apartheid South Africa, Margaret Thatcher, the British prime minister, constantly harangued the ANC and referred to it as a dangerous terrorist organization that had to be crushed. As for the

United States, it officially listed Mandela as a "dangerous terrorist"; he needed special permission to enter the country until July 2008.

As the president of a democratic republic, Mandela could, as James Barber puts it, freely punch above South Africa's weight on the international stage.[32] The government often found itself having to meet former foes, including the United States, Great Britain, and France at multilateral platforms such as the UN. It was apparent to all that post-1994 South Africa could not be held captive by manipulative Western countries. As a result, and unlike the majority of African countries, South Africa was not afflicted by the international donor syndrome perpetuated by the Bretton Woods institutions. Mandela and his cabinet could thus not be held ransom when asked to apply for unsolicited loans by loan sharks representing the International Monetary Fund and the World Bank. For historical reasons and compared with other African leaders, Mandela did not view the West as big brother to whom he was accountable.

Peace Building and Conflict Resolution on the African Continent

In stereotypical Western discourses Africa is habitually otherized as the epicenter of conflict: it is the continent that harbors endemic disease, is engulfed in unending warfare, and practices primitive, barbarous rituals. But the truth is that conflict is a fact of human existence and is universal, as, indeed, Mandela remarked in an address to the fifty-third session of the UN General Assembly in September 1998:

> A whole range of areas of conflict confront us, in Africa, Europe and Asia. We are all familiar with these, which range from the Democratic Republic of the Congo, Angola and Sudan on my own continent, to the Balkans in Europe and Afghanistan, Tajikistan and Sri Lanka in Asia.... [U]rgent steps are also required for a just and permanent peace in the Middle East, on the basis of the realisation of the legitimate aspirations of the people of Palestine and respect for the independence and security of all the states of this important region. We also look forward to the resolution of the outstanding issues of Western Sahara and East Timor.[33]

Nelson Mandela's presidency duly marked many diplomatic and peacemaking efforts that extended worldwide.

As I noted earlier, the ANC leadership of the time was not prone to a high level of animosity or conflict, and this is what helped Mandela's rise to the leadership position after Tambo had passed away. To be sure, there were instances when the ANC leaders on Robben Island clashed: the arguments between Harry Gwala, Govan Mbeki, and Mandela are well documented.

But these internal dynamics were resolved within organizational structures. The unity of purpose characterizing the ANC made Mandela's task easier in terms of ruling the country.[34] Such unity also made it possible for him to deal with conflict resolution in other parts of the African continent and the international world. His broad perspective on these matters (based on the simple idea that "charity begins at home") is captured in his speech on March 18, 1995, when he accepted the African Peace Award:

> We are all too aware that peace is more than just the absence of war. The dark clouds still hovering above our landscape, particularly in Lesotho and Angola, are matters of serious concern.... One could go further to refer to political conflict in other parts of Africa; or even the deaths, though on a much smaller scale, that plague the province of KwaZulu-Natal.... In promoting peace and preventing conflict, South Africa will work hand-in-hand with our neighbours and in multi-lateral forums such as the SADC and the OAU. In this regard, we welcome and are part of the OAU initiative for an early-warning mechanism and the shift from conflict management to conflict prevention.[35]

The spirit of internationalism combines here, and in Mandela's diplomatic achievements, with an African practice of consensual conflict resolution. When Mandela came to power in 1994, new conflicts emerged in the continent: the Rwanda genocide of 1994 and upheavals in Sierra Leone, Angola, Liberia, Côte d'Ivoire, Ethiopia and Eritrea, the Democratic Republic of the Congo, Zimbabwe, Lesotho, Burundi, Madagascar, Uganda, and Sudan. He steadfastly implemented the ANC's political traditions based on internationalism, consensual politics, and dialogue. A politically stable and democratic South Africa had to reconsider its geostrategic position in the world, which meant a move from being a nuclear power and military aggressor on the continent toward assuming a constructive role as peacemaker. In order to keep the continent of Africa nuclear-free, South Africa facilitated the drafting and eventual adoption of the 1996 Pelindaba Treaty. Mandela's words on this occasion, which echo those of his inaugural speech, are revealing and moving: "Never again," he declared, "shall South Africa be fountainhead of conflict in the region and further afield. Never again shall our country be the source of armaments used to suppress communities and to wage aggressive wars against neighbours. Never again shall we spend our people's resources to develop weapons of mass destruction."[36]

That the role of consensual conflict resolution is now downplayed in contemporary African societies is perhaps due to the pervasive influence of Western values, in terms of which (often counterproductively) one is either completely right or absolutely wrong. Thanks to Mandela's efforts, a pragmatic, consensual diplomacy of conflict management and prevention was often adopted in order to broker peace. This was no easy task. Indeed, the persistent violence in KwaZulu-Natal, which plagued South Africa during the transition and the early years of Mandela's presidency, drove peace-loving and concerned South Africans to the breaking point. Mandela spearheaded conflict mediation and facilitation through preventive diplomacy and negotiations. (Lesotho was the only exception to this rule, when, for the first and last time South Africa intervened militarily to roll back a coup d'état in September 1998.[37]) President Mandela sought to broker a peace deal to end the two-decade-long civil war in Angola between the National Union for the Total Independence of Angola (UNITA) and the People's Movement for the Liberation of Angola (MPLA, an ANC ally) by reviving the Lusaka Peace Process. However, relations became frosty when Mandela's government refused to sell arms to the MPLA to use against UNITA, a particularly tense situation because of the apartheid regime's previous support for the latter organization.[38]

Mandela continued his peacemaking efforts in the Great Lakes area as early as 1997 when war broke out in Zaire with Mobutu Sese Seko and Laurent Kabila as the main protagonists. Kabila prevailed and took control in May 1997 and renamed the country the Democratic Republic of Congo (DRC). The situation was complicated by the involvement of rebels from Rwanda and Uganda, and much of the conflict centered on gaining control of natural resources rather than on issues of identity and ethnicity. Rebel groups, regional actors, and multinational corporations were profiting from the war by developing political, military, and business elite frameworks. The net effects were disastrous for the ordinary people of the DRC. South Africa refused to sell weapons to Kabila, so its relations with Zimbabwe's Robert Mugabe and Angola's Eduardo Dos Santos, who sided with Kabila, plunged to an all-time low. At one stage, Sam Nujoma, the president of Namibia, Mugabe, Dos Santos, and Kabila all accused South Africa of promoting regional apartheid and of siding with Uganda, Rwanda, and the rebels in an effort to topple Kabila – even for harboring Congolese rebels in South Africa.[39]

But Mandela faced his stiffest challenge from General Sani Abacha, the ruthless Nigerian dictator, who accused him of being a stooge of the West, not a true African nationalist. This was because Mandela dared to challenge him about atrocities committed against the Ogoni. At first Mandela adopted a diplomatic stance, but when Ken Saro-Wiwa and eight others were executed by the Nigerians, Mandela challenged Abacha head-on. His dedication to bringing Abacha down was made clear in an interview in the *Sunday Independent* (also broadcast on BBC World Service). Stung by criticism that he had not acted forcefully enough to stop the Nigerian executions,

Mandela went at Abacha with guns blazing. He vowed that South Africa would press ahead with "strong action" against Nigeria, including oil sanctions, to ensure that democracy be attained in "the shortest possible time." He declared, "We are dealing with an illegitimate, barbaric, arrogant, military dictatorship which has murdered activists, using a kangaroo court and using false evidence." He also rejected criticism that South Africa was to blame for Saro-Wiwa's death.[40] As a result, Abacha petulantly barred the national football team from competing in the Confederation of African Football 1996 African Cup of Nations, which was hosted – and won – by South Africa.

Challenges and Accomplishments

When the ANC won the 1994 elections it won political power but did not control the administration; the public service did not reflect the demographics of the country, and most civil servants were white Afrikaners. Transforming the public service was thus an early priority. Careful political decisions had to be taken. Significantly, Mandela's first minister of finance was Derek Keys; the president retained Keys (and later also Chris Liebenberg) specifically so that he could keep the captains of industry at bay. He wanted to command the confidence of the corporate chiefs, big multinationals (the majority of them from outside the country), and international financiers (most of whom happened to be white). He argued that if they saw the new president had retained the incumbent minister, they would be reassured that there would be some stability in the South African economy. Trevor Manuel, a prominent ANC member, however, was the first deputy minister of finance.

Another hurdle was that none of those who were appointed as ministers and deputy ministers had any idea of how to run a government, let alone a ministry and a national department. Although they had experience in running the ANC, South African Communist Party, and United Democratic Front and although there were some who were prominent in the trade unions, they collectively lacked experience in running a government. For the first time in their lives they had to come to grips with things like cabinet memos, cabinet committees, and the like that had been set up by the previous regimes. The president also had to work out how to distribute the chairing of cabinet committees between Mbeki and De Klerk. It was clear that Mbeki was the more senior deputy president, although this was never officially spelled out by Mandela. Given that the ANC was the dominant party, policy issues were driven essentially by the ANC.

Some commentators have underestimated the difficulties faced by Mandela and his cabinet when they took over the government and introduced the concept of a government of national unity. Mangosuthu Buthelezi of the IFP was brought in as minister of home affairs. His colleague Ben Ngubane was appointed as minister of arts, culture, science, and technology. A political scenario arose wherein the ANC, totally inexperienced in terms of running a country, had to co-govern with former opponents. Although the negotiations at CODESA did help a great deal in forging links with NP politicians, it was now a question of working together for a common cause. Mandela, as the president, had to give political direction. One should also be aware that, unlike Mandela and Mbeki, De Klerk had a highly experienced staff of some sixty public servants at his disposal, people with whom he had worked prior to 1994. In contrast, Mandela and Mbeki had to start from scratch in terms of setting up office at the Union Buildings and building the necessary administrative backup. Essop Pahad, then the parliamentary counselor to Thabo Mbeki, remembers the haphazard bureaucratic situation clearly:

> Remember there's no paper, there's no pen, there are not even paper clips ... it was only an office with beautiful wooden panelling and some furnishing. Then these two support staff ... a man and a woman, white....[t]wo good people and without them it would have been very difficult.... Mandela brought Barbara Masekela with him from the ANC office and we had to work hard to set up his office.[41]

Another challenging issue for Mandela was dealing with policy matters – both minute and far-reaching. In contrast to the situation in more established democracies, entirely new policies had to be devised, as it was unwise (and unpalatable) to simply continue with old apartheid policies or just tinker with them, as would suffice for a newly elected leader in the United Kingdom or United States. In South Africa, a complete revision – indeed reversal – of former practices was necessary. For example, in the legal system it took a long time to wipe off all the discriminatory apartheid legislation and regulations. The newly appointed government did its best and was still trying to draw up a list of all the petty racist and discriminatory legislation that had to be amended when Mandela left office in 1999. Before the ANC assumed power in 1994, it had established various working groups that focused on health, education, and other crucial issues, in which the ANC brought together its own people and consultants of international repute. They had worked on the necessary policy issues for the new government, which provided some direction. However, the *implementation* of policies proved to be the biggest challenge of all. Mandela's presidency was bedeviled by the fact that for the first two or three years, because of inexperience, ministers did not cost their new policies when developing them. It was only later that the cabinet began to play a stricter role in terms of estimating the financial implications of policy options. Linked to this was the difficulty, after the adoption of the 1996 Constitution, that the national government was faced with the issue of how to relate to the provinces. In the existing system the provinces did not have original powers delegated to them by the Constitution. When the cabinet took a policy decision at the national level it was binding on provincial and local governments as well. But if the responsible minister and the public servants who served under that minister did not have the necessary infrastructure or budget for those policies, it was virtually impossible to implement them efficiently. Mandela's cabinet had to learn this the hard way.

Yet despite these enormous challenges, Mandela was able to end the presidency in the same manner in which he started it: a spirit of collectivism and healthy respect still prevailed by the time Thabo Mbeki was designated to take over as the second president of South Africa. This is apparent in Mandela's speech at the final sitting of the first democratically elected parliament, in which he expressed confidence in the caliber of the next generation of ANC leaders:

> Deputy President Thabo Mbeki, whom we all expect to be President of South Africa, exemplifies ... [an] approach which is critical to the unity of our country. I call on all to give their support to his leadership, across all political parties. His and other voices are those of a new generation of leaders that are emerging in answer to new historical challenges. They are the voices of good men and women who exist in all communities and all parties, and who define themselves by their capacity to identify the issues that unite us as a nation. Together we must continue our efforts to turn hope into reality. The long walk continues.[42]

The unity Mandela invokes here did not last. However, the importance of keeping in mind the living legacy of African traditional values has remained, as was only too clear in the months of his illness in 2013, when questions of custom, the role of chieftaincy, and even the importance of ancestral memory were again brought to the fore.

NOTES

1 Toni Morrison captures the problem as follows: "The world does not become raceless or will not become unracialized by assertion. The act of enforcing [universal] racelessness ... in discourse is itself a racial act." *Playing in the Dark: Whiteness and the Literary Imagination* (Cambridge, MA: Harvard University Press, 1990), 46–47.

2 Martin Meredith, *Mandela: A Biography* (New York: Public Affairs, 1997), 541.

3 The ideology and politics of naming in colonial times deserves a study of its own. See David Theo Goldberg, *Racist Culture: Philosophy and the Politics of*

Meaning (London: Blackwell, 1993); Campbell Shittu Momoh, "Philosophy in African Proverbs," in *The Substance of African Philosophy*, ed. C. S. Momoh (Auchi: African Philosophy Projects Publication, 2000), 359–76.

4 Jabulani Sithole, "Zuluness in South Africa: From 'Struggle' Debate to Democratic Transformation," in *Zulu Identities: Being Zulu, Past and Present*, ed. Benedict Carton, John Laband, and Jabulani Sithole (Pietermaritzburg, UKZN Press, 2008), xiii; Jabulani "Mzala" Nxumalo, "The National Question in the Writing of South African History: A Critical Survey of Some Major Tendencies," Working Paper 22 (Open University, n.d.), 29.

5 Mandela has two official signatures; one is "Nelson Rolihlahla" and the other "Nelson Dalibhunga." For a discussion of the meanings of "Rolihlahla," see Chapter 6.

6 Moses Hadebe, "John Langalibalele Dube," *Thinker* 21 (2010): 56; Nelson Mandela, *Long Walk to Freedom* (New York: Little, Brown, 1995), 617–18.

7 Nelson Mandela, "Posterity Will Prove That I Was Innocent," in *In His Own Words*, ed. Kader Asmal, David Chidester, and Wilmot James (New York: Little, Brown: 2003), 20.

8 Ibid.

9 Mazisi Kunene, "Introduction," in *The Ancestors and the Sacred Mountain Poems* (London: Heinemann, 1982), xiv–xv; Kunene, *Anthem of the Decades: A Zulu Epic Dedicated to the Women of Africa* (London: Heinemann, 1981), xi.

10 Mandela, "Election as President," in *In His Own Words*, 63–64.

11 As Dubow notes, the ANC's National Executive Committee declared itself in support of a justiciable bill of rights based on fundamental freedoms in 1987 (thereby re-endorsing the commitments of the early ANC and the Freedom Charter); the Harare Declaration of 1989 also included the clause "All shall enjoy universally recognized human rights, freedoms and civil liberties, protected under an entrenched Bill of Rights." See Saul Dubow, *South Africa's Struggle for Human Rights* (Cape Town: Jacana, 2012), 97–98 and the introduction. For a different view, one that traces an unbroken line from the African Claims, to the Freedom Charter, to the Women's Charter, and to the 1996 Constitution, see Kader Asmal with David Chidester and Cassius Lubisi, *Legacy of Freedom: The ANC's Human Rights Tradition* (Johannesburg: Jonathan Ball, 2005).

12 African National Congress, *The ANC and the Bill of Rights, 1923 to 1993: A Seventy Year Survey* (Marshalltown: ANC Department of Information and Publicity, 1993); Mandela, "Before Inauguration as President," in *In His Own Words*, 66. The African Claims document actually dates from 1943.

13 Mandela, "The Long Walk Continues," in *In His Own Words*, 176.

14 On violence after the 1994 elections, see Mary de Haas, "Violence in Natal and Zululand, 1980s–1990s, Part 2: The 1990s," in SADET, *The Road to Democracy in South Africa*, vol. 6: 1990–1996 (Pretoria: UNISA Press, 2012), ch. 3.

15 Mandela, "African Peace," in *In His Own Words*, 540.

16 Chris Landsberg, *The Quiet Diplomacy of Liberation: International Politics and South Africa's Transition* (Johannesburg: Jacana, 2004), 13. See also Sifiso M. Ndlovu, "The African National Congress and Negotiations," in SADET, *The Road to Democracy in South Africa*, vol. 4: 1980–1990 (Pretoria: UNISA Press, 2010), ch. 2.

17 Mandela, "Labour," in *In His Own Words*, 212–13.

18 The representation of women in parliament increased from 2.7 percent during the apartheid era to 27 percent after the historic 1994 elections in South Africa and reached 44 percent after the 2009 elections. Several women (e.g., Nkosazana Zuma, Sankie Nkondo-Mahanyele, Stella Sigcau, Geraldine Fraser-Moleketi, Susan Shabangu, Lindiwe Sisulu, Thoko Didiza, Phumzile Mlambo-Ngcuka, Brigitte Mabandla, and Gill Marcus) were appointed full-fledged ANC cabinet ministers. In this Mandela was not, in my view, inspired so much by the feminist movement as by African traditions, not least the tradition of warrior-queens, who in southern Africa included Ndzinga of Angola, Kaipkire of the Herero, Manthatisi of the Batlokwa, Mkabayi of the amaZulu, Ntombazi, Queen Mother of the Ndwandwe, and Modjadji, the powerful Rain Queen. The role of women in the ANC leadership deserves a separate study, outside of Mandela's shadow.

19 Peter Limb, *Nelson Mandela: A Biography* (Westport, CT: Greenwood Press, 2008), 111.

20 Mandela, "African Peace," 541.

21 Examples are "Health and Human Rights," delivered on March 6, 1995; "Rural-Anti Poverty Programme" (October 13, 1998); and "A Clinic for Nobody" (September 20, 1997).

22 Mandela, "Planet and Humanity," in *In His Own Words*, 226–27.

23 Limb, *Nelson Mandela*, 116.

24 Mandela, "Reconciliation Day," in *In His Own Words*, 137–38. On the history of December 16 see F. A. van Jaarsveld, "A Historical Mirror of Blood River," in A. Koning and H. Keane, eds., *The Meaning of History* (Pretoria: University of South Africa Press, 1980), 8–59. This is an incisive essay by an Afrikaner historian exposing the myth of the commemoration of "Dingaan's Day." See also Isabel Hofmeyr, "Popularising History: The Case of Gustav Preller," in *Regions and Repertoires*, ed. Stephen Clingman (Randburg: Ravan Press, 1991), 60–83.

25 On the House of Traditional leaders, see M. P. Sithole and Sifiso M. Ndlovu, "CODESA at the Centre of a Complex Moral Question: Traditional Leadership in Negotiated Political Settlement in South Africa," in SADET, *The Road to Democracy in South Africa*, vol. 6, ch. 31.

26 Consider, for instance, the strong views expressed by Phathekile Holomisa, one of the leaders in the House of Traditional Leaders, that women did not "belong" in traditional leadership roles. His chauvinist viewpoint was rejected with the contempt it deserved.

27 Francis Meli, *South Africa Belongs to Us: A History of the ANC* (Harare: Zimbabwe Publishing House, 1988), 26–27.

28 Ibid., 54.

29 See Aziz Pahad, "Reflection on the International Scene," *Thinker* 5 (2009): 42–43; Landsberg, *Quiet Diplomacy*; Joe Matthews, "South African Foreign Policy Today," *Thinker* 5 (2009), 54–5. On Ubuntu and non-racial democracy in the international context, see Horace Campbell, *Barack Obama and Twenty-First-Century Politics: A Revolutionary Moment in the USA* (London: Pluto Press, 2010), ch. 2.

30 Brendan Vickers, "Pulpit Morality or Penny-pinching Diplomacy? The Discursive Debate on Mandela's Foreign Policy," *Politea* 21.2 (2002): 80–100.

31 See the following chapters in SADET, *The Road to Democracy in South Africa*, vol. 3: *International Solidarity* (Pretoria: UNISA Press, 2010): Christabel Gurney, "In the Heart of the Beast: The British Anti-Apartheid Movement, 1959–1994," 255–351; Sietse Bosgra, Jacqueline Derens, and Jacques Marchand, "France–South Africa," 667–77; Gottfried Wellmer, "A History of the Anti-Apartheid Movement in Federal Republic of Germany," 677–91; and William Minter and Sylvia Hill, "Anti-apartheid Solidarity in United States–South African Relations: From the Margins to the Mainstream," 745–822.

32 James Barber, *Mandela's World: The International Dimension of South Africa's Political Revolution, 1990–99* (Oxford: James Currey, 2004): 196–200. The metaphor is an appropriate one, given Mandela's prowess in boxing.

33 "Mandela's Address to the UN, 21 September 1998," in *In His Own Words*, 528–29.

34 Interview with Essop Pahad, conducted by Sifiso M. Ndlovu. See also Ndlovu, "The Relationship between the Collective and the Individual," South Africa Democracy Education Trust Oral History Project (Pretoria: SADET OHP).

35 Mandela, "African Peace," in *In His Own Words*, 539–42.

36 Ibid., 541. See also Landsberg, *Quiet Diplomacy*, 166.

37 The invasion was ordered by Chief Mangosuthu Buthelezi, who was acting president at the time.

38 Landsberg, *Quiet Diplomacy*, 166.

39 Ibid. See also Emmanuel Kisiangani, "Conflict in the Democratic Republic of the Congo," *Conflict Trends* 2 (2009): 38–44; and Khareen Pech, "The Hand of War: Mercenaries in the Former Zaire, 1996–97," in *Mercenaries: An African Security Dilemma*, ed. Abdel-Fatau Musah and J. Kayode Fayemi (London: Pluto Press, 2000), 117–54.

40 "Mandela Guns for Nigeria's Dictator," *Independent*, November 27, 1995.

41 The insights in this section are based on my series of interviews with Pahad (SADET OHP, Pretoria).

42 Mandela, "Long Walk Continues," 176.

PART III

Representing Mandela

9

DANIEL ROUX

Mandela Writing/Writing Mandela

At the time I was writing this chapter, every bookshop in South Africa seemed to have Heidi Holland's *100 Years of Struggle: Mandela's ANC* on display.[1] The book's cover boasts the green, black, and yellow of the African National Congress (ANC) flag with a picture of a raised fist, the defiant symbol of unity in struggle ineradicably associated, in this context, with Nelson Mandela. In the work, Holland makes the valid point that Mandela was instrumental in the militarization of the ANC and therefore responsible for its identity as a liberation movement. But the logic of the title belongs to mythology, not history. With the title's genitive case, Mandela comes to embody a history that precedes him and to own a party that he led, in actual fact, quite briefly from 1991 to 1997. Mandela's story is one of extraordinary individual achievement, but it is also, as Elleke Boehmer points out, "the collective many-voiced story of a nation coming into being."[2] Holland's book invokes this mythical "many-voiced" Mandela, a person who retroactively accounts for and abridges a long and complex history. To talk about Mandela is, in fact, to talk about what he has come to represent: triumph over adversity, dignity, the struggle for human rights.

When Mandela was released in 1990, he stepped into a symbolic role that had been scripted largely in his absence, and somehow the surprisingly avuncular, rather elderly man who walked out of Victor Verster Prison managed not to disappoint. If anything, his physical presence galvanized the myth – the "Madiba magic" discussed by Deborah Posel in Chapter 3 – and extended its scope. In his article "Mandela Comes Home: The Poets' Perspective," Russell Kaschula translates a Xhosa poem delivered by an unknown *imbongi* (praise poet) at a welcoming rally at the University of Transkei on April 23, 1990:

> They call him even if they don't know him
> They call him even if they have never seen him before
> That is why we need to be humble and respect one another,
> Because we have seen him at last.

An example of Jesus followed by many people,
He has come with them in truth and dignity,
That is where we can witness and hear his words,
That is where we have confirmed that his words are true.[3]

What is striking about this poem is the way it uses the language of Christ's advent to suggest that Mandela's physical presence serves to confirm his words; moreover, the poem suggests that the people who witness Mandela in person are constituted, in the act of witnessing, as a community. The real Mandela confirms the truth of his words, and his words acquire potency because of his presence. In *Living in Hope and History*, written in 1999, Nadine Gordimer attempts to insist on the historical reality of Mandela the man, but ends up seeing him as the embodiment and ideal of being human and a reflection of the global zeitgeist:

> Far from assuming a celestial status, Mandela has a quality that is, on the contrary, so fully and absolutely that of a man, the essence of a human being in all the term should mean, could mean, but seldom does. He belongs completely to a real life lived in a particular place and era and in its relation to the world. He is at the epicenter of our time; ours in South Africa, and yours, wherever you are.[4]

It is as if the figure of Mandela always points away from itself, toward an epoch, an ideal; he is like a smooth, impenetrable surface.

Remarkably, he seems to accommodate almost every projection, no matter how contradictory. For at least half a century, Xhosa praise poets have represented him as a lion, a resolute ox, a dangerous snake, a savior in a Christian tradition, a peacemaker, a warrior, Xhosa royalty, and an internationalist.[5] In Lewis Nkosi's slyly tongue-in-cheek novel, *Mandela's Ego*, Mandela becomes so closely associated with masculinity and sexual prowess in the mind of the young Zulu protagonist, Dumisani, that Mandela's eventual arrest by the Security Police results in decades of sexual impotence. In the earliest recorded poem about Mandela, "Chief Rolihlahla Nelson Mandela (Hail, Earth Tremor!)," written by Phakamile Yali-Manisi, one can already see the kaleidoscopic quality of subsequent representations: Mandela's internationalism ("mighty nations are puzzled, / for small nations are writhing, / straining, striving to burst their bonds"), his pan-African nationalism ("you've bridged nations great and small, / forging African unity: / all its nations are gripped in one birth pang"), his striking physical appearance ("Piercing needle, / handsome at Mthrikrakra's home"), his politicized masculinity ("Speak out fearlessly, Thembu! There are still men! / Speak out fearlessly, there're still men in Africa!"), and his potential martyrdom ("Even if death's in store, / you've been readied to serve / as blood offering for blacks").[6]

One of the difficulties that attend on writing about Mandela, then, especially in biographical and fictional modes that privilege interiority and individuality, is a sense that there is something missing from the depiction: to talk about Mandela becomes a conversation about what Mandela represents, and what Mandela represents becomes identical to his life, as if his life is always already an instrument in the service of some larger narrative. In the mythologized figure of Mandela, South Africans encounter a kind of limit to their attempts to demythologize their past and to reach more complex understandings of the genealogy of the present.

The Missing Manuscript: Finding the True Mandela

Mandela claims that he based his autobiography, *Long Walk to Freedom*, on a manuscript that he prepared in prison in 1975 and managed to smuggle out in 1976, and that subsequently went missing in Lusaka.[7] This missing manuscript, as David Schalkwyk points out, acts as a kind of non-presence, an awkward supplement to the future-oriented, nation-building agenda of *Long Walk to Freedom*. The published autobiography "displaces or acts as a substitute for the original, which, unlike the later work, was forged in the actual conditions of incarceration. The later memoir thus represses or suppresses the former."[8] It is, of course, entirely possible that *Long Walk to Freedom* represses nothing, but the point is that it is difficult to read Mandela's memoir without the sense that it substitutes for something else or to encounter any representation of Mandela without feeling that it overshoots its mark, even as it fails to include some essential detail. When Gordimer pursues her desire to demythologize Mandela she ends up discovering not the human being, but the "essence of a human being": a quality that is both larger than any particular individual and too limited to convey the singularity of a person.

In her book *A Change of Tongue*, the Afrikaans poet and journalist Antjie Krog describes a disastrous television interview with Mandela at his house in Qunu. Armed with some anodyne pre-approved questions, she encounters a fatigued, angry Mandela, whose dismissive, militant responses leave her feeling deeply embarrassed and somewhat brutalized. For a moment, it is as if she catches a glimpse of a wholly other Mandela: a rather unfeeling revolutionary behind the customary gracious mask. After the interview, Mandela's personal secretary acknowledges that she had never seen Mandela as severe as during his interview with Krog and explains that the election campaign was running him into the ground. Krog remarks, rather disconsolately, that "it is his good right not to like a journalist. Or to ridicule the questions. But it feels a bit like finding out that God doesn't like you."[9] This is probably the closest that any recent writing comes to producing an alternative to the dominant post-apartheid stories about Mandela. Krog goes on to recount a conversation with a friend soon after the interview. They discuss the nuances of Mandela's surprising response, and the friend concludes with some advice, couched as a question: "Why are you unwilling to grant him a nuanced space in which he can reach out and reprimand because he knows and believes all people are equal, while at the same time feeling free to let his frustration surface at times, and be accepted for it? The space of sainthood is not really a space – besides, one cannot learn from a saint how to live in this world."[10] Krog manages to use this dialogue in her narrative to humanize Mandela by showing us his inhuman face. Instead of disclosing some private, interior dimension to the public persona, Mandela's remarkably personal, charming public facade seems here to conceal something much more formal: an instrument of history, a servant to the struggle, who speaks on behalf of a collective and not himself.

What is revealed here is not some secret, authentic content that belies the myth, but an absence of the more human qualities with which Mandela is popularly associated. However, the brief and shocking disclosure of the militancy behind the genial mask serves, almost paradoxically, to make Mandela seem more like an ordinary person, by suggesting that he is susceptible to fatigue and irritation, a human being like everyone else. In fact, Mandela's responses to Krog during the interview are perfectly consonant with claims that Mandela has often made about himself and that tend to be read as evidence of his humility: he lacks warmth; his personal life is irreducibly connected to his public role; he plays the role of a cosmopolitan celebrity because that is his job in the post-apartheid moment, in the same way that being a revolutionary soldier was his job under apartheid. What Krog "uncovers" is really no more than what has always already been on the surface.

This desire to disclose some hidden truth about Mandela is a recurrent theme, especially in more recent attempts to come to grips with his personality, history, and legacy, but at the same time Mandela seems at some level simply to defuse this kind of scrutiny; it is as if all revelations about Mandela paradoxically end up consolidating his familiar public image. Even Max du Preez, a veteran renegade Afrikaner journalist, concedes an admiring kind of defeat in his encounter with Mandela. In his book *Pale Native*, Du Preez recalls his first live television interview with the state president at the time, F. W. de Klerk. He remarks that De Klerk seemed annoyed afterward by his tough questions but adds that the man nonetheless handled the interview well: "If only politicians would realise that soft, sycophantic television interviews don't do anything for them in the eyes of the public – if you can hold your own with an aggressive interviewer, you win." [11] After sharing this insight, the *enfant terrible* of South African journalism goes on to name the one exception to his interview philosophy. "My television interviews with the new president, Nelson Mandela, were in stark contrast. I simply could not be aggressive, or even mildly assertive. He was such a gigantic presence; when he talks, you shut up. Sometimes, when he paused, I would try to jump in to speed up the pace of the interview. He would just fix you with a stare and continue with what he was saying." [12] Perhaps one needs to be embedded in South African society to understand how surprising this admission is, coming from Max du Preez: he allowed Mandela to set the pace and the content of his television interviews.

In his recent book, *Young Mandela*, David Smith makes a concerted effort to escape from the silencing effect of Mandela's "gigantic presence." Smith's biography is a sustained attempt to sketch a revisionist portrait of Mandela, a "warts and all" appraisal of his life before his incarceration. "My plan was to rescue the sainted Madiba from the dry pages of history," Smith maintains, "to strip away the myth and create a fresh portrait of a rounded human being, setting his political achievements in the context of his natural character." [13] Thus Smith focuses on Mandela's mistreatment of his first wife, Evelyn, speculates that he had affairs with Lilian Ngoyi, Dolly Rathebe, and Ruth Mompati, neglected his children, and so on. Nonetheless, the book hardly manages to dislodge Mandela's mythical status. In fact, Mandela has always conceded that he made mistakes in his youth and that he was intemperate. If anything, Smith's book simply sharpens the contrast between the youthful and the mature Mandela, a contrast that has always been central to Mandela's self-representation. As Mandela notes in his unpublished sequel to *Long Walk to Freedom*: "As a young man I ... combined all the weaknesses, errors, and indiscretions of a country boy, whose range of vision and experience was influenced mainly by events in the area in which I grew up and the colleges to which I was sent. I relied on arrogance to hide my weaknesses." [14] Smith's book represents Mandela's maturation as a transformative – even transmutational – event in a way that verifies rather than undermines Mandela's numinous authority. Thus, when Mandela meets Esmé Matshikiza in London in 1962, we are told that "he was not the same person any more, not the person she had known back home. Esmé had the feeling that he was up there, way above them all somewhere, a visionary, with an aura of someone special." [15] Smith's book, for all its revisionist impulses, simply seems to reproduce a familiar narrative trajectory – one that was essentially created by Mandela himself – and ends up leaving Mandela's iconic status intact.

The Illusion of a Unitary Subject

How do we account for this sense that the figure of Mandela is unassailable, a figure whose mythical status seems paradoxically fortified rather than diminished by his more sublunary human qualities? Representations of Mandela, no matter how varied or even contradictory, continue to produce the effect of a unitary subject, one who is deeply familiar and simultaneously essentially inscrutable. In fact, Mandela's self-representation seems to resist appropriation. Mandela is recognized as an individual with unique but universalizable qualities – despite, or perhaps even because of, his human failings: his irascibility, his occasional intolerance. Indeed, part of his allure rests precisely in his ability to admit his shortcomings, to overcome his own limitations.

What makes this sense of representational continuity even more remarkable is that Mandela's life in the public eye can be divided into three overarching and quite distinct phases. First, between 1947, when he was elected to the National Executive Committee of the ANC, and his incarceration on Robben Island in 1964, he consolidated his identity as a passionate and flamboyant young revolutionary at the vanguard of the struggle against state oppression. Next, between 1964 and 1990, when he was finally released from prison, his invisibility facilitated his mythologization. In many ways, he became a site for the projection of many disparate fantasies and aspirations. What these representations had in common, however, was their insistence on Mandela as martyr, a condition for his elevation to sainthood: an elevation that Mandela registered, while in prison, and felt troubled by. In the unpublished sequel to his autobiography, Mandela observes:

> One issue that deeply worried me in prison was the false image that I unwittingly projected to the outside world; of being regarded as a saint. I never was one, even on the basis of an earthly definition of a saint as a sinner who keeps on trying.[16]

It was also during this period that Mandela increasingly became identified as the (absent) face of the ANC, and the ANC, somewhat misleadingly, as the principal representative of the more general struggle against apartheid. The third phase, dating from after his release in 1990, was the era of Madiba, the elder statesman, role model, peacemaker, and global celebrity, whose occasional patrician severity always found a counterpoint in his sense of humor, his colorful clothes, his gentle flirtatiousness, and his sociability. Throughout this historical trajectory, there were also very strong competing representations, like the Nationalist Party's Mandela, a Communist and terrorist with the blood of innocents on his hands, and the Black Consciousness Mandela, a man whose willingness to collaborate across ideological and racial boundaries marked him as an unsatisfactory substitute for Robert Sobukwe, Robben Island's other important (and commonly neglected) prisoner.

How, then, did these different images of Mandela, often yoked to competing aspirations, solidify in an essentially congruent way in a single person? With the benefit of hindsight, it seems a superfluous question to ask; the intuitive answer is simply that Mandela impressed everyone with his principled, forgiving stance and that the impression that he made of a self-reflexive, deeply humane person whose ideas matured over time tended to displace or obscure some of those abiding and jarring "antinomies" discussed by Philip Bonner in Chapter 1. Perhaps it is worth pausing here to note that the former view is predicated on the understanding of Mandela as an exceptional human being who exemplifies certain ethical values that enjoy eminence during this phase of global modernity. It is not a view that I would quarrel with. But what such a judgment omits, even if it is essentially reasonable and correct, is a focus on the process that rendered these qualities visible and widely intelligible. In the transitional period from 1990 to 1994, in particular, South Africa was a volatile nascent democracy, the country seemed on the brink of civil war, and acts of violence and brutality were attended by a cacophony of voices making use of new freedoms to claim public platforms and to speak through the media. The figure of Mandela, specifically, was charged with meaning: when he walked out of prison, he was a profoundly overdetermined figure. It is a remarkable achievement, under such conditions, to present an image of a complex yet coherent subjectivity and almost universally comprehensible moral probity. How was this feat accomplished?

Part of the answer to this question is, of course, that it was achieved through many different public performances and statements that coalesced over time. His biographer Tom Lodge makes the point that "[f]or Mandela, politics has always been primarily about enacting stories, about making narratives" and remarks that Mandela and his associates in some respects made a conscious decision to construct Mandela as a mythological figure while he served as the commander of Umkhonto we Sizwe (MK), the military wing of the ANC.[17] Indeed, as many commentators (most notably Boehmer) have pointed out, Mandela has always exercised extraordinary care to determine how he is represented. This preoccupation with self-presentation surfaces, in quite instructive ways, at key moments in the narrative of *Long Walk to Freedom*. Consider, for instance, Mandela's description of an incident that occurred during the early years of his incarceration on Robben Island. One particular day, the prison officials issued the prisoners some worn jerseys to fix, instead of their usual hammers for work in the courtyard. The prisoners soon discovered that the reason for this change in routine was a visit from two journalists from the London-based *Daily Telegraph*. Mandela observes that the prisoners treated this visit with skepticism, since the journalists "were brought in under the auspices of the government" and the *Daily Telegraph* had a reputation as a conservative paper. Mandela observes that "it was in the government's interest to show that we were not being mistreated."[18] Nonetheless, he agreed to be interviewed and talked candidly about the Rivonia trial and about prison. When he was asked whether the photographer could take his picture, he reluctantly consented because he felt that friendly publicity abroad might do the liberation cause some good. On an earlier occasion, however, he invoked prison regulations in order to prevent a warden from taking his picture "on the ground that it is generally demeaning to be seen as a prisoner."[19] In this latter instance, Mandela simply refused to have his image appropriated and used by the prison. He insisted on maintaining control over his own image, and, in a typical gesture, he did so by invoking the rules of the very institution that wanted to represent him. The encounter with the *Daily Telegraph* reporters is not as clear-cut. On the one hand, Mandela insisted on a degree of influence over the picture by demanding that Walter Sisulu join him; in this, he refused the individualizing operation of the prison and composed an image of solidarity and cooperation (a gesture that underpins the entire autobiography). On the other hand, his acerbic remark that "the reporters were barely out of sight when the warders removed the jerseys and gave us back our hammers" serves as a reminder that the picture was ultimately staged by the prison, and the fact that he "never saw the article or heard anything about it" implies a certain anxiety about his lack of control over the use of the picture and the meanings it was made to generate: the picture became marked by a worrying ambivalence, an uncertainty appertaining to ownership and control.[20]

What we should recognize here is an incessant, thoughtful engagement with his own image, its contexts, and its uses: for Mandela, part of the struggle against apartheid oppression is precisely a struggle for control of the terms of representation. In this sense, he fulfilled a particular mandate of the ANC, one that became absolutely crucial in South Africa's transition to democracy. As Rita Barnard observes, "For an organization so long underground, officially erased from view, the politics of symbolic display – the task of visually reconquering the national and international public sphere – was inevitably of great importance."[21] Mandela was uniquely situated to fulfill this requirement, not only through visual self-display, but essentially by scripting a narrative to anchor and naturalize his different representations.

However, to claim that Mandela exercised careful control over his image is really only a partial answer to the question, what was it about the image he projected that made it so resilient and capacious? What linked Mandela's self-representations was an overarching narrative; in fact, it is the story that he presents in his autobiography, *Long Walk to Freedom*. Another anecdote recorded by Krog is relevant here. She learns from a friend of Mandela's (identified only as Rebecca) that someone who visited Mandela the previous day was struck by the way he tended to repeat certain stories almost verbatim as they appear in *Long Walk to Freedom*. Rebecca discussed this assertion with Mandela's right-hand man, who claimed Mandela did it only with some stories: "Mandela is doing it intentionally.... As if Mandela wants to say that there are certain truths which should always exist as truths, and that these important truths should continue to exist in precisely the same way."[22] To understand the overall cohesion of the many ways in which Mandela is portrayed across diverse media ultimately means paying attention to his powerful, widely disseminated autobiography, which brings together Mandela's personal life story, the history of the struggle against colonial domination and apartheid, many of Mandela's speeches inside and outside the courtroom, ANC policy documents, Mandela's philosophical and ethical ruminations, and his speculations about the future – all in a single narrative object. To some extent, then, the question about the foundation of Mandela's resilience and stability as a public icon is a question about literary form.

The Literary Foundations of Mandela's Public Image

There are two interlocked ways in which *Long Walk to Freedom* serves to stabilize the figure of Mandela. First of all, it consistently employs a form of metaphoric inversion (chiasmus) that allows Mandela to advance specific counterintuitive propositions. Second, its plot traces the processes of maturation and development of an individual from youth to maturity in the generic form of the bildungsroman. To be clear, my primary interest is not to attempt some classification of *Long Walk to Freedom* in a taxonomy of literary tropes or genres; rather, like the figure of Mandela himself, his autobiography seems accommodating to various classificatory schemes.[23] Moreover, as almost all commentators on the genre point out, the bildungsroman is in some ways an impossible classification, perhaps even, as Marc Redfield argues in *Phantom Formations*, an invention of academic literary criticism rather than an actually existing type of story with determinate characteristics.[24] What I would like to suggest, instead, is that when *Long Walk to Freedom* is read as a bildungsroman, aspects of the technical way in which it represents causes and effects become foregrounded. Once these elements become visible, it may be quite possible to discard the term and to use other critical lenses to achieve the job at hand. In other words, I am saying that when we investigate Mandela's autobiography as a bildungsroman, a certain dimension of its allegoresis becomes visible.

We can grasp something of the formal method that sustains Mandela's self-representation by considering how *Long Walk to Freedom* develops the metaphor of the garden and the idea of Mandela as a gardener. Boehmer comments on the role that gardening on Robben Island and later at Pollsmoor Prison played in Mandela's personal development: "With his cultivation of a patch of earth – discovering a common love of soil and plant-rearing with his captors – Mandela developed important insights into the qualities of forbearance and cooperation, and into the accommodations that eventual mastery, including self-mastery, would entail."[25] To this one could add that Mandela also employs the garden as a literary device, a metaphor that establishes a certain kind of narrative continuity as a marker of character development. The gardens that we encounter in *Long Walk to Freedom* are not merely descriptive, particularly because the autobiography is so powerfully performative: it provides a frame for viewing self and nation, not just a depiction of a life, or a historical moment, or some sort of propaganda, although it might contain elements of these.

The first extended description of a garden in *Long Walk to Freedom* is Mandela's account of Reverend Harris's garden at Clarkebury, the Thembu college Mandela attended as a young man and where he first encountered a Western way of life: "a new world," as he says, "whose rules were not yet clear to me."[26] Clarkebury, Mandela notes, was run in an authoritarian fashion by the severe Harris, a principal who was "feared more than loved" by the students. However, when the young Mandela assists him in the garden, he recognizes that "Reverend Harris had a public face and a private manner that were quite different from one another."[27] In the garden, Mandela finds a respite from the rather Victorian discipline of the school and encounters a stern white man's more human side. Mandela claims that this experience instilled his lifelong love of gardening. The garden becomes a meeting place, a place of crossings and encounters, even though it is also the Reverend Harris's private place, removed from the normal social sphere of the school. The thematics of public and private on which Mandela draws in these recollections has literary currency in many South African (anti-)pastoral fictions (including J. M. Coetzee's *Life and Times of Michael K*), and it recurs in subsequent references to gardens in the autobiography. On Robben Island, for example, Mandela is eventually allowed to cultivate a small garden on the prison grounds. This garden seems at first to offer, as at Clarkebury, a pleasant diversion from the harshness of prison life. However, Mandela metaphorizes the space in a different way. As Boehmer remarks, Mandela's prison garden "afforded a readily available correlative for the strategies of political transformation he was sketching in his mind."[28] It acquires, in other words, a political dimension, not least because Mandela has to win the right to garden by petitioning the prison authorities year after year. While the garden remains a solitary retreat, its privacy, its association with the individual rather than the collective, is transformed into an allegory for leadership. "In some ways," Mandela writes, "I saw the garden as a metaphor for certain aspects of my life. A leader must also tend his garden; he, too, sows seeds, and then watches, cultivates and harvests the result."[29]

This strategic transformation of solitary endeavor into the prerogative of leadership occurs elsewhere in *Long Walk to Freedom*. When Mandela makes the contentious decision to negotiate with the apartheid government, he decides not to inform his comrades of his decision. "There are times when a leader must move out ahead of the flock, go off in a new direction," he explains, "confident that he is leading his people the right way."[30] Mandela represents the figure of the leader as a servant of history; in this way, his individualism becomes but a stage in the realization of the collective will. If the garden offers an allegory and testing ground for leadership, Mandela also recognizes the garden as an occasion for autonomy, a form of individual freedom in a penal environment that is by definition hostile to this kind of liberty: "A garden was one of the few things in prison that one could control. To plant a seed, watch it grow, to tend it and then harvest it offered a simple but enduring satisfaction. The sense of being the custodian of this small patch of earth offered a small taste of freedom."[31] By deploying the garden as a trope that yokes individual liberty, autonomy, and private reflection to leadership, Mandela, as it were, discovers that the private is always already political and that individual agency is a retroactive realization of the collective revolutionary agency of the people. The garden metaphor is a narrative device that facilitates and naturalizes this inversion. Mandela takes the "humanizing" aspect of the garden (which remains closely tied to the European pastoral and its conception of the garden as a place of private self-cultivation, a place where nurturing kindness can flourish) and decisively transforms this symbolic plot of soil into the space of the political par excellence.

This transformation renders the trope of the garden and gardening somewhat ambivalent in the autobiography. This ambivalence is beautifully illustrated in a photo of Mandela taken in 1977 – against his will and

Figure 9.1. "A Prisoner in the Garden," 1977. Courtesy of Nelson Mandela Centre of Memory.

not in his garden, incidentally, though it nevertheless came to be titled "A Prisoner in the Garden" (Figure 9.1). Dressed in the impeccably neat and ironed clothes of an English gentleman at leisure, Mandela stares at the camera with undisguised hostility, his foreboding dignity at variance with the caption. As Boehmer remarks about the same photograph: "Here we see the political prisoner laying claim to his patch of ground, his island rock, a piece of his nation, making it fruitful."[32] This is the gardener as revolutionary, a bit like Wittgenstein's "duckrabbit": now it is the globally recognizable figure of a leisure gardener, and now the highly masculinized, forbidding figure of the revolutionary. I would argue that Mandela's ability to appeal to different constituencies across the divided South African landscape has always had to do with the polyvalent, ambiguous nature of his signs and performances.

Self-Narration and Human Rights

The very title of his autobiography, *Long Walk to Freedom*, is itself an example of the kind of inversion I have outlined. In the last paragraph of the book, Mandela transforms the destination of the metaphoric walk into a point of departure: "I have walked that long road to freedom.... But I can rest only for a moment, for with freedom come responsibilities, and I dare not linger, for my long walk is not yet ended."[33] Such transpositional metaphors are essential to Mandela's technique of self-representation: they yoke fundamental divisions, such as the personal and the political, individual and collective, freedom and service, destruction and growth, and the local and the global together in the narrative equivalent of a non-orientable curved surface, like a Möbius strip. One of the ways in which this metaphorical artifice of reversal and reconciliation is naturalized is generic. For the garden at Clarkebury and the one at Robben Island are also moments in a narrative, the logic of which becomes visible when we think of *Long Walk to Freedom* as a bildungsroman: a novel about growth and education, where, as Wilhelm Dilthey puts it, "the dissonance and conflict of life appear as necessary crossing points for the individual on his road to maturity and harmony."[34]

In *Human Rights Inc.*, Joseph Slaughter identifies two aspects of the bildungsroman that are important for this argument. The first is that a bildungsroman deals with someone who, through interactions with others and introspection, develops into the person he or she has always already been. The bildungsroman shows how the underlying nature of the protagonist both propels the plot and is created by it, as the outcome of a series of windfalls, setbacks, interactions with others, ruminations, crucial choices, and so on. At the end of the bildungsroman, the protagonist can say, "Now I am finally the person I was destined to be at the outset"; the mature narrative voice is the expression of the personality of the character that provoked the story in the first place, that caused its telling.[35] As Franco Moretti notes, a bildungs-narrative "ends as soon as an intentional design has been realized: a design which involves the protagonist and determines the overall meaning of the plot."[36] The second aspect of the bildungsroman that is germane to my argument relates to its relationship to the social. Slaughter claims that the Enlightenment philosophy of *Bildung* "imagines a humanist process of transubstantiation by which the individual concretizes its abstract species image and realizes the intellectually enabling fiction of a harmonious, natural human personality through self-contemplation and self-cultivation of 'a universal sense' – a transcendental sense of identification with humanity in general."[37] The classic idealist bildungsroman is a literary attempt to

comprehend and express this process. In the bildungsroman, the protagonist's full individualization is coterminous with the full assumption of social
responsibility: it is subjectivization at its purest. The bildungsroman provides, Moretti observes, "one of the most harmonious solutions ever offered
to a dilemma conterminous with modern bourgeois civilization: the conflict
between the ideal of self-determination and the equally imperious demands
of socialization."[38] If we regard *Long Walk to Freedom* through this generic
lens, what becomes striking is precisely the way in which it realizes this
essentially modernist project of internalizing and working with the contradiction between individual freedom and social responsibility by unfolding
the tension into a narrative form.

The final pages of the autobiography provide a potent summary of
Mandela's bildungs-motif. "I was not born with a hunger to be free," he
writes. "I was born free – free in every way that I could know."[39] However,
this boyhood freedom is revealed to be an illusion, and the young Mandela
starts to desire personal freedom: "I wanted freedom only for myself, the
transitory freedoms of being able to stay out at night, read what I pleased and
go where I chose."[40] Gradually, Mandela explains, this hunger for freedom
acquired a social dimension, and membership in the ANC became coterminous with this articulation of personal and collective liberty: "I saw that it
was not just my freedom that was curtailed, but the freedom of everyone
who looked like I did. That is when I joined the African National Congress,
and that is when the hunger for my own freedom became the greater hunger for the freedom of my people."[41] This increasing orientation toward the
social, the fulcrum of a bildungs-narrative, is understood through a series of
binaries that are reversed: it accounts for Mandela's purported transformation from a frightened young man into a bold one, a law-abiding attorney
into an outlaw, a family-loving man into a person without a home, and a
sociable man into one who lived like a monk.[42] Finally, on this deceptively
neat timeline, the desire for collective freedom is realized through the struggle for *universal rights*: rights that serve the former oppressors as much as
the oppressed. "I knew as well as I knew anything," Mandela remarks, "that
the oppressor must be liberated just as surely as the oppressed."[43] When
Mandela finally achieves a provisional version of the personal freedom that
he mistakenly believed he had in the first place – a mistake that acts as the
catalyst for the story of his life – it is only through a rights-driven process of
universalization that is accomplished in narrative time.

The structure of this overarching bildungs-narrative is tirelessly iterated
in Mandela's writing and speeches. Indeed, *Long Walk to Freedom* is structured like a Russian doll, with modularized versions of this transformative

process assembled into a large bildungs-narrative with the prison at its center. Almost all the conflicts that Mandela describes on Robben Island – between prisoners and warders, between common-law and political prisoners, between the different political parties and between the different generations of activists – follow a similar pattern.

When confronted with the militancy of the young Black Consciousness prisoners after the Soweto riots of 1976, for instance, Mandela responds to the threat that this new generation of combative prisoners posed to the relatively ordered life on Robben Island by invoking precisely the chronological template that I outlined earlier:

> Just as we had outgrown our Youth League outlook, I was confident that these young men would transcend some of the strictures of Black Consciousness. While I was encouraged by their militancy, I thought that their philosophy, in its concentration on blackness, was sectarian, and represented an intermediate view that was not fully mature. I saw my role as an elder statesman who might help them move on to the more inclusive ideas of the Congress Movement.[44]

In the face of ideological opposition, Mandela typically represents his own ideological view, which is fully conflated with that of the ANC, as the more mature, transcendent resolution. By presenting the Black Consciousness point of view as a kind of inchoate, underdeveloped manifestation of the ANC position, he is in effect universalizing the ANC's perspective. His role becomes to help others realize that their standpoint is always already the position of the ANC, which in turn is simply a resolved reflection of all possible points of view. In this way, the ANC's specific political stance starts to function as a stable position *above* the political, a position that might serve as the collective voice of a *nation* rather than a political faction.

Needless to say, this notion of factionalized self-interest that comes to realize its universal, social potential by passing through the crucible of struggle, persecution, and imprisonment under the guidance of the ANC did not always coincide with day-to-day reality. Mandela regarded the common-law prisoners that were present during his early days on Robben Island "not as rivals but raw material to be converted" and duly explains how he and his comrades fought to improve conditions in prison for everyone. [45] However, Mandela's description of the relationship between the political prisoners and the common-law prisoners on the Island ends rather abruptly with a betrayal rather than the more typical narrative conclusion of assimilation and conversion. Mandela recounts how he tried to help a convict called Bogart, who was assaulted by a warder at the quarry. His attempt to assist his fellow prisoner collapsed when Bogart accepted a bribe and denied that the assault ever took place, humiliating Mandela in front of the commanding officer.[46] "From that point on," Mandela ends this curious chapter, "I demanded a signed and written statement from a prisoner before I agreed to take up his case."[47] A bildungs-narrative is, in fact, well equipped to recuperate these aporetic moments in which the genre encounters obstacles to its logic: obstructions can always be reformulated as learning experiences or challenges for the future, so that descriptive limitations become assimilated by the future-orientated trajectory of the narrative. As a senior statesman, Mandela proved disarmingly adept at reframing criticism in terms of precisely such an understanding of learning and progress.[48]

Long Walk to Freedom's central preoccupation is the ability of rights discourse – a discourse that is closely associated with the ANC – to transform the oppressive social sphere into an enabling one. For Mandela, an insistence on rights is a form of resistance, but it is ideally effected through consensus and legal compliance. The prison and its various spaces – the cell, the quarry, the garden – provide both a stage and a narrowly circumscribed stock of spatial metaphors that allows Mandela to speak simultaneously as an individual compelled to record the facts of his life and the history of his personality in a situation that denies the legitimacy of a black person's experience, as a revolutionary subject-instrument in the service of freedom, and as a venerable leader who needs to consolidate a new state and translate his personal experiences into a kind of parable to render recent South African history intelligible.

The composite character of Mandela's autobiography, which Philip Holden also remarks on in his *Autobiography and Decolonization*,[49] is negotiated and to a certain extent veiled by precisely such metaphoric spaces that allow multiple, even apparently contradictory roles to be understood as logically congruent aspects of a single subjectivity: the prison, the courtroom, the school, the garden. Mandela yokes the bildungsroman format securely to a sophisticated understanding of the reformist nature of human rights law – an unrevolutionary resolution to a romantically revolutionary life, which manages to draw on the energy and spectacle of a legitimating revolution in order to secure a peaceful civic sphere. In this way, for instance, Mandela takes the benign, even banal idea of the gardener and reinvents it: the revolutionary leader is reborn as a gardener, the revolutionary energy that threatens to dissolve the social bond becomes the energy that insists on the proper, legal constitution of a social bond and on the primacy of the social. Indeed, one might say that on Robben Island the prisoners eventually turned into their own warders: "In a way that even the authorities acknowledged," Mandela observes, "order in prison was preserved not by the warders but by ourselves."[50] Mandela's notion of freedom sometimes seems almost paradoxically to coincide with prison that adheres fully to its own rules, its own purported reformative goal, and therefore – in true Benthamite fashion – stops being a prison.

If *Long Walk to Freedom* can in some respects be read as a classic bildungsroman it is, in fact, also a sophisticated translation of the themes of *Bildung* into a language of rights: where the classic bildungsroman is preoccupied with personality, Mandela conflates the idea of an (individual) personality with the more technical idea of a legal person. In this way, Mandela's much-feted personable character becomes entangled quite explicitly with the abstract notion of a rights-bearing individual. Mandela casts his own life as a journey toward a person-ness that then becomes generally applicable, a template for being a person in a just society. In the final instance, Mandela's self represents a remarkable superimposition of the literary idea of the fictional bildungs-protagonist onto the fiction of the person of human rights law.

This culmination of Mandela's particular life story in the figure of a rights-bearing person allows Mandela to link an eminently local, specific identity to a formal legal template that is by definition universalizable. Mandela's realization of his rights is represented as the natural outcome and expression of his personality, and his personality, as he constantly reminds us, is what set the long walk of the narrative in motion in the first place: "I was young and impatient, and did not see the virtue in waiting."[51] *Long Walk to Freedom* creates a narrating voice that is poised between individual and the social, but also one that is eminently global. In this precise sense *Long Walk to Freedom* strains against the limitations of a "national allegory," to use Fredric Jameson's term;[52] the concept of rights that animates it is always in excess of a particular communality and linked to a particularly deterritorialized modernist ideal.

Mandela, in sum, has provided a compelling and highly transportable generic form for understanding the "lessons" of history alongside the story of the self, one that can accommodate disjuncture, contradiction, multiplicity, and paradoxes by appealing to a complex notion of development that unfolds in narrative time. If it is difficult to look behind Mandela's mask or to challenge some of the dominant myths about the man, it is because Mandela's self-representation always already anticipated such challenges and incorporated them. To talk about Mandela differently we would have to talk outside his understanding of time, a possibility that is still to come, as we stand at the very edge of the persuasive and influential national historical imaginary of Nelson Mandela.

NOTES

1 Heidi Holland, *100 Years of Struggle: Mandela's ANC* (Johannesburg: Penguin SA, 2012).

2 Elleke Boehmer, *Nelson Mandela: A Very Short Introduction* (Oxford: Oxford University Press, 2008), 5. This is a point also made by Sifiso Ndlovu in Chapter 8, this volume.

3 Russell Kaschula, "Mandela Comes Home: The Poets' Perspective," *Oral Tradition* 10.1 (1995): 100.

4 Nadine Gordimer, *Living in Hope and History* (London: Bloomsbury, 1999), 153.

5 Noxolo Bobelo, "IsiXhosa Poetry on Nelson Rholihlahla Mandela," MA thesis (Johannesburg: University of Johannesburg, 2008), 67–92.

6 The full poem, co-translated from Xhosa with Manisi, appears in Jeff Opland's "The Early Career of D. L. P. Yali-Manisi, Thembu Imbongi," *Research in African Literatures* 33.1 (2002): 20–22.

7 Nelson Mandela, *Long Walk to Freedom: The Autobiography of Nelson Mandela* (London: Abacus, 1994), 467.

8 David Schalkwyk, "Mandela's Missing Manuscript," in *Leaves to a Tree*, ed. Robin Malan (Cape Town: South African Council for English Education, 2005), 207.

9 Antjie Krog, *A Change of Tongue* (Cape Town: Random House Struik, 2003), 246.

10 Ibid., 259.

11 Max du Preez, *Pale Native: Memories of a Renegade Reporter* (Cape Town: Zebra Press, 2010), 263.

12 Ibid., 263.

13 David James Smith, *Young Mandela* (London: Weidenfeld & Nicolson, 2010), vii.

14 Mandela, *Long Walk*, 467.

15 Smith, *Young Mandela*, 260.

16 Nelson Mandela, *Conversations with Myself* (London: Macmillan, 2010), 410.

17 Tom Lodge, *Mandela: A Critical Life* (Oxford: Oxford University Press, 2006), ix.

18 Mandela, *Long Walk*, 470.

19 Ibid., 471.

20 Ibid., 470–71.

21 Rita Barnard, "Contesting Beauty," in *Senses of Culture: South African Cultural Studies*, ed. Sarah Nuttall and Cheryl-Ann Michael (Oxford: Oxford University Press, 2000), 355.

22 Krog, *A Change of Tongue*, 256–57.

23 Zodwa Motsa, for instance, claims that the conflation of individual and national aspirations in *Long Walk to Freedom* places it in the tradition of the African epic. See Zodwa Motsa, "*Long Walk to Freedom* and the Mutating Face of the Epic," *Journal of Literary Studies* 25.2 (2009): 7–24.

24 Marc Redfield, *Phantom Formations: Aesthetic Ideology and the Bildungsroman* (Ithaca, NY: Cornell University Press, 1996).

25 Mandela, *Long Walk*, 174.

26 Ibid., 38.
27 Ibid., 41.
28 Boehmer, *Mandela*, 162.
29 Mandela, *Long Walk*, 583.
30 Ibid., 627.
31 Ibid.
32 Boehmer, *Mandela*, 163.
33 Mandela, *Long Walk*, 751.
34 Wilhelm Dilthey, *Das Erlebnis und die Dichtung: Lessing, Goethe, Novalis, Hölderlin* (Leipzig, 1922), 395, my translation.
35 Joseph Slaughter, *Human Rights Inc.: The World Novel, Narrative Form, and International Law* (New York: Fordham University Press, 2007), 97–98.
36 Franco Moretti, *The Way of the World: The Bildungsroman in European Culture* (London: Verso, 1987), 55.
37 Slaughter, *Human Rights Inc.*, 111.
38 Moretti, The Way of the World, 15.
39 Mandela, *Long Walk*, 750.
40 Ibid.
41 Ibid.
42 Ibid.
43 Ibid., 751.
44 Ibid., 578.
45 Ibid., 484.
46 Ibid., 485–86.
47 Ibid., 486.
48 Peter Limb recounts how the journalist John Pilger confronted the retired Mandela about his presidency's financial support of the notorious Suharto regime in East Timor. According to Limb, "Mandela asked Pilger if he had perhaps been too soft on Suharto, conceding that to him such things were often 'a dilemma.' Pilger in turn could not but concede Mandela's grace." See Limb, *Nelson Mandela: A Biography* (Westport, CT: Greenwood Press, 2008), 124.
49 Philip Holden, *Autobiography and Decolonization: Modernity, Masculinity, and the Nation-State* (Madison: University of Wisconsin Press, 2008), 143.
50 Mandela, *Long Walk*, 464.
51 Ibid., 65.
52 Frederic Jameson contends that in "Third World" narratives, "the story of the private individual destiny is always an allegory of the embattled situation of the public third-world culture and society." See "Third-World Literature in the Era of Multinational Capitalism," *Social Text* 15.1 (1986): 69.

10

LITHEKO MODISANE

Mandela in Film and Television

Oh, cameras in space, hurtling to pierce planets
In search of light
In search of life
Show us the thoughts of an old man kept in a cage.
John Pepper Clark, "Mandela"[1]

There are many Mandelas. A revolutionary hero, a prisoner of conscience, a social being, a media personality, and in some eyes a traitor, Nelson Mandela, aka Rolihlahla, Dalibhunga, Madiba, and at one point David Motsamai, is many things to many people. A subject of many memoirs, political treatises, popular reference works, films, graffiti, even "art" purported to be of his own making, the figure of Nelson Mandela attracts diverse platforms and perspectives.[2] He has inspired the birth of a whole industry, partly dedicated to his ideas, but mostly trained on the magnetism of his persona. The signification of Mandela has become more important than the man, and his value as an article of commerce knows no bounds.[3] Nelson Mandela is an object and an effect of various forms of representation, catapulting him beyond mortal foibles and ordinary political agency.

Though Mandela has always been conscious of his public persona and made serious efforts to cultivate it, it was only in the 1970s that his comrade and fellow inmate Ahmed Kathrada proposed the idea of a memoir "to boost the growing cult of Mandela."[4] This was a politically calculated move, which would gain momentum in the 1980s when the African National Congress (ANC) formally took the decision to develop and exploit the Mandela name. In the throes of anti-apartheid activism and the buildup to his release, Mandela served as a rallying point for the liberation movement. Though he was absented from public life by the white minority regime, his powerful name made up for his lack of visibility. By virtue of its absence, Mandela's actual "image" stimulated curiosity, but public opinion about him was informed more by fascinated imagination than by knowledge of the man. Rob Nixon observes that "Mandela's jailers assumed that if media visibility opened the door to fame, invisibility would shut it."[5] However, his jailers could not have been more wrong: they "set up a gigantic photo opportunity in reverse. Mandela became an off-camera phenomenon and his silence grew more eloquent than words."[6] When the opportunity for visual renderings came, the media, including cinema, readily embraced it.[7] Mandela's re-emergence into public life attracted massive public attention at a time when the media in South Africa were just undergoing democratization. In this, television played no small role. According to Martha Evans, "The first live broadcast – Mandela's release – hailed the collapse of apartheid, and consolidated Mandela's saint-like image."[8]

The creation of "Madiba magic" and its effects are the subject of Chapter 3 by Deborah Posel. Here I ask how films about Mandela portray him. Mindful of the fact that this chapter cannot possibly do justice to the many films about Mandela, I do this principally through the lenses of *Mandela* (1987, directed by Phillip Saville) and *Invictus* (2010, directed by Clint Eastwood). My objective is not to examine filmic portrayals of Mandela against actual historical events, but to inquire into how film has constructed Mandela and assess the discursive implications of such constructions. What critical reflections arise when the life of the twentieth century's most revered and admired statesman is committed to the screen? I put forward several such reflections. I show that filmic representations of Mandela (and sometimes the Mandelas) have not only individualized the political struggle against apartheid, but also mystified the historical personality of Mandela. The films I am concerned with achieve this by casting Mandela in the garb of a modernist crusade and messianic tropes. Such representations ostensibly elevate Mandela, but fundamentally succeed in deflating his subjectivity and the revolutionary impetus of his political background. Where *Mandela* introduces him as the awaited savior of black South Africans, *Invictus* deflects this role by using him as a vehicle to contain and delegitimize black social and political aspirations.

My focus on film is both an acknowledgment of and a reaction to the dominant role of print media in the construction of the image of Mandela. Commentators tend to locate him within either the domain of print capitalism or cultural sites like museums.[9] His stature, to be sure, is provocative and problematic for cinema. The film medium and the cognate visual arts have encountered in Mandela a figure whose towering dignity poses an aesthetic and intellectual challenge – precisely because he may seem to leave so little for the filmmaker's imagination. His overwhelming "shadow" – the legendary presence that seems to always precede any creative endeavor to portray him – is the culprit here. All his acknowledged laudable qualities and his self-representation across the genres of autobiography, speech, and interview form a deceptively complete narrative. Infused with larger-than-life symbolism, Mandela's life story is intertwined with the hopes and pains of South Africans and, to an extent, of the whole world.[10] It may, therefore, appear risky for filmmakers to subject it to critical or disappointing representations that threaten to undo the aspirations of so many.

Yet reverential imagery should not replace film's capacity for valuable critical engagement; mere celebration would contradict Mandela's own efforts to "dismantle the cult of personality constructed by the media" around him.[11] A critical appraisal of Mandela as a subject of filmic and televisual representation is a challenge that filmmakers and scholars alike can ill afford to disregard. Without an appreciation of the cinematic Mandela, any attempt to understand the cultural and political impact of his persona remains incomplete. Tom Lodge describes Mandela's continuing influence as "a product of stories enacted by him and told about him, and the particular power of these stories to reach a multiplicity of audiences inside and beyond South Africa."[12] As a mode of telling stories, film is by far the most powerful, hegemonic, and transnational, due to its formal complexity (its visual, oral, and aural elements), its technological portability, and its immersion in intricate global corporate and cultural relations.[13] For an understanding of Mandela as sign, we should concern ourselves with all of these aesthetic and expressive attributes, considering not only cinema's indexical relation to the historical, sensory world and its generic modes of appeal to particular audiences, but also the limitations of a system of representation immersed, as is often the case, in the commercial concerns of the United States and Hollywood. (These concerns explain, among other things, why black South African voices are all too often mediated by African-American actors – a state of affairs lamented by local artists.)[14]

Though there has been some important work by film and media scholars, especially on the film *Invictus*, the exploration of the cinematic Mandela is still a surprisingly open – and extensive – terrain.[15] Mandela's life story attracted the motion picture medium for the first time in the mid-1960s. Although not about Mandela per se, the West German television series called *Rivonia Trial* (*Der Rivonia-Prozeß*, 1966) sets the precedent for filmic portrayals of Mandela. Starring the actor and later director Simon Sabela in the role of Mandela, *Rivonia Trial* was made shortly after Mandela's incarceration on Robben Island. The film was never shown in South Africa. In the late 1980s, with the momentum of the Release Mandela Campaign and the anti-apartheid struggles in South Africa, Euro-American filmmakers again turned their camera lenses on the Mandelas. *Mandela* (1987), the made-for-television biopic, re-enacts the high points of his life: his philosophical shift from passive resistance to armed struggle, the treason trial, and his lengthy imprisonment. Mandela's release from prison and ascendance to the presidency elicited new interest in his life from global networks. The ABC News documentary film *Mandela: The Man and His Country* (1990) chronicles the life of Nelson Mandela against the backdrop of South African politics. Discovery Channel also produced a documentary, *Mandela's Fight for Freedom* (1995). *Mandela: Son of Africa, Father of a Nation* (1996), produced by Jo Menell and Jonathan Demme, followed on its heels and garnered an Oscar nomination. Renderings of Mandela in fiction films also abound, including *Drum* (1997), the American Cable Network television production *Mandela and De Klerk* (2005), *Goodbye Bafana*, released on DVD in the United States as *The Color of Freedom* (2007), and *Winnie* (2011). Other films about Mandela are under way. At the time of writing, an adaptation of *Long Walk to Freedom* is on circuit in North America. This film was produced by Anant Singh and stars Idris Elba. The controversial British filmmaker Peter Kosminsky is in the process of making a film focusing on Mandela's early years, especially the formative period of Umkhonto we Sizwe, the armed wing of the ANC. Reportedly, the film will seek to "expose" Mandela's "terrorist" past.[16]

While I will refer to other films in this chapter, I will, as noted earlier, focus on two films from different historical moments: one from the height of the anti-apartheid struggle and one from the beginning of the Obama presidency, from which vantage it looks back on the Mandela republic with a kind of appropriative curiosity. My aim is not to give extensive textual analyses, but rather to highlight what I see as the most distinctive characteristics of the cinematic Mandela over the past three decades.

The Awaited Messiah

Mandela provides an insight into the mediation of Mandela in the 1980s, especially in light of US domination of film production. As an anti-apartheid film that employs elements of the Hollywood romantic genre, it today invites a critical examination of the political impasse of its historical moment. This rather lengthy made-for-television film, starring the African-American actors Danny Glover and Alfre Woodard as Nelson and Winnie Mandela, respectively, covers Mandela's life from 1952 until 1985 at the time of his incarceration in Pollsmoor Prison. Shot on location in Zimbabwe, it was targeted primarily at British and later US television audiences and not South African ones, a fact that certainly interfered with the integrity and purpose of its choices.[17] At the very outset, the film presents the problem of audience.

According to Victoria Marshall, "The film was produced to appeal to a US audience with violence, conflict, heart-throb emotions, and romance."[18] *Mandela* mediates the political significance of the historical Mandela via the cultural currency of Glover and Woodard, whose very accessibility to North American audiences reveals the film's detachment from the cultural and political context of the anti-apartheid struggle in South Africa. Though broadcast in the heyday of the United Democratic Front and the international campaigns to free Mandela, the film was an export product: a translation of the struggle for sympathizers abroad.[19]

The film introduces its subject's life in *medias res*. It opens with the broadcast of a parliamentary speech by Prime Minister D. F. Malan extolling white supremacy and apartheid in the wake of the National Party election victory in 1948. The speech, in which the off-screen Malan triumphantly celebrates white ownership of South Africa, is accompanied by a montage of police harassment amidst the brutal destruction of a shantytown. This is followed by a sequence of a train moving across an uncluttered rural landscape and coming to a halt at a desolate settlement. A confident-looking man of obvious patrician manners in a suit, briefcase in hand, alights. It is not long before we know the man's identity and purpose. He is Nelson Mandela on a mission to recruit country folk to join the Defiance Campaign, a non-violent attempt to weaken the apartheid system by deliberately breaking its laws. From the outset, then, *Mandela* establishes white supremacy as the ideological bogey against which history must find a virtuous adversary. Mandela's very modern bearing and assignment present the first counterblast to Malan's rabid racism, a notable prelude to the film's treatment of Mandela's confrontation with the state. Undertaking the campaign alone, Mandela enlists a dignified number of *amadelakufa* – people who are prepared to die for the anti-apartheid cause. The message is clear: if he is a self-sacrificing hero, Mandela is also the jovial, affable, and peaceful individual around whom the collective political struggle against apartheid takes shape.[20] The strategy of introducing Mandela immediately after the racist speech casts him as a forceful leader at the helm of the struggle against apartheid – which would seem, thereby, to begin with him. His individual, even isolated leadership, as well as his repeated harassment and arrest by the Security Branch, is mitigated largely by the solace he finds in his wife, Winnie. She becomes increasingly politicized and is also harassed and later jailed for her defiance of banning orders. The film ends with Mandela, in the later years of his incarceration, hand in hand with Winnie, making a promise that he will return to public life. By not honoring the ultimate American cinematic formula of "a closed plot" and "happy ending," *Mandela* acknowledges the then–"ongoing tragedy" of apartheid and its protagonist's imprisonment; but this avoidance of convention is, of course, overridden by the heroics of the lead actor and the spectacle of heterosexual love.[21]

Two major narrative arcs unite in the film: the romance of Nelson and Winnie and its historical emplotment in the linear documentary tradition. Nelson and Winnie's courtship and eventual marriage add color to the film. It is here that historically factual aspects retrospectively coincide with fictive elements. According to Harwood, the inclusion of Winnie was deliberate: "I wanted in the screenplay to balance Mandela's political activities with his private life. I was drawn to this shape because of the remarkable qualities of Winnie Mandela, the woman with whom he fell in love and later married."[22] Intimate scenes of Nelson and Winnie dominate the screen, accompanied by a heated exchange of intimate letters at different stages of the couple's imprisonment. For Harwood, the point was not only to "tell the story of the Mandelas' fight against apartheid," but also "to reveal something of the extraordinary bond between the man and the woman, a bond which sustained them through their struggle against a brutal and inhuman social system."[23] However, their romance does something else: drawing on the deeply emotive appeal of a love relationship in the mode of the Hollywood romantic film, the film attempts to establish a rapport with its Euro-American audiences. The fear is, of course, that Euro-American audiences will find a "purely" political story about an African liberation hero unappealing. For Marshall, the personal relationship between Winnie and Nelson is "the real focus of the film."[24] "*Mandela*," she declares, "is a simplistic dramatization of the political issues of apartheid, so simplistic that the issues effectively become a sub-plot to the 'romance and turmoil' the Mandelas suffered under the oppression of apartheid."[25]

While this is the case, the romance is itself not devoid of political mythmaking. The sexualized bodies of the protagonist and his partner are also politically charged. It merits pointing out that the Mandelas' relationship embodies the import of the feminist insight that the personal is the political, as Munro also acknowledges in Chapter 4. The film humanizes the political symbolism of Mandela with the help of the popular register of a romantic relationship. Therefore, it is also via the bedroom that Nelson and Winnie become the property of politics. The private Mandela is also a man of love writ large, at the level of the home and the "nation." It is on the body of the lover and his beloved that the pain and pleasure of black South African experiences are sensually inscribed. If the film seeks to romanticize the Mandelas' relationship for emotional value, it also inadvertently foregrounds their bodies as sites of political persecution. Equally insinuated in Nelson and Winnie's romance are conservative religious codes about sex and sexuality. This is achieved partly by instituting several lacunae in Mandela's private life: the total absence of

Evelyn Ntoko Mase, his first wife, and possibly numerous other paramours. The film envelops the Mandelas' relationship in a Protestant ethic of courtship and marriage in which divorce and adultery are unthinkable. Ultimately, the persecution of Mandela and the idealization of his relationship with Winnie satisfy the moral standing expected of a political messiah.

Occasionally relying on the strategy of "voice-off" in the mode of radio news announcements about specific historical events in Mandela's life, the film reconstructs history visually in a manner that is reminiscent of documentary film and newsreels of yesteryear.[26] Along with "voice-offs," it intermittently displays dates to mark the passage of time in the mode of the newsreel. The muting of news media in South Africa makes the reportage angle resonant for its times.[27] However, where *Mandela* achieves the rhetorical integrity of a factual program, it is weakened as a fictional representation. The film's use of media reportage makes it appear more concerned with the recorded events of Mandela's life than with representing him in a nuanced way as a person: history trumps subjectivity. The fast editing, moreover, especially in the first half of the film, gives the effect of a history that does not march but gallops along. The overall effect is a symmetric interpellation of the film's principal subject within a monumental and fast-paced historical narrative. Within this narrative, Mandela's every move is made to be compatible with the succession of historical events in the struggle against apartheid. Ultimately, he indexes the entire struggle against apartheid in a mechanistic and foreordained manner.

At the same time that it summons Mandela alongside, if not subject to, the historical past, the film is also self-reflexively presentist in the depiction of its materials. *Mandela* relies on the traces of the man's past; it raids the archive for Mandela's own reflections and gives ample screen time to the performance of his speeches and the reading of his letters. Glover's re-enactment of the words from the past both reflects and undercuts the limits that history might impose on the film as representation. We are offered a visual and aural proxy of Mandela's actual voice, representing him as though he were free and addressing viewers directly and in the present. The apparition of Mandela, as it were, haunts the present of the film's circulation in real/reel time. The inclusion of speeches and letters inadvertently enjoins the viewer not just to bear witness to history via the cinema screen, but also to help realize the banished popular leader's unfulfilled political vision.

In the light of its overall narrative structure, its adulatory bias toward the Mandelas, as well as the circumstances of its production and release, it is nearly impossible to reflect on *Mandela* other than as an anti-apartheid propaganda film. The editing of the early sequences illustrates the point sharply. Malan's triumphalist speech of 1948, as we have seen, is followed by a sequence of Mandela's 1952 recruitment drive for the Defiance Campaign: a temporal jump linking Malan to Mandela in mortal ideological combat. The sound of Malan's opening address to parliament set against visuals of forced removals (which historically were, of course, to follow only later) instates the birth of apartheid as the originary moment, the year zero of white supremacy, already containing all of its violence. Apartheid becomes not just the kernel of white supremacy at a particular historical moment, but a fixed ideology, interchangeable with white supremacy at all times. This act of historical synecdoche effectively constructs apartheid as an aberration of Western modernity and not a part of its antinomies. The editing of the opening sequences also suggests that apartheid is the instigating condition for the emergence of Mandela, who must carry the burden of undoing it. Yet the anti-apartheid bias of the film is underwritten by a discourse of the struggle in accordance with the West's fantasy of a universal humanism, safely carried in the person of Mandela. It is in Mandela that the progressive modernity in which the Malan regime is so utterly lacking finds a genuine custodian. In a flash of irony, the film works against apartheid by making Malan invisible, while it grants cinematic visibility to the "absent" Mandela. It is as though the film subjects Malan to a "spatial displacement outside time" and therefore outside history.[28] In this way, the film enhances Mandela's image – first, by granting him privileged access to history and, second, by instituting surface distinctions between him and his political rivals.[29] The off-screen depiction of Malan prefaces the film's construction of Afrikaners and Afrikaner authority in a succession of thin character studies. "Afrikaners in *Mandela*," William Sudderth observes, "are practically comical in their evilness at times. They are so gruesome as to be unbelievable."[30] Such depictions guarantee their mechanical contrasts with Mandela, aimed at heightening his stature above his enemies.

However, Glover's character study of Mandela itself raises questions as to its richness and complexity. The question arises in spite of the character's implausible contrast with his political rivals and the instances of his other dimensions as a lover, husband, and father. The film extends a far greater role to Mandela than he actually fulfilled and projects certain values onto this expanded historical agency. The viewer's first impression of Mandela is that of a complete gentleman with all the accoutrements and mannerisms of an English baron. Stripped of background but deeply absorbed in the struggle, Mandela manifests a cultural ideal of modernity that his African followers must emulate. Without any reference to the African cultural aesthetics in the mold, for instance, of the Xhosa attire that Mandela wore to court during his 1962 trial, the film confines him to a Western ideation of a modern subject. His appearance betrays the political out look of an autonomous Western rational subject, stable and forthright in its conviction. The certitude of this kind of subjectivity presents a problem because of its univocality that makes historical agency an individual endeavor. Ultimately, the collectivist ethos of the political struggle against apartheid and other forms of discrimination falls away.

In the film, the sweep of history is intermeshed with fictional representation, the story of an ordinary family man who means well. But it reverts, in a dialectical assertion, to being a prophetic undertaking: "I will return." *Mandela* prefigures its subject's "return" to public life, envisioning his release from prison. Committed to film, Mandela's words assume a life of their own and place him at the center of South Africa's history.[31] In light of this very resonant promise, the film's intimation of the motif of resurrection cannot be disavowed. This can be seen in the contrast between the beginning and the end of the film. In both instances the rhetoric is built and consolidated on the palette of religious sentiments and appeals to the divine. Borrowing freely from Afrikaans poet and racial theorist J. D. du Toit ("Totius"), Malan opens the film by asserting that apartheid is "Divine Will."[32] At the end of the film, having rejected President P. W. Botha's conditional offer of his release, Mandela declares with prophetic finality, "I will return." Here, white supremacists lose the rhetorical battle to a more ambitious project of messianic impersonation by its principal challenger. Embracing the messianic narrative of return, the film anoints Mandela ahead of Malan in the role of a visionary prophet. *Mandela* obviously lifted this piece of speech from its subject's actual letter written in prison and meant for public rendering by his daughter Zindzi. However, its re-enactment in the film gives it acute resonance, thanks to the image of Mandela's intense expression in the final extreme close-up frame. This image leaves the viewer with a lasting impression of determination and even threat to his jailers. These visual images match his promise of return, a motif with actual political ramifications, thanks to the increasingly urgent calls for Mandela's release in the late 1980s. At the same time, Mandela's promise of return is the high point of the film's politics of individualism, according to which the individual carries the weight of history. The end of the film, then, is reflective of the individual's resolve in the beginning and cannot be imagined otherwise. The message is clear: Mandela's return is the ultimate historical event that will "normalize" South Africa. He serves history by exorcising its iniquities.

Mandela is thus interpellated within a Christian paradigm of deliverance. His molding in messianic terms can be seen in the light of the implicit Christian inclination, which Hayden White sees as the latent drive of Western historiography. According to White:

What is unique about the Western idea of history is the notion of rebirth, revival, or reformation, the idea that it is possible always to begin again. Whence the popularity of the notions of Renaissance, Reformation, Revolution, Rebirth, and so on for characterizing historical processes in the West. These notions of revival and rebirth derive, it would seem, from the peculiarly Christian idea that meaningful temporality describes a process of expectation and fulfillment."[33]

This idea finds a ready subject in *Mandela*. In the film, the future remains in abeyance until Mandela's return. Thus the messiah, who is charged with the termination of apartheid and delivery of liberation, stands to fulfill his historical task of bringing a new nation into being.

Mandela grapples with and proffers the interpretation of the struggle via the person of Mandela, who is himself interpellated in a pre-text of Christian struggle and deliverance. In the film, Mandela's persecution only serves to highlight the disruption of a conjugal unit, and not the regalvanizing of the struggle into the mode of revolutionary violence. His struggle succeeds more in inserting him in a universalistic template, significantly devoid of a revolutionary message. The protagonist of *Mandela* is not only a loving father and husband, but significantly clean, a gentleman: the very picture, not of a revolutionary, but of hegemonic civic virtue.

If political intervention were a criterion for assessing the critical significance of texts, *Mandela* would certainly garner accolades. Here is an anti-apartheid film made and broadcast in a context of intense anti-apartheid activity, bringing into circulation the memory of a symbol consigned to an apartheid jail. This was undoubtedly a momentous time, considering the ban on the images of Mandela in South Africa and censorship of free expression in general. We may ask, however, what kind of critical questions *Mandela* poses, in addition to its negative display of apartheid, which was, even then, universally condemned. I would suggest that, although it demonstrates the moral repugnance of apartheid and encourages mainly British and US television audiences to embrace the anti-apartheid struggle and the Free Mandela Campaign, the film's anti-apartheid agenda in fact precludes it from posing questions. I would also speculate that the realities of the Cold War, in which Africa was seen as a terrain of struggle between the West and East, may also have left their trace on this film; they may have informed this fairly moderate picture of Mandela three years before his release from prison. The urgency of political imperatives, it would seem, makes substantive questions about the nature of the struggle, leadership, and the political future of black South Africans seem superfluous. The function of the filmic trope of the messiah is to trump analysis.

Messiah: The Return

The motif of resurrection in *Mandela* (later imported to the 1988 film *Remember Mandela*) foreshadows future imaginings of Mandela in cinema and other media.[34] His emergence from prison after twenty-seven years was indeed portrayed as a messianic return, especially during his adulatory visit to the United States in 1990. This acclaim, however, annoyed at least one person: Mandela's deeply religious first wife, Evelyn, who promptly rebutted such religious codifications. Reacting to the media hype about his release, she expressed her dismay at the event being likened to the second coming of Christ. "He is only a man," Evelyn reportedly told an interviewer. "It's very silly when people say this kind of thing about Nelson. How can a man who has committed adultery and left his wife and children be Christ? The whole world worships Nelson too much."[35] Evelyn's words signal the tension between media constructions of Mandela in a saintly vein and the fallible social being she knew him to be. Her protest unmasks the media construction of Mandela, but it also underplays the historical magnitude and discursive productivity of the media events themselves. It is precisely due to such events that the name of Mandela gained immense global currency, to the extent that his attributes as a historical figure are often ignored.[36]

The cinematic recall of Mandela's return to public life in the 2000s also bears critical scrutiny. If *Mandela* laid the ground for the imaging/imagining of Mandela the historical figure within a Christian paradigm, films from the 2000s gave it a post-apartheid expression. In these films young white disciples have the privilege of benefiting from Mandela's teachings. In *Goodbye Bafana* (2007), for instance, Mandela's racist and politically naive jailer learns about the wrongs of racism from him. In *Invictus* this correlation of Mandela's embodiment of Christian-inspired morality and the redemption of young white men is also foregrounded. The film offers, one might say, a gospel according to Hollywood. By moralizing and sanctifying the figure of Mandela, *Invictus* is able to install a dehistoricized version of the man, delinked from revolutionary connotations but available as a "postracial" figure of unity.

Directed by Clint Eastwood, *Invictus* is an adaptation of the journalist John Carlin's book, *Playing the Enemy: Nelson Mandela and the Game That Made a Nation* (2008). The film is based on historical events of the past two decades but focuses mostly on the Rugby World Cup, held in South Africa in 1995. A fleeting montage of Mandela's release from prison in 1990 and his ascendance to the presidency in 1994 precedes the film's narrative. The montage, which takes the form of reportage or historical synopsis designed for international audiences, also documents events following Mandela's release: the violent clashes between the Inkatha Freedom Party and ANC supporters and Mandela's pacification drive. *Invictus*, however, revolves around Mandela's mentorship of Francois Pienaar, the captain of the national rugby team. Drawing wisdom from his own experiences on Robben Island and his vision for democratic South Africa, Mandela offers leadership advice to the overwhelmed captain. The end is a glorious victory by South Africa's rugby team, a moment relished by every South African across the color line and in every space across the land.

Featuring Morgan Freeman in the role of Nelson Mandela and Matt Damon as the team captain, Francois Pienaar, the film also bears what Stéphane Robolin calls "the hallmarks of a movie tailored by and for a predominantly American standpoint."[37] One of the ways in which this happens is through "the flattening of South Africa's black political scene."[38] However, I will show that *Invictus* does more than that: it contains the black political scene within the universal humanist precepts on which the portrayal of Mandela is based.

The relationship between the newly elected black president of a non-racial South Africa and the leader of a predominantly white sporting team did indeed open a new chapter in the history of South African sports.[39] This is brought into sharp relief by the encounter in the film of the extremes of rugby's unspoken history of right-wing politics and anti-black racism with Mandela's non-racialism and magnanimity. Thus *Invictus* thoroughly exploits the Rugby World Cup, a perfect occasion for what Carlin believes to be an act of political genius by Mandela: the selling of reconciliation on a global scale. In the film, a member of Mandela's staff tells him that the World Cup will be beamed to television screens throughout the world and watched by a billion viewers. Mandela's enthusiastic response to the information betrays his calculated intent to use the event as a showpiece of "the rainbow nation" – the trope of multiculturalism coined by the Reverend Jesse Jackson and later appropriated by Desmond Tutu, the former archbishop of Cape Town. To this can be added Mandela's endorsement of humanism above politics:

CHIEF OF STAFF: "So this rugby ... it is just a political calculation?"
MANDELA: "No it is a human calculation. If we take away what they cherish, the Springboks, we just reinforce the cycle of fear between us."

But it is, of course, also a media calculation. The film sets up Mandela's historical opportunity for marketing abstract values, but not for opening a debate on them. The euphoria of South Africa's victory in the Rugby World Cup provides an occasion for the film to translate the abstraction into a reality. By focusing on the Rugby World Cup, *Invictus* elevates a media moment into a signifier of nation building, courtesy of another overdetermined signifier of non-racialism and post-apartheid nation building: Mandela himself. Thus the play of signifiers at the center of the film makes possible the film's ritualization of symbolic rebirth through play. In *Invictus*, the nation is conceived in terms of the sinuous spectacle of white masculine prowess on the rugby field – the nod to the only black player, Chester Williams, regardless. The enthusiastic response of the "de-raced" body of rugby fans and well-wishers provides a stamp of approval to this national re-beginning. Mandela enters the fray of these displays, as both surrogate patriarch and moral conscience, offering advice on personal growth as a template for realizing a new national consciousness. Mandela, in the film, *is* the custodian of the consciousness of the nation, and it is ultimately through his moral suasion that the nation can be imagined into being.

The film plots Mandela's performance as sage in a manner that draws indexical correspondences between his highly mediated "public self" and a thrilling Hollywood spectacle. There is an undeniable link between his representation in the film and his media-saturated performance of his own historical celebrity: the manner in which he appears before the crowds – the waving hands, the unctuous smile, and the stoop. These are signifiers of a signifier, in Morgan Freeman's impersonation. The stadium, where most of the narrative action occurs, is a stage of and for national spectacle. Other sites of the narrative action, including Mandela's presidential mansion, the Union Buildings, parliament, and the street, are overshadowed by the super-visibility that the stadium accords him. It is in the stadium that the viewer witnesses Mandela's magnanimity and is invited to celebrate his political morality, which here is virtually equated with his popularity and crowd appeal.[40] The spatial configuration of Mandela's movements in the film, in other words, reduces and instrumentalizes his subjectivity in order to highlight the historic importance of his values.

Two scenes in the film portray his private side, away from the spectacle of sporting performance and endorsements. In the first, Mandela's coldly disapproving daughter Zindzi visits him. In the second, Mandela's white bodyguard asks him about his family, only to be reprimanded by a black colleague: "We never ... *never* ask him about his family.... Think about it, man, he is separated from his wife, his family. How often do you see them here"? The turn to family here seems to acknowledge the intersection of Mandela the historical figure with Mandela the man, especially when Mandela retorts that he has a family of 51 million people, a remark simultaneously indicative of his deep-seated national allegiance and the pain of being an absentee father and husband. The film also uses this moment to make the point, through the black bodyguard, that Mandela is "not a saint, he is a man with a man's problems."[41] However, denying Mandela sainthood is not guaranteed by the verbal reprimand; it only draws attention to the effect that he has on people. However much it may disavow his sanctity, *Invictus* portrays Mandela in terms of the virtues that are extended to saints – notably, selflessness and forgiveness. Moreover, the film does not interrogate Mandela's separation from his family, thereby denying the viewer any real sense of the messy contingencies of his life – symptomatic, perhaps, of an overall tendency of the film to keep all those nitty-gritty historical realities – realities that refuse to submit to symbolic redemption – off-limits.

It is important to consider, then, how the film's moralizing approach relates to the historical contradictions of the post-apartheid era. The narrative structure of *Invictus* seems to magnify its shortcomings as a romantic and jejune study of South Africa's "post-racial" fantasy: a fantasy the film entirely shares. This is already registered in the opening sequence of the film. The motorcade transporting the recently freed Mandela proceeds along a road dividing two playing fields. On one side of the divide, impoverished black children play a game of soccer on a desolate field. On the other, white children play rugby on a lush green pitch, complete with a coach. This introduction of stark structural inequality provides the backstory of the checkered history on which the film is based. It is against this background that the film visualizes the story of Mandela's efforts at advancing racial reconciliation through the game of rugby. Race and class are therefore acknowledged as social problems that Mandela inherited from the apartheid era and that he is compelled to address. However, the scene does not outlive the moment of its appearance; it is a superficial and rote acknowledgment of deep-seated social and economic problems at the dawn of the eventful 1990s. And that is all it amounts to: acknowledgment. Examined in light of the subsequent events in the film, the opening scene actually unmasks *Invictus*'s refusal to address the weight of the past, both on and off the rugby field. What is foregrounded, instead, is the demonstration of (a rather attenuated version) of Mandela's ideas and personal aura and their ostensibly positive outcome in a sporting triumph.

Invictus portrays an unctuous old man who befriends and mentors the captain of the rugby team, while dissuading his black assistant, bodyguards, daughter, and comrades from being vengeful and "selfish." It is interesting that white South Africans and their views are largely ignored until they mysteriously realize their errors. To be sure, we do see racist, unwelcoming whites waving the old South African flag at the beginning of the film, but they magically disappear as it progresses. More is made of the fact that blacks need to be persuaded, lest they "overturn all vestiges of white minority rule" as the National Sports Council is wont to do.[42] In this regard, the scene of the town hall meeting is illuminating. The argument against the rugby team's historically problematic, racially exclusive symbol of the springbok is undermined by the excessively insurgent iconography of the council's chairperson, with his flippant swagger. While his studious colleagues are in suits like Mandela, he appears at a formal meeting of national importance in loose-fitting casual clothes and a tweed cap to boot. The unnamed chairperson's very manner signifies aversion to hegemonic civility: he does not even have to speak to draw the audience's antipathy. The chairperson's incendiary attitude is one step from releasing the animus of black response against the symbolic configuration of the game of rugby. It follows, then, that his character must not be developed: he serves only to represent views against which the characters of Mandela and the captain – and the very thrust of the narrative – must prevail.

By focusing its lens on Rugby World Cup triumph and placing a halo on its subject's personality, *Invictus* yokes abstracted versions both of the public imagination of the event and of Mandela. Thanks to the melodrama, aura, and euphoria of a sporting event, a nation is imagined into being. Considered on these terms alone, *Invictus* can be considered a masterstroke of cinematic signification. But the transient pleasure and honor of a game (or a film) do not a nation make. On the very margins and fringes of the stadium, there are social and political convulsions that the game cannot possibly address. If the fictive Mandela that *Invictus* represents draws a lot from the historical figure's known principles, it also overstates their cogency. In the film, the Mandela of reconciliation and nation building also comes through as the Mandela who delegitimizes black South African sentiments, as one who basks in the glory of spectacular, but ultimately illusory moments. *Invictus* commits Mandela to a "silencing project" under the sign of a new nationhood. By urgently overturning the National Sports Council's decision and by his reprimand of Zindzi, Mandela commissions silence about the present and amnesia about the past as a way of achieving what are supposed to be the higher goals of unity and reconciliation. Thus the fascinating lure of Mandela's personality is also history's vanishing point. He is a transformative figure, in Eastwood's film, not because of his political background and organization, but because of his awe-inspiring role in the legitimizing of South African rugby – and with it, the delivery of a national consciousness devoid of political contestation. It is, no doubt, the film's release a decade after Mandela's presidency and its intended audience of mainly North American viewers that permits these elisions. One might say that its concerns are not with the peculiarly South African structural inequities and historic rifts marked in the opening scenes; rather, much like Eastwood's previous film, *Gran Torino* (2008), it embodies a kind of feel-good multicultural tolerance that is also a familiar part of the Hollywood gospel.[43] Its virtue is perhaps to be found precisely in its blatant reminder of the relationship between media events and the spectacularization of national politics.

Conclusion

In Mandela, film inherited an already overmediated icon pervading multiple forms of representation, especially print and other forms of news media. Buoyed, no doubt, by the imperatives of history and by Mandela's actual performance of his subjectivity, such representations are invariably in consensus with regard to his moral greatness. The portrayal of Mandela in glowing and elevated terms is therefore neither surprising nor peculiar to the cinema and its cognate forms. However, the circumstances of their production do not necessarily exempt films from an obligation to trouble received knowledge. Unlike certain contemporary interventions in the literature about Mandela, film has not begun to treat Mandela from a critically grounded historical and social perspective. By and large, it has located him within a monumental historical frame, obviating the need for a nuanced subjectivity. The cinematic Mandela is a central player in a teleological narrative, the foreordained outcome of which he must fulfill. This pre-scripted outcome requires mystification and abstraction: emptied of conflict, disappointment, and doubt, the Mandela of my two chosen films appears totally free of psychic dissonance – of those "antinomies" that Philip Bonner discusses in Chapter 1. What these texts proffer, instead, are instantiations of a modern subject who conforms to modernity and its historical project of emancipation – and actually realizes it. However, the cinematic Mandela must achieve his goals in a manner that is not only philosophically fulfilling and narratively satisfying (and entertaining), but potentially hostile to radical evaluations of the historical project of emancipation itself.

NOTES

1 John Pepper Clarke, *Mandela and Other Poems* (Lagos: Longman Nigeria, 1988), 4.
2 See "Mandela Wins Case on Fake Artworks Sale," www.artinfo.com/news/story/428/mandela-wins-suit-over-fake-artworks.

3 At the time of writing, as Mandela grows ever frailer, global media networks have already descended on Qunu, Mandela's village. In a morbid fascination with what they believe to be his imminent death, the networks are already carving perches for the best shot of his coffin.

4 David James Smith, *The Young Mandela* (London: Weidenfeld & Nicolson, 2010), 96.

5 Rob Nixon, "Mandela, the Media, and Messianism," *Transition* 51 (1991): 44.

6 Ibid., 44.

7 With Mandela unavailable to provide the basis for an image, *Time* magazine commissioned an artist to sketch what Mandela "should" look like when he stepped out of prison. However, Ron Krabill observes that the image ironically bore little resemblance to Mandela; "instead the image looked strikingly similar to Danny Glover, who played Mandela in an HBO miniseries three years earlier." Krabill, *Starring Mandela and Cosby: Media and the Ends of Apartheid* (Chicago: University of Chicago Press, 2010), 119.

8 Martha Evans, "Mandela and the Televised Birth of the Rainbow Nation," *National Identities* 12.3 (September 2010): 311.

9 There is a welter of published books on Mandela, yet surprisingly little on the filmic reconstructions of his life. The only biography to provide a list of films is Max du Preez's popular biography, *The Rough Guide to Nelson Mandela* (London: Penguin Books, 2011), 276–77. Ciraj Rassol refers to the genre of biography as part of what he calls "the cultural production of Mandela." Quoted in Okechukwu Nwafor, "Mandela and the Politics of Representation," *AFREV IJAH* 1.2 (2012): 136. Nwafor also argues that "print capitalism emerges to entrench Mandela as a symbol of hero in the annals of South African political history" (ibid.).

10 Nixon, "Messianism," 43.

11 Ibid.

12 Tom Lodge, *Mandela: A Critical Life* (Oxford: Oxford University Press, 2006), x.

13 Ibid.

14 For an article critical of the many attempts by international actors to portray Mandela, see Basia Lewandowska Cummings, "Nelson Mandela (Hollywood; Plural)," africasacountry.com/2012/02/15/nelson-mandela-hollywood-plural/ (accessed January 15, 2013).

15 Ruth Teer and Keyan Tomaselli (1990, 1991), Keyan Tomaselli and Bob Boster (1993), and Keyan Tomaselli and Arnold Shepperson (2008) have contributed to the understanding of the representation of Mandela in the mass media. More recently, the journal *Safundi* has published a round table of incisive readings of the film *Invictus*; 13.1–2 (2012): 115–50.

16 "Terrorist Nelson Mandela" portrayed in film by Peter Kosminsky; m.guardian.co.uk/world/2011/may/08/kominsky-makes-film-on-mandela?cat=world&type=article (accessed July 8, 2012).

17 The film could not possibly target audiences in South Africa due to the legislative environment curtailing free speech. However, its projection to British and North American audiences raises questions with regard to its interpretation of the anti-apartheid struggle in Thatcherite Britain and Reaganite America. According to William Sudderth, "To pacify American fears, the ANC's desire to

first avoid violence; and then killing, is repeated over and over. The Congress' ties to the SA Communist Party are also minimized." ccms.ukzn.ac.za/index. php?option=com_content&task=view&id=335&Itemid=44.

18 Victoria Marshall, "Mandela on TV," *Black Film Review* 3.4 (Autumn 1987): 19.

19 *Mandela* was a late fictional installment in a series of mostly documentary films produced in the 1980s by organizations such as the International Defence and Aid Fund (IDAF), seeking to intensify the call for the release of Mandela. The documentary films include *Nelson Mandela* (1981), by Ben Rea for BBC TV; a film produced in Germany called *Freiheit für Nelson Mandela* (1986), by Ebbo Demant; *Mandela* (1986) and *Remember Mandela* (1988), both by Peter Davis and Villon Films; and *Free Mandela* (1988), by Barry Feinberg and produced by and for IDAF.

20 In the scene of his Defiance Campaign assignment, Mandela advises prospective activists to be peaceful in their march against apartheid laws and not strike back against the police. However, note the point made in Chapter 7 by Jonathan Hyslop disputing the representation of Mandela as a man of peace in the mold of Gandhi and Martin Luther King.

21 Marshall, "Mandela on TV," 19.

22 Ronald Harwood, *Mandela* (London: Boxtree, 1987), ix.

23 Ibid., ix. The film, of course, predates the infamous case involving Stompie Seipei, for whose kidnapping Winnie was later convicted but not jailed. Yet even at this time Winnie's fall from grace had already been precipitated by the infamous 1985 speech in which she declared "with fire in her eyes" (as Anthony Sampson dramatically puts it): "We have no guns – we have only stones, boxes of matches and petrol. Together, hand in hand, with our boxes of matches and our necklaces we shall liberate our country." Sampson, *Mandela: The Authorised Biography* (London: HarperCollins, 2000), 349.

24 Marshall, "Mandela on TV," 19.

25 Ibid.

26 On the relationship between newsreel and documentary, see Parker Tyler, "Documentary Technique in Fiction Film," *American Quarterly* 1.2 (Summer 1949): 99–115.

27 In one poster of the film, published in *Variety*, October 23, 1987, there are clear references to this situation; the film is commended for fulfilling the role of the news media in their absence. A review cited in the poster declares, "Now that the South African government has squashed the flow of news through censorship, *Mandela* is even more valuable." The publication of a book by Ron Harwood to complement the film (providing background information, parts of the script, and visual stills) also draws attention to its informative intention. See Harwood, *Mandela*.

28 Leo Bersani and Ulysse Dutoit, *Forms of Being: Cinema, Aesthetics, Subjectivity* (London: British Film Institute, 2004), 4.

29 Interestingly, though, Malan and Mandela's public endorsements of the film adaptation of Alan Paton's novel *Cry, the Beloved Country*, Malan (in 1951) and Mandela (in 1995), uncannily make them each other's alter ego. Though Malan's endorsement took place in a segregated theater and Mandela's in an open,

non-racist context, they both hailed and consecrated a liberal but paternalistic text in spite of their differences. See Mark Beittel, "What Sort of Memorial? *Cry, the Beloved Country* on Film," in *To Change Reels: Film and Film Culture in South Africa,* ed. Isabel Balseiro and Ntongela Masilela (Detroit: Wayne State University Press 2003), 70.

30 ccms.ukzn.ac.za/index.php?option=com_content&task=view&id=335& Itemid=44.

31 The end of *Mandela* (1987) is also iterated in the end of Peter Davis's documentary, *Remember Mandela* (1988), an explicitly adulatory film about Mandela and his symbolism of the struggle against apartheid.

32 See Saul Dubow, "Afrikaner Nationalism, Apartheid and the Conceptualization of "Race," *Journal of African History* 33.2 (1992): 237.

33 Hayden White, "The Metaphysics of Western Historiography," *Taiwan Journal of East Asian Studies* (June 2004): 2.

34 In the film *Fools* (1997), for instance, a man interrupts a passing church choir singing a gospel song, "Somlandela u'Yesu" ("We Will Follow Jesus"); singing along, he replaces the name "Jesus" with the name "Mandela," thereby politicizing the hymn.

35 *Sunday Telegraph* (London), February 25, 1990.

36 Evelyn expresses a sentiment shared by others who felt anxious about the "disconnect" between Mandela the political activist, the husband and absent father, the celebrity he had become, and the near sainthood foisted on him. See Bongani Madondo, "Fawning over St. Nelson Is No Way to Do Justice to Mandela," *Sunday Times,* February 25, 2007 (accessed April 11, 2012).

37 Stéphane Robolin, "Of Color and Blindness in *Invictus,*" *Safundi: The Journal of South African and American Studies* 13.1–2 (January–April 2012): 121. Robolin demonstrates how the South African situation and, particularly, the social realities of black South Africans are simply interpellated into North American viewpoints in the film.

38 Robolin "Blindness," 121.

39 For a long time black South Africans and anti-apartheid activists regarded the Springboks with open hostility, seeing in the team the symbolic expression of a rabid right-wing and anti-black ideology. The Springboks also became a target of the global anti-apartheid movement. A little more than a decade earlier, their 1981 tour to New Zealand "resulted in street battles between protesters and rugby enthusiasts at every fixture in the programme." Lodge, *Mandela,* 155.

40 Comparatively, *Goodbye Bafana* (2007) is like a retrospective amendment to the historical aporias of *Invictus.* If the latter is a spectacular, media-saturated take on Mandela's enactment of national reconciliation (albeit one restricted to the cultural space of the post-apartheid rugby game), the narrative of *Goodbye Bafana* lies within the domain of suffering and martyrdom. In almost stolen moments, we can see Mandela suffering in dignified silence. Yet in lieu of Mandela's persecuted body, the film accentuates the moral angst of his guard, who carries Mandela's burden of suffering.

41 Mandela has often reiterated his rejection of sainthood: "One issue that deeply worried me in prison was the false image I unwittingly projected to the outside

world; of being regarded as a saint. I never was one, even on the basis of the earthly definition of a saint as a sinner who keeps trying." *Conversations with Myself* (Oxford: Oxford University Press, 2011), 410.

42 Robolin, "Blindness," 121.

43 For a discussion of the relationship between *Invictus* and *Gran Torino*, see Lily Saint, "Regarding the History of Others," *Safundi* 13.1–2 (January–April 2012): 132–36.

11

LIZE VAN ROBBROECK

The Visual Mandela: A Pedagogy of Citizenship

At the final game of the 1995 Rugby World Cup, which seemed to consecrate South Africa's transition to non-racial democracy, Nelson Mandela handed Francois Pienaar, the captain of the victorious Springbok team, a copy of Theodore Roosevelt's famous 1912 speech, "Citizenship in a Republic."[1] This symbolically charged gesture was meant to inspire the team to greatness for the morale of all "new" South Africans. But it also demonstrated the profound value Mandela himself attached to the ideal of citizenship – not only in its narrow sense as a social contract (a set of legal rights and duties conferred by the state), but as a model of exemplary subjectivity. How he came to embody this ideal, not just to South Africans but to the world, is the focus of this chapter. I will first consider the role of portraiture in this process, showing how notions of modern subjectivity and ideal citizenship are conflated and encoded in three striking representations of Nelson Mandela. Next, I will explore narrative – specifically graphic narrative – as a pedagogic device: one that is driven by the demands of nation building in a postcolony divided on the basis of race, class, and culture. The text I focus on here is the Nelson Mandela Foundation's officially sanctioned comic book version of his life. The comic's visual translation of Mandela's autobiography, *Long Walk to Freedom*, renders several competing notions of citizenship harmonious and even complementary; it works to yoke together incommensurable events in Mandela's life and to reconcile apparently irreconcilable binaries in the South African cultural landscape (such as the urban vs. the rural, the traditional vs. the modern, and the communitarian vs. the individualistic).

It must be clear from the outset that I do not regard Mandela's iconicity as a mere construct orchestrated by nationalist ideologues and the media. It is certainly true that the African National Congress (ANC) chose to exploit the propagandistic capital of his evident physical and moral stature and helped to fix his exemplary role in public consciousness. But Nelson Mandela himself was also an active shaper of his image: a complex image, since Mandela deeply internalized and sought to live up to the ideal of masculine subjectivity encoded in Western discourses of nation and citizenship but also strenuously resisted the Eurocentric tenor of these constructs by Africanizing them in strategic ways. What I wish to stress, above all, is that the visual aspects of his media image as model African and global citizen – the cumulative result of both his public performances of self and his depictions by others – are indispensable in the shaping of his international reputation as moral hero.

Iconicity and the Subject as Citizen

Mandela is consistently represented as a coherent, stable, and admirable subject, despite revelations of his human frailties and despite a life characterized by shape shifting and role playing. In Chapter 9, Daniel Roux observes that the myth of an essential, enduring Mandela owes much to his long physical absence from the visible field of politics and media, which ensured that his reputation and his words fixed him as a role model in the consciousness of the world's disenfranchised long before his physical advent in the 1990s. Much of the anticipation and apprehension surrounding his release centered on whether the embodied Mandela would be a suitable vehicle for this painstakingly constructed legend. And he was – perhaps more than anyone could have anticipated or hoped for. Mandela's physical presence miraculously exceeded his larger-than-life reputation. The yoking together of an overdetermined signifier (the physical presence of Mandela) and a pre-established signified (the legendary Mandela as the essence of moral citizenship) seemed to happen naturally and seamlessly. Yet the process whereby representations of the physical Mandela came to encode the values of good citizenship relies on centuries of visual convention and theories of subjectivity.

The etymology of the word "icon" is a good starting point. In its original usage, the term referred to Byzantine and Greek Orthodox Christian traditions in which images of holy personages were revered as spiritual objects; they were distinguished from mere representational or narrative art by their sacred power.[2] Traces of this power persist in the contemporary use of the term to refer to very famous individuals. Indeed, it has been argued that religious icons were the precursors of the portrait in Western art and that something of their spiritual aura of immanent power was transferred to secular portraiture in the modern era.[3] The emergence of the portrait as a major genre was, in other words, coextensive with the emergence (and globalization) of the modern subject.

The relevance of this genealogy of portraiture to a study of Mandela as model citizen is immediately evident in a cover of *Time* magazine, which

Figure 11.1. Mandela as icon, *Time* magazine cover image, May 9, 1999. ©Time-Life, Inc.

appeared in 1999, at the culmination of his presidency (Figure 11.1). The visual promotion of the man as moral presence is seldom as deliberate as in this image. Mandela is portrayed in the stern, full-frontal pose associated with sacred imagery, complete with a halo of flowers and golden rays emanating from his head. The bright, translucent colors evoke gold leaf and jewels; the wooden, medieval proportions enhance the precious otherworldliness of the image. Even the hand, raised in the clenched-fist black power salute, mirrors the iconic Christ figure's right hand, which was conventionally raised in benediction. This portrait's appropriation of the stylistic features of the religious icon tells us much about the world's perception of Mandela as a messianic figure – about how his appearance on the international political stage has been cast not as the product of ordinary causal processes, but as the unfolding of destiny. While the

Time cover's deployment of sacred iconography is not exactly subtle, it demonstrates the persuasive power of visual portraiture in the construction of Mandela as the global model – the patron saint, even – of ethical citizenship.

Just as religious icons depended on ritualized repetition (revealing, no doubt, the anxieties underpinning icon formation), the endless portraits of celebrities in our day serve to fabricate and entrench their exemplary status in public consciousness. This all too familiar phenomenon affirms the ongoing suitability of portraiture as a medium for iconicity, however redefined: the facial features of the celebrity are the locus of his or her intelligibility and instant recognizability. However, the more time-honored notion that the face – the eyes in particular – offer us a "window to the soul" often lifts the portrait out of the domain of indexical description and into the realm of the old iconic immanence. To evoke this sense of immanence, the photographic image, for all its ubiquity, is not the most suitable visual medium. The technology of photography allows it to capture a fleeting moment in a circumscribed space, but the contextual detail that inevitably accompanies this process is not conducive to the production of profound, transcendental statements.[4] Much more suitable for such effects – precisely because it lacks the photograph's quotidian indexicality – is handcrafted portraiture: the painted, sculpted, or drawn image. The artist differs from the photographer in his or her vaunted ability to capture the "true, timeless self" behind the excessive mobility and distracting vicissitudes captured by the camera. Because of its claim to exteriorize the sitter's inner singularity, the handcrafted portrait also tells us more about our conception of the modern subject, whose individuality, after all, has never been reducible to the physiognomic uniqueness of a face.

A striking case in point is the London-based South African artist Paul Emsley's monumental drawing of Nelson Mandela. This work offers a powerful example of the artistic portrait's capacity to produce something in excess of mere resemblance and description – and this excess, it seems to me, is essential to the pedagogic effectiveness of the portrait (Figure 11.2). At 46.1 × 34.8 inches (117 × 88.5 cm) in size, this is a very large drawing; its overwhelming scale contributes to the claustrophobic intimacy of this full-frontal representation. The background is a depthless, opaque black against which Mandela's features emerge with almost hallucinatory clarity.

Not so much appearance as apparition, Emsley's portrait allows no context to intrude. The historicity of Mandela is betrayed only by his trademark Indonesian print shirt (about which I will say more later) and his white hair, which introduce some sense of contingency to disrupt the universality and timelessness of the image. While this is not young Mandela the firebrand, it

Figure 11.2. Portrait of Nelson Mandela by Paul Emsley, 2010. Black chalk and pencil drawing, 88.5 × 117 cm. Nelson Mandela Foundation Collection. Courtesy of Paul Emsley.

is also not the distressingly mortal and vulnerable elderly Mandela, whom we have seen only very occasionally in the media. Mandela is depicted at a suitable age for a role model, as a man who devoted his entire life to achieving what he set out to do, who looks back at a life well lived. His gaze is direct and penetrating, his mouth closed; the dignity and composure of the expression convey a sense of gravitas and self-discipline.

The discourse of immanence surrounding this artistic portrait emerges explicitly in an interview with Emsley, in which he recounts that he found Mandela "as engaging and warm as [he] expected" but that he had to request that his famous subject stop smiling because the artistic aim was to capture "the man behind the smile."[5] Although Emsley used photographs as source material, he insists on "a difference between the portrait and the photographs." "I made aesthetic judgments," he declares. "It was intuitive."[6] The artist thus intervenes to eliminate any accidental, fortuitous, or superfluous detail that might betray the source photograph's indexical nature.

The logic underlying Emsley's artistic decisions is that emotions are fleeting and context distracting – that they interfere with the transmission of the sitter's "true nature," which is conceived as timeless.

In this portrait, then, Emsley espouses a long (and much-debated) model of the subject: one that proves to be significant given Mandela's status as politician, freedom fighter, lawyer, humanist, and statesman. In his influential work on the philosophical origins – and contradictions – of modern subjectivity, Étienne Balibar has argued that the modern subject originated not so much in Descartes's *cogito* as in Kant's conception of the "free and autonomous" and politically active citizen. (We should, of course, acknowledge immediately that not all commentators on Mandela would be happy to see him cast as such a modern Western subject, pure and simple; indeed, this is a reductive perception I will eventually complicate in this chapter.) Though presented as a universal abstraction, this conception of the subject belongs to a particular historical moment. It is firmly rooted in the era of bourgeois revolutions and in accompanying notions of citizenship defined by rights. Kant's influential conflation of subjectivity and citizenship, Balibar reminds us, "never ceased to refer to a very precise history, where it is a question of progress, conflict, emancipation and revolutions."[7] I would suggest, therefore, that the "inner man" that Emsley chooses to represent is Mandela as the model Kantian subject: not only stable and autonomous, but also a historical agent in an emancipatory narrative that has accomplished its aims – a freedom fighter, if you will; or, more exactly, a man for whom liberty is destiny.

But Balibar also complicates the idea of freedom when he raises another important question about subjectivity that pertains to Emsley's portrait of Mandela: "Why is it that the very *name* which allows modern philosophy to think and designate the *originary freedom* of the human being – the name of 'subject' – is precisely the name which *historically* meant suppression of freedom, or at least an intrinsic limitation of freedom; i.e., *subjection*?"[8] The Mandela that emerges from the dark in Emsley's portrait is "subject" in this sense too: he is a man in command of himself and therefore, paradoxically, also obedient to himself. In this model of subjectivity, self-subjection is fundamentally a willing act, an obedience or submission to a model of selfhood prescribed by the notion of responsible citizenship, which becomes the subject's ultimate telos: "This subject," as Balibar puts it, "has to respond, to give an account ... of himself, before another person, who righteously interpolates him. Not a Big Brother, but a Big Other – as Lacan would say – always already shifting ... between the visible and the invisible, between individuality and universality."[9] Mandela's famous stoic discipline, his self-subjection to a physical regime of exercise and moderate diet, the way he coached himself to be "the master of his fate; the captain of his soul," betrays the extent to which he was conditioned (via his missionary schooling) by the same faith in the Enlightenment as emancipatory ideology that informed the Victorian poet William Henley's "Invictus," Mandela's favorite poem.[10] Emsley's portrait, then, reveals to us – for our own edification and emulation – Mandela the accountable, self-disciplined, and self-aware citizen, for whom freedom came at enormous personal costs. Mandela, one might say, is held up as our Big Other; he exhorts us to exercise similar restraint, discipline, and gravitas in the exercise of the rights conferred by the citizenship he fought and sacrificed for.

Nelson Mandela's own high estimation of citizenship as ethical modality (as demonstrated by his symbolic gesture at the Rugby World Cup) suggests something of the global dissemination of this Enlightenment model of the modern-citizen subject and its eventual appropriation by anti-colonial nationalists. To suggest, however, that Mandela uncritically appropriated this Eurocentric "derivative discourse"[11] throughout his long political career, and bought with it, wholesale, the entire epistemological legacy of Western nationalism, would be extremely reductive of the complex subject positions and sometimes conflicting ideological formations that characterize African nationalism in general and Mandela's varied repertoire of political subject positions in particular.[12] Later in this chapter, I will suggest that the mode of subjectivity foregrounded by Emsley masks the contradictions and tensions Mandela had to navigate between the quintessentially liberal-humanist citizenship model (which translated, from the mid-twentieth century onward, into non-racialism) and the call of black nationalism to look after specifically African interests – tensions that continue to play out in South African politics today.

National Narcissism

But let me note for now that, in the political sphere, the term "representation" has two meanings: representation as depiction and representation as standing for or speaking for. Both definitions apply to the visual Mandela. In my discussion of Emsley's portrait I have so far focused on representation as depiction: how Mandela's visage is taken to represent his instantly recognizable self-as-citizen. But we should remember that, in the case of Mandela as politician and statesman, the other sense of "representation" also comes into play: Mandela, as it were, represents the nation to itself and to the world, "holding up a mirror so the nation can admire itself."[13] This narcissistic aspect of the national imaginary forms an essential part of the pedagogic function of the portrait.

A fascinating case in point here is an advertisement for the city of Pretoria that appeared in the British Airways magazine, *High Life*, in June 1996. The advertisement reproduces twelve different images of Mandela – or more exactly, it reiterates the same smiling headshot that appeared on the historical 1994 ballot, but now sporting twelve different headdresses and costumes, each associated with a particular leisure activity or tourist attraction in and around the city. Thus a Mandela in a Voortrekker hat and bandolier is captioned "Historical Monuments"; a Mandela in beads and a skins is captioned "African Art"; a Mandela with a crash helmet and parachute pack is captioned "Skydiving"; a Mandela in a pith helmet and safari suit is captioned "Botanical Gardens"; a Mandela with a miner's hard hat and lamp (but sporting a supervisor's white coat, not overalls) is captioned "Mine Tours"; and so forth. The slogan reads: "See Pretoria with New Eyes: He Did."[14] There is something deeply satisfying and enjoyable about the play of sameness and potentiality we see in this composite of inventively manipulated images, which registers both Mandela's mutable, sartorially deft public performances and the varied new possibilities that the end of apartheid has opened up – not only for the tourist, but also for the black South African citizen, who under the old regime might have worn the miner's helmet but not the tuxedo, the skins and beads but not the rugby lineman's protective headgear. The advertisement presents us, above all, with an image of the newly democratic nation (whose centrifugal diversity the repeated portrait overrides): a nation that can now represent itself in new ways to the outside world and also eagerly consumes this new, pleasurably varied image of itself. It is an image in which differences – South Africa's endemic polyculturalism – are visually held together by the comforting stability of the great man's visage.

The idea that Mandela holds up the mirror so the nation can admire itself is crucial here, especially in that the metaphor alerts us to the narcissistic aspect of the national imaginary, an essential aspect of the pedagogic function of the portrait. For, after all, the advertisement invites us not only to look at Mandela, but to adopt his position, his gaze, his attitudes; to respond to the advertisement's slogan is, as it were, to be interpellated by the Big Other, to accept, by contemplating these pleasurable representations of Mandela, his political representativeness. Psychoanalytic theorists have suggested that nationalistic feelings may arise from the transference that occurs when the infantile sense of omnipotence makes way for realization of the emerging subject's actual weakness and helplessness: a realization that is often compensated for by strong identification with a powerful, idealized Other, who functions as an internalized role model – a national superego, if you will. There is something very persuasive about this psychoanalytic narrative in relation to the pedagogical function that Mandela's portraits – from the serious and putatively timeless Emsley portrait to the humorous advertisement with its play on sameness and mutability – seem to serve. Given the insecurities of the newly invented South African national imaginary post-1994, the idealized Madiba met the intense needs of a population eager to shed the traumatic past and formulate a cohesive and stable identity. The transformation of Mandela into an idealized parental imago is particularly evident among white South Africans, who find redemption in his legendary forgiveness and who, presumably, are reassured by his evident embodiment of Western liberal democratic values. There is, in other words, an element of ideological projection in the neat fit of Mandela in the visual and philosophical frameworks I have put forward so far. Indeed, the myth among some white South Africans that Mandela's death would be accompanied by the mass slaughter of whites indicates the degree to which the idealized self-object furnishes a sense of "safety that results from faith in the strength and omnipotence of another who is seen as a protector."[15]

Numerous writers, including Daniel Roux and Litheko Modisane in this volume (Chapters 9 and 10, respectively), have mentioned the elusiveness of the "real" Mandela and how attempts to uncover the "real" Mandela are largely frustrated because his face is always already an overdetermined sign in a media-saturated world. This begs the question why portraits such as Emsley's seem to have such a powerful pedagogical dimension. The many photographs of Mandela sporting his approving, avuncular smile (and their commercial appropriation in the tourist advertisement for Pretoria or Mandela paper dolls with many costumes) serve to affirm the nation's grandiose narcissism by feeding our sense of specialness. Emsley's portrait, however, has the merit of working in a somewhat different way: it allows the viewer no escape from Mandela's piercing gaze; the eyes look into us and we are judged. This consciousness of our own objectification (that we are objects in the eyes of others and that others perceive us as we can never perceive ourselves) induces a strong sense of self-awareness: of being watched and weighed. This experience suggests precisely how, once internalized, the idealized Other furnishes "the rules of conduct that represent the culture's values and ideals."[16]

To this we could add the idea that the sacred objects of political identification are successful as master signifiers precisely because they do not refer to anything "real."[17] On a conscious level, most people know that Mandela cannot possibly be perfect and that his iconicity is largely a media fabrication; yet his sustained idolization indicates a willing disavowal of that knowledge: people believe in Mandela precisely because they do not have knowledge of the "actual" Mandela. Particularly in today's media-saturated sphere, which fuels both cynicism and the desire for icons, belief in Mandela amounts to a kind of fetishism. Belief in the Other amounts to belief through the Other; so, on the deepest level, belief in Mandela resides in the blind faith that, while one may lack it oneself, an admired Other has access to a deeper, extra-political Truth. Though the political icon functions in what Lacanian psychoanalysis would call the symbolic field, it is effective precisely because it manipulates and reproduces a kernel of enjoyment that originated – and remains – in the fantasy of the imaginary.

Destiny as Narrative Pedagogy

If the images I have discussed so far tend to elide history, the graphic narrative to which I now turn acknowledges it, but shapes temporality in a particular way. On the acknowledgments page of the authorized comic book based on *Long Walk to Freedom*, Verne Harris comments: "The constellation [of stories about Nelson Mandela] is the story of the country, South Africa, for which Tata Nelson Mandela sacrificed so much."[18] Addressed to children and young adults, the comic's aim is clearly pedagogical; it is based on what Elleke Boehmer has called the "the metaphorical substructure of the long walk and the slow upward climb" and deploys the "exemplary patterns of pilgrimage and metamorphosis."[19] It is an allegory, in short, in which Mandela's story is retold as the unfolding of a nation's destiny and it delivers, as we can by now predict, a lesson of exemplary citizenship. The pictorial and narrative devices employed here stitch together Mandela's mutable persona and fragmented life story into a unbroken trajectory of gradual modernization and emancipation, to arrive eventually at the telos of national fatherhood.

The title page offers a sequence of renderings, read from left to right in the tradition of Western writing, of Mandela at various stages of his life: as infant and child in a rural context; as young pupil; as cosmopolitan young lawyer; as unshakable revolutionary; as prisoner; and finally, hand raised in victorious salute, as the mature, international icon in his Indonesian print shirt (Figure 11.3). The drawing recognizes, in other words, the many different roles that Mandela has adopted and it effectively translates these differences into steady growth. The fact that the composition of the image is reminiscent of those familiar renderings of human evolution, from bent and apelike hominids to the upright *Homo sapiens*, is entirely to the point.

We might account for this effect in a more theoretical way as well. The visual encoding of developmental time in this summary of Mandela's life brings to mind Paul Ricoeur's conception of the relationship between

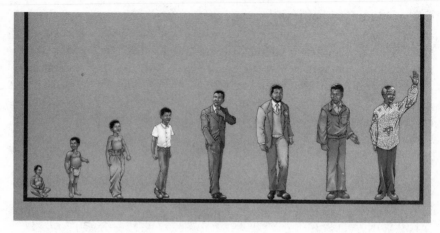

Figure 11.3. Title page of *Nelson Mandela: The Authorised Comic Book*, Nelson Mandela Foundation and Umlando Wezithombe, 2009. Courtesy of Nelson Mandela Centre of Memory.

subjectivity and narrative: a conception that acknowledges the contradictions inherent in abstract formulations of the subject as unique individual. Ricoeur proposes that there are two seemingly irreconcilable aspects of identity, which he names *idem* and *ipse*. *Idem* is identity as sameness – that which remains recognizable and unchanged despite the vicissitudes of life events and physical mutation. It points to a permanence that survives the ravages of time and guarantees an individual's uninterrupted continuity throughout the various stages of life.[20] *Ipse*, by contrast, refers to the selfhood as a dynamic entity that can accommodate change, action, and mutability (and, in this sense, equals promise or agency). The function of narrative, then, is to synthesize essential sameness and evolving selfhood.

The title page image of Mandela at various ages does precisely this synthetic work: though occupying a single frame (and though graphic art is inevitably static), the composite image offers a narrative, a temporal progression. Indeed, it captures the entire comic's core strategy, which is to convert Mandela's serial, contingent, and strategic performances of self into destiny. The unfolding narrative, in other words, mediates between *ipse* and *idem*; the comic's "emplotment," as Ricoeur might observe, "transforms the succession of events into one meaningful whole … which makes the story followable" – and, I would add, pedagogically effective.[21]

Consider, for instance, the comic's treatment of Mandela's rural childhood and, specifically, a scene in which he is shown playing *thinti*, a stick-throwing game in which, we are told, the young Rolihlahla excelled (Figure 11.4). He

Figure 11.4. The young Mandela playing *thinti*, from *Nelson Mandela: The Authorised Comic Book*, Nelson Mandela Foundation and Umlando Wezithombe, 2009. Courtesy of Nelson Mandela Centre of Memory.

wins the game, as seems to be his habit (his propensity for victory is revealed by one of his competitors, who thinks, "Not again"), but instead of gloating, he puts his arm around the defeated boy and comforts him with the reassurance "Next time you may have more luck, my friend." A commonplace activity of Mandela's youth is therefore emplotted as the unfolding of his destiny to become a paragon of conciliatory leadership. The youthful Mandela's graciousness in victory, his reaching out to comfort his defeated friend, prefigures his later political victories and his legendary kindness and graciousness toward the Afrikaners he defeated. The comic book, in other words, uses this small incident from Mandela's childhood to demonstrate the ethical essence of selfhood, which Ricoeur describes as that ability to "keep one's word" despite changes in circumstances.[22]

The comic's construction of Mandela's narrative identity thus admits to the dimension of time, which could otherwise wreak havoc with the notion of the continuous subject – with the timeless and iconic Mandela captured in Emsley's portrait. At any given moment in the narrative, the comic book's Mandela does not simply live through events, but constitutes himself as a merger of his past and future. A good example of this effect is the title page to the first chapter, which captures something of the retrospective character of *Long Walk to Freedom*, while also bringing the future-oriented element of destiny into play. Even though the narrative that follows immediately concerns Mandela's childhood, the image represents the adult Mandela, wearing his black AIDS campaign shirt with his prison number emblazoned

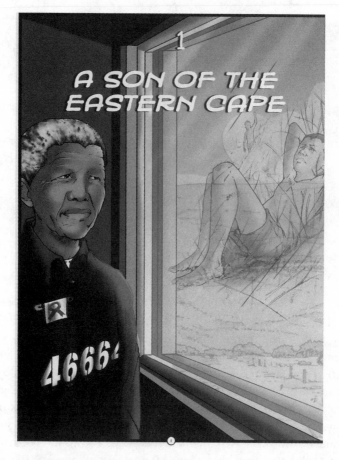

Figure 11.5. A son of the Eastern Cape, from *Nelson Mandela: The Authorised Comic Book*, Nelson Mandela Foundation and Umlando Wezithombe, 2009. Courtesy of Nelson Mandela Centre of Memory.

on it; but he is staring through a window at his youthful incarnation, who is lying on his back and gazing at the sky, dreaming, one supposes, of what he might become (Figure 11.5).

The culmination of the process initiated by these introductory images is fittingly captured in the final panel, showing Mandela, now retired (as evidenced by his cane and Graça Machel at his side), walking into a rural sunset with the instruction "Nelson Mandela's legacy is in all our hands" (Figure 11.6). The elderly statesman thus bequeaths to the youth of South Africa his legacy of fulfilled promise. It is here that the pedagogic import of the bridging of the evolving self and the abiding, quintessential self – the self that is the narrative's fulfillment – is spelled out most explicitly.

Figure 11.6. Nelson and Graça, from *Nelson Mandela: The Authorised Comic Book*, Nelson Mandela Foundation and Umlando Wezithombe, 2009. Courtesy of Nelson Mandela Centre of Memory.

Changing Models of Citizenship

Although the visual plays a vital role in the constitution of Nelson Mandela as model of the ideal citizen, it would be a mistake to infer that this role is merely a cultural construct with scarcely a nod to Mandela the flesh and blood person. On the contrary, the comic (which in this shares the essential purpose of *Long Walk to Freedom*) reveals the extent to which Mandela modeled himself on the ideal of citizenship. Mandela's narrativization of his own development as a political subject demonstrates how, at different times in his life, his perception of duty, rights, and civility was shaped by various distinct conceptions of citizenship, derived from diverse sources. The comic depicts each of Mandela's successive identifications with different forms of citizenship, acknowledging some of the antinomies between the various models – the tribal democracy of his early years, the Thembu and Christian assertions of stoic self-discipline, the definition of the legal person (the ultimate Western signifier of rights and duties) that he encountered in his later studies, the resistant African nationalist and revolutionary, and so forth. But, by and large, it emphasizes their compatibility, if not complementariness. The occasional tear in the seamless weave between one value system and the next, as when, say, Mandela absconds from Mqhekezweni to avoid an arranged marriage, only serves to imply destiny at work (see Figure 11.7).

Figure 11.7. Rolihlahla rebelling, from *Nelson Mandela: The Authorised Comic Book*, Nelson Mandela Foundation and Umlando Wezithombe, 2009. Courtesy of Nelson Mandela Centre of Memory.

Since other chapters in this volume have also reflected on these various modes of subjectivity (see, e.g., Chapters 1, 5, and 6 by Bonner, Ngwane, and Sitze, respectively), I pick up the discussion at the moment of Mandela's flirtation, during his years in Johannesburg, with a variety of ideologies: from communism to Garveyism and an exclusive African nationalism. The comic is frank about this ideological vacillation, but it is pedagogically employed (in true Ricoeurian fashion) to show us how ethical citizenship entails a commitment to change, experimentation, and growth, which inevitably result in some failures and errors. More important, these chapters of the comic promulgate a vision of citizenship in which human rights and human worth are articulated as the products of *ubuntu*, as much as the legacy of the Enlightenment.[23] While the term *ubuntu* is never used in the comic, it serves as an implicit blueprint for the cohesive imaginary of "the people," who are here, as in *Long Walk to Freedom*, implicitly of African descent. What conjoins them in an imagined community is a shared heritage of suffering, humiliation, and dispossession. Insofar as it vests sovereignty in the collective, "the people," it signifies modern power, as opposed to more vertical, traditional forms of authority.[24] But this rhetorical device necessitates a Manichaean polarity of good and evil, in which the oppressive state and its functionaries are visually encoded with signs of their inhumanity and fascist perversion. Prison guards are therefore invariably shown shouting and slavering at the mouth, and some even have swastika tattoos (Figure 11.8). General Magnus Malan and President P. W. Botha, both of whom resisted negotiation, are shown shouting, grimacing, and pointing admonishing fingers.

Figure 11.8. Prison guards, from *Nelson Mandela: The Authorised Comic Book*, Nelson Mandela Foundation and Umlando Wezithombe, 2009. Courtesy of Nelson Mandela Centre of Memory.

The comic book also spends an entire chapter on Mandela's famous appearance in a kaross, the royal Thembu costume during his 1962 trial (see Figure 11.9).[25] Here, flaunting the signifiers of its alleged barbarity, he portrayed African traditional leadership as custodian of human rights, yet convincingly expressed those rights in the modern rhetoric of citizenship – thus harmonizing the seemingly irreconcilable tropes of tradition and modernity and stripping democratic rights of their Western exclusiveness. It is no accident that the relevant image should be particularly heroic and striking: the politics here are symbolic, strategic, and visual, and the comic book's representation capitalizes on and in a sense repeats (in a way reminiscent of the oft-reproduced icons I discussed earlier) Mandela's own visual staging of himself.

It is interesting to contrast this image with the comic book's portrayal of Mandela during the years of the transition, when he emerges as a global statesman. He appears here as a stern and authoritative figure and is shown mostly wearing a dark suit, which, in Western semiotics, marks him as a man among men. Though he is portrayed as conciliatory and reasonable, he is also revealed to be capable of anger, and hence demonstrates his unwillingness to compromise his revolutionary ideals – in these situations, the illustrators use red text boxes to indicate heated speech. Here we see Mandela adapting the oppositional version of citizenship that he staged in court to more moderate political action, as he negotiates for constitutional rights and duties – for citizenship proper, in the conventional understanding of the term. His persona is now presented as the familiar, "reassuringly banal" face of national politics, and the notion of "the people," correspondingly, gets stripped of its revolutionary exclusiveness, as evinced in his victory speech, to make way for "the people" as all South Africans, regardless of race.[26] Thus, as Michael Billig puts it, "[T]he radical [joins] the world system; he

Figure 11.9. Mandela in court, from *Nelson Mandela: The Authorised Comic Book*, Nelson Mandela Foundation and Umlando Wezithombe, 2009. Courtesy of Nelson Mandela Centre of Memory.

[speaks] presidentially, like other presidents addressing their peoples … in the serious clichés of nationhood."[27]

The comic's treatment of Mandela's presidency visually registers yet another change, heralding an even more expansive vision of citizenship. Mandela's newfound freedom is signaled by emerging idiosyncrasies: he is shown dancing his trademark dance for the first time at the victory celebration; his sense of humor is featured more strongly, and, most significantly from a visual and semiotic point of view, his penchant for tie-less Indonesian print shirts is revealed. The frontispiece of the final chapter of the comic, which portrays the fruition of Mandela's destiny (chapter 8, "Mr. President"), situates him in a rural environment, dressed in his trademark shirt and surrounded by children (Figure 11.10).

Figure 11.10. Mr. President, from *Nelson Mandela: The Authorised Comic Book*, Nelson Mandela Foundation and Umlando Wezithombe, 2009. Courtesy of Nelson Mandela Centre of Memory.

The idyllic tableau is haloed – and hallowed – by the setting sun. The stern, suited, professional statesman makes way for Mandela the avuncular *pater familias* in his ancestral rural environment. This image signals Mandela's final incarnation of ideal citizenship: the international icon and global citizen who has not forgotten his origins. The colorful printed shirt he wears is devoid of any specific cultural reference, yet carries a distinct aura of exoticism. Eschewing any sign of cultural parochialism or any overt mobilization of traditional African symbols of power, Mandela's final incarnation denies neither his traditionalist roots nor his commitment to the polis. The drawing suggests that his assumption of global iconicity does not undo any of the models of subjectivity he previously endorsed, by situating him in an idyllic ancestral context (the past become present) and by showing him among those most promising representatives of "the people": the children, who, as beneficiaries of Madiba's legacy, are the embodiment of the future of accountable citizenship.

Some reflections on the semiotics of the suit and Mandela's decision to abandon it are appropriate here. As a symbol of Westernized masculine authority, the suit may confer power on the wearer, yet also, paradoxically, signifies submission to Western signs of civility; it is a uniform that confers power, while simultaneously disempowering the wearer by erasing his singularity and cultural specificity.[28] Mandela's idiosyncratic shirts (now, of course, avidly marketed) signal his freedom to take or leave Western conventions of power: they are the sartorial embodiment of a vision of global citizenship. While the suit speaks the language of legality, constitutions, and contracts, the Mandela shirt speaks the language of freedom and self-constitution, of a humanism that is not exclusively defined by the West. This semiotics of emancipation is beautifully communicated in the comic book when a young girl points at Mandela and asks, "Excuse me, but why do you wear a shirt like that?" Mandela laughingly replies, "You must remember that I was in jail for 27 years. I want to feel freedom!"[29]

Conclusion

One might note here that Mandela's pedagogy of global citizenship, visually encompassed in this comic book primer, has reached far beyond the national borders of South Africa. It is quite feasible that Barrack Obama's successful bids for the presidency (especially the first), which finally managed to breach the normative whiteness of Western political power, owed much to Mandela's example. Actor-comedian Chris Rock's (instantly viral) satirical spoof of Barack Obama as someone to vote for "because he is white" is echoed by more serious critics, who have raised concerns that both Mandela and Obama, by de-racing and thus sanitizing a quintessentially Western liberal outlook, represent the interests of capitalism and white economic supremacy rather than any black cause.[30] While these criticisms are harsh, there is something to the argument that the fit, disciplined self-presentation of these two men, the strategic ways they present themselves as subjects of history (amplified, of course, by the iconic way they are mediated by the print media and television), render them non-threatening to the global liberal elite.

If Mandela's confident cosmopolitan self-presentation and his durable love affair with the media soothed white fears and fostered black hopes, the current South African president, Jacob Zuma, has managed to rekindle white anxieties and shatter much of the strategic harmony Mandela managed to effect between Africanist symbolic power and the demands of global neoliberal realpolitik. The media's open hostility toward Zuma, coupled with the less than optimal conditions under which he rose to eminence, has opened up deep and seemingly ineradicable fault lines in the South African political and cultural spheres.[31] It is, again, in the field of visual representation that these schisms become most apparent. A case in point is the satirical painting by the white artist Brett Murray of Zuma in a heroic Stalinesque pose with exposed genitals. The ensuing "Spear controversy" elicited unprecedented public emotion and provoked government intervention, thereby not only revealing how divided South Africans really are, but demonstrating the power of visual culture to provide masks – and rip them apart.

Mandela's painstaking stitching together of African traditional values, Western democratic liberal structures, global capitalism, and pan-African communitarianism is in the process of being unraveled. The harmonious multivocality of Mandela's formulation of citizenship, captured in both the advertisement and the comic book I have discussed here, has now deteriorated into a cacophony of incoherent voices: the tenuous center established by Mandela is not holding, and things are beginning to fall apart. This is perhaps not surprising. One of the most frequently raised problems concerning postcolonial nationalism is that it is extremely difficult to inculcate citizenship in such polycultural social spaces, where the identification between the state and the nation is notoriously weak.[32] If, as we have seen, the construction of the ideal of citizenship is partly a visual matter, it makes sense that its destruction in contemporary South Africa should be ruthlessly exposed in the visual field, where the difference between Mandela and Zuma could not be more striking. The latter has been increasingly subject to scathing iconoclasm, while the figure of Mandela continues to be the image of good citizenship – not least on Mandela Day (July 18), when photographs of his smiling paternal face preside over and officially sanction "good will and good works." We might also note here the 2012 launch of South Africa's new banknotes, sporting portraits of Mandela. This event spurred the cartoonist Zapiro to publish another "new South African banknote," depicting not Mandela but a caricature of Zuma (complete with the ubiquitous showerhead that, in Zapiro's work, signals the man's womanizing and ignorance about the transmission of AIDS), to the value of R 200,000,000 – a reference to Zuma's profligate spending on personal luxuries.[33] Zuma's traditionalist lifestyle, in particular his polygyny and numerous children in and out of wedlock, seems to reawaken, in the white imaginary, colonial tropes of an atavistic Africanism that is fundamentally inimical to the (*symbolically* Africanized*) liberal values Mandela has come to represent. Yet it is precisely Zuma's traditionalist ways that generate the trust of a significant percentage of the black South African population, especially ethnic Zulus from KwaZulu-Natal, where he hails from and where his controversial expensive homestead is situated. The stark difference between the visual Zuma and the visual Mandela brings to mind Jean Comaroff's point that "for the modernists, history exemplifies the triumph of secular civility over parochial distinctions, a view that makes culture a matter merely of the ceremonial; it might give local color to citizenship, but it cannot provide its substantive basis."[34] Whereas Mandela laid claim (perhaps more than he was entitled to) to his royal Thembu heritage to signify his primary allegiance to Africa in a white man's court, that performative and fundamentally visual gesture was generally accepted for what it was – a strategic and dramatic invocation of precolonial Africa for political ends. Zuma's traditionalism, however, has reawakened the specter of a divisive ethnicity that has been the downfall of many a postcolonial nation.

Added to this, the commodification of nationalism in the new South Africa (already visible in the 1996 advertisement I analyzed) commits a banalization of Mandala's image that threatens to undo his exemplary potential. The proliferation of Mandela items for sale, from fridge magnets to Madiba shirts to a line of Mandela-inspired sportswear, confirms Wole Soyinka's warning that the commercial "Santa-Clausification" of Mandela threatens to subvert his legacy.[35] In light of all this, and particularly given what Franz Fanon has called the "occult instability" of the postcolony, the ideal of citizenship as represented by Nelson Mandela is not to be lightly dismissed.

NOTES

1   In the American film based on this significant moment in post-apartheid history, Mandela hands Pienaar a copy of the poem "Invictus" – a poem that Mandela relied upon in times of hardship. Both the speech and the poem encode post-Enlightenment Western masculine ideals of fortitude and agency.
2   On this aspect of the icon, see Catherine Soussloff, *The Subject in Art: Portraiture and the Birth of the Modern* (Durham, NC: Duke University Press, 2006), 10.
3   Ibid.
4   Since it entails a technological process whereby light is directly captured on photosensitive paper, the photograph can be described as an indexical sign – hence its overdetermined and much-debated "truth" value in the social sciences and the documentary tradition.
5   Jan Cronjé, "Emsley's Moment with Madiba," *Lip* (University of Stellenbosch, Department of Journalism, 2012).

6   Amanda Botha, *Paul Emsley Retrospective Catalogue* (Cape Town: Brundyn + Gonsalves, 2012) 10, media.withtank.com/ba952e7806/emsley.pdf.

7   Étienne Balibar, "Subjection and Subjectivation," in *Supposing the Subject*, ed. Joan Copjec (London: Verso, 1994), 7.

8   Ibid., 6 (emphasis in original).

9   Ibid., 9.

10 See also David Schalkwyk's discussion of Mandela and stoicism in Chapter 2.

11 Partha Chatterjee, *Nationalist Thought and the Colonial World: A Derivative Discourse* (Delhi: Zed Books, 1986).

12 In *Long Walk to Freedom*, Mandela mentions that while "[he], too, had been susceptible to paternalistic British colonialism and the appeal of being perceived by whites as 'cultured' and 'progressive' and 'civilized,'" he later adopted, under the influence of Lembede, militant African nationalism as the "antidote" to these coercive desires (Randburg: Macdonal Purnell, 1994), 91.

13 Michael Billig, *Banal Nationalism* (London: Sage, 2006), 97.

14 In her analysis of this advertisement, Rita Barnard points out that while the slogan acknowledges historical change, the illustration does the opposite: "by implicitly equating such diverse institutions as the gold mine and the Voortrekker Monument (both become pure spectacle), it erases their specific histories and social significance in classically mythical fashion." See "The Final Safari: On Nature, Myth, and the Literature of the Emergency," in *Writing South Africa: Literature, Apartheid, and Democracy, 1970–1995*, ed. Derek Attridge and Rosemary Jolly (Cambridge: Cambridge University Press, 1998), 139.

15 Joseph Palombo, Harold K. Bendicsen, and Barry J. Koch, *Guide to Psychoanalytic Developmental Theories* (New York: Springer, 2009), 264.

16 Ibid.

17 On this matter, see Slavoj Žižek's *The Sublime Object of Ideology* (London: Verso, 1989) and *For They Know Not What They Do: Enjoyment as a Political Factor* (New York: Verso, 1991).

18 Nelson Mandela Foundation with Umlando Wezithombe, *Nelson Mandela: The Authorised Comic Book* (Johannesburg: Jonathan Ball, 2008).

19 Elleke Boehmer, *Nelson Mandela: A Very Short Introduction* (Oxford: Oxford University Press, 2008), 7–8.

20 This aspect of identity corresponds to the Kantian notion of identity as an unshakable essence that remains immutable and recognizable – the immanent "inner self" or "soul" on which, as I have suggested, Emsley's portrait relies.

21 Paul Ricoeur, *Time and Narrative*, vol. I, trans. Kathleen McLaughlin and David Pellauer (Chicago: University of Chicago Press, 1984), 67.

22 Eftichis Pirovolakis, *Reading Derrida and Ricoeur: Improbable Encounters between Deconstruction and Hermeneutics* (Albany, NY: SUNY Press, 2010), 92.

23 Mandela's endorsement of the values of *ubuntu* is evidenced in a televised interview with Tim Modise, in which he articulates it as a form of communitarian humanism. He makes it clear that *ubuntu* does not mean that self-enrichment is unacceptable, but that it must be accompanied by the intention to better the lot of those around you. This articulation of consanguinity between individual and group interests overwrites the commonly understanding of *ubuntu* as a collectivist phenomenon that precludes any form of individual realization.

24 Ivor Chipkin, *Do South Africans Exist? Nationalism, Democracy and the Identity of "The People"* (Johannesburg: Wits University Press, 2007), 2.

25 For other readings of this dramatic performance, see Chapters 5 and 6 by Ngwane and Sitze, respectively.

26 The speech began: "My fellow South Africans – the people of South Africa.... We may have our differences, but we are one people with a common destiny in our rich variety of culture, race and tradition." Quoted in Billig, *Banal Nationalism*, 97.

27 Ibid.

28 Edmund Burke put it beautifully when he suggested that the suit represents "all the pleasing illusions which made power gentle and obedience liberal." In David Kutchta, *The Three-Piece Suit and Modern Masculinity, England, 1550–1850* (Berkeley: University of California Press, 2002), 6.

29 *Authorised Comic Book*, 164.

30 Eduardo Bonilla-Silva, for example, suggests that "Obama has reached the level of success he has in large measure because he has made a strategic move towards racelessness and adopted a post-racial persona and political stance. He has distanced himself ... from anything or anyone who made him look 'too black' or 'too political.'" *Racism without Racists: Color-Blind Racism and the Persistence of Racial Inequality in the United States* (Lanham, MD: Rowman & Littlefield, 2006), 212–19.

31 Apart from charges of racketeering and corruption, Zuma also faced, but was acquitted on, rape charges in the buildup to his presidency.

32 For reflections on this dilemma, see Chipkin, *Do South Africans Exist?* 35, and Jean Comaroff, "The End of History, Again? Pursuing the Past in the Postcolony," in *Postcolonial Studies and Beyond*, ed. Ania Loomba et al., (Durham, NC: Duke University Press, 2005), 130–31.

33 In the run-up to the presidential election at Mangaung in 2012, Zuma was accused of spending in excess of R 250 million of state monies on his private home, Nkandla, in Kwa-Zulu-Natal. The showerhead sprouting from Zuma's bald dome was first drawn by Zapiro after the rape trial and refers to Zuma's statement in court that he protected himself against possible AIDS infection (his alleged rape victim was HIV-positive) by taking a shower after intercourse. This motif has since been adopted by Zuma's political enemies (including the ANC's own Youth League) as a derogatory physical gesture. Zuma's irresponsible ignorance about the epidemic is thus contrasted with Mandela's highly visible activism for HIV prevention.

34 Comaroff, "*End of History*," 137.

35 Wole Soyinka, "Views from a Palette of the Cultural Rainbow," in *The Meaning of Mandela: A Literary and Intellectual Celebration*, Xolela Mangcu (Cape Town: HSRC Press, 2006), 24.

12

SARAH NUTTALL AND ACHILLE MBEMBE

Mandela's Mortality

The law of mortality, Hannah Arendt wrote, is "the most certain and only reliable law of a life spent between birth and death."[1] To be sure, these two most important events in human existence are never directly experienced by the subject; they are always an "already-happened" (birth) and a "not-yet-happened" event (death). Nelson Mandela was not a witness to his own birth, but he did, more than once, contemplate his own death. Not only did he embrace his mortality on these occasions, he strove to be the owner of his death. In the opening section of the chapter, we will trace out Mandela's attitudes to death – the deaths of others and his own. We will explore his thinking, across several decades, about the obligations of the living to the dead and about his own inner world as he experienced deep suffering and loss, states of being that one "never wants to experience ever again."[2] In order to foreground the drama of Mandela's death and its singular ability to speak to the living, we will pay attention to the dialectics of presence and absence, of disappearance and reappearance, which have been a hallmark of his life from the time he went underground in 1961 until his re-emergence to freedom in 1990. His was anything but a sudden death – his life having been lived as a long oscillation between encounter and separation, solitude and conviviality, the life of the day and the life of the night. Nor, we argue, does his death open onto total absence. We see the prison cell (of which Mandela speaks a great deal in his writings) as a prefiguration of his final departure: a purgatorial space in which his self, or double, undergoes transformation, his death appearing in this context as the final station in an endless process of transfiguration.

In later parts of the chapter we consider Mandela's bodily mutations as he approached old age and death. The images we focus on reveal his bodily frailty, increasing inability to walk properly, and aging face. We examine, too, the active planning for his death that was already taking place as we first conceptualized this essay (2012) and the nature of the controversies that arose from the preparation for his final passing and burial. As we reflect on his death, we consider the anxiety it elicited in so many people.

We examine the pervasive feeling in South Africa that Mandela's death might reveal a void at the heart of a country that has always tried to mask such an emptiness at its center: a country that has struggled to define itself as a nation and draw together its many fragments into a sustained sense of commonality in the wake of a long racist past. More than anybody else, Mandela embodied this sense of commonality, and his passing is likely to reignite the metaphysical anxiety that South Africa is neither a concept nor an idea – just a place, a geographical accident. In the closing part of the chapter we ruminate on whether Mandela might not be one of the world's last heroes – in a specifically modern, twentieth-century sense of the term.

Mandela on Death

In his autobiography, *Long Walk to Freedom*, as well as in *Conversations with Myself*, Nelson Mandela reveals unexpected facets of himself, at odds with the public image of the victorious political icon and liberation hero who went from prison to power, forgave his foes, reconciled his fractured nation, and ushered his country into a new age of freedom. Instead, we are faced with a man acutely aware of his own vulnerability, at times at war with himself and his passions, a man whose loyalties are divided between his family and "the family of the people" (LWF, 215) and whose encounter with his own destiny, although irreversible, happened in stages, almost by accident. After a lengthy prison sentence, he emerged as a man who suffered in his body and psyche – hard labor, tasteless meals, and grim boredom: "the frightful frustrations of a life in which human beings move in complete circles" and land each day exactly at the point where they "started the day before."[3] Mandela knew pain and devastation, suffered countless indignities, severe and irrecoverable losses, dramatic separations and invisible wounds, grief, helplessness, and mourning: the kinds of experiences that "eat too deeply into one's being, into one's soul" (CWM, 172).

Throughout his active life, Mandela drew a veil over his wounds and misfortunes. He turned his pain into a private secret he was loath to exhibit in public. While he offered his outer self to the political sphere of men, he shared his inner self with privileged women friends. "The truth," he wrote to his daughter Zindzi in 1970, is that "my appearance had nothing to do whatsoever with the state of my feelings" (CWM, 189). The ethos of the struggle, he argued elsewhere, required that the freedom fighter suppress many of "the personal feelings that make one feel like a separate individual rather than part of a mass movement" (LWF, 215). But his stoic attitude to pain, suffering, and loss – his effort to discipline his emotions – were things he learned to cultivate in childhood at crucial moments of separation. In *Long Walk to Freedom*, as in his later accounts of life underground and in prison, such moments reveal his personhood to be double: the inner self is released from the shackles of the outer self, and both are kept at a distance from each other. For this distancing to occur, the inner world of the person must cease to mirror the outer world of the public figure.[4] The release of the *soma*, its disconnection from the psyche, allows the sublimation of pain and the transfiguration of the self to take place; in the face of death, silence becomes the privileged form of language and speech.

The split between the inner and outer self is nowhere as manifest as in the scene of circumcision and seclusion, of which Mandela offers a vivid and arresting tableau in *Long Walk to Freedom*.[5] To enter manhood, a piece of one's own body has to be cut and buried in the earth in the middle of the night. The newly circumcised man has to paint his naked and shaved body from head to foot in white ochre. He must inhabit the appearance of a ghost (LWF, 27). The untying of one's foreskin, discarding a piece of one's own flesh, and burying it in the earth are followed by what Mandela calls a "re-emergence" (LWF, 27). The last act before "re-emergence" consists of the burning of the seclusion lodges. In Xhosa tradition it is forbidden to look back while the seclusion lodges are burning – a taboo Mandela transgressed. But all he sees are "two pyramids of ashes," in which, he thinks, lies "a lost and delightful world" – that of his childhood (LWF, 29).

Early on in Mandela's life, "leaving" and "departing" became intricately intertwined, as did "leaving" and "looking back." Leaving Qunu – "all that I knew" and "loved ... in the unconditional way that a child loves his first home" (LWF, 14) – was a direct consequence of the passing of his father. Again and again in his life, leaving not only meant walking toward some other place, some other world, but also mourning the world left behind, usually in silence. "The silence of the heart" (LWF, 14), as Mandela calls it – his characteristic mode of relating to his mother – always entailed a backward glance, a kind of ritual Mandela would repeat throughout his life under similar circumstances. "Before disappearing behind the hills," he says in connection to his departure from Qunu, substituting words with a gaze, "I turned and I looked back for what I imagined was the last time at my village" (LWF, 14). This Orphean retrospect was not only a way of holding onto memory; it was also a manner of speaking to the future as the name par excellence of the unknown and the uncertain, the name of what might never happen again – or if it did, one might never witness it again, because it might be "the last time" (LWF, 14).

The first death Mandela witnessed was that of his father, Gadla Henry Mphakanyiswa. About his father's passing, Mandela cannot remember "experiencing great grief so much as feeling cut adrift." For Mandela, having defined himself through his father, the latter's death signaled the end of a world, especially since his mother had decided that he had to leave Qunu, his first home, after the event. From childhood on, then, death and parting, mourning and leaving became for Mandela expressions of that first "last time" (LWF, 14). Many times during his life, he would have to mourn, leave, and part ways. The pattern initiated by this original encounter with death repeated itself at crucial moments.

Mandela viewed every death as "a frightful disaster no matter what the cause and the age of the person affected." He distinguished between a gradual, slow death, as in the case of illness – when "the next-of-kin are at least forewarned and the blow may not be so shattering when it ultimately lands" – and the kind of death that claims "a strapping and healthy person in the prime of his life" (CWM, 170). Living through the second type of loss could be "paralyzing." Each death was nevertheless a singular and unrepeatable event, its meaning often ungraspable at the moment of its occurrence. For it to fully become an event for those who mourned the loss, it had to trigger a remembrance of the deceased, as well as memories of other deaths; it had to emerge into consciousness as actuality. In Mandela's case, each death of a family member (his daughter, his son, and his mother) produced its full effects only after the fact, when it was remembered on the occasion of other deaths – a repetition that often became its own spectral presence.

Significantly, Mandela missed the burial of many of those who meant a great deal to him. Such was the case of the regent Jongintaba in the winter of 1942. Such, too, was the case of his mother and his eldest son, Thembekile. His applications to the prison authorities were ignored on the death of his mother: not only was he not permitted to attend her funeral, his letter was "not even favoured with the courtesy of an acknowledgement" (CWM, 170). Missing burials always triggered intractable questions, chief among which was the specific nature of one's duties to the deceased. After the regent's funeral, Mandela spent nearly a week in Mqhekezweni, in conflict with himself: "Had I no obligations to the dead?" "Was I not permitted to make my own choices?" he wondered (LWF, 79). He found, moreover, that no death prepares one for the shock of a second. "Nothing I experienced in the late Forties and in Sept[ember] last year," he declared, "can be likened to what I went through on July 16 [1969]" (CWM, 171), the day his son, Thembi, died in a car accident. Thembi was not the first child of Mandela's to die. The first was his nine-month-old baby daughter with Evelyn, Makaziwe. He describes her death in this way: "She had been hospitalized and had been making good progress when suddenly her condition took a grave turn and she died the same night. I managed to see her during the critical moments when she was struggling desperately to hold within her tender body the last sparks of life which were flickering away. I have never known whether or not I was fortunate to witness that grievous scene. It haunted me for many days thereafter and still provokes painful memories right up to the present day; but it should have hardened me for similar catastrophes" (CWM, 171).

Or so the stoic might muse. But the news of Thembi's death at age twenty-three, while Mandela was on Robben Island, was devastating to him: "The news was broken to me about 2.30 pm. Suddenly my heart seemed to have stopped beating and the warm blood that had freely flown in my veins for the last 51 years froze into ice. For some time I could neither think nor talk and my strength appeared to be draining out. Eventually, I found my way back to my cell with a heavy load on my shoulders and the last place where a man stricken with sorrow should be. As usual my friends here were kind and helpful and they did what they could to keep me in good spirits" (CWM, 173). Or, as Mandela describes the experience in *Long Walk*: "I do not have words to express the sorrow, or the loss I felt. It left a hole in my heart that can never be filled. I returned to my cell and lay on my bed. I do not know how long I stayed there, but I did not emerge for dinner. Some of the men looked in, but I said nothing. Finally, Walter [Sisulu] came to me and knelt beside my bed, and I handed him the telegram. He said nothing, but only held my hand. I do not know how long he remained with me. There is nothing that one man can say to another at such a time" (CWM, 432).

In later years, after his release, the deaths of Oliver Tambo and Walter Sisulu also proved difficult for Mandela in terms of resisting the public expression of his pain. He likened the death of Tambo to "the falling of a giant oak tree" (CWM, 345): "I felt very lonely and seeing him lying there I couldn't believe that he was dead." Walter Sisulu's death left him "almost prostrate with grief" (CWM, 345). What we observe in all these descriptions is Mandela's dramatic expression of emotion, the quasi-physiological and somatic effects of the tragedy upon him, and the nature of his response (withdrawal to his cell) in a context of extreme powerlessness in which he can strictly do nothing.

Mandela's closest encounter with the prospect of his own death occurred during the Rivonia trial in 1964. A police raid on Liliesleaf Farm in Rivonia had resulted in the arrest of almost all of the high command of Umkhonto we Sizwe. Put on trial in October for sabotage, Mandela faced the real possibility of being sentenced to death. "The critical phase lasted a few hours only," Mandela tells us, "and I was a worried and exhausted man as I went to bed the day I heard of the Rivonia swoop. But when I got up in the morning the worst was over and I had somehow mustered enough strength and courage even to rationalize that if there was nothing else I could do to further the cause we all so passionately cherished, even the dreadful outcome that threatened us might serve a useful purpose on wider issues" (LWF, 124). This belief, Mandela continues, served to "feed and replenish my slender resources of fortitude until the last day of the proceedings." It was reinforced by the conviction that their cause was just and by the wide support they received from "bodies and individuals from both sides of the Colour line." But, he admits, "all the flourish of trumpets and the hosannas sung by us as well as our well-wishers in the course of the trial would have been valueless if courage had deserted us when the decisive moment struck" (LWF, 124).

In his book, *The State vs. Nelson Mandela*, defense attorney Joel Joffe describes a visit to the accused around this time: "They were calm, living now in the shadow of death. The strain and tension was becoming almost unbearable, yet the only matter they wanted to discuss was how they should behave in court if the death sentence was passed."[6] Informed that the judge would ask him whether he had any reason to advance why the death sentence should not be passed, Mandela responded that he was "prepared to die for his beliefs, and knew that his death would be an inspiration to his people in their struggle." There is "no easy walk to freedom. We have to pass through the shadow of death again and again before we reach the mountain tops of our desires," he concluded.[7] The trialists themselves thought it likely that they would receive a death sentence. "We discussed it," Mandela reports of a conversation with Ahmed Kathrada, "and we said that it was necessary for us to think, not just in terms of ourselves, who were in this situation, but of the struggle as a whole. We should disappear under a cloud of glory, we should fight back" (CWM, 122–23). This was quite different, he acknowledges, from being in his cell alone and trying to confront the fact that he was likely "to not live." In a 1969 letter to Sefton Vutela, he was more explicit about his will to live: "We should be ready to undertake any tasks which history might assign to us however the price to be paid may be.... I must however, confess that for my own part the threat of death evoked no desire in me to play the role of martyr. I was ready to do so if I had to. But the anxiety to live always lingered" (CWM, 123).

The Cell as a Shroud

Some of Mandela's most momentous engagements with death occurred while he was in prison. The pivotal space during his carceral years was the cell. It might not have presented the strict appearance of a grave. Measuring seven by eight feet, its features were more a mixture of a coffin and a catacomb. It was the concentrated instantiation of the harshness and grimness that surrounded him for decades. Whenever death struck, as we have seen, it was to his cell that he withdrew. A physical space of confinement and solitude, the cell became a shroud, a space of mourning and confrontation with oneself and the memory of the dead. Mandela's life underground, in his own account, was already a kind of twilight zone, tipping this way and that between the worlds of living and dead, day and night, visibility and invisibility, presence and absence. He would surface in the midst of an increasingly hazardous life, only to disappear again. Living underground, he remarked, "you cannot be yourself; you must fully inhabit whatever role you have assumed" (LWF, 245). "The key to being underground is being invisible," he wrote in his autobiography. The transition from life underground to life in a cell was significant, marked as it was by the penal ritual of *thawuza* (a degrading form of anal inspection). When, in 1952, Mandela was taken to Johannesburg prison, he and his comrades were stripped completely naked and lined up against the wall. He was then taken into "a tiny cell with a single drainage hole in the floor which could be flushed only from the outside ... the blankets were encrusted with dried blood and vomit, ridden with lice, vermin and cockroaches, and reeked with a stench that actually competed with the stink of the drain" (LWF, 228). Rituals of nakedness were complemented by isolation, usually associated with the deprivation of meals, except rice water. Of his first experience of isolation, Mandela remarks: "I found solitary confinement the most forbidding aspect of prison life. There was no end and no beginning: there is only one's own mind, which can begin to play tricks. Was that a dream or did it really happen? One begins to question everything" (LWF 401–402). Or: "I had nothing to read, nothing to write on or with, no one to talk to. The mind begins to turn in on itself, and one desperately wants something outside oneself on which to fix one's attention.... After a time in solitary, I relished the company even of the insects in my cell and found myself on the verge of initiating conversations with a cockroach" (LWF 321–22).

But it was especially the regime of hard labor that put a ghostly stamp on Mandela's prison experience. For decades he worked at the quarry, with the heat and the sun's rays reflecting off the lime into his eyes. The glare hurt his eyes, which streamed, while his face became fixed in a permanent squint and the dust swirled all over him. "By the end of the day, our faces and bodies were caked with white dust. We looked like pale ghosts except where rivulets of sweat had washed away the lime. When we returned to our cells, we would scrub ourselves in the cold water, which never seemed to rinse away the dust completely" (LWF, 392). During the Robben Island years, Mandela's dreams were ghostly narratives, usually about arriving at his house in Orlando and finding no one at home. This dream was preceded by an actual event involving Evelyn, his first wife, who left him during a two-week imprisonment in 1957: "When I left on bail," he recalls, "I found that she had moved out and taken the children. I returned to an empty, silent house. She had even removed the curtains, and for some reason, I found this small detail shattering" (LWF, 193). Mandela wrote to Winnie, "Sometimes I feel like one who is on the sidelines ... who has missed life itself."[8]

The prison cell in these accounts appears, then, as a space of isolation and loneliness, capable of jeopardizing Mandela's personhood. But it is also a place of ascetic detachment and mourning. It operates as a shroud over his prisoner's existence. Yet it also allows Mandela to perform a practice of regeneration. In prison he struggled with letting go of attachment; it was here that he felt the loss of beloved objects as losses of his own self. The objectively wretched conditions of prison separated his ego from his restricted and confined body, his selfhood from the most brutal aspects of pain and, thereby, from the threat of complete objectification. What David Schalkwyk describes as Mandela's stoicism in Chapter 2 can also, as we suggested earlier, be grasped in terms of a division he created between psyche and *soma* in order to attain a certain state of detachment. An aspect of this removal is his sexual life, his celibacy, of which he speaks very little. He held onto the assurance that joy was possible when almost everything (except the right to be human and free) had been given up. In prison he encountered the void, but he was able to build a bridge back to the world left behind. This bridge was built with trusted others, especially women. In his letters, he deliberately tried to remain in contact with a universe wider than his prison cell.

It is worth considering the transition from the cell as a shroud or a catacomb to the cell as a house of Mandela's first freedom. Mandela's Qunu house is built on the model of the warder's house at Victor Verster Prison, where he spent his last period of captivity. In *Long Walk To Freedom*, Mandela writes: "I have always believed that a man should have a home within sight of the house where he was born. After being released from prison, I set about plans to build a country house for myself in Qunu.... It was based on the floor plan of the house I had lived in at Victor Verster. People often commented on this, but the answer is simple: the Victor Verster house was the first spacious and comfortable home I ever stayed in, and I liked it very much. I was familiar with its dimensions, so at Qunu I would not have to wander at night looking for the kitchen" (LWF, 599). Isaac Ndlovu has observed how, for Mandela, "life after prison keeps reproducing its logic, even its architecture."[9] We could remark, too, that during apartheid both the macro-spaces of segregation (like the bantustan) and the micro-spaces (like the matchbox township house) were loci for the staging of humiliation. Mandela makes the counterintuitive move of embracing the prison house not only as the final staging post on the path to freedom, but also as the most comfortable house he has ever lived in, thus subverting the logic of the system that sought to contain and break him. Conversely, we might consider how, in small ways, Mandela made his prison cell a house, a process born, Verne Harris suggests, of "holding his mistakes close to him."[10] Mandela felt that he had made mistakes in his domestic life, that he had neglected the realm of the home in favor of his political career. Seeking to remedy this, he nurtured a domestic space in prison, by gardening, cleaning, caring, and administering to others. His gardening, in turn, as shown by Daniel Roux in Chapter 9, led to a revised political vision. Within the spectral seclusion imposed by the life sentence, observes Elleke Boehmer, gardening allowed the prisoner to explore the spirit of certain key ideas – of regeneration and reconstruction.[11]

Bodily Mutations

Throughout his life, Mandela was able to project multiple images of his self and his body. Each of these images has contributed to the making of his aura. That he was "one of the world's longest serving prisoners" (CWM, 410) served to cement his iconic stature. Yet Mandela's auratic power preceded his prison years, during which, by his own admission, he unwittingly projected to the outside world "the false image" of a "saint" he "never was, even on the basis of an earthly definition of a saint who is a sinner who keeps on trying" (CWM, 140). This power also stemmed from his charisma and the enigma he ended up becoming. Both the charisma and the enigma were enhanced (as other contributors to this volume have also pointed out) by his physical appearance, including his height, and the aesthetic dimensions of his bodily control, projection, and movement. That he was willing to maintain his body and enhance it through physical exercise and acutely nuanced sartorial practices only helped to accrue its powers. He occupied many image ages: the hip young lawyer (with only one suit, we later learned in his autobiography, with which he nevertheless managed to convey the image of an elegant man, charming women and doing politics); the defendant in court in his kingly regalia; the prisoner whose image became shrouded with mystery, a subject of speculation and, increasingly, fabrication; his years as president and world statesman.

There have been many images available of the aging Mandela, especially in the years before 2010. Since 2010, however, there have been far fewer, the most striking of which are images of frailty, low activity, and unsteadiness. In most of these, Mandela is no longer seen walking tall, but is bowed, often seated, and homebound. A painful example is the photograph taken on June

Figure 12.1. Mandela mourning for his great-granddaughter Zenani, 2010. Photograph by Siphiwe Sibeko © European Press Photo Agency.

11, 2010, at his granddaughter's funeral, on the morning after the opening ceremony of the FIFA World Cup (Figure 12.1).

On the night before the opening of the event, which was hosted in South Africa, Mandela's thirteen-year-old granddaughter Zenani was killed in a car accident. Her death recalled the many losses Mandela has suffered in relation to children in his family. (His third child, Makgatho, died of AIDS-related illness in 2005. Another Mandela, the seven-year-old Kefuoe Seakamela, known by her friends to be a good swimmer, drowned in a school swimming pool in 2008.)[12] In the funeral image, Mandela's cheeks are so sunken as to completely change the shape of his face. The pall of his skin is different; he looks far older than he does in other pictures from this time, and his grief and despair are revealed in the slackness of his mouth and the angle from which he looks into the camera. It is significant to recall here Joffe's description of Mandela after a year on Robben Island: "He had

Figure 12.2. Nelson Mandela, 2011, photograph by Tyrone Arthur. Courtesy of Tyrone Arthur.

withered during his year in a South African jail, and looked thin and miserably underweight. His face, formerly well filled out and a rounded, deep glistening brown, was now hollow-cheeked, a sickly pale yellowish colour. The skin hung in bags under his eyes."[13] The body, it would seem, carries its affective past with it.

This photo can be contrasted with a much happier one taken in September 2011 of Mandela with his new great-grandson on his knee, an image that was published on the front pages of the country's Sunday newspapers (and that readers can easily view online).[14] Here Mandela's face appears round and full again – the face of a much younger man than the one photographed more than a year before. It is a joyful image, in which Mandela looks straight at the viewer and appears healthy and glowing.

Another arresting image of the aged Mandela, by Tyrone Arthur, appeared in *Business Day* in late 2011 (Figure 12.2). This is a remarkable image, a brilliant study of the human face. A shadow hangs alongside it, as if a shroud. Mandela's eyes appear watery – probably the water of aging eyes rather than tearfulness. Facial skin, of course, changes over time, becoming thinner, most notably around the eyelids, a process accelerated by sun exposure, which damages the skin. But Mandela's eyes have years of Robben Island's light-exposure abuse written in them too. We may bring to mind here Elleke Boehmer's idea, drawing on Derrida's *Spectres of Marx*, that during the period of the treason trial, winning freedom came to be equated with overcoming an attachment to life itself and that in prison Mandela experienced the feeling of being a "living ghost": "not present, not presently living," of "living on the sidelines" of the world.[15] A number of these phrases and formulations could be applied to old age: the inevitable approach of death, the feeling of being in life but not entirely of the world anymore, of existing on the edges of national politics and public life. The ghostliness that was prefigured by life in the cell is recalled in this final image: a life in a shroud, a life across which the shadow of death is already falling.

Mandela's image remained outside of time for many years during his imprisonment and therefore came to embody the eternal potential of the revolutionary moment. These much later images may embody – or may encourage one to project onto his aging features – anxieties about South Africa's future in a moment when the revolution has failed to materialize or to achieve its full potential. Mandela's aging seems to correspond to the diminishing power of the vision of 1994 and of the hopes that were so alive during the years of his presidency.[16]

Political Autopsy

The image is an unsettling form of the deconstruction of a human being and the dismantling of his or her double: its danger lies in its capacity to liberate signs from the control of their maker. An image of a cadaver is even more perilous, especially when looked at from outside its proper sphere, the funeral. An image of the corpse is an object of fear and dread; it is possible to imagine that creating such an image could unleash forces that might cause the death of the person whose cadaver is depicted. This explains something of the furor that was caused in South Africa in 2010 when, reworking Rembrandt's seventeenth-century masterpiece *The Anatomy Lesson of Dr. Tulp*, the Johannesburg artist Yiull Damaso conjured up the scene of an autopsy: a dissection of Mandela's corpse (Figure 12.3). While the dead body in the image is not repulsive, the painting nevertheless foregrounds the gory physicality of Mandela's death.

In Rembrandt's painting, an autopsy is being performed in front of a small group of spectators – mostly doctors who paid to be in the painting. In Damaso's 2010 version, the late AIDS orphan Nkosi Johnson performs the autopsy on Mandela, while Archbishop Emeritus Desmond Tutu and politicians F. W. de Klerk, Jacob Zuma, Cyril Ramaphosa, Trevor Manuel, Thabo Mbeki, and Helen Zille take the place of the spectators. The African National Congress (ANC) responded to the representation of Mandela's autopsy by likening it to witchcraft. The charge seemed to be haunted by much earlier African traditions in which the image is imbued with power and ambiguity. The painting drew out, through the scandal it created, multiple anxieties that center around Mandela's body.

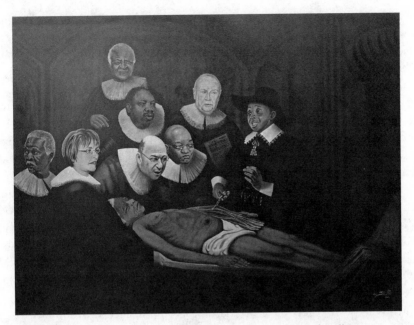

Figure 12.3. Yiull Damaso, *The Night Watch*, 2010. Courtesy of Yiull Damaso.

Damaso's view was that "the eventual passing of Mandela is something that we will have to face, as individuals, as a nation."[17] Nicola van Kan, marketing manager of Hyde Park Shopping Center, where the painting was displayed, observed, "We feel it is a controversial piece, but we support freedom of expression and art."[18] An article in the *Mail & Guardian* on the same day reported that "the painting's reproduction on the front page of this newspaper's edition on Friday provoked a furious response from the ruling party." "The ANC is appalled and strongly condemns in the strongest possible terms the dead Mandela painting by Yiull Damaso," said Jackson Mthembu, a party spokesman. "It is in bad taste, disrespectful, and it is an insult and an affront to values of our society. In African society it is a foreign act of *ubuthakathi* [bewitching] to kill a living person and this so-called work of art ... is also racist. It goes further by violating Tat'uMandela's dignity by stripping him naked in the glare of curious onlookers, some of whom have seen their apartheid ideals die before them.... Why would anyone dream of a dead Madiba?"[19] Commenting on Damaso's painting, the deputy editor of the *Mail & Guardian*, Rapule Tabane, said the artist was grappling with the state of the country's current politics and the meaning of Mandela in that context. "You might say that it asks the question 'what killed the special spirit that Madiba brought to our national life?'" he wrote in a text message to the South African Press Association. "It should not be seen as a reflection on or anticipation of the literal death of Madiba as a person, but as an inquiry into the state of the nation and its iconography."[20]

Tabane's comments point to an anxiety about the loss of a form of politics deeply associated with the person of Mandela. We could think here of Thabo Mbeki's conflictual relation with Mandela's politics of reconciliation, of Nkosi Johnson's dramatic death as a commentary on Mandela's slow response to the AIDS crisis, and of the way the Democratic Alliance, the official opposition in South Africa, has, under Helen Zille, tried to lay claim to Mandela's legacy, claiming that the ANC has abandoned all or most of what he stood for.

The prickly relationship between Mandela and his immediate successor, Thabo Mbeki, is sharply dissected by Mark Gevisser in his biography *Thabo Mbeki: The Dream Deferred*. In a chapter entitled "One Good Native: Mbeki and Mandela," Gevisser reminds us of the following potent public incident in the life of South African politics. "Madiba," Thabo Mbeki said as he stepped up to the podium to accept the mantle of ANC president from his predecessor at the party's conference in Mafikeng in December 1997, "members of the press have been asking me how it feels to step into your shoes. I've been saying I would never be seen dead in such shoes. You wear such ugly shoes!" Gevisser rightly describes this as "the awkward braggadocio of someone whose performance is measured, perpetually, against the stature of a father figure," the symptom of a conflict between the atavistic patriarch and the rational manager.[21] Mbeki, Gevisser writes, "wished to be nobody's father, and nobody's son either"; he called Mandela's outsize popularity "Mandela exceptionalism" when he was being polite and the "one-good-native syndrome" when he was not.[22] A key difference between the two men, according to Mbeki, was their different approaches to racial reconciliation: for Mbeki racial reconciliation was "unrealisable" unless it was "accompanied by the fundamental transformation of the entire social-economic fabric of South African society. Therefore you can't have reconciliation without transformation."[23] Mandela, meanwhile, was taking tea with Betsie Verwoerd and donning Springbok rugby jerseys. So, as Gevisser notes, they had different understandings of history, of healing, and of transformation as a social and psychic process. It was Mbeki's view that Mandela's status precluded good government and that his executive style privileged personality over process. Yet ultimately, most commentators agree that Mandela's political style won out, most pointedly as a critique of Mbeki's defensive, wounded form of doing politics and his destructive blind spots.[24]

Damaso's painting, then, drew into focus a complex and toxic brew of necropolitics: political patricide, the AIDS crisis, which has killed thousands of South Africans, and conflicting claims to the dead man's body and legacy. A symbolic act of autopsy thus gets externalized as a series of questions about the nation, and Mandela's body becomes a complex site of interplay between private body and public narrative. It dramatizes an attempt to pierce the secret within: the feeling that Mandela is both of and not of South Africa, that he is at odds with the place and deeply inside of it, that he represents South Africa's fight with itself, that he has managed to find the secret of the quest for the *pharmakon*, the future – and that perhaps it is hidden inside of his own body. Significantly art – and, increasingly, money – have emerged as central in debates about Mandela's death and the processes of memorialization (in contrast to, say, pronouncements from the Nelson Mandela Centre of Memory).

Filthy Lucre

Various attempts to turn Mandela into a commodity and use his appeal as a source of revenue have predictably reared their heads in recent years. Arguments have been waged over whether his corpse will be the property of the state, the ANC, or his family. Related to this are attempts at making him into an effigy and conceiving of such an effigy as a permanent, inalienable component of the South African nation. The recent inscription of Mandela's face on the national currency turns Mandela into a fiscal thing, a sign of the South African commonweal: the common property of all, imprinted on banknotes exchanged daily across the country. Though intended as a sign of respect and longevity, it works, too, as the conversion of a moral debt into a monetary asset.

Many of the arguments over plans for Nelson's Mandela's funeral and burial, which arose in 2012 and again in June 2013, involved the controversial figure of his grandson, Mandla Mandela, a chief in Mvezo, Mandela's birthplace, who seemed eager to capitalize on his grandfather's impending death. One of Mandela's biggest preoccupations during his life was his inability to properly take care of his family, his wife and children first and foremost, but his wider family too. But while he recognized his debt to his family, he never formulated this debt in monetary terms. Mandla's attempt at turning the event of Mandela's death into a source of private revenue involved the deployment of two sets of symbolic capital: his lineage with Mandela and his position in the politics of chieftaincy. Along with the already complex politics of lineage and legacy, we must also consider Mandela's complex history of family making. Married three times and divorced twice, he has many children and grandchildren, several of whom claim a part of his aura and inheritance. All of this, in turn, complicates the hard question of who "owns" his corpse: his family? but what family? the state, the ANC – or his widow, Graça Machel?

In late May 2010 a feud began to brew in the extended family following the surprise reburial of three of Nelson Mandela's children. The remains were exhumed from the family cemetery in Qunu and reburied in Mvezo, about forty kilometers away, by a local funeral parlor and officials of the Department of Health. The exhumations were ordered by Mandla Mandela. The move angered family members, who maintain they were not consulted about the exhumations, and threw arrangements for Madiba's funeral (like the building of roads and pavements by the state) into disarray. The exhumations took place four days after Mandela arrived at his homestead for his first visit since being discharged from hospital in Johannesburg in January 2010; he and his wife, Graça, were not present at the exhumations. (The dispute over this action, as it turns out, was only resolved in July 2013, when, after a court order, the coffins were reinterred at Qunu.) The event became entangled with disturbing allegations in the *Sunday World* not only that Mandla Mandela sold the exclusive rights to Madiba's funeral to the SABC, but that he pocketed R3 million from the deal. He was also accused of hiding details of the transaction from his family. The paper reported that the deal was code-named Project M and R700 million had been budgeted for it. It quoted an insider saying, "We have already done about 15 packages for the M project, and have secured exclusive interviews with a number of people who are very close to Madiba." The SABC, however, said that it had investigated the allegations and found "nothing."[25] "The very thought of the eventuality [of Madiba's death] sends shivers down our spines," said Mandla, who reportedly became very angry when he learned that an SABC crew was driving to his homestead to film the exhumation of Madiba's sons and infant daughter, contacted senior officials in the organization, and demanded that the crew from Mthatha be recalled.

In a further controversy, which unfolded in December 2011, South African police opened an investigation after two international news agencies set up surveillance cameras outside Mandela's home in Qunu. Police declined to name the media outlets, but British-based Reuters and the US news agency Associated Press both confirmed they had set up cameras outside the former president's home. After the cases were opened, police spokesman Vish Naidoo said that the media outlets could face criminal charges for violating a law that restricts access to sensitive areas. "The cameras were positioned some time ago, with the knowledge of the authorities. The cameras are not turned on. They are not spying on Mr. Mandela's home," AP spokesman Paul Colford commented. "They are part of the preparedness that AP and other large news organisations customarily make in the event of a major news story involving a former world leader."[26] But the profit motif again raised its head: Chieftainess Nokwanele Balizulu, who lives near Mandela's house, said, "I agreed to having those cameras there, but I'm not going to say anything else."[27]

Letting Go

In 2011, when asked about the former president's passing, Verne Harris, chief archivist at the Nelson Mandela Foundation, observed: "We feel that he is already gone – as an active voice who offers us a last resort. He is no longer with us. He has been frustrated by our dependence on him. He wants to see us walking without him.... We must allow him to go." Harris recalled Mandela's words to the Foundation at the moment of his "retirement from retirement": "it is now in your hands." In urging them to move forward, Harris recalls, Mandela suggested they keep in mind three working principles: that justice should be their guiding argument in any decision reached, that they should not turn the Foundation into a "mausoleum" to Mandela, and that they "don't need to protect him." As people learn to live without Nelson Mandela, as Harris put it, memory itself has to be subject to the dialogical, to contestation, to "different versions." He offered two examples of how the Foundation espoused and encouraged ideas in action and in memory of a form of politics to which Mandela subscribed as an active politician. The first was the Foundation's involvement with people who had perpetrated the vicious and shameful xenophobic violence of 2008, when "foreign" Africans were attacked in several South African townships, and its attempt to work through with them "why they did what they did." Another was a round table discussion the Foundation organized between National Intelligence officials and activists from the Right to Know Campaign, in which they could confront and discuss their differences relating to the impending Freedom of Information Act. People who wouldn't usually talk to each other are, in these situations, asked to confront one another in the same room. Rather than being a gatekeeper or custodian of Mandela's legacy, Harris suggested, the Foundation would pursue "memory work ... from the inside out," as a living activity in the present and one that aims to render memory productively unstable and open in order to continue addressing the emerging complexities of the present – even, if necessary, to "find the loose threads which unravel the tapestry."[28]

One can't help noting the similarities between Mandela's "stepping back" in Harris's account and the many instances recorded in this chapter of Mandela's desire or political need to disappear, to go underground. Moreover, while Harris and the Foundation might strive to "let him go," as Mandela himself requested, many South Africans seemed to be yearning, even in Mandela's extreme old age, for him to be a political presence, to say something when it matters. Elleke Boehmer, for example, writing on the occasion of Mandela's ninetieth birthday in 2008 (not long after the xenophobic violence of that year), observed that, while South Africans turned to

Mandela to respond to and condemn the attacks, he remained silent on the matter. Only a day or so before the 46664 birthday concert celebration in London did he express his regret at the violence against fellow Africans in his home country. It was impossible not to notice, Boehmer commented, that his statement had been delivered extremely late in the political day and that it took place abroad, at a dinner with Bill Clinton and Gordon Brown.[29] But more notable than this, arguably, was the desire so many felt that Mandela, despite his great age and frailty, might somehow articulate their own feelings about these events.

The Emptiness of Words

This penultimate part of our chapter will focus on the struggle to give a meaning to Mandela's death: the struggle, that is, against the regurgitation of vacuous words, words that we have heard too often before. What kind of language will rise to the occasion, might fill the emptiness with significance, rather than produce hollow eulogies and thereby unbearable disappointment?

Roland Barthes has written that the stereotype is the word repeated without any magic, any enthusiasm, as though it were natural – as though, by some miracle, this recurring word could be adequate to every occasion rather than operate as a "constraining form," unaware of its own insistence. Barthes speaks of his distrust of the stereotype as opposed to the bliss of the new word. The stereotype, Barthes writes, is the "nauseating impossibility of dying."[30] For Barthes, then, language usually assumes, in its reiterations, the character of the stereotype. The bliss of language, its sharp and new edges, he thinks, are to be found when we depoliticize what is apparently political and politicize what is apparently not. He longs for a form of speaking that resists becoming "a moral site cleansed of any linguistic sensuality."[31] His call is for a language lined with flesh, a text where we can hear the grain of the throat, the patina of consonants, the articulation of the body, the tongue: a bodily language.

Elleke Boehmer has remarked on the curious immobility of Mandela's own verbal performances compared with the extraordinary versatility and expressive force of his bodily and sartorial performances. She comments on the strained, affectless tones that marked his early attempts at public speaking and persisted throughout his career, with only some modifications. This stiffness characterizes not merely his speeches but also his polemical articles written for publications like *Liberation* and his political pedagogical statements in prison. How, she wonders, did his seemingly wooden language – his *langue de bois* – coordinate with the versatility of his statesmanlike behavior and his more impressive speaking practices in court, as a lawyer? Boehmer suggests that Mandela consistently avoided appearing to be a demagogue. To encourage political support, he used pared-down language, the verbs straightforward and workmanlike, the nouns often abstract – invoking freedom, democracy – but unadorned. "In all cases, whether in the dock and on the podium, his reasoned stage-by-stage progressions and set phrases were designed to control the expression of emotion," Boehmer writes. Except on those rare occasions when his anger at an abuse of power yielded a sharp exhortation, Mandela's was a public discourse from which the affect had been extracted: "We were not to know how Madiba felt, how Rolihlahla felt," Boehmer writes. "He was looking for consensus and it made no sense," she argues, "to amplify or over-qualify his words. He left little room for us to do so."[32]

If we want to find a shape-shifting language in which to talk meaningfully about Mandela's death, a language that has the power of undercutting stereotype, we must instead look at the extraordinary artifact, the creative genius, not only of Mandela's public life but of the way he approached a state of transfiguration through his attempts (not always successful) at recasting his inner and outer lives, producing his own difference. In this lies the message he most wanted us to hear: the beauty and subtlety of his person and his life must be mapped onto his invocation of the "we" of a community, of a public in which he partakes and that he personifies. Any more purely subjective meaning is so deeply buried inside of Mandela that we can't get at it – except through his public persona and its images.

In other words, Mandela left long ago. Or, as Winnie Mandela might say, he was never there in the first place. This predicament recalls the reflections in Umberto Eco's *Opera Aperta* on a text that is so shut that it is paradoxically open – open to all interpretations.[33] Nelson Mandela has long been a set of surfaces, completely readable and completely flat at the same time. He has been a screen on which to project wishes and dreams, often contradictory ones. So Mbeki's irritable reading of him, or Winnie Madikizela-Mandela's judgmental one, or even F. W. de Klerk's adversarial one, might turn out to be the strongest readings of him, even though they seem to contradict the views held by admirers, who are more taken in, perhaps, by the projection of their own wishes.[34] The fact that Mandela has become, in many respects, a projection of a projection is the result, as we have suggested in this chapter, of his ways of coping with the painful and often brutal experiences of his prison years and his life in politics. What Mandela seemed to be intimating at the end of his life is that we should take it as a national moment and give it meaning. "Use my body and remember me," he might have been saying, by "opening another space in politics; a space that has been hitherto unthinkable, but that is possible, that is the supersession of what we have today, especially in relation to racism, poverty, oppression."

So the fitting language to accompany his death, a language that will escape the emptiness of reiterated words, must do what Barthes suggested: it must be the language of life, not the zombie discourse of the stereotype that refuses to die – but the language, also, of mortality, of letting go and making something out the gift we already have: the transition to democracy of 1994. This would require us to make the language and the event of Mandela's death *political*, even if it is apparently not – but not in the way that a political funeral is accustomed to doing. The task is, in fact, to depoliticize what is apparently political and to make political what is apparently not. This message is extraordinary: take a political project into your life and reconstitute it as a common practice for change. It is impossible to break the mirror of Mandela – for it will always deflect our gaze back to the same place: to the work of politics as a deep philosophical place that must always be about action in the world. We cannot avoid that place, that task, as we encounter and reflect on the extraordinary body of Mandela. This is the message that will hover well after his body is lowered into his grave: "It is not me, it's you." And along with that collective meaning, there is a deeply personal and intimate one, for this was, after all, a man going into his grave alone. It is precisely this tension, this contradiction that will make us think, "Here is the last hero of our time" – a hero, though, in a deeply self-sacrificial and generative sense: a sense that implies an act of worlding, an act that insists on doing away with the "I" that is not also a "we." At stake here is an insistence on the possibility of a dreamworld: an insistence that constitutes the greatest longing of the twentieth century.

Dreamworld

In *Dreamworld and Catastrophe*, Susan Buck-Morss suggests that the dream of the twentieth century, its collective political desire, was for a social world in alliance with personal happiness.[35] She borrows the notion of a dreamworld from Walter Benjamin, who used it not only as a poetic description of a mental state, but as an analytical concept: one that was central to his theory of modernity as the re-enchantment rather than the disenchantment of the world. The dreamworlds of modernity – political, cultural, economic – are, for both Benjamin and Buck-Morss, expressions of a utopian desire for social arrangements that transcend existing forms. The mass democratic myth of modernity – the belief that the industrial reshaping of the world was capable of bringing about the good society by providing material happiness for the masses – has come under profound challenge in the wake of the disintegration of European socialism, the demands of capitalist restructuring, and fundamental ecological constraints. For some, that dream is being left behind, as consumerism appears to become what Buck-Morss terms "the first global ideological form."[36] Commodities, she suggests, have not ceased to crowd people's private dreamworlds, and they still have a utopian function on a personal level. But "when the larger social project is abandoned, this personal utopianism becomes political cynicism, because it is no longer thought necessary to guarantee the collective good, but only that which is pursued by the individual. Mass utopia, once considered the logical correlate of personal utopia, is now a rusty idea."[37] The work of so many critical theorists at present is, it seems, an attempt to come to terms with mass dreamworlds at the moment of their passing. That passing, Buck-Morss suggests, marks the true ending of the Cold War; it also marks, more profoundly than any of its other more immediate political effects, the end of the twentieth century.

Mandela stands, at this moment of his passing, for the twentieth century in some of its deepest dreamscapes. We have seen this in the materials traced out in this essay and in so much of the recent writing generated about his legacy. But who is to say that the dream has passed or that it has died? South Africa is a conundrum, a volatile mix of all the currents of the twentieth century – and Mandela stands at its center. He is of our time, the time of our world, as an African. And yet who is to know what will happen now that he has gone – when another temporal order might begin, and what the chaotic, volatile, fecund dream-space of a life like his can produce after death? What has passed and what is coming is unclear, though we may feel a set of unmistakable currents moving around all of us, as we speak, as we move through time, and as we absorb the news that he has slipped away and that we are now without him.

June and November, 2012 and December 6th, 2013.

NOTES

1 Hannah Arendt, *Essays in Understanding* (New York: Harcourt, Brace, 1994), 222.
2 Nelson Mandela, *Long Walk to Freedom* (Boston: Back Bay Books, 1995), 389. Subsequent page references will appear in the text.
3 Nelson Mandela, *Conversations with Myself* (New York: Farrar, Straus and Giroux, 2010), 172. Subsequent page references will appear in the text.
4 See also David Schalkwyk's discussion of these matters in Chapter 2.
5 Zolani Ngwane also discusses this incident in Chapter 5.

6 Joel Joffe, *The State vs. Nelson Mandela* (Oxford: Oneworld, 2007), 246.

7 Ibid.

8 Elleke Boehmer, *Nelson Mandela: A Very Short Introduction* (Oxford: Oxford University Press, 2008), 154.

9 Isaac Ndlovu, "An Examination of Prison, Criminality and Power in Selected Contemporary Kenyan and South African Narratives," Unpublished PhD dissertation (Stellenbosch University, 2010), 27n.

10 Verne Harris, "Mandela and the Centering of Memory," Seminar presented at Duke University, October 2011.

11 Boehmer, *Nelson Mandela*, 162.

12 The deaths of all these children bring a different perspective to Mandela's so-called exceptionalism. It is striking how many men of that generation and the next did not know their children, lost their children, and suffered the deaths of children, both in accidents and through disease. A stark pattern emerges from the stories of the loss of these children: a pattern that is all the more striking for its typicality and painful predictability.

13 Joffe, *State vs. Mandela*, 24.

14 See, e.g., abcnews.go.com/blogs/headlines/2011/09/nelson-mandela-welcomes-new-great-grandchild. The child's name, Nkosi Queya II Zanethemba, chosen by Mandela, harks back to a period of Thembu heroism in the mid-1800s.

15 Boehmer, *Nelson Mandela*, 152.

16 We thank Carli Coetzee for her discussion with us on this point.

17 "ANC Outraged over Mandela Painting," *Mail & Guardian*, July 9, 2010, mg.co.za/article/2010–07–09-anc-outraged-over-mandela-painting.

18 Ibid.

19 "Fury over Nelson Mandela Autopsy Painting," *Mail & Guardian*, July 9, 2011, mg.co.za/article/2010–07–09-fury-over-nelson-mandela-autopsy-painting.

20 Ibid.

21 Mark Gevisser, *Thabo Mbeki: The Dream Deferred* (Johannesburg: Jonathan Ball, 2007), 697.

22 Ibid., 703.

23 Ibid., 708.

24 Edwin Cameron writes that when Mandela donned one of the Treatment Action Campaign's "HIV Positive" T-shirts, he "may have marked a turning point in our national struggle about the meaning of AIDS." Cameron believes that Mandela's "intervening moral voice" played a significant role in shifting the government away from its resistance to anti-retrovirals. It also gave members of Mbeki's cabinet the courage to take on the president on this score. Cameron, *Witness to Aids* (London: I. B. Tauris, 2005), 130.

25 Andile Ndlovu, "Mandla, SABC Deny Mandela Funeral Deal," *Times LIVE*, July 22, 2011, www.timeslive.co.za/thetimes/2011/07/22/mandla-sabc-deny-mandela-funeral-deal.

26 Sapa-AFP, "Police Probe News Agencies over Mandela Surveillance Cameras," *Times LIVE*, December 16, 2011, www.timeslive.co.za/local/2011/12/16/police-probe-news-agencies-over-mandela-surveillance-cameras.

27 Chandré Prince, "Madiba Spied On," *Times LIVE*, December 15, 2011, www.timeslive.co.za/news/2011/12/15/madiba-spied-on.

28 Harris, "Mandela and the Centering of Memory."

29 Elleke Boehmer, "Beyond the Icon: Nelson Mandela in his 90th Year," *Open Democracy*, November 12, 2008, www.opendemocracy.net/article/beyond-the-icon-nelson-mandela-in-his-90th-year.

30 Roland Barthes, *The Pleasure of the Text*, trans. Richard Miller (New York: Hill & Wang, 1975), 42–43.

31 Ibid., 54.

32 Boehmer, *Nelson Mandela*, 135. Rob Nixon argues that Mandela's slow speech reinforced his moral weight in the eyes of the world against the sound-bite postures of contemporary politicians who were accustomed to dealing with television. See Nixon, "Mandela, Messianism and the Media," in *Homelands, Harlem, and Hollywood: South African Culture and the World Beyond* (New York: Routledge, 1994), 175–92.

33 Umberto Eco, *The Open Work*, trans. Anna Cancogni (Cambridge, MA: Harvard University Press, 1989), 24.

34 We thank Carli Coetzee for her discussion with us on these points.

35 Susan Buck-Morss, *Dreamworld and Catastrophe* (Cambridge, MA: MIT Press, 2000), ix.

36 Ibid.

37 Ibid., x.

RITA BARNARD

Afterword

Nelson Mandela died on December 5, 2013, at his home in Houghton. The ten days of national and international mourning that followed produced a dense web of commentary, speeches, and imagery, much of it official and sentimental, but some of it of high quality, well worth the attention of readers of this book. The most soaring tribute was offered by US President Barack Obama at the official memorial service at the FNB Stadium in Soweto. Obama recalled that when he first learned about Mandela and the anti-apartheid struggle, something stirred in him: "I woke up to my responsibilities – to others and to myself – and that set me on an improbable journey that finds me here today. And while I will always fall short of Madiba's example, he makes me want to be better. He speaks to what is best inside us."

Obama's words return us to where this book began: to what I identified in the introduction as Mandela's politics of the sublime. Indeed, the speech conforms so perfectly to classic definitions of the term – an effect of expansion and transcendence, of falling short in the face of an object (Mandela's "largeness of spirit") too imposing to encompass – that we must recognize that we are in the sway of a time-honored rhetorical trope. The politics of the sublime is a matter of language and of moving hearts; indeed, some might protest that, in the nitty-gritty sense, it is not politics at all. So it was not surprising that while Obama lauded Mandela as the "last great liberator of the twentieth century," many commentators noted that Mandela's revolution remains incomplete: the sharp inequalities that remain in his country damage democracy and constrain the experience of freedom.

Such sober reminders, however, did not prevent Mandela's passing from eliciting a language of superlatives, verging at times on the metaphysical: thus we learned that the brightest nova of the millennium flared up in the firmament after his death and that the rain that poured down on the day of the memorial was a sign that the ancestors were receiving Mandela in heaven. Even those who declined to think in religious terms had to admit that Mandela was with the stars; the media response to his death was

291

adulatory and omnipresent. The event made headlines across the world; special issues of journals were printed; Tweets and Facebook posts proliferated. Corporate tributes appeared on Web sites and in newspapers, so that Mandela filled even the business and advertising pages. The man's status as global celebrity was no news. But the panegyrics of a legion of famous entertainers sharply brought home the mirror-like character of celebrity culture: like the corporate tributes, these testimonies might well have been heartfelt, but they could not be separated entirely from (self-)promotional aims. Mandela's fame confirmed the fame of others.

There were, however, constant reminders that Mandela was a celebrity with a difference: that, while he was, as Mac Maharaj put it, "a man of gestures," those gestures were not managed and false, as with lesser politicians with PR teams. They were based on Mandela's recognition of the dignity of others, irrespective of status. An Afrikaans writer recalled a moment when, as a peace monitor in 1994, she broke protocol and shook Mandela's hand as he walked through the crowd at a political meeting. The experience differed from all her subsequent encounters with famous people: "He saw *me*, not just another peace monitor or another potential vote for his party. Even in the commotion of the day, he took the time to establish a *connection* with a stranger through a simple greeting." Similar recollections abounded. An especially touching story was that of the dry cleaner who for years took care of the trademark Madiba shirts. He revealed that Mandela actually came to his house to thank him for his labors: "I'm a normal guy," he marveled. "I do nothing but work and go home and sit with my family. He met every day with ministers and kings and queens. How the hell did he remember the dry cleaner?" The story testifies to Mandela's humanity and his respect for ordinary work – enhanced, no doubt, by all those years of breaking rocks on Robben Island. It defetishizes an item that otherwise threatens to become a meaningless sign, a piece of celebrity paraphernalia. One photograph among the thousands published touched me deeply: it showed Mandela in his presidential jet, carefully polishing his own shoes.

The big events during the ten days of mourning all raised questions about the scales, codes, and rituals of political expression. A bizarre figure inevitably stands out: that of the schizophrenic sign-language interpreter, Thamsanqa Jantje, who failed to execute the duties he was hired for at the official memorial. Overcome by a vision of angels entering the stadium, he resorted to meaningless, yet quite solemnly performed gestures. The troubled interpreter, however, was meaningful in himself: he embodied something of the linguistic complexities of the event as a whole. The memorial, in which the ANC government clearly intended to stage a geopolitical reconfiguration by inviting leaders from Brazil, India, China, and Cuba – rather than Europe – to speak, failed to address its multiple audiences effectively. And how could it succeed, given the bad sound system and wooden encomiums? The crowd, braving the incessant rain, dissatisfied with being mere spectators, yearning to sing, mourn, and celebrate in their own way, booed President Jacob Zuma, whose misuse of taxpayer money made national headlines before Mandela's death. They were reprimanded by ANC vice president Cyril Ramaphosa in Zulu – not translated for the global audience – and asked to bring up their issues with the ANC leadership once the foreign dignities had departed. The scolding underscored the disjuncture between the thousands who were bodily present and the millions watching on television; the event left many South Africans feeling dissatisfied and embarrassed. Without Mandela's own charismatic mediation, the connection between the global and the national shorted out.

But the mourning became dignified again as thousands lined up, in scenes reminiscent of the 1994 elections, to view Mandela as he lay in state at the Union Buildings in Pretoria. And at the memorial concert in Cape Town, where organizers were free of the responsibility of providing translators and security for important foreigners, the expressive culture of South Africa came into its own. Madiba was mourned and celebrated in a way he would have enjoyed. The crowds danced and cried, waved flags, and swayed to the music of Johnny Clegg, Annie Lennox, and Ladysmith Black Mambazo. They sang along with the melancholy 1980s hit "Asimbonang' uMandela thina" ("We have not seen Mandela") and with the stirring revolutionary song that last resounded at the funeral of the slain MK leader Chris Hani: "Hamba kahle, Mkhonto weSizwe!" ("Go well, Spear of the Nation!").

The funeral in Qunu seemed more fluent and eloquent than the official memorial. It was a syncretic event. Christian hymns and military rituals blended with Xhosa customs: the welcoming home of the deceased, the slaughter of a spotless ox, the beautiful black and white cattle skins on which the coffin was placed. The language of personal grief emerged for the first time when Ahmed Kathrada, a fellow prisoner, struggling to control his voice, described the loss of Mandela as the loss of an older brother: "My life is in a void and I don't know where to turn." But Kathrada also introduced something signally absent from the official memorial: a remembering of the language and rituals of the liberation struggle. He invoked the generous performatives of the Freedom Charter ("South Africa belongs to all who live in it, black and white") and drew on a trope often deployed by Mandela himself: the naming of comrades who had gone before. Jacob Zuma, who among the world leaders in Johannesburg had nervously gripped the pages of his speech, finally did what he does best: he led the mourners in a rendering of

"Thina Sizwe," the revolutionary lament of the nation for their colonized land. It seemed perfectly fitting amid the open, green hillsides of Qunu.

Nelson Mandela understood the meaningful gesture; he grasped the importance of the right touch, the right clothing, the right expression. The silence of prison taught him to value words and not to use them idly. In a country where language was always a fraught issue, he was an old-school nationalist, declaring that "language is the highest manifestation of social unity" and that it is "the inherent right of each group of people to use its language without restriction." During these days of mourning, Afrikaners frequently recalled that he once said (in Afrikaans, which he learned in prison) that "when you speak a language that a man understands, you address his intellect; but when you speak to him in his mother tongue, you address his heart." Having translated himself from herd boy to global hero, Mandela also understood that certain things – like love – must sometimes remain untranslated and that even a man whose influence travels far must finally be brought home to ancestral ground. Let us take leave, then, in Mandela's own language.

> Lala ngoxolo, tat'uMandela.
> Nkosi Sikelel'iAfrika!

FURTHER READINGS

Biographies, Autobiographies, Memoirs

Asmal, Kader, David Chidester, and Wilmot James, eds. *Nelson Mandela: In His Own Words*. New York: Little, Brown, 2003.

Benson, Mary. *Nelson Mandela: The Man and the Movement*. New York: Norton, 1994.

Bernstein, Lionel. *Memory Against Forgetting*. London: Viking, 1999.

Bezdrob, Anné Marié du Preez. *Winnie Mandela: A Life*. Cape Town: Zebra Press, 2003.

Bizos, George. *Odyssey to Freedom*. Houghton: Random House, 2007.

Boehmer, Elleke. *Nelson Mandela: A Very Short Introduction*. Oxford: Oxford University Press, 2008.

Callinicos, Luli. *Oliver Tambo: Beyond the Engeli Mountains*. Cape Town: David Philip, 2004.

Couper, Scott. *Albert Luthuli: Bound by Faith*. Pietermaritzburg: University of KwaZulu-Natal Press, 2010.

Daniels, Eddie. *There and Back: Robben Island, 1964–1979*. East Lansing: Michigan State University Press, 2001.

De Klerk, F. W. *The Last Trek: A New Beginning*. London: Macmillan, 1998.

Gevisser, Mark. *Thabo Mbeki: The Dream Deferred*. Johannesburg: Jonathan Ball, 2007.

Gilbey, Emma. *The Lady: Life and Times of Winnie Mandela*. London: Vintage, 2004.

Goldberg, Denis. *The Mission: A Life for Freedom in South Africa*. Johannesburg: STE, 2010.

Gregory, James. *Goodbye Bafana: Nelson Mandela, My Prisoner, My Friend*. London: Headline Books, 1995.

Harris, Verne, ed. *A Prisoner in the Garden: Opening Nelson Mandela's Prison Archive*. Johannesburg: Nelson Mandela Foundation, 2004.

Hyslop, Jonathan. "Gandhi, Mandela, and the African Modern." In *Johannesburg: The Elusive Metropolis*. Ed. Sarah Nuttall and Achille Mbembe, 119–36. Durham, NC: Duke University Press, 2008.

Kathrada, Ahmed. *Memoirs*. Cape Town: Struik, 2004.

Lodge, Tom. *Mandela: A Critical Life*. Oxford: Oxford University Press, 2006.

Luthuli, Albert. *Let My People Go: The Autobiography of Albert Luthuli*. New York: McGraw-Hill, 1962.

Maharaj, Mac. *Reflections in Prison: Voices from the South African Liberation Struggle*. Cape Town: Zebra Press, 2001.

ed. *Mandela: The Authorized Portrait*. Kansas City, MO: Andrews McMeel, 2006.

Mangcu, Xolela, ed. *The Meaning of Mandela: A Literary and Intellectual Celebration*. Cape Town: HSRC Press, 2006.

Mandela, Nelson. *Conversations with Myself*. New York, Farrar, Straus and Giroux, 2010.

Long Walk to Freedom: The Autobiography of Nelson Mandela. Boston: Little, Brown. 1994.

Mandela, Winnie. *Part of My Life Went with Him*. New York: Norton, 1985.

Meer, Fatima. *Higher Than Hope: The Authorized Biography of Nelson Mandela*. New York: Harper & Row, 1990.

Meredith, Martin. *Nelson Mandela: A Biography*. New York: St. Martin's Press, 1997.

Naidoo, Indres. *Island in Chains*. New York: Vintage, 1983.

O'Malley, Padraig. *Shades of Difference: Mac Maharaj and the Struggle for South Africa*. New York: Penguin, 2007.

Sampson, Anthony. *Mandela: The Authorized Biography*. London: HarperCollins, 1999.

Sisulu, Elinor. *Walter and Albertina Sisulu: In Our Lifetime*. Cape Town: New Africa Books, 2011.

Smith, David James. *Young Mandela: The Revolutionary Years*. New York: Little, Brown, 2010.

South African History, Law, and Politics

Alexander, Neville. *An Ordinary Country: Issues in the Transition from Apartheid to Democracy in South Africa*. New York: Bergahn Books, 2003.

Asmal, Kader, David Chidester, and Cassius Lubisi. *Legacy of Freedom: The ANC's Human Rights Tradition*. Johannesburg: Jonathan Ball, 2005.

Barber, James. *Mandela's World: The International Dimension of South Africa's Political Revolution, 1990–99*. Oxford: James Currey, 2004.

Broun, Kenneth. *Saving Nelson Mandela: The Rivonia Trial and the Fate of South Africa*. Oxford: Oxford University Press, 2012.

Buntman, Fran. *Robben Island and Prisoner Resistance to Apartheid*. Cambridge: Cambridge University Press, 2003.

Carlin, John. *Playing the Enemy: Nelson Mandela and the Game That Made a Nation*. New York: Penguin, 2008.

Chipkin, Ivor. *Do South Africans Exist? Nationalism, Democracy, and the Identity of "The People."* Johannesburg: Wits University Press, 2007.

Drew, Allison. *Discordant Comrades: Identities and Loyalties on the South African Left*. Pretoria: University of South Africa Press, 2002.

Dubow, Saul. *The African National Congress*. Stroud: Sutton, 2003.

South Africa's Struggle for Human Rights. Cape Town: Jacana, 2012.

Ellis, Stephen. *External Mission: The ANC in Exile.* Johannesburg: Jonathan Ball, 2012.

Ellis, Stephen and Tshepo Sechaba. *Comrades Against Apartheid: The ANC and the Communist Party in Exile.* London: James Currey, 1992.

Fredrickson, George M. *Black Liberation: A Comparative History of Black Ideologies in the United States and South Africa.* New York: Oxford University Press, 1995.

Gerhart, Gail. *Black Power in South Africa: The Evolution of an Ideology.* Berkeley: University of California Press, 1978.

Glaser, Clive. *The ANC Youth League.* Auckland Park: Jacana, 2012.

Guelke, Adrian. *Rethinking the Rise and Fall of Apartheid: South Africa and World Politics.* Basingstoke: Palgrave Macmillan, 2005.

Holland, Heidi. *100 Years of Struggle: Mandela's ANC.* Johannesburg: Penguin SA, 2012.

Irwin, Ryan M. *Gordian Knot: Apartheid and the Unmaking of the Liberal World Order.* Oxford: Oxford University Press, 2012.

Joffe, Joel. *The State vs. Nelson Mandela: The Trial That Changed South Africa.* Oxford: Oneworld Publications, 2007.

Johns, Sheridan and R. Hunt Davis, eds. *Mandela, Tambo, and the African National Congress: A Documentary Survey, 1948–1990.* New York: Oxford University Press, 1991.

Kane, John. *The Politics of Moral Capital.* Cambridge: Cambridge University Press, 2001.

Landsberg, Chris. *The Quiet Diplomacy of Liberation: International Politics and South Africa's Transition.* Johannesburg: Jacana, 2004.

Lodge, Tom. *Black Politics in South Africa since 1945.* London: Longman, 1983.

Politics in South Africa from Mandela to Mbeki. Cape Town: David Philip, 2002.

Sharpeville: An Apartheid Massacre and Its Consequences. Oxford: Oxford University Press, 2011.

MacDonald, Michael. *Why Race Matters in South Africa.* Cambridge, MA: Harvard University Press, 2006.

Mandela, Nelson. *Nelson Mandela Speaks: Forging a Democratic, Nonracial South Africa.* Ed. Steve Clark. Cape Town: David Phillip, 1994.

No Easy Walk to Freedom. Ed. Ato Qayson. New York: Penguin, 2002.

The Struggle Is My Life. New York: Pathfinder Press, 1986.

Marks, Shula and Stanley Trapido, eds. *The Politics of Race, Class, and Nationalism in 20th Century South Africa.* New York: Longman, 1987.

Marx, Anthony W. *Lessons of Struggle: South African Internal Opposition, 1960–1990.* New York: Oxford University Press, 1992.

Matthews, Anthony S. *Freedom, State Security, and the Rule of Law: Dilemmas of the Apartheid Society.* Berkeley: University of California Press, 1986.

Meli, Francis, *South Africa Belongs to Us: A History of the ANC.* Bloomington: Indiana University Press, 1989.

Nash, Andrew. "Mandela's Democracy." *Monthly Review* 50.11 (1999): 18–28.

Ndlovu, Sifiso M. "Mandela as Public Face of the African National Congress," *Thinker* 52 (2013): 58–61.

O'Meara, Dan. *Forty Lost Years: The Apartheid State and the Politics of the National Party: 1948–1994.* Athens: Ohio University Press, 1996.

Sachs, Albie. *Justice in South Africa.* Berkeley: University of California Press, 1973.

Seekings, Jeremy. *The UDF: A History.* Cape Town: David Philip, 2000.

Sparks, Allister. *Beyond the Miracle: Inside the New South Africa.* Chicago: Chicago University Press, 2003.

The Mind of South Africa: The Rise and Fall of South Africa. New York: Knopf, 1990.

Tomorrow Is Another Country. Chicago: University of Chicago Press, 1996.

Spitz, Richard and Matthew Chaskalson. *The Politics of Transition: A Hidden History of South Africa's Negotiated Settlement.* Johannesburg: Wits University Press, 2000.

Turok, Ben. *Nothing but the Truth: Behind the ANC's Struggle Politics.* Cape Town: Zebra Press, 2003.

Van Kessel, Ineke. *Beyond Our Wildest Dreams: The United Democratic Front and the Transformation of South Africa.* Charlottesville: University of Virginia Press, 2000.

Waldmeir, Patti. *Anatomy of a Miracle: The End of Apartheid and the Birth of a New South Africa.* New York: Penguin, 1998.

Welsh, David. *The Rise and Fall of Apartheid.* Charlottesville: University of Virginia Press, 2010.

Literature and Cultural Studies

Arnold, Millard, ed. *Steve Biko: Black Consciousness in South Africa.* New York: Vintage, 1979.

Attwell, David. *Rewriting Modernity: Studies in Black South African Literary History.* Pietmaritzburg: University of KwaZulu-Natal Press, 2005.

Atwell, David and Derek Attridge. *The Cambridge History of South African Literature.* Cambridge: Cambridge University Press, 2012.

Bartlett, Richard and Morakabe Raks Seakhoa eds. *Halala Madiba: Nelson Mandela in Poetry.* Wiltshire: Aflame Books, 2006.

Biko, Steve. *I Write What I Like.* Ed. Aelred Stubbs. London: C. R. Heinemann, 1987.

Chapman, Michael, ed. *The Drum Decade: Stories from the 1950s.* Pietermaritzburg: University of Natal Press, 1989.

Cole, Catherine. *Performing South Africa's Truth Commission: Stages of Transition.* Bloomington: Indiana University Press, 2010.

Coombes, Annie E. *History After Apartheid: Visual Culture and Public Memory in a Democratic South Africa.* Durham, NC: Duke University Press, 2003.

Coplan, David. *In Township Tonight! South Africa's Black City Music and Theatre.* Chicago: University of Chicago Press, 2008.

Davis, Peter. *In Darkest Hollywood: Exploring the Jungles of Cinema's South Africa.* Athens: Ohio University Press, 1996.

Derrida, Jacques and Mustapha Tlili, eds. *For Nelson Mandela.* New York: Henry Holt, 1987.

Erlmann, Veit. *Music, Modernity, and the Global Imagination: South Africa and the West.* New York: Oxford University Press, 1999.

Gordimer, Nadine. *Living in Hope and History*. New York: Farrar, Straus and Giroux, 1999.

Herwitz, Daniel. *Race and Reconciliation: Essays from the New South Africa*. Ann Arbor: University of Michigan Press, 2003.

Holden, Philip. *Autobiography and Decolonization: Modernity, Masculinity, and the Nation-State*. Madison: University of Wisconsin Press, 2006.

McDonald, Peter D. *The Literature Police: Apartheid Censorship and Its Cultural Consequences*. Oxford: Oxford University Press, 2009.

Modisane, Bloke. *Blame Me on History*. London: Thames & Hudson, 1963.

Munro, Brenna. *South Africa and the Dream of Love to Come: Queer Sexuality and the Struggle for Freedom*. Minneapolis: University of Minnesota Press, 2012.

Ndebele, Njabulo. *South African Literature and Culture: Rediscovery of the Ordinary*. Manchester: Manchester University Press, 1994.

Nkosi, Lewis. *Home and Exile*. London: Longmans, 1965.

Mandela's Ego. Cape Town: Umuzi, 2006.

Nixon, Rob. *Homelands, Harlem, and Hollywood: South African Culture and the World Beyond*. New York: Routledge, 1994.

Nuttall, Sarah and Cheryl-Ann Michael, eds. *Senses of Culture: South African Cultural Studies*. Oxford: Oxford University Press, 2000.

Nuttall, Sarah and Carli Coetzee, eds. *Negotiating the Past: The Making of Memory in South Africa*. New York: Oxford University Press, 1998.

Pityana, Barney N. *Bounds of Possibility: The Legacy of Steve Biko and Black Consciousness*. London: Zed Books, 1992.

Salazar, Philippe-Joseph. *An African Athens: Rhetoric and the Shaping of Democracy in South Africa*. Abington: LEA, 2002.

Sampson, Anthony. *Drum: The Making of a Magazine*. Cape Town: Jonathan Ball, 2005.

Sanders, Mark. *Ambiguities of Witnessing: Law and Literature in the Time of a Truth Commission*. Stanford, CA: Stanford University Press, 2007.

Sandile, Dikeni. *Soul Fire: Writing the Transition*. Pietermaritzburg: University of Natal Press, 2002.

Schalkwyk, David. *Hamlet's Dreams: The Robben Island Shakespeare*. London: Continuum, 2013.

Soyinka, Wole. *Mandela's Earth*. New York: Random House, 1988.

Wenzel, Jennifer. *Bulletproof: Afterlives of Anticolonial Prophecy in South Africa and Beyond*. Chicago: University of Chicago Press, 2009.

Select Filmography

Come Back Africa. Dir. Lionel Rogosin. New York: Milestone Films, 1959.

Dear Mandela. Dir. Dara Kell and Christopher Nizza. New York: Sleeping Giant Films, 2012.

Endgame. Dir. Pete Travis. London: Target Entertainment, 2009.

Free Mandela. Dir. Barry Feinberg. San Francisco: California Newsreel, 1988.

Goodbye Bafana (The Color of Freedom). Dir. Billie August. Chatsworth, CA: Image Entertainment, 2007.

Have You Seen Drum Recently? Dir. Jurgen Schadeberg. Princeton, NJ: Films for the Humanities and Social Sciences, 2003.

Invictus. Dir. Clint Eastwood. Burbank, CA: Warner Bros. Pictures, 2009.

Mandela. Dir. Peter Davis. Vancouver: Villon Films, 1986.

Mandela. Dir. Philip Saville. New York: HBO, 1987.

Mandela: Long Walk to Freedom. Dir. Justin Chadwick. New York: Weinstein Company, 2013.

Mandela: Son of Africa, Father of a Nation. Dir. Jo Menell and Angus Gibson. London: Island Pictures, 1996.

Mandela and De Klerk. Dir. Joseph Sargent. New York: Hallmark Entertainment, 2005.

The Man Who Drove with Mandela. Dir. Greta Schiller. New York: Jezebel Productions, 1999.

Mrs. Mandela. Dir. Michael Samuels. London: Diverse Productions, 2010.

Nelson Mandela: Life and Times. Dir. Robin Benger. Ottawa: CBC, 2004.

Reconciliation: Mandela's Miracle. Dir. Michael Henry Wilson. Burbank, CA: Warner Brothers, 2011.

Remember Mandela. Dir. Peter Davis. Vancouver: Villon Films, 1988.

The 16th Man. Dir. Clifford Bestall. Bristol, CT: ESPN Films, 2010.

INDEX

Abacha, Sani, 196–97
ABC News, Mandela documentary by,
226–27
Achmat, Zackie, 104–5
Act of Union of 1910, 40–41
African-American jazz culture, Sophiatown
Renaissance and, 93–94
African Democratic Party (ADP), launching
of, 35–37
African Freedom Movement, 44–45.
See also Organization of African
Unity (OAU)
African independent churches, 85–86
African National Congress (ANC).
See also ANC Women's League; ANC
Youth League; Umkhonto we Sizwe
(Spear of the Nation)
autopsy painting controversy and, 278–80
banning and unbanning of, 1–2, 41–42,
165–66
Black Consciousness movement and, 219
collaboration with OAU, 44–45
democracy, reconciliation, and, 187–90
disagreements within leadership of, 29–30,
194–95
economic policy shift of, 190–92
gay rights and, 104–5
human rights initiatives and, 220
iinkokheli zoluntu (people's leaders)
in, 120
independent Africa's support for PAC
over, 130
Indian Congresses and, 38–39
Inkatha Freedom Party and, 234–35
internationalism of, 192–93
lawyers in, 145
Madikizela-Mandela's leadership roles in,
105–6
Mandela's association with, i, 3, 9–10,
29–47, 176–77

media coverage of, 93–94
militarism and military activities
of, 18, 126, 165–66, 167–72,
175–76
mortality of Mandela and, 278–80
mythologizing of Mandela supported by,
74–75, 80–82, 210–13
negotiations between National Party
and, 77–83
non-African alliances of, 130
party discipline and collective leadership
of, 29–30, 38–39, 40–45
peace-building efforts of, 164–65,
194–97
post-apartheid transformation of, 12–13
in post-transition period, 178–79
presidency of Mandela and influence of,
197–99
Reconstruction and Development Program
of, 14–16, 190–92
Release Mandela campaign and, 73
South African Communist Party and,
172–75
women's leadership in, 201
Women's League of, 105–6
Youth League of, 17, 148–50
African Peace Award, Mandela as recipient
of, 194–95
African Survey (Hailey), 137–38
Africanism. *See also* nationalism
atavistic compared to symbolic, 264
global anxiety concerning, 262–64
Mandela's changing views in light of, 37
Mandela's court appearance in light of, 16,
21–22, 94–95, 116–17, 121, 125–31,
151–52, 259
Mandela's presidency in light of, 182–99
non-racialism and, oscillation between,
10–11, 35–37
women's leadership and, 201

Cambridge Companions to...